W9-BNH-373

THE FOUNDATIONS OF BELIEF

THE FOUNDATIONS OF BELIEF

Leslie Dewart

Theodore Lownik Library
St. Procopius College
Lisle, Illinois

HERDER AND HERDER

201
D515f

1969
HERDER AND HERDER NEW YORK
232 Madison Avenue, New York, N.Y. 10016

Library of Congress Catalog Card Number: 69-17777
© 1969 by Herder and Herder, Inc.
Manufactured in the United States

Contents

Philosophical study is not for the sake of understanding what men have thought, but how reality truly obtains.

THOMAS AQUINAS

Dogmatic theology today has to be theological anthropology.

KARL RAHNER

Though our vista of history is rather short up to date—extending back, as it does, over no more than a few thousand years—it is already long enough for us to see that all secular institutions, whether they are states or nations or governments or languages or civilizations, have comparatively short lives compared with religions. We can be sure that the Western civilization's role in history is going to be a minor one compared with the role of Christianity.

ARNOLD TOYNBEE

Acknowledgments

An earlier version of section 2 of chapter V first appeared in *Commonweal,* and parts of section 4 of the same chapter were originally written for publication in the volume *The Presence and Absence of God,* the collected lectures given during 1968 in the series of the same title at Fordham University's Cardinal Bea Institute. I am grateful to the editors of *Commonweal* and to Professor Christopher Mooney, S.J., for permission to include this copyrighted material in this book.

The Publisher and the Editor of Herder & Herder have been most helpful to me in a variety of ways, but I should make special mention of the latter's conscientious, most valuable editorial advice. I also wish to acknowledge my debt to Professor Bernard Black, C.S.B., and to Mrs. Margaret McGrath, of the St. Michael's College Library, for generous assistance with my library needs.

To Professor Arthur Gibson and my other colleagues in the St. Michael's College Faculty of Theology and in the Department of Religious Studies of the University of Toronto I am deeply grateful for having welcomed me to their ranks and, moreover, for their stimulation, friendship and thoughtful, scholarly criticism.

I am greatly indebted to Professor J. Edgar Bruns, Chairman of the Faculty of Theology. Since this book was written as a course of formal lectures to be given in the Graduate Faculty of Theology in the Fall of 1968, it would not be inexact to state that, in a sense, it was commissioned by him. It is only fitting, therefore, if I hereby present it to him—and, through him, to my other departmental colleagues.

Preface

As its title should convey, this volume gives form to an enquiry which falls within the ambit of that discipline which in Catholic academic circles has long been known as Fundamental Theology but which among Protestant scholars has been more commonly called the Philosophy of Religion. Both these designations have advantages and disadvantages. Fundamental Theology is descriptive enough in some ways, but it overstresses theology—rather, it connotes neither the basically philosophical nature of the style of thinking it demands, nor its historical situation within the philosophical tradition which, to be sure, has always been associated in Western Christendom with theology, but from which it has been distinguished since at least the age of Descartes. The name Philosophy of Religion does at least recall some of these things. On the other hand, it does not lend sufficient emphasis to the specifically theological relations and preoccupations of this order of speculative thought. Philosophical Theology has been occasionally suggested as a third alternative. But this—at least so far as I am concerned—is uncomfortably close to the "natural theology" of neo-Scholasticism. I believe that *Theological Philosophy,* which is my own preference, may be at least as good as any of the more usual expressions, and I hope that this coinage will gain favour and come to fill a useful role in the contemporary Christian academic world.

Not the least benefit to be expected from this appelation may

11

be its aptness for putting in relief the theological task which philosophy should normally and naturally undertake when it is practiced by the Christian intellect. This may be an especially timely reminder to offer to Catholic philosophy today. I do not imagine that Catholic philosophers, generally speaking, consciously believe that all theological problems to which philosophy could make a contribution have already been solved—though a few of them, evidently, implicitly assume precisely that. But it would be a pity if by default or by inertia the Catholic philosophical community were to adopt in practice a position that few of its members (or so I estimate) would care theoretically to espouse.

But whatever the name that may designate its subject best, this enquiry complements that which I undertook in my earlier book *The Future of Belief*. I will, of course, discuss the nature of the problem below in more detail, but I should explain here briefly its relation to my previous work. In *The Future of Belief* I addressed myself to the question: can the Christian faith be deemed truly to develop and unequivocally to evolve (and not merely to change the outer, worn-out garment of its pristine, spotless nudity) even if it is assumed that this faith is *supernatural* and that its object is *revealed*? The question to which I address myself here, however, is more fundamental yet: can the Christian faith be said truly to develop and unequivocally to evolve, on the assumption that this faith is *true* and that its object is *real*? The two enquiries, thus, have a common background, namely, a common Christian faith and a common preoccupation with what I take to be the crucial, real-life problem of Christianity today, namely, whether it will consciously undertake to direct its own evolution, or whether it will continue to evolve, but at an obsolete

12

rate and in a pre-conscious and, as it were, strictly zoological mode. The principal difference, beyond that which I have already noted, namely, that the second question is more fundamental than the first, is that the first is narrower than the second. My earlier publication was synecdochically devoted, in effect, to the future of *Christian* belief, whereas the present one is elliptically concerned with the foundations of *religious* belief.

Given the wider compass of the latter, the question may occur to the reader why, except for three brief and incidental moments in Chapters II, III and V, I do not in this volume mention religious belief outside the Western Christian world. It may appear as presumptuous to speak generically of the foundations of belief on the basis of a study of Christianity, as to universalize from a sample of five thousand middle-class Americans to the *Sexual Behaviour in the Human Male*. My ratio is somewhat less unfavorable than that of the late Alfred Kinsey, but not decisively so. There are several hundred million Christian believers, and they straddle several continents and they walk all modes of life —but Christianity is a minority religion among the faiths of the world. (It is indeed a minority religion even within the Christendom of the West.)

In reply I must acknowledge that my study is specialized; there are unavoidable limitations to any enquiry which is by definition and design devoted to specific aspects of a broader topic in relation to which a scholarly contribution is conceived. I need hardly stress the obvious truth that a comprehensive, catholic study of the foundations of religious belief would necessarily require the contribution of scholars who would base their research on their understanding and appreciation of other religious traditions—and not least of all on the peculiar approach of the comparative re-

13

ligionist, who can correlate differences and similarities which at first may be deceptive or insufficiently to the fore. In a sense, one of the principal conclusions of this book is precisely that in this ecumenical age of man's history a cross-cultural approach to the study of all religion has become indispensable to the understanding and development of any given faith. On the other hand, it is the nature of the question more than the range of the evidence that tends to determine the scope of the reply. My question has to do with the foundations of religious belief, namely, the concepts of *reality* and *truth*. To the extent that my findings may be valid, their provenance from Christian experience should not altogether void their applicability, *mutatis mutandis,* to other forms of religious belief.

There are, moreover, two other mutually complementary reasons why it is not altogether unfitting that an enquiry about the foundations of religious belief should be approached by the Christian, to begin with, from the viewpoint of the Christian faith itself. The first is that the incipient unification of the human race in a world-wide system of federated civilizations is taking place under the sign of Westernization—this may yet change, but for the foreseeable future it is likely to remain the fact it now is. Thus, Christianity has been willy-nilly thrust in the position of the only likely candidate for the post of world ecumenical religious leadership. The progressive integration of the human community will unavoidably require a measure of eventual religious integration—or at very least synergic co-ordination and interaction among the higher world religions; and if Christianity does not undertake this pursuit, it is possible that no other faith may be in a position to do so. Christianity could profitably begin

14

to train itself toward this eventual role by attempting to understand, in its own terms and from its own inner resources, the nature of the foundation of all religious belief: Christianity must, as it were, universalize itself to itself in the first instance, before it is in a position effectively to discharge its leadership in the universalization of the religious belief of man.

The second reason is that, apart from the peculiarities of the contemporary historical situation of *homo sapiens,* Christianity itself has always believed itself to have a call to universalize the religious belief of man. That is why Christianity's true name is *Catholicism*—I mean, unqualified Catholicism. Catholicism aspires to be the catholic religion. But I stress that it so aspires, that this is its vocation, because Christians have not always realized the eschatological nature of the catholicity of Catholicism— to tell the truth, scarcely all Christians realize this even today. Thus, the catholicity of the Universalist Common Body of the Spirit of God (more usually but less significantly known as the Catholic Church—again, unqualified Catholic Church) has been mistaken for a divinely granted privilege and, indeed, for an actual property, a "note" of the Church. Catholicity is, however, a divine call to contribute to the religious development of the human race, entire and as such; it is, therefore, also Christianity's undertaking to become worthy of thus serving the interests of man. Likewise, the uniqueness and distinctiveness of the truth of Universalism does indeed imply that Universalism has a correspondingly unique and distinctive religious contribution to offer to man. But this has been frequently mistaken for the exclusiveness of Christian truth, supposedly implying a correspondingly exclusive right to the religious allegiance of every man. In what may well turn out, in the long run, to have been its most consequential and revolutionary doctrine, Vatican II disposed of this view—hopefully once for all:

The Catholic Church rejects nothing which is true and holy in [non-Christian] religions. She looks with sincere respect upon those ways of conduct and life, those rules and teachings which, though differing in many particulars from what she holds and sets forth, nevertheless often reflect a ray of that Truth which enlightens all men. Indeed she proclaims and must ever proclaim Christ, "the way, the truth and the life" in whom men find the fullness of religious life, and in whom God has reconciled all things to Himself.

The Church, therefore, has this exhortation for her sons: prudently and lovingly, through dialogue and collaboration with the followers of other religions, and in witness of Christian faith and life, acknowledge, preserve and promote the spiritual and moral goods found among these men, as well as the values in their society and culture.[1]

The style retains a self-contradictory shade of Roman traditional, but the novel doctrine shines through undimmed, and the patronizing language fails to hide the unarrogant truth: the evangelical mission of the Church is not a proselytic, but an ecumenical task.

In a world increasingly characterized by the self-organization of man on a global scale, the catholicity of the Catholic faith must seek the ultimate religious integration of mankind. Catholicity means, in Raymond Panikkar's expression, "ecumenical ecumenism."[2] The Universalist Religious Community must seek,

[1] *Declaration on the Relationship of the Church to Non-Christian Religions*, sect. 2; in Walter Abbott and Joseph Gallagher, eds., *The Documents of Vatican II*, (New York, 1966), pp. 662–663.

[2] "We would like to widen and to deepen . . . Christian ecumenism into an *ecumenical ecumenism*, if this expression is permissible; that is

in the first place integration (not necessarily uniformity or judicial unity) within itself. (The model of its inner integration may well be a paradigm for later use). Beyond this, the three semitic-scriptural religions must likewise seek integration in some form which cannot as yet be remotely envisaged or usefully defined. Ultimately there remains the goal of integration (in some valid, however unforeseeable, meaning of the term) with the higher religions of the Far East.

I need hardly stipulate that this is not an immediate prospect, except perhaps for the first step. Nevertheless, the contribution that this book would wish to make keeps very much in mind the more distant possibilities. This is not an idle preoccupation, even at this early date. The rate of human evolution has accelerated to the point that planning must take place on a much longer scale than has been reasonable and sufficiently prudent in the past. Economists and technologists are already laying plans for the

---

to say, into an ecumenism that is really ecumenical, catholic, engaged not only in the dialogue and encounter between Christian confessions, but also between religions. It is certain that this catholic ecumenism would at the same time help to a great extent the issues at stake in Christian ecumenism, as well as in other specifically Christian problems. Latin-Greek disputes appear almost as family quarrels, which do not transcend the Mediterranean horizon, from the perspective of an encounter between Christianity and Hinduism, for instance. This observation should not minimise the Latin-Greek tension, but could perhaps centre it in its proper place. Nor should we lose sight of the fundamental differences between the *dia-logue* among Christians and the *dia-lectic* among 'believers' of several religions," *The Unknown Christ of Hinduism,* (London, 1964), pp. 31–32. Cf. also H. R. Schlette, *Toward a Theology of Religions,* (New York, 1966); and Eugene Hillman, *The Wider Ecumenism,* (New York, 1968). But I am especially indebted to the work of Arnold Toynbee, particularly to *An Historian's Approach to Religion,* (London, 1956), and to *Christianity Among the Religions of the World,* (New York, 1957).

beginning of the third millenium of the Christian age.[3] It may not be too early for the student of religion to begin to look ahead to a world which may yet be several hundred—perhaps several thousand—years away. In sum, my suggestions concerning the foundations of belief point beyond the narrow circle of Christian belief, even if they begin only within the confines of Christian belief.

Some readers may detect an apparent inconsistency between envisaging objectives which reach almost unrealistically into the future—although, on that score, may I add that for all its high abstraction and theoretical hue, the study of religion is at least as close to real life as nuclear physics is, in the age of overkill—an inconsistency, I say, between this study's orientation towards the future and its pronounced preoccupation with the fairly distant past: more than a third of this book is devoted to an interpretation of the role of Greek thought and of the philosophy of St. Thomas Aquinas in the Hellenic-Western tradition that leads to our own day. The reasons why this is, on the contrary, eminently consistent may become fully apparent as we proceed. At this point I will merely remark that the longer the range of one's envisaged consequences, the more thorough the understanding of the antecedents must be, if for no better cause, (such as those which I hope will become apparent from this book), because, as a fellow-Spaniard, English-language philosopher once said, "those who forget the past are condemned to repeat it."

Finally, I should also preface my work with a caution about the term *meta-metaphysical,* which I have coined with reference to the mode of philosophical thought which alone can, in my

[3] Herman Kahn and A. J. Wiener, *The Year Two Thousand,* (New York, 1967).

opinion, effectively restore the foundations of Christian belief today. I wish to call attention to the adjectival form which I usually give to it. It would be a thorough misunderstanding of my intent if I were attributed the suggestion that there is a distinctive philosophical discipline, or a division or "branch" of philosophy called meta-metaphysics—least of all one which would share with other philosophical divisions like logic, ethics and metaphysics, the totality of philosophical science. I have not in this book suggested this. What I have suggested is that philosophy today must give itself a meta-metaphysical orientation. I have suggested that philosophy should transcend its metaphysical stage of development and, thus, initiate its meta-metaphysical age. I have even suggested, in a sense, that philosophy develop, as it were, a meta-metaphysical metaphysics. I have above all suggested that Christian philosophical thought in particular should become meta-metaphysical thought. These suggestions may be worthwhile or they may not. They are, at any rate, the suggestions I have actually made.

THE FOUNDATIONS OF BELIEF

1.

The Contemporary Problem
of Belief

PROLEGOMENA

We live today in a period which began as the first, patristic-
mediaeval age of Christianity came to a close—a period of rapid
development which has reached its proper stride (or since it
may be too early yet to call it proper, let us say its unprecedentedly
lengthy stride) in our own generation, and perhaps even as
recently as the second half of a 20th century which is only beginning its last third. The weight of this affirmation, however, does
not fall on any one of the dates I have imprecisely alluded to—
dates which must in any event be arbitrarily selected, and which
are not always the same for different aspects of one and the
same period of the history of our world. For, from the viewpoint adopted in this book, namely, that of the course of human
evolution as a whole, it does not matter very much whether we
choose to mark the beginning of our age by the century which
Averroes almost lived to see and which St. Thomas almost
spanned, or by the century in which Søren Kierkegaard and
Karl Marx began to reconstruct Western thought on a conceptual
basis which, in reaction to Hegel, diverged from the very roots
of the uninterrupted philosophical tradition which had come to

them from the Greeks. Indeed, this whole epoch of seven centuries or so might very well be considered as a broad band of transition from an earlier age to the present. For the continuity of history back from our own day to that of earliest man underlies every historical division. Even pre-history is historical, and the term *pre*-history makes sense only in reference to our reflective awareness of the continuity of the historical process: the process of human development is from the outset historical. Man's reflective awareness of the nature of this continuous process has enabled him merely to become aware of what has always been the case, namely, that the history of man is an evolutionary one.

Thus, it is a strictly arbitrary and relatively unimportant matter whether the age in which we live should be called "atomic" rather than "post-mediaeval," or "contemporary" rather than "modern". What is not arbitrary, and what is important, is that man has crossed the threshold of a level of development that liquidates the age that began with the discovery of agriculture and which produced the mode of human self-organization known as the *city*. Man is entering into the time of "post-civilization," as one economist has called it.[1] It is also, by the same token, the age of the "global village,"[2] a mode of human self-organization

---

[1] Kenneth E. Boulding, "Post-Civilization," in Paul Goodman, (ed.), *Seeds of Liberation*, (New York: 1964), pp. 12–23: "We are living in what I call the second great change in the state of man. The first is the change from pre-civilized to civilized societies. . . . We are in the middle of the second great change in the state of man, which is as drastic and as dramatic, and certainly as large, as, if not larger than, the change from pre-civilized to civilized society. . . . These great changes can be thought of as a change of gear in the evolutionary process, resulting in progressive acceleration of the rate of evolutionary change," pp. 12–13. Cf. also his *The Meaning of the Twentieth Century*, (New York, 1964), p. 2.

[2] Marshall McLuhan, *War and Peace in the Global Village*, (New York, 1968).

that is at once more fragmented and more highly integrated—it is a "mosaic" [3]—than every human culture of the past. It is, by any other name, the beginning of the planetary stage of human development. Having passed, about 100,000 years ago, from the *herd* to the *tribe,* and less than 10,000 years ago, from the *tribe* to the *city,* in 1,000 years or so man has traversed most of the distance between *city* and *world.* Only in relation to such historical perspective is it possible to integrate one's understanding of the multiplicity of critical events of the last few centuries, and particularly the increasingly spastic recurrence, since the end of the middle ages, of scientific, ecclesiastical, philosophical, technological, political, industrial, economic and social revolutions, the end of which is not apparent to sight.

These various revolutions have not been successive, but cumulative. None of them is over. Each one has added its turmoil to the previous one, and the prospect is that at least for some time to come we shall have more of the same. Perhaps the latest revolution is the historical revolution. Man has become aware of historicity.[4] Man has always evolved; he has always existed in

---

[3] *Idem, passim.*

[4] Among the earliest and most influential philosophical sources of the historical revolution was John Locke, who was one of the first philosophers to realize that the empirical nature of human consciousness requires all intellectual investigation to follow an "historical, plain method," *Essay Concerning Human Understanding,* I, 1, 2. Christian thinkers have always been more or less aware of the historical nature of man's situation —more in patristic times, less perhaps since Aristotle was rediscovered in the West. We have but to recall St. Augustine's *De Civitate Dei* to note that Christian thought has always been permeated with a sense of the historicity of man. But there is a very important difference between being aware of the historicity of the human situation and being aware of the historicity of human consciousness—and, in particular, the historicity of intellectual investigation, that is, the historicity of man's conscious attempt to heighten his consciousness, as in scientific and philosophical thought.

history. But now he is conscious that he evolves, that he has a history, and this consciousness affects every other mode of human conscious life. Every earlier revolution has become all the more upsetting because man has now found an additional reason for wishing to change the world. Since everything evolves, the real problem for contemporary man is not whether the world will change or whether it will remain the same; the alternative is whether the world will change of its own accord, without human management, or whether it will be changed deliberately, consciously, with the self-regulation which is possible for the world only if its evolution is directed by man.

If this is what defines the historical situation in which we exist today, the question arises: can religious belief remain essentially unaffected by human evolution? Now, if faith were not a form of human consciousness, man would not be pressed to decide for himself and to do so immediately. But religious belief is an intrinsic part of human experience. The question does not really mean whether, but how, religious belief will evolve as man enters the epoch of self-directed evolution. Will it evolve disruptively, under the sign of inner division, inadequately fulfilling, (or not fulfilling at all), its role as the centre of meaningfulness for human life? Or will it evolve consciously, aforethought, reflectively, intelligently, in a less animal, more spiritual, manner than any other conscious attempt at self-evolution undertaken by man so far? Either possibility, and many another between these two extremes, is perfectly real. Which of them will in fact come to happen cannot be foretold. However, what should happen, what might well happen, why it might happen, and what to do to make it happen—these questions are very much the legitimate subject of philosophical enquiry. They define the broad area within which ranges the discussion to which this essay seeks to contribute its suggestions and remarks.

PROBLEM

I have alluded to the discussion within the Christian church on the problem of the evolution of Christian belief. This term may be adequate enough to describe what is taking place within Reformed Christianity, but it understates what is happening in the Roman Catholic Church (with which I shall be predominantly concerned here, largely for the sake of simplifying an enquiry which will not be brief even after being restricted in this way). In relation to the Catholic Church the terms *crisis* and *conflict* would much more aptly describe the contemporary situation of belief. *Crisis,* because in the customary Catholic attitudes, in the established Catholic institutions, in the received Catholic structures, in the traditional Catholic theology, and in the official Catholic teaching, little if any provision has been made for the possibility of undergoing, let alone initiating, evolutionary change. *Conflict,* because, for reasons connected with the very epistemological issues which shall be discussed below, those who think that the evolution of Catholic belief is impossible, naturally (but, I stress, not necessarily or always) tend by the logic of their position to be intolerant of those who think otherwise. But whatever we may call it, there can be no doubt that the contemporary situation of the Catholic Church is definable only as an abyssal division, on the very question of the evolution of the Christian faith, between groups which are most frequently, and not entirely imprecisely, called traditionalists and progressives.

27

Of course, traditionalists are not against all progress, and progressives do not for the most part think that whatever is traditional is therefore to be rejected. There is, in point of fact, a spectrum of opinion, not a dichotomy. On the other hand, the full range of opinion quite visibly clusters around two poles, especially on the three critical issues: (a) how is the present historical situation of mankind to be assessed, (b) what is the basic orientation which should be given to (or retained in) the Church, and (c) in what way should believers most meaningfully relate themselves to the situation of the Church within the contemporary world of man, and to the situation of the world of men within the universe of reality and truth.

Thus, the division is not precisely on whether Christianity is to develop, but on whether Christians are to initiate and consciously direct the development. Traditionalists admit that *natural* changes, as it were, do occur in the faith of the Church; but they believe that the Christian's task is to ensure that these developments are kept within such bounds as will result in the preservation of the sacred deposit of faith entrusted to the Church. Progressives, on the other hand, assert (or assume) that the natural development of Christianity appears to have been arrested, and that, in any event, even if the hitherto normal evolution of Christianity were unfettered, its "natural" pace would probably not be enough for the needs of the Christian faith today. Therefore, they propose that the Christian community actually *promote* the development of doctrine. Fitting the action to the word, they have seized the initiative and have proposed concrete reforms in a variety of speculative and practical respects. Thus, traditionalists are right when they judge that but for the interference—or the intervention, according to one's preference—

28

of progressives with the natural course of Christian events there would be no crisis of Catholic faith today.

The traditionalist stand rests on two distinct though closely related considerations. The first is that Christian belief cannot be equated with natural religion. Christianity was revealed by God, and the Christian faith is supernatural in origin. To suppose that Christianity could substantially evolve would be to suppose that it is not really revealed or supernatural, since only human creations are subject to change. To attempt to initiate and direct the evolution of Christianity would be to render it false and corrupt.

Traditionalism usually recognizes that the Christian Church has developed its understanding and appreciation of the truth which it has always possessed since it received it from God. What was known in principle may become known in greater detail; what was believed vaguely or simply may be drawn out clearly and in complex form; what was only implicit may be unfolded explicitly into new articles of the same faith.[5] Traditionalism further recognizes that the Christian truth may sometimes stand in need of purification from whatever undesirable, or no longer desirable, accretions may have been superadded to it by strictly human hands. In these, and in other similar ways, they admit, there may be development in Christian belief. But there is at least one respect in which there cannot be evolution at all, namely, in the essence of the truth which, having been revealed (and perhaps also in respect of every other truth which, though not in-self directly revealed, is necessarily connected with what has been revealed), cannot be supposed by the believer to be subject to development without impugning the perfection of the truth of

[5] St. Thomas Aquinas, *Summa Theologiae*, (henceforth *ST*) II–II, 1, 7.

revealed religion and the veracity of the revealing God. This is why the supernatural, revealed truth of Christianity must be defended from the danger of progressivism.

I have elsewhere discussed this question in some detail, adducing some evidence which indicates that the traditionalist position may not be well taken, and suggesting some arguments in support of the alternative view that the consciously undertaken, creative development of Christian belief is not only compatible with its supernatural and revealed character, but actually demanded by it.[6] I will therefore not consider this topic again here, except insofar as it is connected with the second, yet more basic difficulty opposed by traditionalist thought—a difficulty with which this study shall be directly concerned.

For the traditionalist objection to Christian self-evolution has two levels which are not always kept clearly distinct. Traditionalism emphasizes that it is concerned with the truth of Christian belief and with the reality of its object, precisely insofar as (a) this belief is supernaturally held, (rather than arrived at through the use of unaided human reason), and insofar as (b) its object reveals itself, (rather than is discovered by the human intellect). Thus, traditionalism defends above all the truth and the reality of *supernatural, revealed* religion, namely the religion of the Christian Church.

However, the traditionalist concern for the supernatural, revealed character of Christian truth is logically dependent upon the prior assumption that Christian belief is true and that its object is real. For example, the traditionalists hesitate to draw from the major premise that the truth of Christianity evolves, the conclusion that Christian belief does not have a supernatural, re-

[6] *The Future of Belief*, (New York, 1966).

vealed character. But why should they hesitate, if not because such a conclusion would be incompatible with the character of Christian belief as *true?* Traditionalists sometimes say that they believe Christianity to be true because it was revealed by God, and that they believe that it was revealed by God because they have supernatural faith. Let us suppose that this is correct, and that Christianity is revealed and faith supernaturally had: could anyone believe that Christianity is false, though revealed by God? Could anyone assert that although Christianity is false he nevertheless professes it, because he has received the supernatural gift of faith?

The belief that Christianity is a supernatural, revealed religion is, indeed, part of Christian belief. But this belief can be held only as a function of a logically antecedent belief in the truth of Christian belief and in the reality of the revealing God. The traditionalist hesitates to jeopardize, (as he imagines that progressivists do), the supernatural, revealed character of Christianity only because he hesitates to jeopardize the truth of Christianity. Without a prior concern for the truth of Christian belief and for the reality of its object, he could not very well be concerned with the supernatural character of the truth of Christian faith in the reality of the revealing God.

In other words, traditionalism has a second, more fundamental objection than that which is more immediately evident, to the suggestion that believers should consciously undertake to redevelop Christian belief. Prior to every consideration concerning the supernatural, revealed status of the Christian religion, traditionalists think that any opinion that would consciously or unconsciously, implicitly or explicitly, assume the evolutionary development of Christian belief and practice, strikes at the Christian truth

31

precisely *as truth* and at the reality of the Christian God precisely *as real*. For, if Christianity *was* essentially true, it cannot *become* true in any essential respect, and if the Christian God is not *actually real,* the question whether Christianity has been *actually revealed* cannot possibly arise. Thus, if the Christian revelation was not essentially true to begin with, its becoming true would amount to the creation of a new belief, a new religious truth. Traditionalists would grant that, to be sure, if Christianity had no claim to truth and thus had always been false, then the creation of a new, true religion might not be entirely out of place. But they would insist that those who retain Christian belief cannot very well agree to admit, by however subtle and indirect implication, that their belief is false and their commitment misplaced. The taproot of the negative reaction of traditionalism to the historical situation that presses Christianity to undertake its own creative evolution, is the concept of truth as it is traditionally understood and, in strict correlation with it, the concept of reality which corresponds to that concept of truth.

This is why traditionalism finds it very awkward to grant to progressivism the status of a tenable opinion. For traditionalists find it extremely difficult to imagine that a historical situation that would press Christianity to deny its own truth could be in any way created or facilitated by the Spirit of the God who originally revealed that truth to man. It must be granted, traditionalists say, that such a historical situation does as a matter of fact exist. Evidently, however, it must be the child of human wickedness—if not worse.[7] But whatever the level of their origin (which is in any event certainly sub-celestial), the emergence and

[7] "We know very well to whom the paternity of these lies should be traced," Jacques Maritain, *Le Paysan de la Garonne,* (Paris, 1966), p. 16.

the strength of the historical forces that urge Christianity substantially to change itself do not indicate that there is anything faulty with Christianity in its traditional and surely perennial form. They can only reveal that there is something wrong with the world. The Church must, therefore, patiently suffer this trial, and confidently wait until the tempters pass away and the *saeculum* dissipates.

The traditionalist posture is logical and consistent. And there can be little doubt that, generally speaking, it is struck only in obedience to the purest motives. But, having brought up the issue of motives, I should also voice the opinion that progressivism must be judged in this respect to be the close match of traditionalism. This must be said not only because upon analysis the assertion can be shown to be true, but also because mutual respect is the necessary precondition to any meaningful dialogue. Division of opinion and even certain forms of competition are not necessarily unprofitable in any human enterprise. But division of opinion or intellectual strife in the Church must not, any more than in any other human enterprise, be a wound in the flesh, and it may not under any conditions become, in Arnold Toynbee's expression, a Schism in the Soul.

It does not take a prolonged enquiry or a scientific survey—it takes only some openmindedness and common sense—to observe that both traditionalism and progressivism have common objectives which stem from common religious motives. Consider, if not, the inner logic of progressivism. Why should a progressivist wish to *change* Christian belief, if not because he too has a prior belief in its truth? For if he thought that Christianity was not true, and had never been true, would he not abjure Christianity and pursue the new religious truth which

33

he supposedly wishes to create? Evidently, the progressivist must be, by definition, a believer, and a believer cannot consistently presume to create a religious truth which would falsify the truth of his religious belief. Thus, he must surely intend to profess as true the faith that Christianity *has* traditionally professed— though he may add that this faith has been traditionally professed in a form which may no longer reveal, and which may now even hide, the Christian truth. Any reasonably unbiased view of the situation should manifest not a little reciprocity between traditionalism and progressivism—both in the better and in the worse respects. The current Catholic crisis is in every essential respect a looking-glass war.

I would, however, neither exaggerate nor idealize. It is true that those who congregate around the traditionalist pole of opinion sometimes exhibit little concern for the rights of others and overestimate the relevance of legitimate authority to certain human situations. But it must be allowed that the same intolerance can be found at the other end of the spectrum as well— and if there are differences between the two groups in the frequency with which intolerance is shown, the unequal distribution of power and authority between them undoubtedly accounts for much of it. Of course, traditionalists are not always intolerant, even when they have the power to be so. Nor do they always assume their position unthinkingly or uncritically. It would not be difficult to cite instances where a real humility and sincere soul-searching have been amply shown by traditionalists —with pride of place to be given to Pope Paul VI, whose sincerity and personal humility are above all reasonable suspicion —offsetting the exhibitions of arrogance and moral insensitivity of other traditionalists. The most truthful testimony that can be given at this time is that traditionalists are, on the whole, as sincere and well-meaning as most human beings usually are.

But the same is more or less true of progressivists. They too can count among their numbers some conscious and unconscious opportunists; they have their unthinking and uncritical fringe, their fanatics and their fools, their knaves and their dupes. But only sheer prejudice could imagine that progressives generally adopt their posture because they chafe at uncomfortable truths, or because they have itchy ears, or because they have chosen to "kneel down before the world." [8] Personal bewilderment candidly

[8] *Ibid.*, p. 85. However, Maritain is undoubtedly correct when he asserts that behind the attitudes of progressivism there lies an epistemological inspiration: "the phenomenological method . . . [*has*] changed everything," *ibid.*, p. 17. (Actually, it has not changed quite "everything." This book is substantially concerned with determining what, in the order of Christian belief, has been changed by the phenomenological method and what has *not yet* been changed by it.) On the other hand, Maritain evidently misunderstands the nature of phenomenology: for example, he deems it to be nothing but "the latest among the mutations of idealism," *ibid.*, p. 162. Moreover, Maritain's epistemological misunderstanding begins with idealism itself; his aversion to it has now been revealed to rest upon a mixture of philosophical misunderstanding and religious prejudice (which is itself the result of a misunderstanding of the nature of Christian doctrine itself). Thus, he supposes that "the Bible and the Gospel exclude radically every sort of idealism, in the philosophical sense of this word," and that "Christianity professes, with confident impudence, that which in the philosophical vocabulary is called realism . . . It must be said . . . that a Christian may not be an idealist," (*ibid*, pp. 148–149.) I have no wish to save idealism, but Maritain's opinion, which is close to superstition, is evidently due to an understanding of idealism which is much less sophisticated than one's reading of his earlier *Les Degrés du Savoir* would have led one to suspect. For he continues: "the all-powerful God who created the world and whose voice Moses heard, did he hold his existence and his glory from the mind that knew him? And the people which this God chose for himself, and the land to which he led it, with its vineyards, its olive groves and its wheat—all these men and all these things that the land touches and the eye sees, were they objects without form or

expressed, like the agony of decisions reluctantly taken, should mutually manifest, to traditionalist and progressive alike, the conscientious (though possibly benighted) nature of each other's views.

It is always easy to doubt the sincerity of those with whom one disagrees. Part of the reason is that, whereas one always knows oneself to be interested in the truth, sometimes one does not know how to account for someone else's dissenting opinion, (which must be deemed, of course, to be mistaken) except on the grounds of either intellectual or else moral fault. If truth is but the outcome of looking at what-is and grasping it, those who disagree with one's understanding of the truth cannot be in the same good faith that one knows oneself to be in, unless they lacked intelligence or opportunity. This may be, *prima facie,* not an entirely unreasonable view. Yet, it may be more reasonable still, whenever it is necessary to study the motives of one's opponents—and sometimes this is indeed the case—to rule oneself not by the supposed moral implications of whatever speculative opinions they may entertain but by the positive indications given by their behaviour. But when we do so, we usually find, as we do in the case of traditionalists and progressives, that most people are sincerely interested in the truth. (I shall also suggest in this book why error, however egregious, is not necessarily the sign of deficient intelligence even for those in the best faith.) Failure to attain the truth, even when the necessary wit and

solidity except in dependence upon the mind that knew them? And the Word who came down to take flesh and human nature in a virgin of Israel: does the Gospel ask us to believe in this Word, and in this flesh, and in this human nature that he made his own, as in pure ideas of our mind? And the Christ preaching in the highways . . . ," etc. *Ibid.,* p. 148.

acquaintance with the facts is present, is not a reliable indication of the nature of anybody's personal disposition towards the truth. It may be, however, an indication of the inadequacy of any view of the nature of truth which leads one, by its own inner logic, to intolerance, suspicion and arrogance. It does take some imprudence to think that one's own truth can under any conditions reveal the wickedness of someone else's mistake.

In sum, division of the Church into traditionalists and progressives does not necessarily indicate a moral failure on anyone's part.[9] On the contrary, the division reveals a common concern for the *truth,* which is in turn presupposed by a common act of faith in Catholic doctrine *as true.* It is indeed this very concern which lies at the root of intolerance. For some Catholics, whether traditionalists or progressives, conceive the nature of truth, and therefore also the nature of error, in a manner which requires them in good logic to fear for the faith unless their way of thinking should prevail. They who so believe will be tempted to practice intolerance, whether in defense of traditionalism, or with

___

[9] This is not to say that there is no moral issue involved. Traditionalists frequently appear constitutionally unable to entertain the possibility that they may be mistaken, and so they sometimes fail to take with sufficient seriousness the possibility that the translation of traditionalism into practice may be, objectively speaking, morally wrong. The assumption of some traditionalists, that in case of doubt traditionalism is always "safe," is far from self-evident. In connection with contraception, for instance, (quite apart from the truth of the matter), automatically to resolve any doubt in favour of the traditional prohibition would be most imprudent. For if the progressivist opinion on the subject should be correct, then contraception may be morally imperative under certain, fairly common, conditions; and under such conditions to abstain from contraceptive practices might, be unequivocally wrong. Traditionalists do not often enough entertain the thought that unfaithfulness to the Catholic tradition and the Christian spirit may as surely, though less spectacularly, occur through unwarranted stability as through unwarranted change.

much less consistency, in defense of progressivism; and I repeat that if the more obvious and frequent instances of such intolerance are to be found among traditionalists, the fact that progressives as a whole have fewer opportunities to be intolerant probably has something to do with the fact.

There are, however, other members of the Church who, whether because they are inconsistent with their traditionalism or because they are consistent with their progressivism, whether because their concept of truth so dictates or because their good will compels their prudence so to judge, do not believe that whoever disagrees with their understanding of Christian belief should be invited to leave the Church. For one reason or another, they feel that this is the sort of invitation no fellow Christian can be grateful for, and that he who should issue it might be at least as guilty as he who would in reply accept. However, although tolerance may be practiced in charity by anyone, it may be consistently understood only by him who consciously or unconsciously takes a different view of the nature of truth than that which leads traditionalists to traditionalism. And tolerance can be more aptly justified by a sound understanding of its nature than by charity—though it is, of course, more likely to be practiced well by those whose charity is genuine than by those who can only count upon their understanding of the matter being sound. At any rate, some members of the Church take the view that the truth of their belief demands cultivation and development, that although the truth of tradition must indeed be preserved its preservation depends not upon its reiteration in a traditional form but upon its cultivation and development. They think, in other words, that to remain true, the truth cannot remain the same. For the truth does not really remain, but develop, and the original truth cannot retain its original value for evolving man unless it evolves as man himself evolves. The common concern with the truth of the Catholic faith leads to conflict not because different people begin with belief in different doctrines, but because they begin with different concepts of truth. If the current division in the Church is to be healed, it is necessary to discuss the different concepts of truth implicit in the division itself.

But truth can be conceived only in relation to knowledge, a wider, more basic concept: without some idea of knowledge one cannot very well think of either true or false. And knowledge, or any equivalent way of conceiving man's awareness of, or relation to, reality, is similarly connected to a concept of reality, that is, a concept of that *to which* consciousness relates itself. It seems, then, that the two issues on which contemporary Catholic belief is divided are not, at their most basic and real level, specific doctrinal beliefs, but the very foundations of belief.

This should not be surprising. After all, religion has to do with the most real, vital and important modes of self-disposition of man's free existence; and this is but another way of referring to man's conscious, free, self-relation to reality. Surely the specific way in which man conceives reality, and the specific way in which he conceives what it is for him to be related to reality—for instance, what it is "to know" and "to love"—will determine the limits within which his religious consciousness can expand. Man's implicit or explicit, primitive or elaborate, conscious or unconscious, assumptions about the nature of his self-relation to reality, and about the nature of the reality to which he relates himself, are the two foundations of all religious belief.

The heart of the contemporary problem of Christian belief is, thus, whether the traditional assumptions of Christian doctrine concerning the nature of *truth* and of *reality* remain adequate—that is, whether they remain sufficiently true or whether they do not require improvement—and, if they should be found wanting, what alternative philosophical foundations must be laid by Christian thought in order to reconstruct upon them those forms of Christian religious belief which would correspond to the contemporary level of the evolution of human experience, and which would permit, as it were, the introduction of planification into the religious economy of the Christian Church. This is the problem to which this book addresses itself.

PURPOSE

The progressivist project of consciously undertaking the redevelopment of Christian belief implies the judgment that the traditional forms of Christianity are not only out of phase with contemporary experience, but that these forms are inadequate to contemporary experience. (I stress, in this view it is the forms that are inadequate to experience, rather than the other way about.) Progressivism implies, therefore, a conscious or unconscious, philosophical or common sensical, criticism of the basic principles of all traditional Christian philosophical thought.

As an impression this is not a rare view among Catholics today: the irrelevance of Scholastic philosophy to the 20th century is no longer the uncommon assumption that it had been until recent times. However, although I concur with the general truth which this judgment expresses, certain qualifications seem to me to be in order. First, it is not enough to operate under impressions,

40

THE CONTEMPORARY PROBLEM OF BELIEF

however valid these may in fact be. The contemporary Church, or the contemporary Catholic philosophical community, should beware of dismissing Scholasticism in general, or neo-Thomism in particular, and least of all the thought of St. Thomas himself, either on the basis of impressions or, in any event, in principle or wholesale. No contemporary Christian philosopher should rightly, in my opinion, practice any variety of Scholastic thought or lapse into any manner of discipleship, Thomistic [10] or otherwise. On the other hand, it may not be much worse to be a Thomist than to be an anti-Thomist, to be a faithful follower of St. Thomas than to be a faithful follower of a contemporary philosopher, to be a faithful believer than to be a faithful disbeliever in Thomism. Anyone can sneer at Thomism as *passé* and irrelevant; but the philosopher must know why Thomism is outmoded and irrelevant (to the degree and in the sense that it may be said in fact so to be).

This leads to the second reason why contemporary Catholic philosophy—at least to the degree that it is seriously and professionally practiced—cannot neglect the study and analysis of Thomism and indeed of all past theological and philosophical thought. Regardless of the inadequacy of past thought to present situations, the past can never be *historically* irrelevant to the present. The past *as past* can never lose its truth. The neglect of the conservation, study and appreciation of the Christian past, (philosophical or otherwise), would be the self-mutilation of the present Christian consciousness. It would be a sin against the future, the very future which the present is by nature required to create. Thus, any assessment of the sufficiency or insufficiency

[10] In this connection no distinction need be made between traditional Thomism and transcendental Thomism.

41

of the Christian past, (philosophical or otherwise), which we may have retained *as present* would be worse than useless if it were not critically derived. Progressivism would be ironically reactionary to the very degree to which its implicit or explicit criticism of the foundations of traditional belief failed to be analytically and empirically grounded.

If progressivism ultimately implies, as I believe it does, a sharp divergence from the concepts of *truth* and of *reality* enshrined in traditional Catholic philosophical thought, then progressivism must consciously undertake a philosophical analysis of the inadequacies of those principles—principles which at one time were doubtlessly adequate to the then current level of development of man—and of the process whereby traditional philosophical thought became dysfunctional with the passage of time. This process—may I incidentally remark—is all the more puzzling because its causes must be sought within the confines of the Hellenic-Western Christian culture, since this tradition has never been more than superficially affected by cultural diffusion from other civilizations.[11] These analyses are important not so much

[11] I assume, of course, the fact that Christianity originated in a non-Hellenic (though, especially in the *diaspora,* partly hellenized) culture. I would not minimize the extent to which Hebrew categories permeate Christianity to this very day. My point is rather that the original Hebrew culture forms of Christianity gave birth to Christendom in monogamous marriage with Hellenism. In the middle ages a certain amount of Arabic blood entered the line through the Arab conquest and protracted occupation of Spain; but even this served only to reinforce the Semitic strain of Christendom.

I should also remark at this point, against the opinion of those who promote the contemporary dehellenization of Christianity in favour of its re-Hebraization, (e.g. the substitution of biblical for Scholastic categories), that Christianity has already travelled the road *from* Hebraism. There is no reason or sense in going back. The future lies ahead, beyond hellenized Hebraism, not in pre-hellenized Hebraism.

because they would lend greater certainty to the opinion that the traditional philosophical bases of Christian belief are inadequate: the object of criticism is not evaluation for its own sake, but for the sake of understanding.

To be sufficiently certain that no philosophy of the past, however renovated its terminology and concepts, can speak with direct relevance to the situation of later times—if later times have really witnessed the evolution of man and not merely changes in "accidental" respects—does not require philosophical acumen, it only requires some perceptiveness and realism. Indeed, this may be more evident to the layman than to the philosopher. The deeper reason why progressivism must be based upon an analysis of the philosophical foundations of the past is, however, that no cultural reconstruction—least of all that of basic philosophical concepts—can take place except in and through the understanding of the adequacies and inadequacies of the processes that led to the present difficulties of past thought. (There can be, as it were, no true purpose of amendment without a serious examination of conscience.) We may consider an analogy from psychotherapy: personality disorders cannot be psychoanalytically corrected without first tracing the processes that led to them. In human affairs generally, corrective therapy can hardly be distinguished from aetiological analysis, and the reorganization of consciousness is but the obverse of the interpretation of the unconscious. Likewise, the reshaping of the future is but the other side of the analysis of the past.

Thus, the thesis I will develop in this book falls into two complementary parts. The first part, the burden of which is carried by Chapters 2 and 3, outlines the dynamic of Hellenic-Western philosophical thought in its relation to religious belief. Since the

43

interpretation I will offer is somewhat complex, it may be useful to offer at this point a brief summary of these two chapters to serve as a rough means of orientation through an avowedly intricate exposition of an interpretation of the history of philosophical thought which will be unfamiliar to most readers, as it has not been frequently advanced by philosophers in the past. [12]

[12] I may note, however, the view of Johannes B. Metz, so close to my own, according to which: "the epochal transformation which took place in the middle ages (in Thomas Aquinas) and still influences modern thought, the change in the metaphysical understanding of being and self, and the growing methodical and reflexive independence of metaphysics from theology, did not arise in opposition to the historically developing logos of Christianity but through it, for this logos supposes a growing independent understanding of its own existence as a condition for the grounding of its existence. [Para.] In its encounter with Greek thought medieval Christian theology at first takes on what looks like a closed metaphysical form. But this metaphysical face of theology is not simply Greek metaphysics as received. In its highest expression in Thomas Aquinas it is a genuinely new metaphysical approach, even though it is couched in Greek terms and categories. This is quickly recognized if we look not merely backwards from Thomas to Aristotle but forwards as well. It goes far beyond a thematic enrichment of Greek metaphysics. It changes the whole horizon of the understanding of being and self. In [sic] can therefore be called an epochal turning point in metaphysics, a term to be applied not to every added idea but only to a new way of thinking of being, in whose horizon all thought content is lodged. It is in this sense that the middle ages began to transmit a new epoch in metaphysics, an epoch in which the understanding of being was impressed with the stamp of the Christian logos. [Para.] How does this appear? The man who enters metaphysics within the horizon of the historical and existence-founding Christian logos does so by reflecting upon himself from a certain point of view. He is orientated not primarily toward thing-relationships but toward existence-relationships that are historically unique. He sees himself not as a static world-reason but as subjectivity which in freedom (before God) definitively binds and perfects himself. His way of thinking is not cosmocentric but anthropocentric. Thus we see in the Christian metaphysics of the middle ages the beginning of the great change from Greek cosmocentrism to anthropocentrism, from ob-

Because of the cultural circumstances under which Judaism gave birth to Christianity, namely, the ecumenical prevalence of Hellenism, the universalism of the Universal Faith of Christianity, required, (especially after St. Paul), the rapid substitution of the specifically Hebrew bases of belief by their Hellenic, philosophical counterparts. But despite the considerable adaptation and creative modifications imposed upon Hellenism by Christian thinkers, a certain incompatibility between Christian belief and the pagan attitudes that were incarnated in Greek philosophy never ceased to preoccupy the Christian mind. Christian speculation, itself due in great part to the adoption of the Socratic faith in reason, derived much of its vitality from this inner challenge, that is, from the constantly recurring and ever more trenchant conflict between Greek reason and Christian faith. But the climax was reached in the 13th century, when for the first time a Christian thinker, namely, St. Thomas Aquinas, succeeded in de-

jectivity to subjectivity, or better from an objectively ontic to a transcendental-ontological understanding of the subject, from nature to history, from abstract to concrete universality, from the static thing in space to the person in time. [Para.] In brief, this change has been unfolding conceptually and categorially in modern thought, in Pascal, Leibniz, Kant, and the German Idealists; in Kierkegaard, Nietzsche, up to phenomenology and existential philosophy. *In all this development, with all due reservations in particular cases, we see the growing metaphysical self-understanding of a reason that has encountered the Christian logos,"* "The Theological World and the Metaphysical World," *Philosophy Today*, X, 4 (Winter, 1966), 253–263, pp. 258–259. [Italics mine]. Apart from the fact that I would not wish even momentarily to opt for subjectivism—for, as I shall attempt to show in this book, the difficulty with the epistemology of the Hellenic-Western tradition does not lie with objectivity, but with the dichotomy of objectivity-subjectivity—my only disagreement with this passage concerns the assertion that all thought content is lodged in the horizon of being. I think this view needs considerable qualification. I shall also take up this question in detail below.

veloping a metaphysics which, to be sure, made use of Greek speculation, but which embodied a view of reality which in certain key respects (though not in all) transcended the most basic assumptions of Greek thought concerning the nature of reality. This was a critical moment in the history of Christian, if not also human, evolution. St. Thomas' idea of reality has remained at work in the Christian world to our own day, having undergone many modifications, but no essential change. However, St. Thomas did not depart from Greek thought in any essential respect in what pertains to the nature of human thought, in which sphere his doctrine barely improved upon Greek and earlier Christian philosophy.[13] The course of later philosophical thought in the Christian world has been determined by the attempt of philosophers, taking advantage of St. Thomas' metaphysical insights, to cope with the incompatibility between St. Thomas' metaphysics and his epistemology.

But since St. Thomas' metaphysics was only partly liberated from Greek thought, the eventual success of later speculation in relation to epistemological problems automatically revealed the inadequacies of St. Thomas' metaphysics. Insofar as Christian belief retained the epistemological and metaphysical foundations set down by St. Thomas, (which remained without essential modification in later Scholasticism), Christian belief has naturally become alienated from the historical development of Western

[13] There are some important differences between the Greek (including the Aristotelian) and the Thomistic doctrines on the nature of man, and in particular on the nature of the human soul. These do not gainsay the opinion I have stated. Moreover, St. Thomas' divergence from Greek thought in these respects did not have nearly as subversive consequences for Christian Hellenism as did his divergences in the order of metaphysics.

Christian philosophical thought and, therefore, also from all those areas of the Western Christian world which have been influenced by post-mediaeval philosophy. Conversely, the modern philosophical tradition of Western Christendom, as well as much of the Western Christian world it has helped shape, have found it impossible to profess a Christian belief the foundations of which simply did not take favourable account of the development of post-mediaeval philosophical (and scientific) thought.

After explaining in some detail this historical construction, and after having adduced some evidence in its support, I will develop in the second part of this book the consequences of the conclusion to which the first part shall have led: the project of redeveloping Christian belief cannot rest either (a) on the traditional philosophical foundations, or (b) on those provided by contemporary thought, as they presently stand. Progressivists have correctly concluded the former, but traditionalists have not been altogether mistaken when they have asserted the latter. But traditionalists have been mistaken, however, when they have imagined that a return to the philosophical past was therefore both desirable and possible—when in reality it is probably impossible and in any event a worse remedy than the disease.

It is true that contemporary thought cannot support Christian belief. But the reason, as I shall attempt to show, is only that post-mediaeval philosophy, for all its successful exploitation of St. Thomas' creative transcendence of Greek *metaphysical* thought, (reaping a harvest which St. Thomas himself did not intend to sow, namely, the transcendence of the basic concepts of Greek *epistemological* thought), has at no time since St. Thomas so much as conceived the possibility of transcending certain basic assumptions of Greek metaphysics which were retained by St. Thomas. In other words, the dehellenization of Christian philosophy was initiated in part by St. Thomas, and complemented [14] in *another part* by contemporary thought. Contemporary *Christian* thought should now complete what St. Thomas only initiated, and should revise what contemporary thought has achieved. An exposition of the nature of the essentials of this double task is the burden of Chapters 4 and 5. The concluding chapter sums up the findings, hinting at some of the directions that the consciously undertaken evolution of Christian belief would take, if the project were erected on the philosophical foundations which Christian thought should first reconstruct *ad hoc*.

I assume I need not underline that no individual Christian philosopher could reasonably expect to be equal to the magnitude of the task which proposes itself today to the Christian intellect. Enterprises of this ambitious nature may have been possible at the time of Descartes, but the problem is much more difficult in our time, and the solution correspondingly more complex. A concentrated, cooperative effort of many minds and competences would be mandatory today. But it should not be considered presumptuous of any Christian to attempt to make his own, however limited, contribution to that end. If this enquiry does no more than to raise some of the questions that Christian philosophy should ask at this particular moment in the history of Christian belief, its purpose will have been fully achieved. If,

---

[14] I say complemented, not completed. As we shall see, the incompatibility of modern thought with Christian belief stems from the incomplete dehellenization of the former, and is compounded by the retention of Hellenism by the latter.

beyond this eventuality, it should also happen that these reflections map out with sufficient accuracy, if only in broad outline, the area to be explored, and therefore inspire others to till the same intellectual ground, then its success will have been crowned with an unearned, unexpected reward.

2.

The Traditional Foundations
of Belief

HELLENISM AND FATE

If there is a single word which more accurately than any other sums up all the factors that have shaped the complex civilization known as Western Christendom, that word is *charity*—even if, symptomatically, we are not completely certain what this word means. But if there is a single word which performs the like function for the Hellenic world, that word is *Fate*. The most fundamental concept at work in Greco-Roman culture was the idea that whatever happens, happens necessarily. The course of events is essentially inexorable; the problem of man is how to cope with a world of reality, and with a human situation, the outcome of which is (at least in priciple) set beforehand. Despite a seemingly innate human inclination to endeavour and to strive, all human efforts appear, upon reflection, utterly vain.

The central role of the concept of Fate in Hellenism has been well established.[1] It is more difficult to ascertain why this idea, which permeated the entire Hellenic civilization, should have

[1] Perhaps the most comprehensive study of this subject is William Chase Greene's *Moira: Fate, Good and Evil in Greek Thought*, (Cambridge, Mass., 1944), which includes ample bibliographical information.

taken such early and tenacious roots on Greek soil.[2] One may, however, speculate on certain aspects of human experience which may have rendered this phenomenon possible. Let us recall that pessimism is not peculiar to the Hellenic world. Many primitive cultures and early civilizations have experienced the world as an inhospitable environment in which man is buffeted about by uncontrollable forces: surely the harshness of primitive and early civilized life is a factor in the creation of this attitude. Nor were the Greeks and the Romans unique in the intensity with which they experience reality as frustrating the endeavor of man. The Sumero-Acadians, for instance, exceeded Greek pessimism by far, and regarded the world of reality not only as frustrating, but as positively hostile and malevolent. At least in relation to man, the world was not a friendly habitat, and at least some of the forces that the world manifested were essentially evil. Demonolatry attempted to propitiate fearful deities, and dualism attempted to explain why the world, despite first impressions, was not really all bad, and why there was in reality not only evil, but also good.

---

[2] The process by which Greek philosophy evolved from the Greek religious belief in Fate, but remained to its last days marked by this faith was the object of F. M. Cornford's early, but still unsurpassed, study *From Religion to Philosophy: A Study in the Origins of Western Speculation,* (London, 1912), whose thesis was "that a real thread of continuity can be traced back from the final achievement of [Greek] science—the representation of a world of individual atoms, governed by Necessity or Chance—to the final achievement of Olimpianism, mirrored in Homer's supernatural world of individual Gods, subordinate to Destiny (*Moira*). This subjection of all individual powers, divine and human, to *Moira* is the profoundest, and (at first sight) the most baffling dogma in this type of religion," whence Cornford proceeded to "attempt an analysis of *Moira* . . . with a view to establishing the persistence of this conception, right on through the course of Greek science, in which it holds the place now occupied by Natural Law," (p. vii).

Likewise, many of the higher religions of the Far East offer to man one form or another of ultimate hope, but only on the presupposition that "man is born unto sorrow, even as the sparks fly upwards." For instance, the first of The Four Noble Truths of Buddhism is *duhkha,* suffering; that is, suffering is the basic fact of life.

To a degree unparallelled in other cultures, however, the Greeks diverted their belief in Fate into constructive channels. The creation of tragedy as a dramatic form may be taken as a symbolic instance of the inventiveness which the Greeks brought to their experience of Fate. With unique aptness tragedy exhibits the two principal features of the peculiarly Greek reaction to a fateful world. Tragedy shows, in the first place, the antinomy between man's natural, inevitable dissatisfaction with the way reality is—and therefore the way reality treats him—and the natural, inevitable law which decrees that this situation will forever remain the same. However, this is only the background, the precondition, of Greek tragedy. The essential tragedy of human existence is that not only the world, but man himself is fated, and that his Fate is sealed by himself. For man is condemned to hope for the hopeless, he is fated to struggle against Fate. Endowed by nature with the ability to know good and evil, to discriminate between what actually is and what he would like to bring about, man is doomed, not by the distressing events that befall him, but by the peculiarity of his nature, which makes him able to conceive an alternative to what actually is.

Hence, man's Destiny is fated, not only in the sense that pain, suffering and distress are inevitable, but also the sense that his own ability to suppose that his situation might be otherwise is the source of his deepest unhappiness. Man is frustrated above

52

all by his own impotence to bring about in reality what he can easily fashion in his dreams. And this powerlessness is not even the result of his being deprived of the means to achieve happiness, namely, reason and will: it is the unavoidable consequence of the ineffectiveness of these means in the fact of the machinations of Fate. Thus, man's torture is essentially that of Tantalus. Nature gives man an ambivalent, tormenting gift, namely, the consciousness of his condition. For consciousness means, on the one hand, his awakening to the theoretical possibility of ideal happiness and, on the other, the realization that in point of fact happiness cannot be attained. Though man insofar as he is free and intelligent deserves, as it were, a better fate than that which Fate has in store for him, he remains subject to Fate. For by his very nature, by his intelligence and freedom, he conspires in the creation of his own Fate, as his attempt to escape Fate turns out to be the very mechanism by which Fate overtakes him—let us recall, for instance, the clearest exposition of this belief in *Oedipus Tyrannus*. And the ultimate tragedy of man is that, in this manner his own conspiracy with Fate in the creation of his own undoing renders him guilty and, thus, deserving of his undeserved Fate: man's awareness of Fate and its nature renders him "proud" and, thus *justly* apt to be smitten by Fate. The Fate that smites him is the Fate that he, by his own nature as a conscious being, himself brings about.

Consciousness, awareness of one's self as aware of reality, is, evidently, the first condition of the possibility of perceiving the world of reality as constituted by inevitable necessity. And since it is not at all difficult for man, especially under primitive conditions, to be overwhelmed by unhappiness, even to the point that he will believe himself to be at one and the same time (a) constitutionally entitled, by his very nature, to perfect and unending happiness and (b) opposed by a world which constitutionally, by its very nature, fails to ply him with perfect and unending happiness, it is not without cause (though hardly with sufficient reason) that man sometimes perceives the world in which he exists as the source of all frustration. The converse of this is perceiving the world as pervaded by necessity, and, not surprisingly, primitive cultures have frequently so perceived it. What distinguishes the Greeks is that they were the first human society to have grasped certain further implications which man's awareness of his awareness has for his Fateful situation. For in this very awareness the Greeks found the suggestion of a possible avenue of escape from Fate: the human intellect.

In its original Greek sense *philosophy* was but the disciplined and efficient human use of reason for "speculative," "theoretical" purposes. However, these terms are somewhat misleading unless we strip them of their later, Western connotations. *Speculation* and *theory* do not indicate lack of existential interest; they point to ultimate, rather than immediate, practice and value. Philosophical speculation and philosophical theory emerged in Greece as reason's attempt to exorcise and manage Fate. Thales' idea that "all things are full of gods" [3] is not a statement of animism but, on the contrary, a profession of faith in human reason. It means that the divinities are not actually found in peculiar or sacred places or times, as mythology, (indeed, as all primitive religions), naturally tend to suppose.[4] The divinities lie immediately before us, in things themselves. Of course, this relocation

---

[3] According to Aristotle, *On the Soul,* I, 5 (411 a 7).
[4] Cf. Mircea Eliade, *The Sacred and the Profane,* (New York, 1961), Chapter I.

of the mysterious force of inevitability from sacred places to the interior of "all things" does not diminish the fatefulness of Fate. Nevertheless, its relocation in that which is at hand may make it manageable: at the very least it directs man's attention to the study of the "inner" constitution of things. Thus arises the idea that the philosopher ascertains the "nature" of reality. This nature is nothing other than their inner necessity, for the nature of any reality is what it is "born" to be. To say that "all things are full of gods" is to say that the fatefulness of Fate has its ultimate source in the inner constitution of things; it is to say that necessity is not extrinsic to the reality of the things of the empirical world, but intrinsic to them.

Thus, if Fate is the central concept of Hellenism, *nature* is the central concept of Greek philosophy. In its original non-technical sense, the term φύσις, (*natura,* birthness) already had the connotation of inevitability: a thing was what it was because that was the way it was "born." But with the transposition of necessity from the mythical agencies of the three Fates to the single inner principle of the constitution of things, the *nature* of a thing indicated at one and the same time the source of its invariable behaviour as well as the principle of its constitution in reality. Thus, to ascertain the *real* nature of anything was the same as to ascertain its inner necessity. For instance, the philosopher could be said to achieve the knowledge which was proper to philosophy, namely science, only when he knew with certitude, that is, when he ascertained the necessities that governed the appearance and behaviour of things. For ascertaining these necessities lent to the intellect its necessary truth. The mind was certain when it did not fear the possibility of error; and the mind could discard this possibility reasonably only when its knowledge was necessarily true. But the mind's knowledge was necessarily true only when its affirmations reflected the inner necessities of things. Thus, "the proper object of unqualified scientific knowledge is something which cannot be other than it is." [5]

It is sometimes supposed that behind the Greek creation of science there lay a disbelief in the mysterious quality of reality. Quite to the contrary, Greek philosophy is a reaffirmation of it. The hidden powers of reality are real. They are all the more real because their reality does not obtain outside reality but within it, and because it is not foreign to reality but constitutive of it. The distinction between appearance and reality confirms this: there is an inner truth of things which is not readily evident but which can be extricated from things, as it were, through the use of the human intellect. In sum, the creation of the very concept of philosophy must be interpreted as the peculiarly Greek reaction to the world in which civilized man had made his evolutionary appearance. Greek philosophy embodied man's first act of faith in the intellect, and expressed man's first act of hope that his struggle with the overwhelming reality of a Fateful world might perhaps end in an unforeseeable victory for man.

This was not, moreover, a blind faith; it was not an unreasonable hope. For this fate and this hope were grounded upon an implicit realization that man's consciousness or awareness is what defines his fundamental and constitutive relation to reality. The discovery of the Greeks, therefore, was the astoundingly simple and elementary idea that man *by nature* relates himself to reality: that man's relation to reality is a *self-relation* to reality. Ever since man had become man he had been relating himself to reality. But now he discovered this very fact, namely, that *he*

[5] Aristotle, *Posterior Analytics*, I, 2 (71 b 15).

related himself to reality. This was a discovery which must be counted as a permanent, and most probably irreversible gain in human progress. It was not, of course, the last time that man would make a discovery of comparable import, as we shall have occasion to note in the next chapter. But first we must inquire more precisely into the nature of the Greek conscious discovery of the human mind's relativity to the reality of the world.

KNOWLEDGE AND TRUTH

I have stressed so far one aspect of the Greek reaction to the experience of reality by early civilized man, namely, that aspect which can be accounted for in terms of the nature of man himself and of his experience, as these are found at the level of human evolution to which both Greek and even contemporary Western man belong. If it is true, as we have some reason to believe, that man's nature is to be understood in terms of his awareness of his own awareness of reality, it follows that the Greek discovery of intellect, the discovery of the intellect as a power for dealing with reality as such, was perfectly logical. It was the "natural" step which man would sooner or later take. It was the step which, knowing what we now know about the nature of man, we would have expected man to take. It was a step which, in principle, any other human culture might have taken, but a step which in point of fact the Greeks, and only the Greeks, happened to take. However, perhaps I have expressed this fact in a misleading way. The statement may seem to have carried the implication that the course of human development was itself fated beforehand, at least in the sense that certain potentialities, and no others, were present in human nature, and that human development was but the inevitable resultant perfection of those potentialities as such. This is not, however, what I intended to convey. What I had in mind was that we today can understand the nature of the Greek achievement because we ourselves have been formed by it.

For it is only after man has learned to define himself in terms of his consciousness that he can appreciate the logic of the process by which he became conscious of himself. Like every moment in human evolution, the discovery of the human intellect was ambiguous and ambivalent. With the Greeks man learned to understand himself as relative to reality. But the concrete way in which this was learned, and the precise manner in which it was conceptualized—these were at one and the same time grounded upon the nature of human experience and yet peculiarly and contingently Greek. They constituted a permanent gain, and yet were "destined" to be superseded—to be superseded, indeed, precisely in the same measure that man profited from the insight of the Greeks. Thus, the Greek concepts of man and of his relations to reality are warranted by what human nature *in fact* is. But that the Greeks so conceived man and his relation to reality does have some relation to what human nature is in fact *today*. In other words, though human nature warranted the Greek discovery, the Greek view of man's relation to reality is not eternally valid. The Greek concept of man's relation to reality *can* be superseded; and yet, the view that supersedes it can be historically accounted for only in terms of the peculiarly Greek understanding and conceptualization of the human facts. This is why in order to appreciate the true wisdom of Greek thought it is indispensable to criticize it. The depth of any later culture's appreciation of, and even agreement with, Greek thought is reached not when Greek thought is recaptured and repeated, but only when it is transcended. What, then, is peculiarly Greek—and, therefore, what is to be transcended—in the Greek understanding of man's relation to reality?

I have suggested that, like other peoples, the Greeks thought of necessity as pertaining to the nature of reality, but that, unlike other cultures, the Greek civilization discerned within the self-experience of man the possibility of escaping the fatefulness of reality. I have also implied that, apart from the question whether reality is validly apprehended as constituted by necessity, (and I believe it is not), the Greek attempt to escape Fate was warranted by the nature which human consciousness *does* exhibit. This means: although the problem of man may not have been what the Greeks took it to be, their solution to *their* problem was grounded on facts concerning the nature of human experience which are valid enough. Valid enough, that is, for *their* purpose. For the way in which the Greeks conceptualized their experience of the facts of human experience was itself conditioned, as one might expect, by the nature of the problems to which the conceptualization was directed. Hence, the Greek insight into the human fact which we now call *consciousness* was conditioned by the Greek preoccupation with the fatefulness of reality. This is why the observation that man relates himself to reality was cast by the Greeks, not in such terms as those I have used here—for example, not in terms of *consciousness,* or of any Greek equivalent thereof—but in terms of man's *knowledge* of the world.

The peculiarly Greek conceptualization of man's self-relation to reality in terms of knowledge implied that within man's

59

mental life there was a distinction between the power (or powers) which put man in possession of the necessity of reality—powers which, as it were, handed over and delivered to him the inevitability of reality—and, on the other hand, the power (or powers) which might enable him to manage and manipulate within himself what was delivered to him, and thus to impose upon reality (at least within his own inner world) his own necessity and will. We can in retrospect appreciate the logic of the Greek reasoning—indeed, we can admire the wiliness of their methodology. It is a fact that the world does not necessarily behave in the way man wishes it to do; if this is indeed a fact, it would be foolish to imagine that simply by wanting it badly enough man could make reality conform to his wishes. The facts that man dislikes the way certain things are, and that he is frequently thwarted by events, directly imply that there is a distinction between what he wants or what he may desire, and what is really the case. But what is really the case is definable in terms of that which is not subject to human rule: it is that about which we can do nothing, (except perhaps reflect it and grasp it inwardly at the same time that we inwardly resist its effective rule). Greek philosophy invented the stratagem of joining the enemy that one cannot beat.[6] In other words, the understandable (and even, relatively speaking, justified) Greek preoccupation with Fate, under the sign of which the Greeks became creatively aware of human consciousness, imprinted its form on their discovery of man's relativity to reality. This influence is directly responsible for the division of human consciousness by the Greeks into two realms, cognition and appetition, and particularly into understanding and will.

[6] More precisely, the Greeks erected the stratagem into a *method*.

I stress again that this dichotomy is not entirely arbitrary—philosophical interpretations rarely are. But the idea that there are in man two distinct orders of faculties with distinct operations specified by distinct objects—this is not above criticism, and, as will be suggested below, there may be better and more comprehensive ways of interpreting the experiential facts. I will not, therefore, attempt to explain at this point what in the nature of human experience *does* lend colour to the classical opposition of knowing and desiring. For present purposes it will be enough to note that this fundamental distinction implies that the principal, basic, typical, natural and most proper human relation to reality is that of contemplation, as Plato and Aristotle repeatedly and extensively remarked. The extent to which Christianity adopted —to be sure, only after thoroughly adapting—the Greek outlook on reality is shown perhaps nowhere as graphically and decisively than in the eventual Christian interpretation of "salvation"— which in the Gospel is couched in terms of "heavenly banquet," attaining to "the kingdom of God," "rising from the dead," and so on—in terms of the intellect's Beatific Vision of God.[7]

According to the Greeks, appetition, striving and self-exertion *follow* upon cognition. And they follow contingently: we may or may not desire, will and act after we know. On the other hand, if we are to desire, will and act, it is necessary *first* to know. Moreover, if man's primary, fundamental and necessary relation to reality is, as it were, that of acquaintance rather than friendship, it follows that human awareness must be understood in

---

[7] According to St. Thomas, "the essence of happiness consists in an act of the intellect," *ST*, I–II, 3, 4, and "the ultimate and perfect happiness, which we expect in the future life, consists entirely in contemplation," *ST*, I–II, 3, 5.

relatively passive terms. To be acquainted with reality is not to interact with it; it is to witness it, to reflect it inwardly, to grasp it as it is in itself. It is not, for instance, to converse with it; it is to see it, to watch it go by, to observe it as it follows its own (necessary) way. The idea that there is a pre-condition to man's possible manipulation of reality, to man's attempt to shape the world, and to man's self-determination in relation to it, implies that there must be a prior relation to reality, namely, cognition, that *excludes* manipulation, formation and self-determination.

Thus, when human consciousness was conceptualized by the Greeks as *knowledge,* this term was automatically burdened with the connotation of objectivity which it has retained to our own day. The world is as it is; reality is what it is. That is, reality is not what we may wish it or imagine it to be. (This is, of course, true enough in a *primitive* way.) To know is to grasp reality *objectively*. The facts are *given* by reality, and they are given *in* reality, and the knower can but repeat them (inwardly, to himself) as they are *in themselves*. The universe in which knowledge happens is the universe of two solitudes: man and his world. Man's solitude in the face of the solitude of the world is the immediate, direct and necessary consequence of sundering human consciousness into intellect, which sees but does not touch, and will, which may or may not touch what the intellect sees, but which does not, in any event, communicate with reality but imposes—or, for that matter, gives—itself to it.

Before I continue this analysis of the classical understanding of human consciousness I should suggest briefly two far-reaching consequences of the division of human experience into two distinct modes of self-relation to reality, two orders of mental life which operate in opposite direction to each other. These remarks are not relevant to the immediate discussion, but we shall have occasion to recall them below.

It is sometimes thought that the Greeks were so enamoured of stability and immutability that they defined reality itself in terms of self-identity. It seems to me, however, that this view confuses cause and effect. It is possible that this misconstruction originates in the normal foreshortening of historical perspective, which produces in many students of philosophy the impression that Plato and Aristotle were the creators of the Greek philosophical spirit rather than its climax. The fact is rather that the Greeks were struck by the reality of change at least as forcibly as all perceptive, reflective human cultures have always been. Indeed, some Greeks, particularly among the philosophers, could be said to have been very overwhelmed by the reality of change: the Sophists and Heraclitus are as typical of Greek thought as Parmenides and the Atomists. But the Greeks were not simply struck, and not only overwhelmed, they were obsessed, and they were even haunted, by the reality of Fate. It matters little how convinced one may be of the evident and undeniable fact that the things of the world constantly and ceaselessly change: if one assumes as a fixed point the twofold view that (a) reality behaves in accordance with inner necessities, and that (b) by the act of cognition man but witnesses and reflects inwardly to himself the inner constitution of reality in itself, the unavoidable conclusion is that, *appearances to the contrary,* reality is inwardly necessitated. And to say that it is inwardly necessitated is, therefore, to say not only that it is in its inner reality necessitated, but that it is necessitated by itself: thus, its reality is as such *self*-necessitated. Self-necessitation, despite appearances and even contrary to them, is what defines the nature of reality as such.

This was implicit already in the thought of Thales—but philosophy always moves slowly. It took three hundred years or so for this implication to be drawn out and to be located within the Greek philosophical world as the definition of reality as such. Although there may be a First Cause and a First Mover to account for the multiplicity of beings and for the relations among such multiplicity, the original and primary necessity which constitutes each being as such is entirely self-contained.[8] Hence, every being is, as such, an atomic reality.[9] (I say *as such* because it was

[8] This is why the idea of creation never occurred to the Greeks. If the concept of *creation* (in the Christian sense of this term) implied no more than a *making out of nothing* then there is no reason why this could not have occurred to Plato and Aristotle—who approached it as closely as *Genesis* itself does, namely, as a *making out of chaos*. The Greeks, however, were in no position to proceed, as the Israelites did, from this idea to the idea of *making out of nothing*, because to do so they would have had to conceive the corresponding *creatureliness* of that which is created, that is, its contingency upon the creator. To assume that every being is, as such, constituted by an entirely self-contained necessity, is thus automatically to discard the possibility that it be fundamentally contingent upon another.

[9] I attribute this to Greek philosophical thought generally, despite the fact that not all Greek philosophers by far could be said to be Atomists. This only means that there never was a Greek consensus on whether reality was physically atomic, or only metaphysically so. But all Greek philosophers were agreed that every being was self-identical and self-contained. Even the Monists allowed, each one in his own way, the plurality of empirically given, individual beings. Later, Christian thought preserved the same assumption and, indeed, glorified it. It did so, first, with the doctrine that "person signifies what is most perfect in all nature," (*ST,* I, 29, 4), since this doctrine adds the perfection of rationality to the perfection of individuality; second, with the doctrine that although individuality cannot be predicated of God "insofar as the principle of individuation is matter," nevertheless it is truly predicable of him "insofar as it implies incommunicability," (*ST,* I, 29, 4, ad 4); for God is Being, and existence itself is a principle of incommunicability, insofar as "the specific act of existence of one thing is distinct from the specific act of

evident to the Greeks that in addition to their basic self-containment things *entered* into relations among themselves.) It is not things in general that are what they are: *"every* being is what it is."[10] Before it can enter into relation with other beings, every being is constituted by its being itself. Hence, being as such is self-identical, but not merely in the sense that if it were superimposed upon itself, as it were, it would coincide perfectly with itself. Being is also self-identical in the more important sense that it is constituted by its being-itself. The reality of being is intelligible only because being is whatever it may be in a self-identical way.

In this view, the reality of being, if I may so put it, is neither its being (in the sense of its existing, an idea for which the Greeks did not even have a word), nor its being whatever it is. The reality of being consists in its being self-identically whatever it is. The Greeks were well aware, of course, that there is no substance without "accidents"—that is, without additional "happenings." But these are additional ways of being, and they

---

existence of another," (*De Veritate,* II, 2). At the end of this line of progression stands the doctrine of the "mode of subsistence," whose "proper function is to terminate the substantial essence, to make it be incommunicable, that is, so that *it could not communicate with another substantial essence in the existence which actuates it;* it is to divide it off from every other not only in what pertains to *that which* it is (as individual substance), but divided off from every other *in order to exist,"* J. Maritain, *Les Degrés du Savoir,* (Paris, 1948), p. 848. In Chapter V, below, I will study some of the difficulties of this existential monadism, particularly in relation to God, proposing alternative interpretations which might be more in accordance with the facts of human experience and with the Christian doctrine that *Deus caritas est.*

[10] J. Maritain, *A Preface to Metaphysics,* (London, 1948), p. 93, (Italics mine).

THE FOUNDATIONS OF BELIEF

"accrue." For every being to be is essentially to be itself, and to be itself by virtue of what it is in itself.[11]

From the self-identity which is constitutive of being from the οὐσία, literally the being-ness, the substantiality of reality, the Greeks were rationally to deduce—reluctantly and against the grain, as we may suppose—the essential immutability of reality as such. But whereas the immutability of reality was an apodictic conclusion, directly and intimately connected with all that the Greeks took for granted about reality, the reality of becoming was a matter of immediate experience which must be somehow reconciled with the self-identity of being: not even Parmenides assumed that becoming did not constitute a serious problem for philosophy, and a challenge to the principle that every being is what it is.

The dichotomies which had to be introduced by philosophers as they grappled with the problems of being and becoming are, of course, well known, and need but brief allusion here. Appearance and reality, phenomenon and being: we have seen above how this distinction was logically implied by the very concept of philosophy as an attempt to domesticate the inevitability of Fate. With special reference to the problem of becoming, however, this

[11] As we shall consider below, this was the very metaphysical kingpin which had to be removed by Christian philosophy before the direct influence upon Christianity of the Greek idea of Fate could begin to wane. It was St. Thomas who loosened it. But he did not manage to pull it out altogether, and the later Church has lacked sufficient philosophical creativity to complete the philosophical "revolution" which St. Thomas began. It thus fell to atheism to declare in modern times that man is in no way subject to Fate, the possibility of Christian philosophy doing so having been compromised by the Church's insistence upon defining God, and belief in God, on the basis of the very Greek philosophical notions which of their very nature tend to introduce fatalism into religious belief.

was transformed (as with Plato) into the dichotomy of the "being that truly is" and the "un-being being," that is, into a dichotomy between realms of being; it was also transformed (as with Aristotle) into the dichotomy of "form" and "matter," that is, not into a dichotomy of realms of being but into a dichotomy of principles of being, though this dichotomy still implies that being obtains in various degrees. And with reference to man's knowledge of reality, the dichotomy between ἐπιστήμη, knowledge that is really knowledge, and its various approximations, parallels the dichotomy of the various cognitive powers into the two essential categories, *sense* and *intellect*. As we consider below the problems which arise in connection with these dichotomies we should remember their origin, which is not (as is sometimes supposed) in the opposition between an obvious concept of being and a problematic concept of becoming, but between an empirical fact, becoming, and an interpretation of reality, being.

The Greek belief in Fate helped shape the Greek conceptualization of human conscious experience. But there must be something in the nature of experience which naturally tended to confirm—and indeed, in retrospect, to render seemingly self-evident—the idea that man's fundamental relation to reality is that of "observing" it. I recall the visual component of many Greek verbs which mean "to know." (This is preserved, though to a reduced extent, in modern European languages. For instance, in English "to see" is frequently used in the sense of "to understand.") Among the chief characteristics of vision in comparison with the other human sensory modes is its *di-stance*. (We should note that in the entire segment of the radiation spectrum to which man is sensitive, the visual range comprises the most penetrating frequencies.) It is not in vain that "observing" carries the specific connotation of refraining from all interference and, as it were, of standing off: to observe is best done with one's hands behind one's back. Well, Christian thinkers did not merely fail to share the Greek belief in Fate. They consciously rejected it, diametrically opposed as it was to the central Christian belief in the self-communicating, self-giving, gracious nature of ultimate reality. Nevertheless, early Christian thinkers accepted without question, (as have later philosophical generations until recent times), the Greek distinctions between cognition and appetition (particularly between intellect and will) and the cognate idea of knowledge as observation, as the mind's proximal reflection of a distal what-is.[12] Evidently, Christian thinkers must have assumed not only that the Greek concept of knowledge was separable from the Greek belief in Fate, but also that the Greek concept of knowledge imposed itself upon the philosopher by the sheer weight of its truth. Indeed, it was not until the late middle ages that Christian philosophers began actively to speculate on the *nature* of knowledge—as contrasted with speculation on the process, conditions and mechanism by which knowledge, as it had always been understood since the Greeks, came about. It is not an exaggeration, therefore, to state that the Greek concept of knowledge was assumed by Christian thinkers as a matter of common sense. Had they been asked why they assumed it, most of them would probably have replied that it was a self-evident truth which Greek reason has ascertained, even if Greek reason had not penetrated to other truths also ascertainable by

[12] The proximal-distal mode of perception and its embodiment in modern European languages has been studied in John W. M. Verhaar's *Perception, Speech and Thought,* (Assen, 1963); cf. especially Chapters V and VI.

reason, probably because it lacked the extrinsic aid provided by man's knowledge of truths which were altogether beyond the power of his unaided intellect.

The self-evidence of the Greek concept of knowledge should itself be far from self-evident to anyone who has had an opportunity to teach the doctrines of Aristotle or St. Thomas to *ab initio* students of philosophy in our own time. On the contrary, the idea that through knowledge reality "comes into" the mind, in however analogical a sense, appears fantastic to, and is usually resisted by, the newcomer to philosophy. Its tenacious hold upon philosophy comes rather from its self-validation. The Greek concept of knowledge is, once adopted, very difficult to transcend. It is not for lack of philosophical effort that after the necessary conditions of its transcendence were introduced into philosophy —by St. Thomas Aquinas, as I shall suggest in more detail below—between six and seven centuries were to elapse before a more comprehensive human self-concept could appear. Let us now describe the essential features of this Greek view.

The classical concept of knowledge is as a matter of *fact* grounded upon the human mind's ability to reflect upon itself. It is, therefore, an empirically grounded concept. The Greeks did no come to conceive of knowledge in the precise manner in which they did, either whimsically or gratuitously. The Greek concept of knowledge is grounded upon certain observations performed by the human knower upon knowledge itself.

The basic and irreducible observation with which all classical epistemological thought implicity or explicitly begins is the opposition between self and non-self (or "world"), subject and object, mind and being as such. (I say *as such,* because evidently the mind too is being.) This is a real opposition: one is not the other, and the other is not the one, despite the fact that the two are in confrontation. Moreover, this opposition is entitative; that is, it pertains to the order of being: for, as I have just indicated, the mind is itself a being.[13] Mind and being confront each other as any two other beings confront one another. And this opposition between the being which is mind, and the being which is being, is irreducible; it is an absolutely primary datum for reflective philosophical thought. It is also indemonstrable: it can be observed as a matter of fact, or else not at all.

But the latter alternative is scarcely a real one. In point of fact, everyone who is conscious and rational is in a position to observe this opposition. For no one who is conscious is in any real danger of failing to distinguish between himself and the world, between the self and the non-self. To be conscious is to experience: "there it is;" or—what is the same—to experience: "there it is, here I am." For the *it* which is *there* is known precisely as an *it*, that is, as an *other-than-I*, so that to experience "there it is" amounts to experiencing the reality of something which is essentially distinct from him who experiences—or, at least, essentially distinct from the experience itself, that is, from

[13] For simplicity's sake I have expressed myself imprecisely. I do not intend to convey that in this view the mind is a substance, without qualification, (though a few philosophers in this tradition have so believed), because it makes no substantial difference to the matter at hand whether the entitative opposition between mind and being be the opposition between a mind-substance and another substance, or whether it be the opposition between a mind which is the seat of the powers of a soul which is the substantial form of a body which is a substance which is in turn opposite another substance, and so on. Even if the soul is not a substance, it is *"per se subsistens,"* (*ST*, I, 75, 6). Moreover even for St. Thomas the soul is, in a qualified but perfectly proper sense, a spiritual substance, though it is a spiritual substance which is the substantial form of the human body; cf. *De Spiritualibus Creaturis*, II.

the act by which *it* is known.[14] Thus, the most primitive fact in this epistemological tradition is the fact that the mind, as everyday observation attests, is *other than* the world and, of course, vice versa: the conscious self is other than, and essentially separate in its reality and substantiality from, the non-self, that is, from every being which is other-than-him.

But the very fact that every conscious being is aware of this fact implies that this opposition between self and world, this dichotomy between object and subject, this entitative separation between the knower and the known, is somehow overcome. Even if one knows *it* in no more detailed or profound way than simply as a *thing,* simply as an *it,* to know it at all is to be aware of *it* as such, that is, as other-than-I. Thus, to be aware of the other as such is to overcome its otherness: it is to *reach* it, to in-tend it, despite its original alienation separating it from one.

The overcoming of this original alienation is what is called *knowledge.* To know is, therefore, for the mind to pass from the condition of isolation, the condition of separation from the world of reality within which it exists but from which it is essentially separated by its self-identity, to a certain union—indeed a certain unity—with that world. Thus, according to St. Thomas, who in this respect neither adds nor takes away from Greek thought, "knowledge (*cognitio*) is achieved by the known becoming united, through its likeness (*secundum suam similitudinem*), to the knower," [15] so that "every knower is united to its object by its cognitive power, *and not vice versa.*" [16]

[14] I add the latter qualification in order to cover the specific case of self-experience.

[15] *ST,* I–II, 1, ad 3.

[16] *Contra Gentiles,* II, 59. I underscore St. Thomas' explanation that this union takes place within the knower, that is, the cognitive power brings

The nature of this union, the process by which it comes about, and the conclusions that may be drawn from it, are problems on which the philosophical tradition that begins with the Greeks exhibits little unanimity. But these are subsequent questions, that is, they arise within the common commitment of the Hellenic-Western philosophical tradition to a stable concept of knowledge, to a constant conceptualization of the basic facts concerning man's relation to reality—facts which do not explain but which, on the contrary, stand in need of explanation—in terms of a being's achievement of cognitive union with another being by the former's power and through the latter's similitude. In other words, there is a distinction between the concept of knowledge and the theory of knowledge. The Hellenic-Western tradition has continuously developed the theory of knowledge, while remaining until recent times, generally speaking, committed to the original Greek concept of knowledge in essentially unaltered form. In this tradition there have been *many theories of knowledge* which philosophers have successively developed as they have deepened their understanding of *one and the same concept of knowledge,* a concept which remained fairly stable after the pre-Socratics. The variety of theories of knowledge has been spent on the attempt to find the solution to the problem presented by a single, constant conceptualization of the facts, namely, the conceptualization that I have just described and which I shall now briefly analyze.

But before I proceed I should specify that the continuous de-

---

about the unification of the knower to the known, although the known is not thereby unified to the knower (i.e. it does not know—unless it itself is a knower). And cognition takes place *per similitudinem* because the union of knower and known is intentional, not physical; hence it takes place in the knower, rather than in the known, or in both, or in a third thing.

velopment of epistemology to which I have alluded reached a culminating point and a critical moment with Hegel, when a sort of qualitative change in the history of philosophy began to occur. After Hegel a new conceptualization of the observable fact of knowledge gradually emerged—so gradually indeed that only with the hindsight of a century and a half has it become possible to appreciate the quality of the change and the meaning of the entire range of the historical age that it brackets. Thus, within the continuity of our philosophical tradition of the Greeks to our own day it is possible to discern two principal concepts of knowledge: the classical, and that which has begun to emerge in our own age. Whereas for the period up to Hegel the variety of epistemologies obtained within both a continuity of filiation and the continuity of a common conceptualization of the empirical fact of experience as knowledge, for contemporary epistemological thought—at least in those circles where it is progressively rather than repetitiously practiced—there is exhibited, throughout its variety, only a continuity of filiation with that of the Greek, mediaeval and modern periods. For the former no longer shares with the latter common assumptions as to precisely what epistemology tries to understand and explain.

As already mentioned, even the fairly elementary question of the nature of the union brought about by knowledge between man and the world has been the object of disagreement among philosophers. The Greek philosopher Empedocles appears to have had the simplest and crudest interpretation of the facts of knowledge that the history of Hellenic-Western philosophy records, namely, the theory that the objects of knowledge give off an efflux which is physically captured by the knower, whence knowledge is brought about in the knower as a quasi-physical mental effect. But this is a rare, if not unique, philosophical theory of knowledge. The fairly common opinions have always been that the union is in some way non-physical: let us agree to call it intentional, despite the variety of philosophical interpretations of what intentionality may be. Likewise, the most common opinion, at least after Aristotle, has been that, for all the knower's passive (and intentional) receptivity of the object of knowledge, the knower is active in one essential respect, namely, in positing the act of knowledge. Indeed, with Aristotle this activity received its highest recognition. Distinguishing between the "passive" and the "agent intellect," Aristotle, and those who have followed him, assign to the knower not only the responsibility of positing itself in actual act of knowing, but even the task of rendering actually intelligible the potential intelligibility of the object of human understanding. Other philosophers have not been so generous. Locke, for example, explicitly allowed mental activity, (as contrasted with cognitive receptivity), only regarding the mental manipulation of objects within the mind. But even Locke assumed that the act of knowledge was the act of the knower. If he appeared totally uninterested in the source of the actual intelligibility of the intelligible, assuming that it was somehow actually intelligible, perhaps the reason is that by Locke's time the concept of knowledge as the transcendence of the dichotomy between object and subject had become itself problematic.

But for St. Thomas, for instance, cognition occurred when one being acted physically, transitively, upon another, if the other was a knower—that is, if it had within itself the power to take advantage of this activity upon itself, in order to posit within itself an immanent act the formal nature of which was to render him

THE TRADITIONAL FOUNDATIONS OF BELIEF

(intentionally) one with the known, that is, one with that which was originally *other,* to which the knower was united precisely *as other.* For, as remarked above, the basic observable fact which enables the philosopher to speak of the union of knowledge, despite all absence of physical change in the known and despite the concentration of all the effects of knowledge in the knower himself, is the fact that in every act of knowledge the knower knows an-other precisely as other-than-himself. Thus, the most formal definitions of knowledge according to this tradition are *"fieri aliud a se,"* "to become other than oneself," and, far more common, *"esse seu fieri aliud in quantum aliud,"* "to be or to become the other as other." Although these formulae were not in common use until after the 17th century, when they, especially the latter, were put in circulation by John of St. Thomas,[17] the idea had been present since the pre-Socratics. Except in Scholastic circles this formula lost its popularity in modern times, but the idea that it conveys remained at work among all those who have persistently attempted to explain how the objects of knowledge were "grasped" by the mind. Thus, theories of knowledge in the Hellenic-Western tradition have until very recent times commonly attempted to explain how, despite certain philosophical indications to the contrary, things which were distinct in *themselves,* distinct in the order of being, happened—as the empirical observations made by reflecting upon knowledge indubitably suggest—to become *one for us,* that is, one in the order of

[17] *"Cognoscentia autem in hoc elevantur super non cognoscentia, quia id quod est alterius, ut alterius, seu prout manet distinctum in altero, possunt in se recipere. . . . Cognoscere est fieri alterum, seu trahere ad se formam alterius, ut alterius . . . fieri alterum a se, et recipere illud non ut communicans in esse cum illo, sed ut alterum a se,"* John of St. Thomas, *Cursus Philosophiae, De Anima,* IV, 1.

knowledge, or intentionally one.[18] For this becoming one-for-us was what we called knowledge. The problems of psychology and epistemology had to do with the processes whereby—the conditions under which, and the validity with which—this type of event came to pass and became itself intelligible.

I want to underline at this point a certain feature of the classical concept of knowledge which we shall have occasion to recall below. I have said that the most primitive fact in the Hellenic-Western epistemological tradition is the dichotomy of self and non-self: "there *it* is," or, as Maritain puts it *"scio aliquid esse,"* "I know that something is," I know something which is known; that is, the "something known" is at least implicitly other-than-I. Well, the specific meaning which this view has traditionally carried includes the idea that this opposition of each being to the remainder of the world is not peculiar to knowers. *Every* being confronts *every other* being; for insofar as anything is a being, it is self-contained and distinct (at least as subsistent) from the rest of the universe. What is characteristic of knowing being,

[18] For reasons that will be explained below, this particular "problem of knowledge" does not arise in philosophical traditions outside the Indo-European cultures. Chinese philosophy, for example, "does not demarcate clearly the distinction between the individual and the universe [i.e. the world of objects] . . . In Chinese thought . . . there has been no clear consciousness of the ego of itself, and so there has been equally little attention paid to the division between the ego and the non-ego; therefore, epistemology has likewise not become a major problem," Fung Yu-lan, *History of Chinese Philosophy,* (London, 1952), vol. I, p. 3. However, in the light of certain considerations which I will present below, it appears to me somewhat imprecise to attribute the absence from Chinese philosophy of the typically Western "problem of knowledge" to the unclearness of the "consciousness of the ego of itself" among Chinese philosophers. Perhaps it would be better to attribute it to the specific character of the mode in which self-understanding is experienced in Chinese thinking generally, and in Chinese philosophical thinking in particular.

therefore, is not its self-containment, its separation or alienation from other beings. To be in confrontation with a world which is itself constituted by self-contained beings is not the peculiar condition of the knower: it is the condition of being as such. Thus, knowers are opposed to the world of being around them, not in the first place because they are knowers, but because they are beings. To be is *prior* to both knowing and being known. Knowing, and being known, compensate, as it were, for the isolation, the *entitative* isolation, of every being as such from every being as such. I suggested above that the universe in which knowledge erupts is the universe of two solitudes, man and world. I now amplify: in the Greek *Weltanschauung* the world itself is a conglomeration of solitudes. Every being is, as such, isolated from every other in the order of its inmost reality. Relationships *accrue* to self-existing, self-sufficient substances; but that which is, is as such unrelated to what is not-it. Thus, to say that knowledge must be conceived as some sort of union between the mind and reality, is to say that knowledge is a privilege of certain beings, (i.e. it is the superadded, intentional way of being of certain beings which follows upon the specific nature of their entitative being). This "privilege" consists in their ability or power to overcome the limitations which otherwise restricts them to being (physically) whatever they are. As St. Thomas put it:

Since the specific act of existence of one thing is distinct from the specific act of existence of another,[19] in every created thing of this kind the perfection falls short of absolute perfection to the extent that that perfection is found in other species. Consequently, *the perfection*

[19] I call attention to the basis of St. Thomas' reasoning, namely, the self-containment and isolation of every being from every other, (cf. above, note 9). Note also that St. Thomas offers no justification why his state-

of each individual thing considered in itself is imperfect, being a part of the perfection of the entire universe, which arises from the sum total of the perfections of all individual things.

In order that there might be some *remedy* for this imperfection, another kind of perfection is to be found in creative things. *It consists in this, that the perfection belonging to one thing is found in another.* This is the perfection of the knower insofar as he knows; for something is known by the knower by reason of the fact that the thing known is, in some fashion, *in the possession of the knower.*[20]

To sum up, in the Hellenic-Western epistemological tradition the concept of knowledge has been grounded upon an empirical observation which is primary, undeniable and irrefutable, namely, the dichotomy of object and subject. But this means: the universe in which knowledge occurs can be described in terms of a dichotomy between the self and its world. The opposition between self-

---

ment should be applicable to created being only. We may well conjecture, however, with considerable moral certainty, that his justification might have been this: that no perfection could be denied to God, nor attributed to him imperfectly. Nevertheless, if the basis of his reasoning is the (real) distinction between the act of existence of each being and that of every other being, then, on the assumption that God is being, (and he is, indeed, *a* being, an *"individuum,"* insofar as his being is incommunicable, *ST,* I, 29, 4), it follows either that God is imperfect or else that created being does not exist by an act of existence which is its own and proper to itself. The latter alternative could in turn be maintained (with but certain qualifications) within Christian orthodoxy, as long as being was conceived by Christian philosophers without substantial departure from the outlook of Greek metaphysics. But only so long. Thus, the introduction of St. Thomas' existential concept of being, which implied a substantial departure from the Greek metaphysical outlook, would ultimately facilitate the pantheism of Spinoza and Hegel, insofar as this reality of every created being must be deemed to be intrinsically its own while, at the same time, its own act of existence cannot be other than God's except to the detriment of the perfection of God.

[20] *De Veritate,* II, 2.

contained beings describes the condition of the world in which knowledge takes place. For knowledge is indeed the overcoming of this condition. St. Thomas, as we have just seen, even provides a rationale for the every existence of knowledge in precisely such a world.

Therefore, what is distinctive of a knowing being (as contrasted with being generically) is, according to the clasical view, that the opposition between each knowing being and every other being is not merely a cosmic fact—though it is, in the first place, precisely that—but also a fact which enters into their reality and which affects them in a peculiar way. Every being is, as such, opposite to every other being. Its self-containment, its isolation, its alienation is not to be understood spatially—any more than the overcoming of this isolation is to be understood as a spatial transposition of any sort. The nature of this opposition is best understood in terms of the absence of consequences from it: nothing happens because one being is itself and not another. But if the being which exists in this situation is a knowing being, something does decidedly happen in consequence of its opposition to other beings: a knowing being takes advantage of its entitative opposition to other beings for its own benefit, and perfects itself entitatively by means of it. A knower not only confronts an-other, but confronts an-other precisely as other. For it is this very confrontation with the other precisely as other that we call knowledge. Knowledge is not only the union of the self with the non-self: it is the union of the self and the non-self *despite* their original isolation—an isolation which in the order of physical, substantial existence [21] remains, of course, unaffected

[21] Greek and mediaeval philosophers generally assumed not only the entitative isolation of substances from each other, but also their com-

by this union, which is strictly of a cognitive sort. The event which can be thus described is what philosophers since Greek times have had in mind when they have referred to cognition or awareness. Cognition thus understood, they have assumed, is the fundamental relation of man to the world of reality within which he exists.

More precisely, as an act posited by the knower, knowledge is that *by which* that fundamental relation is established. The cognitive relation itself is identifiable with knowledge only when the latter term is used, in a secondary acceptation, to refer to the perfection worked in the mind by the operation of knowledge. In other words, knowledge means principally the operation by which the mind acquires the perfection of other realities, though in a looser sense the term may mean the perfection of the mind that has acquired the perfection of the things that it knows. But the proper name of the latter perfection of the mind is not knowledge, but *truth*. The ambiguity of the term knowledge is noteworthy: it parallels the ambiguity of the term truth as it is used, for reasons that will be examined below, to refer both to an "objective" and to a "subjective" reality.

---

munication at the level of accidental existence. The first assumption derives, as we have seen, from the Greek concept of being; the second is grounded directly on the empirical observation that things obviously act upon each other and are accidentally related in a variety of ways. As long as the classical concept of knowledge remained unproblematic no question could very well arise as to the possible inconsistency of these two assumptions. But when knowledge became problematic, the problem of the accidental communication (or "interaction") of substances automatically became problematic as well—as Descartes realized. The outcome could only be the rejection of either the accidental communication of substances, as with Leibniz, or else the rejection of the substantiality of the subject of experience, as with Hume.

In any event, the concept of truth evidently originated in the observation that knowledge works a peculiar perfection in the knower. So far we have dwelt on the nature of this perfection, noting, with St. Thomas, that it is definable strictly in relation to the perfection of the world in which the knower exists—that is, in terms of "the other." For to acquire the perfection which a knower in act acquires is not to acquire anything other than the perfection of another. Thus, as Aristotle had already observed, the soul is, "in a certain way, all things." [22] The typical perfection of the human intellect consists not in its having a certain determinate perfection, but in its openness to acquire the perfection of other things. This is why knowledge is describable not only in terms of a union, but likewise in terms of intussusception, that is, inward receptivity. Or, if we wish to stress the fact that this inward reception is due to the activity of the knower alone, we might describe it in terms of an inward, intentional and spiritual grasp of the reality of the world: knowledge is the mind's ap-*prehension* of reality, it is the mind's clutching of being, in order to consume it, that is, in order for the mind to perfect itself by the acquisition of the reality of other things. This is why the classical conception of knowledge essentially and necessarily implies the idea of a certain transposition, as it were, from the known to the knower—a transposition which, to be sure, must be deemed to be "formal" and intentional by any philosopher in this tradition who rises above the level of an Empedocles or a Democritus, but a transposition nonetheless.

Not every philosopher, on the other hand, will agree with the full aptness of Locke's metaphor, somewhat too literally taken, of the mind as a bare cupboard which is furnished with objects

[22] *On the Soul*, III, 5 (430 a 14).

received through experience: "external and internal sensation are the only passages that I can find of knowledge to the understanding. These alone, as far as I can discover, are the windows by which light is let into this dark room. For methinks the understanding is not much unlike a closet wholly shut from light, with only some little openings left to let in external visible resemblances or ideas of things without." [23] As we have seen, what is really *acquired* by the knower when he knows is the inward perfection of truth, not the objective reality, intentionally transmuted, of the object of knowledge. On the other hand, the inward perfection of truth can be acquired only in and through the acquisition of the formal perfection which other things have in the first place in and for themselves. The mind, thus, truly reflects inwardly what lies outside it. This is, to be sure, an inward perfection; that is, the mind reflects for itself, within itself, and according to the mode of itself as recipient, the perfection of the other. Nevertheless, it is truly a reflection, a reduplication of the other—a reduplication which is itself not what is known, but the result, the effect of possessing within itself that which is known.

The point might be made clearer by emphasizing that re-duplic*ation*—not to be confused with a reduplic*ate*—is an activity and a process. Knowledge is not grasping an inward reduplicate. St. Thomas insists on the the falsity of the view that "the intellect understands nothing but its own affections, namely, the intelligible forms (*species*) which it had received; so that, according to this opinion, this *species* is itself what is understood," affirming instead that "it must be said that the intelligible form (*species*)

---

[23] *Essay Concerning Human Understanding,* II, 11, 17.

is related to the intellect as that by which the intellect understands." [24] Nevertheless, all this having been granted, it remains
that, by one means or another—and all the more so if this means
is not itself "what is understood," but only "that by which the
intellect understands"—knowledge is a grasping of "outer"
reality for the sake of one's own perfection: knowledge is a
reduplication of it. When the mind knows, its perfection consists in its reduplication of reality.

St. Thomas expresses the same idea in different terms when he
says that knowledge takes place "by similitude;" that is, it occurs
when "the [thing] understood is in the understanding [power]
by its [i.e. the thing's] similitude (*per suam similitudinem*)." [25]
But to complicate matters, the theory of knowledge of St.
Thomas, like that of most Scholastics, (both mediaeval and contemporary), explains, for its own good reasons, the *process* of
knowledge in terms of the mediation of "species." These philosophers would rightly object to the charge that they conceive
knowledge as the identification of the mind with reality through
the means of a *species* which, being a likeness (*similitudo*) of the
object, makes the object known *indirectly*, somewhat as a picture
makes known to a beholder the reality that it portrays. [26] This

[24] *ST*, I, 85, 2.
[25] *ST*, I, 85, 2, ad 1. Cf. *ST*. I, 5, 4, ad 1; I, 75, 1, ad 2; I, 76, 2, ad 4;
I–II, 28, 1, ad 3; *Contra Gentiles*, I, 72; II, 77; II, 98; IV, 11.
[26] "Descartes saw clearly that the object known is known within
thought; his capital error was to have separated the *object* from the
thing, thinking that the object is in thought, not as intelligibility which
has been rendered present within a mind by an immaterial form with
which the mind identifies itself intentionally, but as an imprint is in a
piece of wax. Thenceforth the intentional role disappears, the object
known becomes part of thought, an imprint or an inborn portrait; under-

would be an incorrect understanding of the *similitudo* by which knowledge is explained. Nevertheless, the classical concept of knowledge is, in the precise sense here indicated, essentially *reduplicative*. As long as knowledge is the transcending of an original dichotomy between knower and known, knowledge could not be essentially anything else but the inward reduplication of that which in itself exists outside the mind. Thus, the classical concept of truth originates in the observation that knowledge works a certain perfection in the knower, a perfection the nature of which, as to form, is neither self-evident nor easily determined, but which, as to matter or content, is self-evident and beyond all possible question: in this respect truth is, obviously, a perfection the nature of which accrues to the knowing mind through the acquisition of the perfection of other things.

This is why "truth" is, at one and the same time, a datum and a problem: not a few epistemological confusions have resulted from this ambiguity. Like "knowledge" (in the sense explained above), the classical concept of "truth" runs constant throughout the varieties of theories of truth. Every philosopher in the classical tradition sets out to explain the nature of knowledge only after presupposing that knowledge is the overcoming of the dichotomy of the object and subject. Likewise every philosopher in the classical tradition sets out to explain the nature of truth only after presupposing that it is the perfection achieved by the mind as a result of overcoming the dichotomy of object and subject. From the viewpoint of logic this is, of course, unexceptionable in itself.

---

standing stops at the idea (now considered as an instrumental sign). This idea-portrait, this idea-thing has as its reduplicate (*a pour doublure*) a thing which it resembles, but which is not itself attained by the act of understanding," J. Maritain, *Les Degrés du Savoir,* (Paris, 1948), pp. 248–249.

But it is important that we note it consciously; it means that since every enquiry into the nature of truth is strictly dependent upon the prior concept of knowledge, the critical analysis of classical epistemology must begin with a critique of the concept of knowledge rather than with a critique of the concept of truth. Conversely, since the only concept of truth which is compatible with the classical concept of knowledge is the clasical concept of truth, once the classical concept of knowledge is assumed it is logically impossible to criticize the classical concept of truth. It is little to be wondered at that some Thomists reject the very possibility of a critical realism,[27] and that even those who, like Maritain, admit it, are careful to stipulate that the task of epistemology is not to *determine* whether its "spontaneous" convictions about the nature of truth are warranted, but to *confirm* that they are, indeed, justified.[28]

If knowledge is the transcending of the object-subject opposition, then truth, the perfection of knowledge, the valuable quality which makes it worthy of being loved and pursued, can be understood only as some sort of conformity to what is. For if knowledge is the intussusception, the intentional possession, or the inward reduplication, of reality, then the perfection which knowledge lends to the mind can be understood only as establishing a relation from the mind to reality of this precise sort, namely, of conformity. For, surely, no cognitive perfection follows, no value accrues to the mind in act of knowing, if the act does not bring about the mind's conformity to being.

How could it be otherwise, if it is true, as suggested above, that

[27] See Etienne Gilson, *Réalisme thomiste et critique de la connaissance*, (Paris, 1939).

[28] *Les Degrés du Savoir*, pp. 142–145.

this epistemological complex took its origin from the view that being is necessarily what it is? To say that being is necessarily what it is is to say that it is unavoidable for man to be related to it except by conforming to it. The effective (though largely blind) purpose of the Greek philosophical distinction between intellect and will was, in the construction of the history of philosophy I have suggested, to explore the possibility of escaping the fatefulness of reality. This distinction tended of its very nature to restrict the scope of the power of necessitation to the area of cognition, leaving open the question whether by that part of him which by nature does *not necessarily* conform to what is, man can escape Fate. For it is clear that any such attempt to escape Fate is reasonable only if it is predicated upon the prior acceptance of the facts, that is, of the necessary character of being as such. Whether or not the fatefulness of reality can be overcome, it is certain that the wise man's attempt to overcome it will begin with respect of what is. Violence will not succeed against necessity, and man's only reasonable hope to overcome it lies, as it were, in circumventing it.

To our own day, therefore, the best part of common sense in the Hellenic-Western world is that whether or not one chooses to abide by the facts, to know the facts is to grasp reality as it is. One philosopher who is conscious of his position within the undiluted mainstream of this tradition goes so far as to claim that the only correct attitude of the mind towards reality is "masochistic," "submissive," and "anal-erotic." [29] Though this may be too extreme a conclusion—at least, I have no wish to sug-

---

[29] "[A psychoanalyst] would say that I have the prejudices and the passions of an anal-erotic. I am trying to be completely submissive to objective truth and order. I am masochistic toward reason," Mortimer Adler, *What Man Has Made of Man,* (New York, 1947), p. 122.

gest that the Greek concept of truth is necessarily psychopathological—the observation is basically valid. The classical concept of knowledge implies that knowledge is true if, and only if, its effect is to make the mind conform to what in fact is; knowledge is true if, and only if, its achievement is the mind's correspondence, its conformity within itself, to that which is established in reality independently of man's wishes and existence. For to imagine that the knowing mind need not conform to what is, would be to have lost one's rationality. Indeed, to attempt to imagine so would be self-refuting. Therefore to know is to be related to what is. And since what is is not made to be, or to be what it is, by man, but is antecedent to him, and since it is determined to be, and to be what it is, by its own constitution, it follows that to be related to what is is to be related to what is *unavoidable by man;* and to be related to what is unavoidable is to conform to it. Truth is the mind's relation of conformity to that which the mind knows.

In this sense, therefore, truth has never constituted a philosophical problem for the Hellenic-Western tradition. It is not without significance that the Greeks did not raise any questions about its fundamental nature. The same assertion is true of St. Thomas— though in his case some qualifications are in order. The statement is true insofar as St. Thomas, (to judge by what he wrote), does not seem ever to have supposed that truth might be conceived, in effect, in any other way than as the mind's conformity to things.[30] For St. Thomas the question "what is truth?"[31]

---

[30] I say *in effect* because this definition of the truth need not have been explicitly made before its meaning was at work and formally assumed by philosophers. As is well known, the classical formula appeared only at a relatively late date in the history of the Hellenic-Western philosophical tradition.

[31] *De Veritate,* I, 1.

does not mean "what is the relation to reality in which man stands precisely as man, and because he is conscious?" St. Thomas assumes that this relation can be none other than conformity. The question means, rather, whether this assumed conformity refers to something in the knowing power or something in being.[32] On the other hand, it is significant that even if this question does not actually explore the nature of truth, the question did occur to St. Thomas, whereas it never occurred to Aristotle. And it is even more significant that St. Thomas' answer, for all its distinctions, leans heavily towards the first alternative. We shall deal with this in more detail below. For the present I will merely remark that although St. Thomas did not himself raise any doubt about the classical concept of truth, some of his doctrines, including this very one, that "the true . . . is found secondarily in things and primarily in intellect," have had the historical effect of making the classical concept of truth highly problematic. In this, as in many other respects, the intervention of St. Thomas in the development of Hellenic-Western philosophical thought must be judged to have had an importance, and indeed a value, comparable to that of only very few other philosophical intellects.

But although truth never constituted a problem within the Hellenic-Western tradition, (in the sense that its nature as a relation of conformity was never doubted until its basis in the classical concept of knowledge had been first deemed inadequate), the classical understanding of truth did essentially constitute a problem, in the sense that certain inner inconsistencies of the classical concept of knowledge became increasingly difficult to avoid once the bases on which it had been erected by the Greeks, namely, the fatefulness of reality, became fundamentally excluded from Chris-

[32] *De Veritate*, I, 2.

tian metaphysical speculation—an achievement directly attributable, again, to the thought of St. Thomas, as the next chapter shall discuss. For epistemology and metaphysics are strictly correlative. St. Thomas' departure from classical metaphysics *eventually* entailed a corresponding departure from classical epistemology as well. For, as we shall now consider, the classical concept of knowledge had been, in the first place, the condition of the possibility of classical metaphysical thought.

REALITY AND THOUGHT

If knowledge is the inward reduplication of the reality which is external to (i.e. other than) man, then reality is intelligible. However, what does it mean to say that reality is intelligible? At a certain level of analysis it means little enough: it means that reality can *in fact* be known, that the expectation that reality will become known when man encounters it is well founded. This is, of course, a direct implication of the very idea of intellectual enquiry into the nature of things, the very idea of "physical" philosophy since early Greek times. But as the Greeks developed the implication of their faith in the intellect as the grounds of their hope in overcoming Fate, they were gradually constrained to pursue the matter: the outcome was the *metaphysical* concept of being.

Reality is intelligible. But why? Is it intelligible merely because it happens, as it were, to stand in the right place at the right time when a knower passes by exercising his intellect? To suppose this is to have failed to grasp in what way human knowledge can be expected to deal effectively, for man's own purposes, with the natural necessity of the world. (Actually, as I have intimated, if the Greeks conceived this expectation in the first place, the reason was that they had managed to look with deeper insight into the nature of human consciousness than had been previously done by any other civilized family of man.) It is true that knowledge is somewhat like other processes of absorption—like nutrition, for instance—in certain superficial respects. But at bottom it is essentially unlike any other mode of reception; it is essentially unlike any other mode of overcoming a separation or a gap. The known, as I have said, is "external" to the knower, not in a spatial sense (though it is usually that too, unless the known is the knower himself, in act of reflection upon himself), but in the very order of reality. This is why even when the known is the knower himself, knowing himself by an act of reflection, the knower is formally other than the known. From this it follows, according to this epistemological perspective, that the reflexivity of human knowledge consists in the knower's ability to take a previous act of knowledge as the object of a new act of knowledge —a point of the greatest importance, which must be kept in mind if we are to understand the criticism that can be levelled at Greek, mediaeval and modern epistemological thought. In any event, the known is external to the knower in the sense that it is, as reality, other than him. But it is this very otherness which is overcome by knowledge. Hence, when the known "comes into" the mind, the inwardness of the act is not spatial, but of the order of reality. Insofar as he knows, the knower *is* the known. The union effected by knowledge is not a joining, but a unification: in knowledge the knower becomes identified with the known.

If we keep this in mind, then the observation which almost any adult Athenian citizen might have made, namely, that "whatever is known is knowable," acquires an unsuspected significance. If to know reality is not merely to capture it, but to capture it by becoming one with it, then the intelligibility of reality indicates not merely a property of reality, but its essential identity. Reality does not merely *happen* to be intelligible; it is intelligible precisely as reality. Intelligibility is its proper and essential name.

But what are we to understand by the intelligibility which belongs to reality itself? Granted that intelligibility belongs to reality because of what it itself is, and not because it happens to be confronted by man,[33] intelligibility appears to name reality extrinsically, that is, in relation to the reality of the knower which acquires it. Intelligibility truly belongs to reality—indeed, it belongs to reality as such. But what describes it in itself? To know is to become the other as such, and therefore the other as such is what is known. But what is the other as such? The answer given by the Greek metaphysicians was: being. Reality is intelligible in itself because it is being; the reason why intelligibility is not merely something that happens to reality, but that which constitutes it in reality, that which makes it real, is that reality's true name is being. In brief, as Parmenides put it, "it is the same thing that can be and can be thought." [34]

[33] Some Greek philosophers, namely, the Sophists and, in a later period, the Sceptics, did take the latter alternative.

[34] Fr. 5, τὸ γὰρ αὐτὸ νοεῖν ἐστίν τε καὶ εἶναι, literally translatable as "for it is the same [thing] to think and to be." But a literal translation may be somewhat misleading. The assertion does not refer to the *acts* of thinking and being, but to the *nature* of thinking and being. The point, as I interpret it, is that "that which can be and that which can be thought is the same," that is, that the nature of being is to be understood by its aptitude for being reflected by thought, and that, at one and the same time, being is thinkable because it is being, while thinking is possible because being as such is thinkable. But this is such a crucial text—it is "the basic

91

To understand the meaning of this answer, and the force of the reasoning which produced it, it is necessary to recall certain features of the Greek language which I shall mention in a moment. But to understand it critically it is indispensable in the first place to make use of certain premises concerning the nature of language —premises which have been suggested to philosophy only by modern linguistic research, which employs an incomparably greater range of facts and observations than were, of course, available to the Greeks, the mediaevals or even modern thinkers until very recent times.

I have in mind the dissatisfaction of many linguists with the idea—an idea of Greek origin, as it so happens—that language is a system of variable signs which stand for constant experiences. According to Aristotle

spoken words are the symbols of mental experience and written words are the symbols of spoken words. Just as all men have not the same writing, so all men have not the same speech sounds, but the mental experiences, which these directly symbolize, are the same for all, as also are those things of which our experiences are the

---

theme of all of Western-Eurpoean thinking," Heidegger suggests, (*What is Called Thinking?* New York, 1968, p. 242)—that evidently every translation must implicitly contain an interpretation of the entire history of Greek philosophy. Heidegger's own interpretation, (*ibid.* pp. 240–244), appears to me, for reasons that may become clear as we proceed, untenable *a posteriori* and improbable in itself. If the true meaning of Parmenides' "way of truth" had died with Parmenides, and every philosopher from Plato and Aristotle to Kant and Hegel had misunderstood what Parmenides meant, there could be no philosopher today, not even a Heidegger, who could doubt the philosophical correctness of the traditional interpretation. It is, on the contrary, because every philosopher from Plato to Hegel has understood Parmenides only too well that it has become possible for later philosophy to criticize him severely and, thus, to diverge from the Hellenic-Western philosophical tradition at its Parmenidean root.

images. By a noun we mean a sound significant by convention . . . The limitation by convention was introduced because nothing is by nature a noun or a name—it is so only when it becomes a symbol.[35]

[35] *On Interpretation,* 1 (16 a 3–28). Given the contemporary connotations of English "symbol," and its equivalents in most modern European languages, it is somewhat misleading to translate Aristotle's σύμβολον as "symbol," as not a few translations, including Hugh Tredennick's and Richard McKeon's (it is the latter I have reproduced above) usually do— that is, as if *sign* and *symbol* were synonymous. Now in this passage Aristotle uses two terms indistinctly to refer to the function of words, and in Greek the two are very closely related. One is σημεῖον, which means "sign," "mark," "token"—or "emblem," "standard," "ensign," "signal," "omen," "trace," or "track." The other is σύμβολον, which likewise means "sign," "mark," or "token"—but also "covenant," "treaty," or "contract." Evidently, both terms are used metaphorically by Aristotle with equal propriety, but the metaphor must span a slightly longer distance in the case of σύμβολον than in the case of σημεῖον. But whereas these two terms are of comparable adequacy in Greek in order to signify Aristotle's meaning—that a word is something that, like a σημεῖον or like a σύμβολον, takes the place of something else and refers to it—the *only* apt English word to signify this is *sign.* For in later ages the Greek σύμβολον acquired the restrictive connotation of a special sort of sign, namely, a sign which not only refers to that which it stands for, but also to something else which in one way or another stands behind that which is signified. For instance, the σύμβολον ἀποστολον was not merely the word-signs by which certain essential Christian doctrines were signified, but also the sign of that which stood behind that which the words signified, namely, the Christian faith that came from the Apostles: the words not only "signify" the doctrines, but "symbolize" the faith in the doctrines.

In modern times the second function of the "symbol" has become predominant, if not exclusive; its original significative function has all but disappeared, and *signification* is now almost divorced from *symbolism.* A flag, for instance, insofar as it is a *symbol* does not act as the *sign* of a certain nation or at least does so very tenuously, whereas in classical Greek it is σημεῖον, *not* σύμβολον that denotes "flag." What a flag signifies, precisely as *symbol,* is the feelings, attitudes, policies, self-projection, etc. of a certain nation: one does not so much *raise* a flag as one *waves* it. As a symbol it does not so much let beholders know the political entity of which it is the ensign, as it makes known certain things about

93

Though linguists are less generally in agreement about positive alternatives to this view than in the negative criticism of it, the common factor of otherwise varied theories of language proposed by contemporary linguists is that language is to be interpreted as a *function* of experience rather than as a *conventional signification of it*. A full-fledged theory of language must comprise many aspects which have little to do with philosophy. But what may be of special relevance to epistemology, as I have suggested eleswhere,[36] is that language gives a human, socio-historical form to experience. Language appears to enter into the very composition of human experience; whatever else may need to be asserted about the nature of language, every indication is that, in any event, language is not *preceded* by experience. As man experiences so he talks, and as he talks so he experiences.

The variability of human languages appears, therefore, to indicate variability in the form of human experience. It is no doubt possible to translate any experience, regardless of its concrete linguistic form, into any other linguistic form. This is only to say that all languages are human because humanity does not depend on any given linguistic form, but rather in the giving of

him who raises it (in relation, of course, to the political entity of which it is the ensign). Likewise, draft-card burning does no damage to the draft laws of the United States: it shows contempt for the draft laws of the United States, and is the *symbol* of such contempt—as those who provide punishment for it fully realize. Thus, for us today a word is not ordinarily a *symbol*, but merely a *sign*, although there is no reason why a word should not *also* be symbolic—as slogans are. A symbol, in short, is in contemporary experience that in which man's specifically human relation to something is projected and embodied. The key difficulty with Aristotle's conception of language is precisely that he thought of language as having a strictly *significative* function, whereas in reality it is *symbolic* in nature.

[36] *The Future of Belief*, pp. 100–107.

some linguistic form or another to experience. But translations can be "faithful" only to the degree that human experience is common to the two linguistic contexts—or else to the degree that the translation provides for a restructuring of experience. If so, the characteristics of any given language reveal the concrete mode of experience of which it is the form. This does not mean that experience is conditioned by language, if by this is meant that language can exist prior to, and independent of experience, and subsequently determine experience to be what it is (except, of course, insofar as every individual is born into a linguistic *tradition* that already exists—a tradition, however, which he constantly modifies and develops according as he himself evolves). But language is the condition of experience, in the sense that experience is human only insofar as it has some linguistic form (or another). Thus, human experience is not independent of its concrete linguistic form. And if, upon reflection, linguistic structures and functions reveal the concrete modality of human experience, the reason is not that these structures and functions pre-determine the modality of experience, but that, in point of social and historical fact, a certain modality of experience happened to develop as it did, as the language developed of which it is the form.

The Greek language belongs to the Indo-European linguistic family; and Indo-European languages generally—in any event, Greek and Latin—possess, almost exclusively among human languages, certain characteristics which are directly pertinent to the philosophical development studied above. I refer to the dual function of the verb *to be,* which in Greek and Latin, as in modern European languages usually (but not always) discharges roles which in other linguistic families are sharply differentiated.

95

Esse in Latin, and εἶναι in Greek, are used indistinctly to indicate
the reality of real as such (let us say "existence," though this,
as we shall see, is an inadequate expression in this context), and
the relation of predicate to subject. This indistinction constituted
a tacit premise of all Greek philosophy, though Parmenides was
the first Greek thinker to take advantage of it for philosophical
ends.

Let us recall the positions already arrived at: (a) by knowledge
the mind receives reality into itself, reduplicating it insofar as
the mind makes itself one with it, (b) therefore, to know is to
become the other as other, (c) therefore, the other is intelligible.
But can we also say that the other is intelligible as such? Yes,
we can also say that the other is intelligible as such, because the
other as such is *being;* that is, its reality is to be self-identically
whatever it is. Every being is whatever it is, and it cannot be
what it is: this is why it exhibits intrinsic necessity and self-necessitation. However, what it is, is precisely what is grasped by
knowledge; for all thought is a self-telling of what things are.
The fact that there can be no complete sentence without the
verb "to be" (or a verb reducible to "to be") [37] is an index of the

---

[37] "Every proposition must contain a verb, or the tense of a verb,"
Aristotle, *On Interpretation,* 5 (17 a 10). It is curious that the original
Greek proposition in which Aristotle cast this thought lacks a verb. This
is not as self-contradictory as it may sound at first. The Greek sentence
follows the syntactic pattern of attributing a predicate, P, to a subject,
S, by means of a copula, the verb εἶναι (to be). Thus, its formula is *S is P.*
If the verb is grammatically other than "to be" the syntactic pattern remains the same, *S is P,* because the predicate is attributed *to* the subject
as what it *is;* this is why the distinction is sometimes made between
predicate and *complement* (of the verb). In other words, P as predicate
actually includes the notion *is;* properly speaking in the act of predication
the attribute is not "P" but "is P." Hence, when the verb is grammatically
other than "to be" is it nonetheless reducible to "to be." In the sentence

fact that all knowledge grasps being, that which is. But to grasp being is to grasp reality, for *to be* designates things in their reality, in themselves. In other words: the reality to which man relates himself can be said to be essentially and formally intelligible—that is, it is in itself and for its own sake, as it were, and not merely for the mind's sake, constituted by intelligibility—because all reality as such is being, and being is the object of the intellect, since all predication occurs in terms of being and predica-

---

"Socrates drinks hemlock" the predicate is not "hemlock" but "drinks hemlock." Therefore, the sentence is reducible to "Socrates is hemlock-drinking;" the copula, i.e. the verb "to be" as the means of predication, is thus *implicit* in the more usual form "Socrates drinks hemlock." The same is true even when the verb is intransitive; e.g. "Socrates drinks" predicates "drinks" of "Socrates" and is, therefore, reducible to the pattern *S is P*. Now, the linguistic convention in Greek permits not only the reduction of all verbs to a form of the verb "to be," but also the omission of the verb "to be" from the sentence as an explicit syntactic element. But since such a sentence, if it is indeed a sentence, *attributes* a predicate *to* a subject, the sentence *implicitly* or *tacitly* contains the necessary verb. Aristotle's sentence in *On Interpretation* is a complete sentence because it contains *tacitly* the verb "to be."

I have defended Aristotle's self-consistency, however, not without an ulterior purpose. It is possible to state that a sentence without a grammatical verb implicitly contains the verb "to be" if, and only if, predication is the attribution of a predicate to a subject: for this already implies the essential copulative function of the verb "to be." In Greek, as in Latin, this is the only possible mode of predication: the very term *predication* is convertible with *attribution of a predicate to a subject*. But should there be a language—as indeed there are several thousand—in which (what *we* call) predication is not, to begin with, the attribution of a predicate to a subject, so that the syntactic pattern of the sentence *never* takes the form *S is P*, then we are *not* entitled to say that the omission of the verb "to be" from such sentences can be reduced to the implicit or tacit use of the copulative verb. There can be exceptions to a rule only if there is in the first place a rule. But where there is no rule there can be no exception. We shall have occasion below to recall these remarks.

tion is but the linguistic expression of the mental reflection of the reality which lies outside the mind in the real world.

Parmenides' formula, "that which is thought and that which is are the same," does not state merely that being is in fact intelligible, but that it is intelligible *because* it is being. Hence, it is *necessarily* intelligible, for it is intelligibility which makes it to be itself, and to be self-identically itself. But this reasoning makes sense only if it is first assumed that the true name, as it were, of reality in itself is being—on the grounds that every true name is a form of being, which is precisely what the Greek and Latin identification of copulative "to be" and, (as I have temporarily agreed to call it) existential "to be," naturally and unavoidably suggests—and that the reality of reality *in itself* is signified by being.

With this double identification—the identification of reality as such with being, and of being as such with intelligibility—is introduced the *metaphysical* concept of being. It is literally *meta-physical*, in the sense that the inner necessity of reality is discerned not in the specific nature of each thing, but in their reality itself, which underlies their specific natures. But the metaphysical concept of being is *meta*-physical in a deeper sense yet. It symbolizes a truth the discovery of which fell to Plato and the exploration to Aristotle: reality as such lies beyond the reality of nature. There are, in other words, *degrees* of reality. The reality which is immediately given, (for it is the reality of the world of which we ourselves form part), namely, the reality of the world of nature, is not simply reality. It is reality *secundum quid*, reality which may, as Plato put it, be "not really real," or which, as Aristotle thought, may be really real yet composed of potency and act—but reality, in either event, which is not identifiable pure and simply with *what-is*. Beyond this reality, therefore, there is that reality which in the strictest sense *is* and which is, therefore, strictly immutable, self-identical and necessary. This is the reality which Greek mythology places even above the gods under the name of Fate. Metaphysics is the study of this reality, and of all reality in relation to reality itself; but since reality's true, scientific name is not Fate but being, it is necessary, if we wish to put the matter formally, to say that metaphysics studies being as such.

As is well known, however, the term metaphysics is a relatively late coinage dating from the first century B.C., and it was not indeed until Christian times that it was used with the specific connotations I have marked above. The terms used by Aristotle himself to describe the study which was later called metaphysics are two: one was *First Philosophy,* that is, philosophy in the primary sense of the word. The other term harks back to the origin of philosophy in the relocation of the divinities and Fate within the reality of things. Metaphysical enquiry was erected upon the premise that reality as such, though revealed to man either on the occasion of his knowing the world of nature (as Plato thought) or else (as Aristotle thought) by his abstracting it from the world of nature, where it is found in either participated or limited form, (limited, that is, by the potency which limits act)—metaphysical inquiry was erected on the premise that *reality as such is divine* and that it is divine *specifically insofar as it is being.*[38] Though

---

[38] Christian thinkers could not very well agree that reality as such is divine, so that whatever is real is thereby divine. But since the force of this assertion depends on the identification of reality with being, they automatically reinterpreted Greek metaphysics to mean the opposite of what it originally meant, namely, that God is being (Itself). (This is the great virtue of self-identities, that they can be turned around at will.) At

physics attempts to reach the gods that all things are full of, First Philosophy attempts to reach the very source of the divinity of the realities which legendary, primitive Greek thought had called "the gods." The true name of First Philosophy is, thus, "theology," in the word coined by Plato [39] and immediately picked up by Aristotle: metaphysics is the study of the divine.

It is not directly relevant to our enquiry, but it may be nonetheless enlightening, to note that for all its monumental significance Greek philosophy did not, as measured by its own standards, achieve the precise success it had originally sought. For as hindsight amply reveals, the failure of the Greek philosophical enterprise was, (if I may so put it), ironically unavoidable.[40] Assuming the premise that the function of reason was that of capturing reality, extracting its necessity and neutralizing its painful sting, and that happiness lay in man's free self-delivery to the necessary good, the only possible outcome of the Greek philosophical odyssey was the paradox of Stoicism and Epicureanism —two conceptual voices harmonizing on the same plaintive ethical note. The ultimate achievement of Greek philosophy was the conclusion that man's only way to avoid the tragedy of life (as the Stoics would have put it), or to reach happiness (as the Epicureans would have preferred) was to submit to Fate. This

---

least, Christian philosophy pointed in this direction from the outset, though it arrived consistently and systematically at this position only with the help of St. Thomas. The divinization of being instituted by the Greeks was completed by the ontologization of the divinity in Christian thought.

[39] Plato, *Republic,* II, 379 A.

[40] It is regrettable that it is not always safe for philosophers to drop unlabelled ironies, but the spirit of Socrates witnesses to the fact. This assertion does not contradict the views expressed elsewhere in this book. I do not really think that the course of Greek philosophy was fated by the inner logical necessities of the premises of Greek thought.

was, to be sure, an intelligent submission: it was not a blind acceptance of the inevitable, but a wise incorporation of oneself into it. But, in any event, it was a submission. The final lesson learned by Greek philosophy was that man should stop struggling against Fate and make friends with it. Man must not, as it were, kick against the goad; it is better to accept its reality gently. Man must not wrestle with *what is,* for what is is necessarily. In short, man is to be reconciled to his Fate and make his peace with necessity, cultivating serenity and impassivity, confident that in the free and intelligent service of the inscrutable purposes of the immanent *logos,* man can find the true realization of the natural purposes of his finite reason and will. Now, it was this religious outlook that defined the heart of Hellenism—and it was Hellenism that Christianity took for its cultural form in order, understandably, to achieve its ecumenical, catholic aims.

CHRISTIANITY AND HELLENISM

Although it cannot very well be supposed that Hellenism had no influence whatever on the development of Judaism, there can be little doubt that this influence was relatively slight. Even after the pronounced, innate resistance of Israel to acculturation is discounted, it remains that the significant contacts between Helenism and Judaism occurred only at a relatively late stage of the development of the religion of the Old Testament and the composition of its Scriptures. With Christianity, however, the case was somewhat different. For Christianity, though conceived wholly out of Israel, was not born wholly in Israel and, in any event, did not take root and grow under the tutelage of Israel.

The division of Jewish and Gentile Christianity was, during the short period it existed, uneven; and judaization was condemned, whereas hellenization was not. For Christians were conscious of the particularities of Judaism, whereas they were not clearly aware that the "universal" culture of the Greco-Roman world unified by the κοινή, the "common [speech]," (i.e. Greek) was in fact quite as particular and contingent as all human cultures must by nature be. The catholicity of Christianity tended to conflict with the Jewish culture wherever the latter had remained inward and provincial. This was especially true, of course, in the religious order. For despite the latter-day Jewish trend towards catholicity—a trend of which Christianity was, in a way, the culmination—the more traditional identification of Israel as an ethnic and political community with the community of the elect, remained distinctive of, and predominant in, Jewish belief. These remarks are, of course, a highly inadequate bare allusion to a complex matter. But the complexities of the matter do not take away altogether the basic facts. When all is said and done, the basic fact remains: whereas Hebrew was the language of the Old Testament, the language of the New was Greek.[41]

Neither the whole, nor even the principal part, of the process of Christianity's hellenization is describable by the mere use of Greek as the main language in which the earliest Christian litera-

---

[41] Arnold Toynbee has explained how "the exposition of Christianity in the Greek language (and Christianity was expounded in the Greek language at a very early stage of its history) implicated Christianity in Greek philosophy, because, by the first century of the Christian Era, the Greek language was long since imbued with a Greek philosophical vocabulary, conveying Greek philosophical ideas. And I think that as soon as the Epistles and the Gospels were written, and written in Greek, Christianity was committed to expressing itself sooner or later in terms of Greek philosophy," *Christianity Among the Religions of the World,* p. 6.

ture was composed and circulated. But most of Christianity's hellenization is prefigured and symbolized by no more complex a cultural and historical fact than this. It is illustrative, for example, that the New Testament writers frequently take certain Greek ideas for granted, assuming them as a matter of universal, human common sense. "Be ye doers of the word, and not hearers only:" [42] this is the formula that spontaneously came to the mind of James when he wished to exort those Christians (if I may put it in the terms of a metaphor which comes from another cultural context) whose spirit was willing, but whose flesh was weak. It is to be expected that some members of every community will exhibit somewhat the same pattern of behaviour to which James refers. But the way in which one will conceptualize one's awareness of the fact will depend upon the cultural mode of one's actual existence and historical situation. James assumed that one first hears and only afterwards does—or, perhaps, does *not* do. Reality comes to man through the senses and in return man directs himself outwards towards reality. This is no doubt a possible conceptualization of the facts of human experience. It is also a fact, however, that it did not occur to James to interpret the same facts of human experience in such a way as might have resulted (to use a fanciful illustration) in the following injunction: "Be ye listeners of the word, and not hearers only" or, (more fanciful yet) "you do not hear the word, unless you utter the word."

I need hardly stress that what is true of James is truer still of St. Paul. But it is not only that St. Paul made use of Greek ideas; it is yet more symptomatic that he frequently made use of ideas which were, indeed of Hebrew origin and undoubtedly foreign

[42] *James*, 1:22.

to the Greek mind—like πνεῦμα and σάρξ—but which, of course, he put in *Greek* terms, thereby transforming, that is, hellenizing, their original natural bent. In St. Paul's doctrine of πνεῦμα and σάρξ there is no question of an inner division within the substance of man: the dichotomy is rather an interpretation of the fact that man finds himself paradoxically existing in contradictory conditions at one and the same time, so that he is, as it were, both strong and weak, both willing and unwilling. But we all know how the doctrine of the "spirit" and the "flesh" gradually became understood dualistically, and that for many centuries it has been very difficult for all but a handful of specialists to read it otherwise. For somewhat the same observations about the human condition are described by the Greek philosophers in terms of distinct faculties, the role of one of which is merely to put man in possession of the truth, whereas the role of the other is to act accordingly. Though the ideas behind the Pauline opposition of πνεῦμα and σάρξ were, as I said, foreign to the Greeks, their translation into Greek altered the original to an extent which graduate theological theses writers continue to this day assiduously to explore. On the other hand, the Greek division of the soul's powers into cognitive and appetitive faculties is altered by James in the text I first used as illustration, in at least one significant respect. For the "word" of which the Christian is to be not only a "hearer," but also a "doer," is distinctly neither the word that is spoken nor the inner reality of the world which is the measure and rule of human thought. The "word" is, of course, the Word of God, in the originally Hebrew sense of the term. The hellenization of Christianity took place in more ways than one.

I have not cited these precise instances at random. I have chosen them because they exhibit in a single parallel the twofold features that Christianity's adaptation of Hellenic forms (a) was most effective when these forms were assumed as a matter of course, and (b) that it was most significant when it helped shape the most basic concepts of Christian faith. The reasons for this can be easily surmised. To the degree that man does anything unconsciously (or, more precisely, to the degree that he does anything without heightening his consciousness), he does it uncritically; and to the same degree that man does anything uncritically, he restricts his freedom by restricting the possibilities that will be open to him in the future. It is not the truth that one altogether misses, it is the truth that one takes for granted that is most difficult to improve upon. The second reason has to do with the specific matter of religion. Religion, whatever else may be said of it, has to do with the most basic relation of man to reality. Therefore, man's explicit or implicit understanding of religion will be a function of his understanding, reflective or not, of the nature of man's relation to the non-self. That is why the essential elements of the hellenization of Christianity are found not so much in the countless other ways in which Christianity adapted Greco-Roman cultural forms, as in the Christian faith's very understanding of the nature of faith and of the nature of its object.

Before we proceed to an analysis of these two concepts, I should make certain explanatory remarks, of a general nature, concerning the hellenization of the Christian faith. I offer these remarks with some reluctance, since they add nothing to what I have written elsewhere on the subject. But it may help clear away some misunderstandings if I repeat here what I had hoped I had made sufficiently clear elsewhere.

The hellenization of Christianity is as well established a historical fact as any historical fact has ever been. Granted all the historical research spent on the subject in the last one hundred years or so, the onus is on anyone who has novel evidence on the subject to offer it for examination. The *nature* of hellenization, however, the interpretation which is to be put on the facts, the meaning which it is to be assigned in one's understanding of Christianity is, of course, another matter. On this subject agreement ceases, and the very nature of the problem requires greater diffidence than does the question of fact.

It would not be unwarranted, I believe, to divide the principal interpretations of the hellenization of Christianity into three categories. The first, of which Adolph von Harnack's in the 19th century is perhaps the most detailed and authoritative, comprises a spectrum of theories with a common element: the early development of Christian doctrine is to be understood as the gradual *substitution* of Hellenic elements for the corresponding original elements of the Apostolic Church, and the accumulation of these changes amounts (for better or for worse, usually the latter) to a substantial change in Christian truth.

Other theories, which also range their own spectrum of variety and detail, stress, on the contrary, the substantial continuity of Christian truth. The adoption of Greek ideas and attitudes is interpreted as affecting only these "expressions of Christian truth," since whenever they might have conflicted with Christianity they were purged or adapted. The partiality of the Hellenic influence of Christianity is emphasized by some scholars who fall in this category, noting the quantitative predominance of Hebrew and Scriptural terms, concepts and ideas in the development of dogma. In short, in this view the historical facts are, though not always minimized, usually explained as having failed to affect the substance of the Christian faith. In a subcategory under this heading must be placed those who, without explicitly or perhaps consciously taking this view, assume it tacitly—some because they are not familiar with the elements of the history of Christian dogma and assume that the doctrine of the early Church was but an anticipated summary of the doctrine of the Council of Trent, or others because they ignore the development of dogma or think that, in principle, it can always be explained away, since the Christian doctrine is true and, therefore, it must have always been substantially the same as it is today.

For all their diametric opposition, these two interpretations share some common premises. And although it is not in itself an adverse criticism of either viewpoint, it is revealing of the nature of both that these premises are themselves traceable to Greek thought. [43] I refer to the ideas that (a) the nature of truth demands the constancy of a substantially unchanging human knowledge, and (b) that culture and history are adventitious to the truth of the human intellect. Both these premises are, I believe, mistaken. On the other hand, I find some truth in each of these positions. The first recognizes that cultural forms are not accidental to, but constitutive of, human experience; I have made some remarks above in this connection, with specific reference to language as a cultural form. The second view is instinctively correct in its belief that Christianity's adaptation of hellenic forms did not corrupt its truth. But it mistakenly assumes that the truth of Christianity prevented it from having a contingent cultural form—and that, therefore, if Hellenism provided the cultural

[43] More precisely, they are not only traceable to Greek thought, but they essentially repeat certain fundamental premises of Greek thought.

forms of Christianity it must have done so not insofar as it was a contingent cultural form, but insofar as this cultural form embodied eternal, necessary truths. Needless to say, it is this very understanding of the truth and of its relation to human culture that is being questioned in this book.

For these reasons I incline to a third type of interpretation—which permits, of course, of many variations. The essential aspect of this type is that the hellenization of Christianity did truly change not only the outward character of Christianity, but even its truth. But assuming that truth (and not merely its supposedly detachable expression) can actually develop, and that human experience acquires its humanity, and indeed its character of truth, only in a social and historical context, this view deems the hellenization of Christianity to have been, *in concreto,* practically inevitable and, in any event, a fortunate occurrence. Though I would not go so far as to claim the intervention of providential design in the emergence of Christianity under historical conditions which, in effect, made its hellenization well nigh unavoidable,[44] Hellenism provided, though not the only imaginable set of conditions under which Christianity could contribute to the evolution of human religious consciousness, certainly a peculiarly privileged intellectual matrix. But, by the same token, the cultural form actually taken by Christianity, (to be sure, not without elaboration and creative modifications of its own), can-

[44] I do not mean that there can be no divine agency involved in the development of history, as if "nature" were inwardly necessitated rather than necessitated from without. What I have in mind is that history is not inwardly necessitated, and that therefore the involvement of any divine agency in the course of history cannot be adequately understood as the intervention of divine providence in the course of natural affairs— for the course of "natural" affairs is not such that it can be either interfered with or else left alone to proceed according to its own laws.

not be supposed to have eternal validity: it cannot be supposed even necessarily to have adequacy for all later times. Not, I repeat, if the truth does indeed change.

But here the circle begins. The complex process known as the hellenization of Christianity includes in highly prominent place the Greek conception of truth. To consider the possibility that Christianity may take, in any basic respect, a conceptual form which differs "substantially" from its traditional form is a useless enterprise unless one also considers the possibility that the Greek conception of truth might be improved upon. But to reject this possibility on the grounds that belief in the truth of the Christian faith requires of its very nature belief in the unchanging nature of truth is to hedge oneself within a circle which may be rooted in good faith but which is impenetrably thorny with dogmatism. In this, as in so many other respects, concern for the truth is not necessarily the same as the truth; not every view advanced in defence of truth is necessarily true, nor does it always profit the truth.

It may be this same sort of zeal, genuine but possibly misguided, that accounts for another frequent misunderstanding about the hellenization of Christianity. To assert that Christianity has long retained for itself a Hellenic form which is no longer adequate to the ends which once it did serve is neither to lodge an accusation against Christianity nor to express aversion for the Greek mind. It should not be necessary to explain the difference between an accusation and an adverse critical judgment (be it right or wrong) concerning the alleged wisdom of consciously perpetuating a certain state of affairs about the original wisdom of which no question has been raised. Nor should it be necessary to explain that the recommendation that contemporary

Christianity should consciously undertake the redevelopment of all its various cultural forms (and in the first place its conceptual forms) has nothing to do with one's evaluation of Hellenism. It so happens that I have great admiration for the Greek mind, and I have no wish to belittle the achievements of Greece. (How could any Western Christian wish to do so, if he should believe, as I do, that the future can be constructed only on the basis of the remembrance of one's own past, and indeed as the reconstruction of one's own past—and that, as I insist, the form of the Christian past is in origin essentially Greek?) It is, however, somewhat exasperating to have to affirm this, not only because one had never stated otherwise, but above all because in respect of what *was* being affirmed no one's inclinations about the Hellenic culture were the issue at stake. It matters very little to the real life of Christendom today whether anyone is or is not fair and grateful *to the Greeks*. What matters is whether one is satisfied with the present shape *of Christianity* and, even more, with the future it portends.

But that is precisely the issue: whether the contemporary Christian should or should not be satisfied with the traditional forms of Christian doctrine and life today, when the world of most people is no longer the world to which those forms correspond. There can be little doubt that for many Christians this is not a serious problem, perhaps not even a problem at all. That may be because they measure the adequacy of contemporary experience by the standard of Christianity's traditional forms, saying, as it were: if the spirit of today's world does not harmonize readily with the spirit of the traditional forms of Christianity, then so much the worse for today's world, for the discrepancy can indicate nothing but the waywardness of the world.

Other Christians experience no problem for a different reason:

110

they believe that there is *no* discrepancy between Christian belief and the contemporary world. (I think these people argue on no sounder basis than I might have, say, for maintaining that the Jovian air is a hospitable environment for Christian belief, and that there is no discrepancy between Christian belief and the cultural forms of Ganymede. You see, I have never travelled beyond Earth's atmosphere.) Of course, if, on the one hand, one assumes that the traditional forms of Christianity are immutable because Christianity is true, and if, on the other, one leaves enough human experience out of account or rejects enough human intellectual progress, then one will not agree that Christianity has a problem. One will believe that the problem is really the world's—or else one will ascribe the dissatisfaction of other believers to their idolatry or to their "chronolatry," [45] discerning the remedy for this situation in some variation of the formula "we must serve God and not man." In other words, it is perfectly possible for the Christian to wave away the problems created by the retention of traditional forms of Christianity which have been rendered obsolete by the developments of human consciousness. All he has to do is to refuse to take part in the development of human consciousness, justifying this procedure by denying the validity (if not also the reality) of such a development, indicting the world on a charge of evil and perversion.

I, for one, find it impossible to reason in this way. It seems to me that for all its real evils and perversions, the emergence of contemporary Western culture cannot be judged in itself either evil or perverse. On the contrary, every line of comparison we may care to take reveals that its achievements are real and in not a few respects must be interpreted as a fulfilment of human na-

---

[45] Maritain, *Le Paysan de la Garonne*, p. 25.

ture. This interpretation has even intrinsic probability on its side. History, development and evolution are in themselves natural. Progress is not inevitable, but it is possible; and given the striving, hopeful nature of man when it occurs it is normal enough. This is not to imagine that whatever is, is justified merely because it has come into being. Nor is it to endorse *a priori* whatever man does with himself, or to forget either the permanent possibility of sin or its evident actuality in ourselves, I mean, in contemporary man. But a confusion between the moral character of contemporary culture—that is, whether or not it projects itself towards the future as it should, given what it already is; whether or not it rises to the opportunities which it itself creates—a confusion, I say, between its moral character, which is debatable, and the factual nature and historical reality of the contemporary world, about which there cannot be a reasonable doubt, would understandably jaundice the Christian's perspective upon the world.

It matters little, however, (to the issue at hand), whether our contemporary culture idolizes science instead of worshipping God—though perhaps if worshipping God in a mature manner were rendered an easier spiritual achievement than it is today, then the craving of the masses for authoritarianism might disappear altogether instead of being merely transferred from hierarchical and priestly technicians to technological and scientific priestcraft—what matters is that the contemporary level of scientific knowledge (and I do not mean merely its technological applications) is a high water mark in the history of man's quest for truth. It matters little to the argument in favour of the dehellenization of Christianity whether we, contemporary Western man, use our skills for such inhuman purposes as, say, genocide

112

—though man's self-disposition in the thermonuclear age might be wiser if Christianity served effectively as a source of realistic inspiration and of sound common sense—what matters, if we wish to determine whether the contemporary world is the only real one, and whether it is the world in which the Christian faith must live and the only world to which it must be relevant, is that our technology is the most powerful in the history of human economy—even, unfortunately, when it comes to killing one another. It matters little, finally, whether the contemporary stage of human self-awareness is a pitfall for human pride, and whether self-worship through the worship of progress comes all the easier to man the more he progresses—though man might have made greater progress in self-guidance if Christianity had not discredited itself by openly declaring itself altogether the enemy of progress [46]—what matters is that "it is not in our power, it is no longer even among our possibilities, to retrograde towards a stage in history in which man could appear to himself as an evident given." [47] What matters, in a word, is whether the contemporary mode of human consciousness is an evolutionary, historical fact. That type of Catholic thinking which would have contemporary human consciousness adjust itself to faith in its traditional form is unrealistic and self-delusive to the point of presumption. For human evolution, the development of human consciousness, cannot be actually stopped, it can at most be slowed down, and it can at worst lose meaningfulness—as it has in point of fact in Western Christendom since the Christian world divided itself against itself into secular and religious halves. Christian

[46] It may be a little trite to refer once again to the last proposition of Pius IX's *Syllabus Errorum*. And yet, *quod scripsit, scripsit.*
[47] Gabriel Marcel, *Problematic Man,* (New York, 1967), p. 52.

belief, however, is a grace and can therefore be altogether lost.

If the expression *dehellenization* should still seem too negative, two remarks might be offered in reply. The first is that I have defined the process it designates in strictly positive terms, namely, as the conscious creation of the future of Christian belief, not necessarily through the *adaptation* of non-Hellenic cultural forms, but ideally through the invention of its own concepts and other forms of experience on the basis of an imaginative, creative evolutionary leap ahead. Dehellenization means the creation of a world which does *not yet* exist, on the basis of the only one that *does* exist. But, second, dehellenization implies, in a very real and necessary way, a corresponding negative phase. *De*-hellenization is transcending the traditional forms. To create the future *is* the same as to transcend the past. The negative expressions, "dehellenization," or "transcending the past" are indispensable and have, in some ways, the edge of advantage, because they stress what the positive expressions alone cannot convey, namely, that the future cannot be created except out of the past. But the Christian's concern is the creation of the future, not the preservation of the past. The continuity of Christian tradition is required by Christian belief, not because the Christian faith *was* true, and therefore must forever remain what it once was: it is required because the Christian faith *is* true, and because we wish it to grow and intensify and fulfill its truth in the time that is yet to come.

3.

The Breakdown of the Foundations
of Belief

CHRISTIAN BELIEF
AND CHRISTIAN UNBELIEF

The eventual outcome of the hellenization of Christianity was
the inward division of the Christian world into a believing church
which ceased to play an inspiring, moulding role in the Christian
world, and a world which is culturally Christian, but which does
not as a whole, or typically, profess Christian belief. That is, the
outcome was the paradoxical situation of Western Christendom
today, a Western Christendom which from the viewpoint of the
historian of culture and of the anthropologist can be called nothing but Christian, yet a Western Christendom which no longer
professes its own faith. Both believing and non-believing philosophers have usually failed to find much *historical* significance
in this event, perhaps because they have devoted more attention
and effort to blaming each other than to understanding a phenomenon which is, when we come to think of it, fairly uncommon in the history of civilizations: cultures do no frequently
repudiate the religion which brought them into cohesive being
in the first place. Believers, preoccupied as they have been with
the truth of their belief, have usually tended to interpret the

115

course of events in the Western world as a malicious apostasy which is explicable only in terms of self-seeking and human pride leading man to prefer himself to God. Unbelievers, in their turn, concerned as they have been with the religious truth of their unbelief, have commonly tended to dismiss religious belief as obscurantism and dogmatism, as irrationalities which cannot defy the light of self-criticism or heed the good sense that comes from experience and realism.

When believers so think, however, they may be confusing pride with the normal maturation of the human mind. To become increasingly self-reliant and to take an ever growing role in the conduct of one's own life is not necessarily the sign of pride or selfishness. There seems to be something in the nature of man which requires this development of the individual; there may be something in human nature which requires it of man collectively as well. Unfortunately, for all the myopia of the contrary claim, there is some truth in it as well. (I say unfortunately, because some believers suffer only additional self-delusion thereby.) The development of man is not necessarily straightforward at all times, not does it exclude human failures, moral and otherwise. On the contrary, the temptations and the opportunities for evil are multiplied as man grows; in these respects too, the processes which can be observed in the individual are parallelled in the collective life of man.

But non-believers, likewise, fail to appreciate that the real obscurantism and dogmatism of believers generally, and of the institutional, official Church in particular, does not necessarily gainsay the adequacy of Christianity as a faith, as a form of religious belief, and non-believers may forget that the same unfortunate failings can be found elsewhere—for instance, in the scientific community which figures so prominently in the formation of the contemporary Western world. Yet, here too, it only adds complexity to a complex matter that non-believers can hardly be expected not to take believers at their word when they —and above all when their official rulers and teachers—express themselves unequivocally, by word and action, in terms which do not always exhibit sufficient common sense, in terms which at one and the same unblushing time proclaim the reasonableness of Christianity and yet ask human beings to believe what Church officials teach, on the grounds that the truth of what they teach is guaranteed by God, as should be self-evident to anyone from the fact that it was God who told them the truth in the first place.

To seek to apportion the blame for the schizophrenia of Western Christendom seems to me a fruitless exercise, not only because the likely outcome would be a draw, but because, in any event, nothing useful could be resolved by this means. A more promising approach would be to attempt to understand how the inner scission of our world occurred, so that we may be in a position to heal it. The broad suggestion offered here is that the explanation may be found in the complementarity of two historical processes. First, as Western Christendom pursued the consequences of its original religious inspiration, it developed human experience to a level of self-consciousness, self-creativity and self-relation to reality which became increasingly incompatible with belief in a Christian doctrine which in its concrete form had given meaning to an earlier, less well developed mode of human experience. Second, the community of Christian believers, as it pursued the consequences of its original adoption of Hellenic cultural forms, became persuaded that Christian doctrine was incompatible with the mode of experience developed by the

Christian world—a world which appeared almost bent upon discarding its original Christian faith.

It is ironic that neither believing nor unbelieving Christendom has succeeded in shaping the Christian world in accordance with its (secular or religious) faith. The present Christian world is a world of both Christian belief and Christian unbelief, but it is Christian both in its belief and in its unbelief. The mistaken diagnosis reached by secular Christianity—attributing the incompatibility between traditional Christian doctrine and the developing Western intellect (particularly in its scientific mode) to Christian belief in principle, rather than to Christian belief in its traditional form—has not facilitated its becoming conscious of its own mistaken retention of certain Hellenic cultural forms.[1]

[1] Although the historical progress of experimental science has distinctly tended, on the whole, towards dehellenization, science has remained curiously bound to Greek epistemology in some of its most basic presuppositions. In its early stages the "new philosophy" was new in no more fundamental way than by supposing that the "forms" ascertainable by scientific enquiry were not substantial forms, but mathematical forms. The inner intelligibility of things was a mathematical constitution translatable into a mathematical formula; hence, it was calculable rather than deducible. The metaphysical principles of intelligibility were transmuted into the Laws of Nature. More modern science gave up the notion of *prescriptive* Natural Laws, but largely retained *descriptive* natural laws. For science remained an *objective* investigation of natural realities—it could hardly have been supposed to be a subjective musing about them. Scientific understanding has continued to think of itself even in recent times as the intentional manipulation of outward reality by means of vicarious conceptual constructs or models which represent the reality itself. (Applied science is the manipulation of reality, insofar as reality does actually conform to the theoretical models which reduplicate it scientifically.) It is only in restricted provinces of contemporary science, notably quantum mechanics, that "what is known is seen [by scientists] to be a product in which the act of observation plays a necessary role. Knowing is seen to be a participant in what is finally known. Moreover, the metaphysics of existence as something fixed and therefore capable of literally

But religious Christianity has hardly fared better, having failed to stop progress, having indeed succeeded only in ensuring that the course of human history remained less adequate than what it might otherwise have been, because the progress of the Christian culture has taken place in the absence of conscious Christian belief.

It would be difficult for any single study or for any single scholarly competence to substantiate every aspect of this complex interpretation. I will be concerned here with only one part of it—albeit a part which is of capital importance. In this chapter I shall try to show how it happened that the very philosophical foundations of Hellenism in epistemology and in metaphysics were undermined by Christian thought—indeed, singularly by St. Thomas Aquinas himself. But I must preface my account with certain considerations which are its necessary background.

---

exact mathematical description and prediction is undermined. [But if this approach is correct] knowing is, for philosophical theory, a case of specially directed activity instead of something isolated from practice. The quest for certainty by means of exact possession in mind of immutable reality is exchanged for search of security by means of active control of the changing course of events. Intelligence in operation, another name for method, becomes the thing most worth winning," John Dewey, *The Quest for Certainty*, (New York, 1960), p. 204. Other notable exceptions are to be found in some areas of psychology (for instance, in the work of such as D. O. Hebb), in orthopsychiatry and in the theory of psychotherapy (where the name of Rollo May immediately comes to mind) and in sociology (where the contribution of David Riesman is among the best known). But much contemporary science remains incurably objectivist, wedded as it appears to be to the realist epistemology of Greek and mediaeval times.

LINGUISTIC FORMS
AND CONSCIOUS EXPERIENCE

I have already alluded to the question of the nature of language and its relation to human experience. It is a common lay opinion, to which even most philologists used to subscribe in the past, that language is the expression of experience, the outward manifestation of an inward phenomenon, the cognition of reality. I need hardly emphasize that the Greek origin of this view accounts for its currency and apparent self-evidence in our world today. This idea, however, is hardly the statement of a fact: it is an interpretation which assumes a prior view, namely, the Greek view, of the nature of human experience. If it is assumed that consciousness is divisible into cognition and appetition, and that cognition is the intentional, inward reception of a reality which is constituted by its cognoscibility, then it will be difficult to avoid the hypothesis that whereas consciousness is an "inner" phenomenon, language is an "outward" one. This automatically creates the problem of the relation of language and *thought* (the latter having automatically become severed from experience). And I say this *creates* the problem because unless we make the foregoing presupposition, it would not occur to anyone to distinguish between *talking,* and *talking to oneself,* or between *thinking,* and *thinking aloud,* except, of course, in the obvious sense that in the one case we use sounds (or a derivative of sounds), or other disposition of ourselves in order to project our experience beyond our immediate selves, whereas silent speech, of course, obtains only when vocalization is suppressed. For the view of language as an outer manifestation makes language essentially definable in terms of sound (or a like manifestation) since without sound (or a like manifestation) language could hardly said to be an *outer* manifestation of thought. If so, it follows that thinking—that is, the *inner* phenomena of articulated consciousness —is not language, since it is not vocal.

By the same token, however, thinking is severed from experience. We have already seen the reason for this: experience, as Aristotle says, is "the same for all," representing as it does "those things of which our experiences are the images," whereas thought enjoys the discursivity, articulation and creativity of speech— without however being speech, but an "inner" mental phenomenon. In brief, if we assume the classical concept of knowledge, language has no role in the processes of human consciousness, but is wholly *subsequent* to consciousness and the mere externalization of it. This subsequence implies that there is an "inner" mental process, thinking, which is distinct from both experiencing and talking. I am not at present concerned with the two intractable problems which follow from this view, namely, the relation of experience and thought, and the relation of thought and language. I am only concerned with pointing out that the introduction of the distinction between the public and the private, the inner and the outer, phenomena of thought and of speech, is further based on the assumption that for all their distinction, experience and thought correspond as perfectly as do thought and speech: that for every conscious experience there is a conceptual counterpart which can be mentally manipulated, and that for each and every concept there is a linguistic sign to which the latter corresponds. I am concerned with this correspondence, because its assumption is what permits Greek thought to contradict itself with logical impunity. If language corresponds to thought, but is distinct from it—particularly in that language uses conventional signs (namely, words) which are not the same for all, whereas thought uses natural signs (namely, concepts), which are the same for all—then it is possible (it is indeed necessary) for the philosopher to ignore for all practical and theoretical purposes the distinction between language and thought, and to treat words indistinguishably from concepts.

The traditional formal logic illustrates this well. The logician supposedly studies thought, with the object of determining the structure of thinking. But what are some of the instances of the thought that traditional formal logic studies? Concepts like "man" and "mortal," propositions like "every man is mortal," and syllogisms like "Socrates is a man, every man is mortal, therefore, Socrates is mortal." If it is remarked that these "thoughts" are to all intents undistinguishable from language, the traditional logician would probably reply that he can only refer to thought by means of language, reaffirming that he is not concerned with the sounds, but with the mental operations which are signified by the sounds. And it is true, of course, that if language is defined as a system of significant (i.e. signifying) sounds (or other outward signs), then the distinction is imperative. But the argument is circular: its only useful role is that of shoring up the classical concept of knowledge. On the other hand, for this function a heavy price is paid: the foregoing reasoning makes it possible for the philosopher to assume that the structure of language reflects point for point the structure of thought, without, however, adverting to the fact that this correspondence can be neither gratuitous, nor left unexplained. Indeed, this procedure permits the philosopher, at the same time that he assumes the distinction between language and thought, to analyze the structure of thought as if there were *no* distinction whatever between language and thought.

But it may be asked: What is amiss with this procedure, if it should be true that language does somehow signify thought? The reply may best be given in a round-about way.

Is sound the only feature of language that is variable from one system to another? The Greeks may be forgiven if they thought so. Even today, when most of us have had more opportunities than they to familiarize ourselves with the great variations in human languages, many of us continue to think that, apart from minor, secondary differences which are of no account, the essential difference between any two languages is that different sounds are used to signify the same thing—that the essential difference is given by the different *words* used for the same thought about the same thing. Critical reflection and some linguistic experience, however, should reveal that beyond the semantic variability of languages there stands a less noticeable, perhaps, but much more important, syntactic, functional variability. Aristotle rightly observed that "all men have not the same speech sounds." But we should also observe that the different "speech sounds" of different languages are put together in quite different ways.

Part of the reason why this fact has not frequently entered into the calculations of philosophers is that the semantic differences between languages are clearly marked, even among closely related languages, whereas the syntactic variability of language is not so readily evident unless one compares languages which are historically and anthropologically somewhat distant from each other—and even this information would not be found striking unless one realized, as we have been able to realize only since the middle of the 19th century, that morphological differences among languages are indicative of historical and other cultural processes. Philology was born only after this idea was conceived.

Thus, a mediaeval scholar familiar with, say, Latin, Greek and Hebrew, would still be likely to assume, as Aristotle might well have done, that the differences between Hebrew and Latin are of the same order as those between Latin and Greek: he would, in effect, naturally tend to reduce Hebrew to a system of speech sounds in which the words are yet more distant from Latin than Greek—but more distant only in the same direction, as it were. A philosopher would be all the more likely to think so if he were acquainted only with languages which are closely related syntactically—say, languages of the Indo-European family. Semantic differences would loom large to him, but syntactic differences would appear only of slight consequence, a matter of simple word order, perhaps, such as the preferred position of the verb in Latin and in German, or the different normal order of adjective and noun in Spanish and English, or the inflectional variations between classical and modern languages. A philosopher who operated under these assumptions would understandably also assume, for instance, that every complete sentence has a verb, regardless of the language it may be uttered in, and that this grammatical rule is not culturally contingent but, indeed indicates an essential property of human thought. And since thought in turn reflects the structure of reality, this property of thought, signified by a property of language, would ultimately indicate a property of reality, namely, the constitution of reality as such by an act; (for verbs are act-words). Such a philosopher would likely assume as well that every noun is either substantive or

124

adjectival, and that this division reveals not the way in which his language functions, but "categories" (i.e. *predicaments*) of thought which ultimately reveal the modalities of being itself. In short, such a philosopher would find it very difficult to avoid attributing to thought in the first place, and ultimately to reality, by reason of their supposed invariability, (which would bar their being attributed to language, which is obviously variable), features which in point of fact are characteristic of the structure of language and which in point of fact may vary from one linguistic system to another. Needless to say, this is precisely what most philosophers in the Hellenic-Western tradition have done until recent times—and it is even what not a few contemporary philosophers in the Western Christian world continue to do to this very day.

If it is a mistake, as I have suggested, to attribute to thought certain features (which in turn supposedly reflect the features of reality, the object of thought) on the evidence given by the features of language, it would be as grievous a mistake—indeed, it would be an absurdity—to imagine that the features of language belong to language alone, and not at all to thought. For thought would still remain the significative expression of reality, and language would become the significative expression of nothing at all. As long as language is understood as a conscious activity which is *by nature subsequent to* the mental activity of thinking (few would maintain that it is chronologically subsequent as well), it is necessary to maintain either that language must be the significative expression of thought, or else that language can have no relation to thought at all. But from the consideration that language cannot be the significative expression of thought (for it is not true that the features of language reflect the features of thought—which presumably discharges a like role in relation to the features of reality—since language does not

125

show variability only in the "different sounds" used to signify "the same thing," but indeed does not show any invariable features at all), from this, I say, it does not follow that language is severed from thought, so that the structure of language has nothing to do with the structure of thought. What follows is that language is *not* a conscious activity *subsequent* to the mental activity of thought. What this consideration really does, therefore, is to undermine the distinction between thought and language as, respectively, an inner, prior mental process and an outer, posterior vocal one. The arbitrariness of the Aristotelian distinction is revealed when we realize that it is not only the words, but the *thinking* of the words, the linguistic function, that is not "the same for all."

From this several important consequences follow, some of which will be positively explored later. At this point I will only make some preliminary negative remarks. The first is that to refuse to make a distinction between an inner, prior thought process and an outer, posterior linguistic process is of itself neither to explain what language or thought are, nor to explain the difference between talking in the usual sense (i.e. out loud) and talking in imagination only. All that we can be sure of at this point is that talking is not making sounds signifying what one thinks. There can be little doubt that making sounds is part of talking—that is, of talking out loud—but linguistic behaviour cannot consist in making sounds to designate thought. Indeed, the essential function of language cannot be that of signifying; that is, language cannot have as its essential function the expression of that which had been *previously* thought (whether by a priority of time or of nature, but least of all by the first). The function of language as such can only be thinking itself—though thinking is not necessarily a private, inner activity in which other minds cannot share. But even this formula is misleading, since it reflects in its turn the traditional distinction between *two* things, language and thought. Let us rather say that the considerations adduced here appear to indicate, upon reflection, that vocalization gives to experience its typically human, conscious form. If so, thought is experience of a linguistic form. Man's experience is conscious; it is conscious because man thinks linguistically. But man thinks linguistically because he can use sounds—sounds which develop in a social and historical context—so as to be present to himself when he experiences the world and himself.[2]

---

[2] I do not mean that only sounds can fill this role. Much of the confusion in linguistic theory comes from the circumstance that although the linguistic function, the self-communicative form of man's self-relation to reality, is in fact vocal, the linguistic function is not necessarily vocal. (Actually, it is not exclusively vocal; the gestures and bodily inflections that we make when we talk are not linguistic complements, they are intrinsic part of language itself; or is it not possible to *say* "yes or "no" with but a lifted eyebrow or a gleam in the eye?). There is no biological reason why many modifications of the environment other than those which fall within the audible spectrum could not be used by man as a self-projection which would be apprehensible by "feedback" so as to serve to make man present to himself. (Cf. Norbert Wiener, *The Human Use of Human Beings,* [Garden City, 1954], especially pp. 74–94). Language is essentially but the mirror of the soul, in which man discovers—rather, creates—his own selfhood. There is no reason why this reflector should not work at frequencies other than those which the inner ear can resonate to.

On the other hand, it does make biological sense, given man's physiological structure, and given the physical constitution of his environment, if the emergence of human consciousness was in fact mediated by the production of sounds rather than by any other physiological means. The peculiar aptness of sound, under the stipulated conditions which obtain in the actual human environment, comes from its susceptibility to modulation over an almost infinitely wider range than any other form of energy output readily available to the human body and, correspondingly, the almost

Second, if language is not a distinct process from thought, but the essential and distinctive form of human experience, there are no "mental experiences [which] . . . are the same for all." But this does not render concepts arbitrary or conventional *signs*. If this is not true of "words" it can be even less true of "thoughts." Thus, this view of language also puts in doubt the idea that by knowledge man possesses reality within himself; and if this be so, concepts are not the signs by means of which[3] man knows. Their function can be no other than that of language itself, that is, to give to experience its typically human, conscious form.

Hence, third, the Greek idea that words are *conventional* signs is likewise incorrect. This idea reflects once again the interpretation of linguistic behaviour as the outward manifestation of a

---

infinitely greater filtering and discriminatory power of hearing over every other channel of energy input of the human body. Thus, St. Thomas was very wide of the mark when he thought that sight was "the most spiritual (*maxime spiritualis*), the most perfect and the most comprehensive (*communior*) among all the senses," (*ST*, I, 78, 3). Granted his interpretation of cognition (and the relatively crude stage of physiological knowledge in his time) this misapprehension is perfectly understandable. Had he conceived consciousness otherwise than as intentional appropriation, at man's proximal end, of a distal object—had he conceived consciousness, say, as intercommunication with reality, as *conversation* with the world—he would have realized that communication would be extremely restricted if it were confined to the visual mode. Hearing has a much better claim to be "the most spiritual" of all the senses. Perhaps it is not altogether a coincidence that, as St. Paul says, "faith comes by hearing," (*Romans*, 10:17).

[3] Thomists insist that unlike language, which has its own reality as sound before it is a sign, concepts are "pure means" or strictly "formal signs" of the objects of knowledge. However, this does not affect the validity of my statement. The point is that concepts cannot make known —i.e., signify, however formally—because they cannot mediate the knower's possession of reality within himself, if knowledge is not the knower's possession of reality within himself.

prior, inner mental phenomenon, thought. For in this interpretation language can have no other function than to communicate one mind's thought to another mind. Since thought cannot be held in common by different minds, precisely because it is a private and inner phenomenon, there must be a means of communicate, it is necessary first to communicate. It will not do to different minds, if there is to be any communication at all.

Apart from the difficulties with this interpretation which arise from extrinsic considerations, its inner consistency is not above criticism. To agree upon conventional signs whereby to communicate, it is necessary first to communicate. It will not do to imagine, e.g. that it is enough to point to a table and utter the sound "table," or produce some other outward sign, for convention automatically to arise. For such a convention would require a prior convention, e.g. as to the meaning of pointing, and, most important of all, as to the use of sounds (or whatever) in a *signifying* way. That is, if language is a system of conventional signs, the creation of a language by convention would require the prior determination, *by convention,* of what language is—and it is not easy to imagine how this could be achieved, in the absence of a means of communication, a language, by means of which such a convention could be agreed upon. The Aristotelian interpretation of language has a superficial plausibility which lasts only so long as the historicity of language is ignored and the role of language in human evolution remains unsuspected. For this interpretation assumes, first, that to learn to speak is simply to learn which signs signify which things, but that one does not have to learn to speak, even in the sense that signs signify things; and it assumes, second, that mankind as a whole never did have to learn to speak.

It is perfectly clear, of course, that language does have a communicating function. But it has such a function only because minds have common experience to begin with. Sounds, or other signs, are significant *after* one knows how to talk or otherwise communicate. And one learns to communicate only after one has learned to self-communicate. As significant—and I stress this can only be a derived function from its essential role as the form of conscious experience—language is in the first place self-communicative, and only subsequently communicative. But as the form of conscious experience, it is in the first place the public, outward, *common* form of human thought. Thus, one can learn to speak one's mother tongue only because one's mother tongue already exists. No one's mother tongue was invented by convention—not even by the convention of mothers. On the other hand, to be in possession of the means of self-communication is to be in possession of a means of communication. A child does not learn to speak, say, English by learning English, but by learning to speak.[4] But he cannot very well learn to speak without learning some language, say, English. By the same token, he cannot very well learn to speak in English, without the English language becoming by that very fact the linguistic form of his thought. Thus, anyone who can speak is thereby able to communicate. But this hardly means that language is nothing but a means to communicate that which had been previously thought. It is not altogether irrelevant to note that "thoughtless" people are people who speak "before" they think. I am not suggesting that this is literally true either; but this common expression does enshrine the unreflective observation that speech is not the translation of

[4] Cf. J. B. Carroll, *Language and Thought,* (Englewood Cliffs, 1964), pp. 33–42.

thought into a subsequent form but, on the contrary, that speech is necessarily and directly connected with the formation of thought.

It is understandable that Aristotle should have thought that "nothing is by nature a noun or a name . . . it is so only when it becomes a symbol." In his scheme, vocalization had no function other than being the sign of something other than itself, namely, conceptual thought: therefore, the variability of sounds signifying, supposedly, the same thought (about the same thing) must have meant that speech sounds were basically arbitrary and must originate in human convention. Now, there is a tenuous, negative sense in which this may still be maintained: no one could possibly attempt to support the view that "the true name" of tables is *table,* rather than *mensa* or *Tisch,* since each of these sounds can function with the same adequacy as every other within one and the same world context. But what this really means is that, despite their morphological differences, different languages can be used by man to relate himself to one and the same world; and since none of these languages is more natural to him than any other, it is always possible for him to translate his thinking from one laguage to another—i.e. to relate himself to reality in a variety of ways which are essentially different (despite the constancy of the world) but mutually transformable (because of the constancy of the world). This alone means, once again, that by thinking man *does* relate himself to reality, but that thinking is not reduplicative of reality or manipulative of it.

In any event, though it is natural to man to speak, to think, to conceive, and to relate himself to reality, no language, no way of thinking, no conceptual form, no unique self-relation to reality is natural or necessary. On the other hand, the artificial and contingent nature of language and of concepts does not make language and concepts arbitrary, since human thought emerges historically and socially. To repeat, *table* is no more "natural" (i.e. necessitated by the nature of what it signifies) a name than *mensa* or *Tisch*. But neither *table, mensa* nor *Tisch* signify (i.e. relate man to) certain realities in the world, by arbitrary convention. The use of these words obeys certain rules: first, man needs in certain given historical contexts to think about "tables;" second, the social context in which these needs have arisen have been met in the past and this has in turn contributed to the evolutionary development of man. It is only because the concept "table" arose long ago in a fairly primitive social context, that it is possible for us today to think of, say, "table manners," "table top photography," "water table," and "table of Napier logarithms"—and to live in the kind of world where tables are used in more or less elegant styles, where picture-taking is as near as the corner drug-store, where provision is made to conserve natural resources, and where mathematical calculations are more rapidly machine-made than by hand. If every generation had to begin anew to relate itself to pieces of furniture, no generation would ever get closer to the Moon than could be done by climbing on top of tables. The truth of the idea that language signifies by convention is that language develops historically, and that we *receive* and *accept* the level of thought to which previous generations have risen and then, if all goes well, proceed thence to elaborate, in whatever measure we might, upon the tradition of human thought.

As I have already stated, my objective here is not to develop a theory of language. I have gone into these elementary matters only in order to indicate the plausibility of the following view:

the concrete, determinate form of any given philosophical doctrine may sometimes be determined by the structure of the language (or languages) in which philosophers think.[5] As I suggested a moment ago, one does not learn to speak in a language by learning the language—although, of course, after one already knows how to speak one can learn to speak and usually does learn to speak in a (second) language only by learning the (second) language. But since one cannot learn to speak at all, in any language, without learning a language, it follows that one cannot very well learn to speak in any language, without that language becoming by that very fact the linguistic form of one's thought.

I must stipulate, however, what my suggestion does not mean: to state that the structure of the philosopher's language may determine the concrete form of certain philosophical doctrines is not to explain away any philosophical doctrine. The suggestion is not

[5] Cf. Angus C. Graham, " 'Being' in linguistics and philosophy: a preliminary inquiry," *Foundations of Language,* I (1965), 223–231, p. 223, and " 'Being' in Western philosophy compared with *shih/fei* and *yu/wu* in Chinese philosophy," *Asia Major,* VII (NS), (1959), 79–112, pp. 79–80. See also, Benjamin Whorf, *Language, Thought and Reality,* (Cambridge, Mass., 1956), and the most valuable collection of papers discussing the so-called Sapir-Whorf hypothesis, by Harry Hoijer (ed.), *Language in Culture,* (American Anthropological Association, Memoir No. 79, 1954). I have already referred to John W. M. Verhaar, *Perception, Speech and Thought,* (Assen, 1963). My debt to Professor Graham goes very far beyond that which the number of my quotations of his work would appear to indicate, and if I have not credited him more often than I have in this book the reason is that I have frequently used some of his insights in application to my own philosophical questions in ways that I cannot be certain are also his own. I remain, of course, solely responsible for what I state in my own person. I am indebted to Fr. Verhaar not only for the above noted volume, but for personal communications which I have found most helpful in my own work.

that some philosophies are "nothing but" rationalizations of the way in which philosophers talk. The point is that if a philosopher uses a certain language—and it is difficult to imagine that he should use none—then by that very fact he has committed himself to, rather he has engaged himself in, certain modes of experience which will in all good logic and consistency claim certain implications for his philosophical thought. To use a certain language *means* to experience reality, to think of reality, in a certain way. This does not mean that when a certain language is used every other possible form of perception of reality is thereby forbidden or proscribed. It does mean, however, that in order to experience reality in a different way one will have to learn to speak about it in a different way. Of course, before one learns to speak in a different way one must become aware of why one's previous way of talking no longer serves the purposes which one now undertakes. This is why

the birth of a new concept is invariably foreshadowed by a more or less strained or extended use of old linguistic material; the concept does not attain to individual and independent life until it has found a distinctive linguistic embodiment. In most cases the new symbol is but a thing wrought from linguistic material already in existence in ways mapped out by crushingly despotic precedents. As soon as the word is at hand, we instinctively feel, with something of a sigh of relief, that the concept is ours for the handling.[6]

Thus, the linguistic form, the conceptual form of human thought, and, correspondingly, the linguistic, conceptual form of philosophical thought, does not of itself constitute an intellectual handicap. On the contrary, linguistic, conceptual forms are in-

[6] Edward Sapir, *Language,* (New York, 1961), p. 17.

134

dispensable to all human experience as such: they are that in which and through which human understanding takes place. It is true, as Bergson amply documented, that conceptual thought handicaps the intellect to the extent that it is fixed and static.[7] But perhaps if Bergson had not assumed certain doctrines of classical philosophical thought concerning the relation of language and experience he might have realized that conceptual thought is fixed and static only for the same reasons, and only in the same restricted sense, and only to the same, somewhat limited, extent that language is fixed and static. For one cannot very well think in any but the same way in which one speaks (whether outwardly or to oneself), since thought is formed by speaking, and speaking is the form of thought. Thus, the linguistic form of thought does not actually hobble thinking except, perhaps, to the extent that one assumes, with the Greeks, that the stability, fixity and atomicity of language (and thought) reflects the condition of reality—or else to the extent that one assumes, with Bergson, that since reality is neither fixed nor stable, fixed and stable concepts, which are reduplicative reflections of reality, are evidently not very faithful reduplicative reflections of reality. The fact is rather that neither concepts nor language—to retain the terminology that separates them—are fixed and immutable (nor atomic), and that, in any event, concepts are not reduplicative reflections of reality.

The linguistic form of human thought is least of all a handicap for the philosopher as long as he is aware—even if only dimly or without full consciousness—of the fact that language does give a concrete conceptual form to all experience (a form which is, more-

[7] Cf. especially *Creative Evolution,* (New York, 1944), pp. 330–343, and *An Introduction to Metaphysics,* (New York), pp. 49–51.

over, historically and culturally conditioned), and therefore also
to philosophical thought. The philosopher will then neither seek
to transcend language (or conceptual thought) nor consent to
become its prisoner, (or hope to be delivered from "the tyranny
of words"). He will, of course, continue to use language: there
is for man, at least in the present stage of his evolution, no other
way to think except linguistically (that is, conceptually). On the
other hand, there is no reason why the philosopher cannot, like
every other man, think, that is, use language, creatively. If so, he
will not make the mistake of attempting to deduce the nature
of reality from the way in which he thinks—or talks—about it,
nor will he assume that the mode of experience implicit in any
given linguistic form is unique and eternally valid. If, on the
contrary, the philosopher should lapse into the assumption that
the fundamental way in which he experiences the world is the
only true one—whether because he also assumes that *his* language
is the natural one, or one which is particularly close to the nature
of things,[8] or because he assumes that there is a distinction between thought and language, and that although languages vary

[8] Only very primitive cultures assume the unique and privileged total
adequacy of their language as a means of self-relation to reality, though
the very young and the unlettered, even in advanced cultures, sometimes
tend in this direction. But even after one knows better one is tempted
to think, if not that tables really are "table" rather than *"Tisch,"* at least that
one's own language has *a few* privileged connections with reality. Even as
perceptive a thinker as Heidegger has incredibly asserted that "along with
German the Greek language is (in regard to its possibilities for thought)
at once the most powerful and the most spiritual of all languages," *Introduction to Metaphysics,* (Garden City, 1961), p. 27. But it is very
instructive that Heidegger has so written: it explains a great deal about
his thought, and in particular his tergiversation of the relation of contemporary thought to Greek philosophy, which would be otherwise incomprehensible.

thought is "the same for all"—then language (and concepts) will indeed constitute a major restriction upon the philosopher's thought.

Man, who is egocentric, ethnocentric and chronocentric to the very degree that he remains unreflective and unable to heighten his consciousness and self-understanding, is also glossocentric to the very degree that he uncritically assumes that his selfhood, his culture and his times are the centre of reality. It is all too easy for him, it is indeed in a sense "natural" for him, to suppose that the linguistic form of his own mode of self-relation to reality is, if not the only possible one, certainly the most natural and true one. However, *all* languages, *all* modes of thought, *all* the basic human ways of relating oneself to reality are in one way or another warranted by reality and by man's self-relation to it. More or less adequately all thought succeeds, by definition, in relating man to reality. And it may well be that some languages offer peculiar advantages; though it is also certain no language, being by definition a partial way of self-relation to reality, can entail no inadequacies whatever. In any event, no language enables man to relate himself to reality with uniqueness and finality. To imagine that languages which differ from one's own are not only transformable but (at least implicitly) reducible to the latter, is to cut onself off from the possibility of developing one's thought beyond the limits of one's own linguistic and other cultural forms.

In this connection I should enter a warning against the two opposite, mistaken conclusions most frequently drawn from the contingency (misleadingly called, sometimes, the relativity) of culture and history by those who become acquainted with this concept, but who cannot follow it through consistently to its end. The first is to imagine that contingency is itself relative to a more basic necessity, and that the contingency of culture, history (and, in this instance, the contingency of the linguistic form of thought) is relative to a more fundamental reality which is itself not contingent. The other mistake is to imagine that contingency cannot be a feature of being as such. In this reasoning, if culture and history (and, in this instance, the forms of human thought which have no more natural necessity than language itself) are contingent, it follows that no cultural or historical consciousness can be valid, that no thought can be true. This, obviously, betrays nothing but a radical misunderstanding of the point. It indicates indeed an inability even to entertain hypothetically the suggestion made, since the misunderstanding hinges upon the re-introduction of the very presuppositions that are being put into question, namely, that the validity of thought and the truth of conscious experience depend upon their a-cultural, a-historical inner reduplication of the ob-jective, a-temporal reality of the external world.

To sum up: the Greek philosophy presupposes, as all philosophy must, a linguistic structure which embodies a given, contingent mode of man's self-relation to reality. It is important to realize this for two reasons, the first of which I have already mentioned: as long as one is unaware of it, this presupposition constitutes a limitation to speculation. But it may be better to put the same idea positively: the philosopher should become conscious of the role of linguistic structures as embodying contingent modes of experience, and he should realize critically, therefore, that all philosophy—since philosophy is a form of thinking—presupposes the mode of experience which its linguistic structures imply. He should become conscious of this, because awareness of the fact enables philosophical understanding to enjoy greater comprehensiveness and depth than it possessed when it proceeded less critically; and in this manner philosophy may liberate itself from unnecessarily inadequate assumptions concerning the nature of man's self-relation to reality.

But there is a second, more concrete advantage, accruing from the realization of this fact—an advantage which is of immediate interest to us in this enquiry. If one is aware of the function of linguistic structures in the production of conscious experience and, therefore, in the creation of philosophical thought, one may be in a position to understand more adequately than otherwise the dynamics of the history of one's own language and therefore of one's own intellectual evolution. In our case this means, of course, an awareness of the dynamics of the history of Hellenic-Western philosophical thought. We may thus be in a better position than heretofore to understand in particular why the thought of St. Thomas Aquinas was not merely the adaptation, or even the transformation, of Greek thought, but also the seed of its eventual transcendence, a transcendence into which we have entered (though scarcely fully achieved) only in very recent philosophical times.

GREEK THOUGHT
AND METAPHYSICAL REALITY

Greek is an Indo-European language. But it is almost a peculiarity of Indo-European languages—and even among these, there are exceptions—that a single word, a verb as it so happens, namely, the verb *to be,* discharges functions which in other linguistic families are sharply differentiated and which indeed are frequently not related at all. Let us, for the sake of simplicity, reduce these functions to two, which we have already referred to as the *copulative* and the *existential*. (The inadequacy of these two terms, but particularly the latter, in reference to Greek and Latin should be apparent below, for the present they will have to do.) The union of copulative and existential functions in the single verb *to be* is, at any rate, true of both Latin and Greek. Or, to be precise, it is most strictly true of the various forms of classical Greek and Latin where the only way in which the existence of anything can be signified is by means of the verbs εἶναι and *esse* —the very verbs which are used to attribute a predicate to a subject. There is in these languages, moreover, another syntactic principle which works in connection with the first. Thinking about reality takes place by attributing something (a predicate) to something else (a subject). And the essential means of attribution is, as we have just noted, a verb, namely, the verb *to be*.

Those of us who belong in the Hellenic-Western philosophical tradition do not usually find these features of Greek and Latin striking, because to a large extent, (though not without qualification), the same structures have been transferred onto the modern European languages in which we philosophize today: what I have just stated is elementary grammar for all those who are born to any modern European tongue. Not unnaturally, therefore, most of us in this tradition, including most philosophers, do not frequently find reason to raise the question whether the syntactic phenomena I have just described are peculiar to certain linguistic forms of experience. Thus, largely by default, we tend to identify the way in *we* in this tradition think, with the way in which *man* thinks. (Conversely, we assume that there can be no more than one unique way in which man thinks—namely the way in which *we* in the Hellenic-Western tradition think.) However, these are far from universal features of language. In point of fact, they are relatively rare.

Thinking about reality need not take the form of attribution, least of all, attribution as an act, that is, by means of a verb. It is, indeed, the creation of the copulative verb *to be* which alone embodies and thus makes possible, this mode of self-relation to reality. As for the further identification of copulative and existential *to be*, its exceptional character is best underlined by citing the fact that the most primitive and purest usage of even our modern European languages does not always identify copulative and existential to be. *Deus est* or *ego sum* is perfect classical Latin. *God is*, or *I am* has become tolerable in English, surely through a philosophical influence which originally derives from Latin and Greek. But the sense of incompleteness of these sentences which is normally felt by all but the philosophical speaker of English points to the decidedly copulative bent of the English verb to be. The French equivalent, *Dieu est*, is scarcely more acceptable, or indeed intelligible, than, say, the Spanish *Dios es*. The ordinary native form to signify existence in German is *geben*, (to give), used as an impersonal verb. In Spanish, it is *haber*, (to have), and in French the untranslatable—indeed, uninfinitizable—*y-avoir*, which combines the Spanish use of *haber* with the English use of the preposition in *there-to-be*. And even in English, the existential verb (other than the verb of philosophical provenance *to exist*), is not really *to be* but, as I have just indicated, (and if I may so put it), *there-to-be*. But the influence of Greek and Latin, which have been strong enough in the formation of the vernacular, have been most marked in philosophy. Philosophers have understandably tended to assume that modern European languages were not quite as responsive as Greek and Latin to the needs of metaphysical thought (though few, even among neo-Scholastics have gone so far in this direction as Heidegger has). The fact that metaphysics was originally developed in Greek (and Christian metaphysics in Latin) was assumed to be a fortuitous coincidence of no special significance or interest.

The conjunction of these two syntactic features of Greek and Latin means that every complete thought in these languages is reducible to the logical form *S is P*.[9] Hence, all reality is a form of "being." The exclusively verbal character of the sentence means that every Greco-Roman thought envisages reality as a subject of action. Thus, everything which is attributable to the subject of predication must be attributable to it as its *act*. When to this is added the ambivalence of the verb *to be,* which is not only the copulative verb, but also and indistinguishably the existential one, the result is that in the Greco-Roman pattern of thought everything which is attributable to the subject of predication is attributable to it as an act of *to be* (whether *to be* pure and simple, or *to be* in one or more categorical modalities of accidental *to be*). In other words, the direct implication of the basic syntactic struc-

[9] As I have noted above, (Chapter III, note 32), Greek permits the omission of the copula. But this is a true case of *omission,* since "to be" has a truly copulative function when it is explicitly used. Hence, in Greek *all* propositions are logically reducible to the form *S is P,* even when the grammatical form shows no verb "to be" or even any verb at all. The same is true, of course, of modern European languages, which not only have close historical and linguistic affinity with Greek, but which have been so heavily influenced by Greek ideology. The only difference is that in these languages, although predication with a merely implicit verb "to be" is extremely common, provided the sentence contains another verb, predication with a tacit verb "to be" and without any other verb is extremely rare. (But it is not totally unknown, especially in idioms, sayings and stock phrases, e.g. "so many men, so many minds.")

ture of Greek and Latin is that all reality is reducible to being: reality is *that-which-is* and anything whatever which is thinkable is, of course, being; for it is *something-that-is*. Greek metaphysics centres, of course, on the concepts of being and being-ness, τό ὄν, οὐσία, that-which-is. Granted the foregoing properties of Greek it is not difficult to understand why the identification of reality with being should so readily occur to the Greek philosophical mind.

But we must be careful not to read back into Greek thought the idea that being, that-which-is, is analyzable into *that-which* and *is*. For in Greek thought *to be,* and *to be something,* are one and the same thing. Consider, for example, the following text of Plato:

"My good fellow, is there any one of these many fair-and-honourable things that will not sometimes appear ugly-and-base? And of the just things, that will not seem unjust? And of the pious things, that will not seem impious?" "No, it is inevitable," he said, "that they would appear to be both beautiful in a way and ugly, and so with all the other things you asked about." "And again, do the many double things appear any the less halves than doubles?" "None the less." "And likewise of the great and the small things, the light and the heavy things—will they admit these predicates any more than their opposites? "No," he said, "each of them will always hold of, partake of, both." "Then is each of these multiples rather than it *is not* that which one affirms it to be?" "They are like those jesters who palter with us in a double sense at banquets," he replied . . . "Do you know what to do with them, then?" said I, "and can you find a better place to put them than that midway between existence or essence and the not-to-be? For we shall surely not discover a darker region than non-being that they should still more not be, nor a brighter than being that they should still more be." [10]

[10] *Republic,* V, 22, (479 A–D). I have presented Paul Shorey's translation in the Loeb Classical Library edition, (London, 1946), vol I, pp. 529, 531, 533. Of course, the original does not say "halfway between existence or

The point of Plato's assertion is that things which are subject to measurement and comparison, as are the things of the empirical world, are both being and non-being. And *being* and *non-being* mean not simply *existing* and *non-existing,* any more than they mean simply *being-something* and *not-being-something.* The whole argument of Plato rests, indeed, on the ambivalence of "being," (οὐσία). It is only we, today, who can speak with the accents of later philosophical thought, which hark back not only to Greek philosophy, but more immediately and recently to mediaeval thought, that can wonder whether in this text οὐσία, "being," means *existing* or *being-something. We* can ask whether "being" can mean *being* without necessarily meaning *being-something,* imagining or assuming that the *to-be* of a being, and *what* the being is, are distinct in reality and separable in thought and speech. For the Greeks, however, these would have been literally unthinkable thoughts. The proof of this is that they would have been unutterable modes of speech.

I do not mean that the Greek mode of experience failed altogether to reach that which, following later usage, I have called the existential function of to be:

---

essence and the not-to-be." It is simply impossible in Greek to say "existence or essence." The Greek expression used by Plato is: τῆς μεταξὺ οὐσίας τε καί τοῦ μὴ εἶναι. But how is this to be translated? If οὐσίας were translated "essence" the point would be lost. If it were translated "existence," apart from the fact that it would be too great a departure, the argument would not make sense (because it hinges on the relativity of what things are, e.g. double, beautiful, etc.). It could be translated as "being," but then the meaning would be ambiguous and obscure. The translator's choice is justified, insofar as οὐσίας in this context means indistinguishably what *for us* is *both* essence and existence: one word suffices to express in Greek what *we* need to say in two. Rather, the doctrine here expounded by Plato hinges on the very indistinctness of concepts which in modern times cannot, on the contrary, be readily identified.

If by a word for existence one means simply an expression which we would normally render into English by 'there is', then it is clear that the Greek verb *esti* often has this sense. But if we understand the phrase 'there is' as representing a univocal concept of existence for a subject of predication, as distinct from the content of the predication itself—as distinct from the 'essence' of the subject or the kind of thing it is . . . —if this generalized positing of a subject as 'real' is what we mean by existence, then I would be inclined to deny that such a notion can be taken for granted as a basis for understanding the meaning of the Greek verb.[11]

Translations of Greek philosophy into modern European languages are apt, of course, to give a different impression. There are innumerable passages in Plato and Aristotle in which εἶναι and cognates have to be translated as *existing* or *existence* or *to exist,* in order to make sense in English—even if by making sense in English they lose the original sense. Angus Graham has analyzed the telling instance of the text from the *Posterior Analytics,*[12] which in a recent translation of irreproachable quality reads:

It is evident also from the methods of defining now in use that those who define do not prove the existence [ὅτι ἔστιν] of the definiendum. Even supposing that there is something equidistant from the centre, why does the object so defined exist [ἔστι]? and why is it a circle? One might equally well assert that it is the definition of mountain-copper. Definitions do not include evidence that it is possible for what they describe to exist [εἶναι], nor that it is identical with that which they claim to define. It is always possible to ask *why*. [13]

---

[11] Charles H. Kahn, "The Greek verb 'to be' and the concept of being," *Foundations of Language,* II (1966), 245–265, p. 248.

[12] II, 7 (92 b 20–25).

[13] The translation is Hugh Tredennick's, in the Loeb Classical Library edition of the *Posterior Analytics,* (London, 1960), pp. 197, 199.

The English terminology used seems clearly to imply a strictly existential use of εἶναι, that is, *being* in contradistinction to *being-something*. But, as Professor Graham remarks, although this translation renders ὅτι ἔστιν (literally, "that it is") as "the existence of the definiendum,"—and it is difficult to imagine how else it could have been translated that did not in the end mean, in English, the same thing—nevertheless, as the context reveals, "the phrase [used by Aristotle] implies both that something described as equidistant from its centre exists and that it is in fact a circle." [14]

In a way, however, Professor Graham may grant to Greek thought a greater proximity to Christian metaphysical thought than is necessary. Aristotle's phrase does not really imply both. Rather, Aristotle's phrase implies one thing which *for us* is two. It would be as apt to say that Aristotle's phrase fuses two things into one—rather, it would be as inadequate, because for Aristotle the two are not fused: they are indistinguishable. The duality is not potentially contained in the unity, any more than the unity could be contained in the duality. It is true, of course, that we do find in Aristotle a certain contrast between the expressions ὅτι ἔστι (that [it] is) and τί ἔστι (what [it] is), and it is possible (for historical reasons that I am in the very process of suggesting) to read this contrast as if it implied, at least in primitive or potential form, a distinction between existence, (that something is) and the subject of existence (what something is). In the *Posterior Analytics* can be found the well known text [15] which distinguishes between "being not this or that, but absolutely" from "being this or that." And the same distinction seems to be,

[14] Graham, " 'Being' in linguistics and philosophy," p. 225.
[15] II, 2 (90 a 10).

perhaps, even more clearly suggested in the *locus classicus* [16] where Aristotle contrasts the question "whether [a thing] is" and "what [a thing] is."

The inevitable temptation is to read the text as if it meant in Greek exactly what the English translation conveys. Nevertheless, it would be unwarranted to suppose that "being absolutely (εἶναι ἁπλῶς)" [17] means "existing," as contrasted with "being something determinate." Likewise, the meaning of the text would be traduced if it were thought that the question "whether [a thing] is" is directed at its existence. What Aristotle evidently intends to do is to distinguish between the objectivity or in-itself-ness of the objects of demonstration, and that which is demonstrated about the object of demonstration. We should recall at this point Parmenides' doctrine that "being is, non-being is not" and that "that which is thought and that which is are the same." Aristotle's εἶναι ἁπλῶς, *esse simpliciter*, appears to me in this context to mean "for a thing to be in itself what is affirmed of it by the knower." If a being is said *simply to be,* it is said *to be itself, self-identically,* as contrasted with being *what it is affirmed* to be. This is especially clear from another text [18] where "being absolutely" (Tredennick's frequent rendering of εἶναι ἁπλῶς) is contrasted with "being one of its attributes." We can further understand the meaning of Aristotle if we also remember the underlying

[16] *Posterior Analytics,* II, 1 (89 b 33).

[17] The fairly common translation of εἶναι ἁπλῶς as "being absolutely" may facilitate the misunderstanding (precisely because it is a somewhat interpretative rendering), whereas the more literal "being simply" (the term "simply" being used in the same sense as when the Latin *simpliciter* is the equivalent of *simpliciter loquendo*) would be closer to the original meaning.

[18] *Posterior Analytics,* II, 2 (90 a 33).

presupposition of all Greek thought, philosophical or otherwise, namely, the necessary character of reality, a necessity which renders impossible every question concerning its being-there. In this respect I agree with Gilson when he states that "Aristotle had no doubt as to the fact that to demonstrate the truth of an essential definition was, by the same token, to demonstrate its reality, its being . . . As he himself conceived it, the universe was both eternal and necessary, so that, in it, the demonstration of the truth of an essence amounted to that of its being." [19]

This interpretation, moreover, explains why "Aristotle ignores the distinction [between 'being absolutely' and 'being this or that,' or any variation thereof] when he analyzes the senses of *einai* in *Metaphysics* V, vii, although he carefully separates being *per se* and *per accidens,* being as 'truth', and potential and actual being, and differentiates being *per se* according to the categories." [20] The distinction is not included by Aristotle in the *Metaphysics* because it is not relevant to the study of being; it pertains only to the study of thinking and, in particular, to the study of demonstration. For in the last analysis, the doctrine of Aristotle is simply that being is the condition of the possibility of demonstration, and, indeed, of all thought: affirmations are warranted not because they are affirmations but because they reflect "that which is *simpliciter.*" For, obviously, not everything which is attributed to a subject by means of the verb to be *is* what the thing really is. What the thing really is, is what it is in itself; and it is only because it is what it is in itself, simply speaking (ἁπλῶς), that we can say that it is such-and-such. In short, Aris-

---

[19] Etienne Gilson, *Elements of Christian Philosophy,* (Garden City, 1960), p. 126.
[20] Graham, " 'Being' in linguistics and philosophy," p. 224.

totle's point is that *to be* is *to be objectively true,* and that it is the objectively-being-true of reality that warrants the truth of our thought about it. But the distinction does not mean, Gilson to the contrary, that "the knowledge of what a thing is does not imply the knowledge of its existence." [21] All it means is that having knowledge of a thing does not of itself imply its correspondence to the thing as it is in reality.

The same interpretation might be conveyed by quite different terms: the distinction between ὅτι ἐστι and τί ἐστι in the *Posterior Analytics* is, in a sense, really included in the *Metaphysics*—but under its proper metaphysical guise. It is contained, namely, in the assertion made by Aristotle that in one sense *being* signifies *truth*. Aristotle thus may be said to distinguish, at least inchoatively, between the truth of things and the truth of knowledge. But there is for him no distinction between existence and the truth of an essence. Of course, Aristole was, shall we say, in touch with the same being as every later philosopher, the same being as even we ourselves are today. The being he knew was the being which did in fact (as *we* say) exist. But that its existence was an element or component or act of being of being, and that the activity or perfection of being-what-they-were depended upon the prior, first act of existing—this could not have been reasonably suspected by him, since the most basic underlying assumption of his thought, namely, the necessary character of reality, would have had somehow to be put in question before the suspicion could arise.

In this respect, as I said, I agree with Gilson. But Gilson further

---

[21] Gilson, *Elements,* p. 126. Gilson's misinterpretation of the text is understandable. It is the same misinterpretation that Al-Farabi and Avicenna put upon it, as will be discussed below.

believes that if the case was otherwise with Avicenna, the reason is that the Moslem philosopher was, unlike the Greek, "well informed about the Judaeo-Christian notion of creation and of the actual gap there is, in reality as well as in logic, between an essence and its existence." [22] This is quite another matter, and at this point I part company with Gilson once for all. For we can be fairly certain that Avicenna's religious views (unlike St. Thomas) had only indirectly to do with this matter. Every available indication leads to the view that Gilson's interpretation of the reasons why Avicenna distinguished between essence and existence is mistaken in fact, and that this is the beginning of a gratuitous and misleading construction of the history of philosophy, particularly in what concerns the relations between St. Thomas' thought and later philosophy up to our own times. Let us examine why.

ARABIC THOUGHT
AND CREATED REALITY

Arabic is not, of course, an Indo-European language: it belongs to the Semitic linguistic family. And although this family is not so distant from the Indo-European as the Far Eastern, the African and the Amerindian groups, it is nonetheless different enough. For our purposes we need remark only upon a certain basic difference which affects philosophy directly, namely, that in Arabic, as in Hebrew, there is no verb (or other part of speech) which combines copulative and existential functions. In fact, the contrast

[22] Ibid.

between the two functions is greater than if it were simply a matter of different verbs or of different, but homologous, parts of speech. The two functions follow a different pattern. Indeed, in this context it is somewhat equivocal to speak of "copulative" and "existential" functions, since these notions correspond rather to a linguistic structure which Arabic parallels and overlaps, but does not altogether coincide with.

Let us consider first the "existential" function. The term "existential" can describe adequately the functions of certain Arabic linguistic structures only if we first divest ourselves of the preconception that existence is an *act* of something. Or, to put it better, the Arabic form of thought does not experience existence as something which a being *does,* but as a fact or event which can be, as it were, come across or encountered by another. There is an Arabic verb, *kana,* which can be translated in ordinary contexts by the English existential "to be." It appears, however, that *kana* carries the connotation of "becoming." This is why it can also be used as part of a sentence in a copulative function: "*kana* A (nominative) B accusative)." Thus, *kana* seems to be in some respects somewhat like the Spanish auxiliary verb *estar* (from Latin *sto*), which is used copulatively in place of the ordinary verb "to be," *ser* (from the same Sanskrit root, *es-,* as Latin *esse*) to indicate a temporary, passing, transitory condition of being, and which can be translated into English only as *to be,* but which nevertheless does not in any way signify existence.

In any event, whether or not we wish to count *kana* as an exception, the fact remains that "while in Greek it is much more difficult than in English to distinguish existential and copulative 'to be', in Arabic there is no convenient word which combines both functions." [23] For instance, to translate Aristotle's εἶναι, when the technical sense required the exclusion of the connotations of becoming, and when the Greek sentence had no complement, Arabic translators of Aristotle were reduced to provide the passive voice of the verb *wajada*, "to find." Thus, "X is" (i.e. "X exists") would become in Arabic "X is found." Therefore, logically enough, the Arab translator would render "existence" or "existing," (which, as we may remember, for the Greeks could not be distinguished from "being something," or from "being something self-identically" or from "being the cause of truth," expressions which in Greek would all have been indistinctly put in the same terms, τό εἶναι, that is, the infinitive of *to be* preceded by an article, and in Latin by *esse*, used as if it were a noun) as *wujud*, the infinitive of "find"; and for being (τό ὄν, *ens* "what-is") he would use the passive participle, *mawjud*, "what is found." [24]

---

[23] Graham, " 'Being' in linguistics and philosophy," p. 225

[24] To judge by his published remarks (in *The Christian Philosophy of St. Thomas*, London, 1957) Gilson is evidently misinformed about the meaning of *wujud*. Gilson seems to believe that it was a somewhat fanciful notion of of Averroes that "the Arabian word meaning 'to exist' came from a root originally meaning 'found,' because it seems to have been a common notion that, for any given being, to exist meant approximately 'to be found there,' " (p. 39). Interestingly enough, Gilson then proceeds to explain what must have surely been the source of this extraordinary idea of Averroes: it was "not at all surprising from the moment existence had become an accident," *ibid*. In other words, according to Gilson the Arabs commonly got the idea that "to exist" was something like "to be found there" only because of the influence of the philosophy of Al-Farabi and Avicenna upon everyday Arabic thought. However, as will be explained shortly, the fact appears to be precisely the opposite: because "to exist" is *aboriginally* and *commonly* in Arabic literally "to be found," the Arab philosophers were practically compelled to think of existence as the accident of the essence. This implies, of course, that Arabs do not conceive existence

But let us remember that *wujud* does not have at all a copulative function. Apart from the exceptional use of *kana* in a copulative pattern, the normal copulative sentence in Arabic is expressed in one of three principal ways—none of which, moreover, can be called copulative except in an extended (that is *translated*) sense of the word, since none of these linguistic patterns actually uses a verb (or for that matter any other part of speech) to *join* to extremes. These might well be called juxtapositional rather than copulative sentences. And, indeed, one of the most common "copulative" patterns used in Arabic consists in merely juxtaposing the "subject" and the "predicate," (both in the nominative), so that "A is B" would become "A B." Philosophers (and others) in the Greek-Western tradition will be tempted, of course, to imagine that the Arabic sentence of the pattern "A B" *really* means "A is B," or that the Arabic construction uses the copulative "to be" only tacitly or implicitly, or else that the Arabic language expresses only defectively that which everyone must really think when he thinks (as *we* say) that "A *is* B." The glossocentric nature of this temptation is, I trust, sufficiently clear. For there is no reason whatever to think that anything at all has been omitted or is missing from the sentence "A B"—except, of course, the mode of self-relation to reality that certain philosophical interpretations assume. As Angus Graham has remarked:

If I say 'The rose red' or 'He in Paris', haven't I left out the relationship between the rose and its colour, the man and the place—a relationship which is exactly defined by the splendidly unambiguous word 'is'? No, for 'the red rose' and 'the man in Paris' are no more

---

in the same way Westerners do. But if this implication is well grounded upon the linguistic facts, then it is to be accepted, even if its acceptance requires a reinterpretation of the doctrine of St. Thomas.

ambiguous than 'the rose which is red' and 'the man who is in Paris'. But these phrases do not pretend to be sentences. 'The rose red' needs a verb, not to show how redness is related to the rose, but to assert the redness; for it is a rule of English that there is no sentence without a verb.

The conviction that a sentence needs a verb is so deeply rooted in us that when we try to define a proposition we find it very hard to resist the feeling that its nature is somehow bound up with the nature of the verb. But this rule is of course merely a grammatical convention,[25] not universal even among Indo-European languages.[26]

The other two "copulative" patterns common in Arabic usage are but variations of the first. One possibility is to interpose the third person pronoun *huwa,* (feminine *hiya*), between the two terms, which retain both the nominative case. Thus, "A is B" may be rendered in Arabic by "A *huwa* B," (that is, "A, he B") or, of course, "A *hiya* B," (that is, "A, she B"). It is clear that the pronoun here has but an emphatic role not unlike that of the Chinese particle *yeh,* as in "A B *yeh,*" ("A, B indeed"), used to render the English "A is [indeed] B." A heavier emphasis yet is evident in the third usual pattern, which uses a particle, *inna,* which requires—note well—the *accusative* case in the *"subject"* of the proposition: thus, *"inna* A [accusative] B [nominative]." (Evidently, this pattern is even less deserving than the earlier ones of the name "copulative." We have to do here with varying degrees of what might well be called "emphatic juxtaposition". This pattern is the most emphatic—and therefore the least "copu-

---

[25] *Convention* is perhaps not *le mot juste*. I suggest it would be better to say: a historically conditioned, contingent event. Moreover, the condition of the possibility of such a linguistic structure must be the nature of human consciousness—or at least the nature of human experience—under the cultural conditions that have historically obtained in most of the Indo-European linguistic world.

[26] Graham, " 'Being' in Western philosophy," pp. 85–86.

lative" of the three.) In any event, it is of secondary importance to this discussion whether or not there are truly copulative patterns in Arabic or whether the apparently copulative patterns are not rather parallel to the strictly copulative—I mean *predicative* —patterns found in classical and other Indo-European languages. The important point is that these patterns are quite distinct in form and in function from those which are used in the Hellenic-Western tradition to signify existence, (or its Arabic parallel). For having noted the differences between the "copulative" and the "existential" syntactic patterns of Arabic, we may be in a position to appreciate what happened to Aristotle's metaphysics when Aristotle's Arabic translators found it necessary to render, for instance, τό ὄν, (*ens,* what-is) as *mawjud,* ("what is found,"), whereas they had no choice but to render, say, "A ἐστιν B" as "A *huwa* B." What happened is that they automatically unavoidably, unintentionally, and without any effort introduced into the Arabic versions of Aristotle a distinction between two quite different meanings of εἶναι, *to be*—a distinction, as we have seen, which was emphatically not envisaged or implicit in the original Greek.

In other words, the Arabic versions of Aristotle "are very literal, yet because of the structure of the [Arabic] language they transform him at one stroke into a philosopher who talks sometimes about existence, sometimes about quiddity, *never about* [the single, undifferentiated] *being* [designated by εἶναι and its derivatives]. In place of the single verb *einai* the Arabs found in [the Arabic versions of] Aristotle a set of abstract nouns, each rooted in either the [Arabic] existential or the copulative sentence pattern."[27] Whereas the Greek language embodies a form of experience of reality in which the indistinctness of what-a-thing-is

[27] Graham, " 'Being' in linguistics and philosophy," p. 226.

and the being-of-the-thing is ordinarily inescapable, the Arabic language, on the contrary, embodies a form of experience of reality in which any relation between the two is ordinarily unimaginable.

As I mentioned above, it is imprecise to speak of "existential" and "copulative" linguistic patterns in general. If used without further qualification, these expressions would be accurate only with reference to languages which are closely related in structure to our own group, whether on account of historical or other reasons. In a wider linguistic context it would be important to keep in mind that many languages may not necessarily exhibit truly "existential" and "copulative" patterns but, rather, *equivalents* thereof. The assumption that all languages fulfill existential and copulative syntactic roles, albeit in different ways, and in ways which are variously related (or even unrelated) does not rest on empirical grounds. These categories, "existential" and "copulative" patterns, (severally as well as correlatively distinct patterns), apply to English and other modern European languages, and as well to *mediaeval* Latin—for, as I will shortly suggest, they were introduced into the Western tradition by St. Thomas Aquinas, thereafter becoming part of the heritage of the Western world [28] —but not necessarily to all linguistic thought forms.

[28] It would be somewhat misleading, and slightly glossocentric, to state, for instance, that whereas the existential and copulative functions are joined in the verb "to be" in most Indo-European languages, they are separate and distinct in other linguistic families. As a first approximation, this would do, but if one took in earnest Whorf's "principle of [linguistic] relativity," (*Language, Thought and Reality,* p. 214), one would not wish to assume that the patterns which are, in other linguistic families, the equivalents of Indo-European "existential" and "copulative" syntactic patterns, fulfill *the same existential and copulative functions* that Indi-European patterns perform, albeit by means of different syntactic patterns.

Thus, Arabic, as a form of self-relation to reality, implies, I do not say merely indistinction, but even lack of all relation between the *being* of a being and *what* a being is; this linguistic, cultural, historical fact is the reason why "it is a misplaced compliment to credit Al-Farabi . . . and . . . Avicenna . . . with the discovery of the ontological difference between essence and existence; it was impossible for an Arab to confuse them, although he might, as did . . . Averroes . . . choose for reasons of his own to identify them." [29]

Understandably, historians of philosophy have characteristically tended to read the history of philosophy backwards, not always

---

This would be, in the end, a retrenched position of the traditional concept of language. On the other hand, there is no reason why we should not continue to refer to the "existential" and "copulative" patterns of non-Indo-European languages, provided we really meant: the equivalents thereof in the non-Indo-European linguistic mode of self-relation to reality.

I have stipulated this precision at this juncture in order to prepare the way for the suggestion I will make below, namely, that even the Arabic distinction between *mahiyyah*, (literally "what-is-it-ness"), and *wujud* (literally "being [apt to be] found"), is not strictly comparable, quite apart from further metaphysical properties, with the distinction between *essentia* and *esse* in St. Thomas. (I say they are not strictly comparable. I mean: as they stand. For evidently, they are *transformable:* every language can be translated—somehow—into every other language. After translation, of course, different languages are, by definition, apt to be compared.)

If this is correct, it follows that although *wujud* is correctly *translatable* into English as "existence," and into Latin and other Indo-European languages accordingly, *wujud* does *not quite* mean the same as the English "existence" or its equivalent expressions in Latin and other Indo-European languages. The English "existence," and its equivalents in Latin and other Indo-European languages sparkles with connotations which derive from St. Thomas' philosophical influence over the course of later Western intellectual history. *Wujud*, of course, does not. It seems to me that Professor Graham's conclusions are weaker than what his premises could comfortably support.

[29] Graham, " 'Being' in linguistics and philosophy," p. 227.

making sufficient allowance, as they have become conscious of the evolution of thought, for the historical fact that their own investigation into the evolution of thought is one of the results of the evolution of thought. (Their own thought, of course, contributes in turn to that evolution.) They have frequently failed, therefore, to grasp the nature, meaning and importance of a circumstance which, as experience reveals, attends all investigation: to understand the past "as it really was" is not to understand it as if it were unrelated to the present but, on the contrary, as leading to the present, which is the only viewpoint from which anyone can ever envisage the past.

The question is important enough to warrant a brief digression. It is fundamentally impossible really to understand the past by attempting mentally to travel back in time, to experience the past (at a later time) as if one (who by definition exists always at a later time) were actually existing in the past. (This is the "historical" procedure which we were taught by the Greeks). That is, it is impossible to understand the past by pretending that one exists in the past, or that one exists outside time altogether, abstracting from every later development which has in fact lead to the very present in which one now exists—for instance, by endeavouring to purify every document, every clue, every remnant, every trace of the past, from its supposedly disfiguring later accretions. It is as if a scientist attempted to reconstruct the palaeozoic by throwing away every fossil he dug up, on the grounds that the materials have been affected—as indeed they have been— by the passage of time. Any attempt to reconstruct history *from its origin* is bound to fail in the end: for this procedure rests upon an assumption contrary to fact, namely, that the historian who is attempting to reconstruct history does not *presently* exist.

If, nevertheless, the past can be understood "as it really *was*," the reason is precisely that, being conscious, man can take advantage of the fact that he does exist *at present,* that is, in a situation that was brought about by processes that originated in the past. If we learn to read historical processes in relation to their (present) outcome, we may be able to reconstruct the past, not from its origin, but *from the present* (which is the only time when we truly and actually exist). Paradoxically, to pretend to reconstruct history (or for that matter, to pretend to reconstruct philosophy, or science, or belief, or any other form of consciousness) as if one could begin at the beginning, without prejudice or tare, without baggage or bent, is to suffer from the worst prejudice of all; it is to be burdened by unhistorical thought and to be crushed under the weight of history itself. To read the forward progression from past to present it is necessary to read history *from* the present. (Rather, it is necessary to be aware that one always does so from the present, since in point of fact no one has ever read the past from any other time than his own: anachronism is indeed introduced, despite the historian's most careful efforts, precisely when, reading the past in point of fact from the present, he assumes a condition contrary to fact, namely, that he reads it as if he existed in the past.) If, on the contrary, the factuality of the present were abstracted from, one's reading of the past would inevitably result in retrojection of the present into the past. To pretend to read the past forwards is to read it backwards; the forward course of history can only be read back.

The application of this to the case at hand is clear. Christian historians of philosophy have read Arabic philosophy with the eyes of Christians. I insist not only upon the fact that there is nothing amiss with this procedure, but upon the yet more important fact that there is no alternative way for a Christian to read history than from a Christian viewpoint. What may not be efficient is to read the history of Arab philosophy from a Christian viewpoint without taking account of the viewpoint from which it is read, that is, pretending that it is being read from a viewpoint that transcends time, because it is the viewpoint of unchanging, eternal truth.

Nevertheless, historians of philosophy have been quite correct when they thought they detected a momentous discovery in Al-Farabi, a discovery which would be completed less than one hundred years later by Avicenna. Now, Al-Farabi did not actually discover the distinction between "what-is-it-ness" and "being-found-ness"; for that form of human experience which is cast in an Arabic linguistic form this was a commonplace. But Al-Farabi did discover something which no Arab had, as best we can tell, ever previously suspected, namely, that the two were *related*. To be sure, Al-Farabi's discovery was inspired by his reading (in the original Greek, as it so happens) of a philosophy in which the two were identified—rather, in which they were indistinct. But Al-Farabi did not merely translate Aristotle (which indeed he did) for the sake of reconstructing Aristotle: he learned from Aristotle and then proceeded creatively to put his learning to work. For there is a difference between the assumed *indistinction* which is found in Aristotle, and the consciously asserted *relation* which is found in Al-Farabi. And Al-Farabi was to draw from his discovery certain consequences from which Avicenna and St. Thomas would eventually derive considerable profit.

Al-Farabi's doctrine, in quotation and reconstruction, runs along these lines: "we have accepted for existing things a distinct essence and a distinct existence," that is, most people [i.e. most

Arabs] naturally assume that what-a-thing-is is totally unrelated to the fact that it stands in the world, in front of us, as it were, ready to be found. Actually, as the Greek philosophers appear to have been the first to have realized, this is not so. For it does not readily occur to us [Arabs] to wonder why things are found in the world. We know, of course, that *Allah* creates them. However, although this may be a true fact, it is not an explanation. When we "come across" anything, should we not be struck by the possibility of its not being there? For, is it not true that sometimes we search without finding? We have never asked why this should be so, because it has never occurred to connect the fact that things are *found* in the world with the fact that those things have a distinct *intelligible* constitution. But is there not a relation between these two? Is there not an intimate connection between the reality of being and its intelligible constitution? The answer, as the Greeks apparently have always known, is yes: for whatever is real, is by that very fact intelligible. On the other hand this is very puzzling. Would Aristotle have us believe that whatever is real is eternal and necessary? Surely this is not so; as we know, the world was created by *Allah* and is watched over by Him. Well, then, on the one hand we know that intelligibility is of the very nature of reality and, on the other, that the intelligibility of anything is not that which, of itself, makes it real. The latter is evident not only to the believer in God: *were it otherwise whatever man understands would be indubitably real.* But obviously this is not true. It is not true because, on the contrary, *a thing must be found before we can tell what it is.* Thus,

Existence is not comprised in the essence of things; otherwise it would become a constitutive element of it, and the representation of what the essence is, without that of its existence, would remain incomplete. Indeed, it would be impossible to separate them in imagination. If the existence of man coincided with his corporeal and animal nature there would be no one who, having an exact idea of what man is and knowing his corporeal and animal nature, could put in doubt the existence of man. But this is not at all the case: we do doubt the existence of things until we have direct perception of it by sense or a mediate perception through demonstration. Thus existence is not a constitutive character [of reality], it is only an accident that accrues to it.[30]

In other words, "being found" is related to intelligibility, as Aristotle knew—but "being found" is not of the very intelligibility of intelligibility, which Aristotle did not apparently remark upon. Therefore, existence is an *accident* of real things. For if existence is not essential to essence, it can only be accidental to it.

If this is in fact the meaning of Al-Farabi's doctrine, then one would be warranted to characterize it as the first halting, but forward, significant, step on the road that was to be followed by the Western philosophical tradition as it began to transcend its own sources and to evolve organically into a new *Denkform*. For Al-Farabi effectively introduced—to be more precise, the diffusion of Arabic thought effectively introduced—into Western Christendom the philosophical notion that would eventually become known as *contingency*[31] as a radical alternative to the most basic

[30] Al-Farabi, *The Gem of Wisdom*, trans. Djemil Saliba, quoted by Etienne Gilson, *La Philosophie au Moyen Age*, (Paris, 1947), p. 348.

[31] I underline I refer to the philosophical concept of contingency, that is, a particular, concrete interpretation of reality which explained a much earlier, traditional Christian belief about created reality and its relation to God—a Christian belief originally conceptualized in the non-philosophical (i.e. non-technically interpretative) concept of "creation," (i.e. "making" or "fashioning"), whether without explicit exclusion of a primordial chaos (as in *Genesis* 1:1), or with explicit exclusion of it (as in *Isaiah*

assumption of Greek thought, namely, the necessary, fatal character of reality, specifically as given to it by its *being*.

On the basis of Al-Farabi's doctrine of contingency Avicenna was to build the doctrine of God on which St. Thomas would in his turn erect his own. Completing the doctrine of Al-Farabi and systematizing with greater precision Al-Farabi's unique insights, Avicenna distinguished between uncreated being, which alone was necessary—indeed, his proper definition was *Necesse esse* (as the Latin translations have it)—and created being, in which the contingency demanded by Al-Farabi obtained by virtue of the fact that in these beings their "being-found-ness" *accrued* to their quiddity, and hence was not an essential part of it. God, thus, is real by virtue of himself. In him and him alone are realized *simpliciter* the characteristics of being as such. Creatures, however, are merely possible. That is, they *can* be; but in order *actually* to be they must be posited in reality by God. However, when they are so posited, they are no longer mere possibles. They now are actual occurrences in the world and, thus, apt to be found by those who come across them.

But, as St. Thomas would realize three centuries later, the doctrine of Avicenna implicitly granted more to Greek necessitarianism than could be readily admitted to be compatible with Christian belief. I do not say that St. Thomas managed, any more than did Avicenna, to avoid granting too much to Aristotle—but it is certain that St. Thomas was aware of Avicenna's pitfall and that he was determined to avoid it. But even St. Thomas was not altogether successful in this respect, and in

---

45:18). Since earliest times, thus, Christians had viewed the empirical world in a certain light. This view was now most adequately and profitably conceived as the *contingency* of created *existents*.

the course of his attempt to achieve this end he introduced such modifications to the doctrine of Aristotle as would ultimately make it necessary for philosophical thought to reach back to its Greek foundations in order to abreact and build better anew, with heightened consciousness, on the very foundations provided by its own origin and childhood. Let us see how this development occurred.

No more than Al-Farabi did Avicenna appear to have thought that the reconstruction of the Greek mind was the same as the creation of philosophy and the ascertainment of the whole and final truth. Every indication is that Averroes, on the contrary, assumed precisely that. The truth of Aristotle, being the truth, could be improved upon in no essential respect. However, when Aristotle is read in Arabic, or even in Greek but by an Arabic mind, Aristotle cannot make sense to a philosophically astute reader unless the reader impose upon him, as Al-Farabi and Avicenna did, a meaning which was not originally there. If one were not too concerned with whether the meaning one derived from Aristotle was originally there, one should not be tempted to look further into the matter. (This, of course, would be a pity.) Averroes' failing was the opposite extreme. He, too, thought that the truth was atemporal. But believing the truth to have been already discovered in the past, he found it logical to identify the search for truth and the search for the past. No doubt, philosophy must care for the truth—though philosophy would do well to avoid spelling Care for the Truth with capitals. But to assume that the whole and final truth (or even the whole of the basic, final truth) is to be discovered by recapturing the past may be methodologically unsound—even if, on the other hand, as we have seen, there is some merit in a view that is implicit and effective even in Averroes' exaggeration of it into his worship of the past: no historical reconstruction of the philosophical past can be adequate if it construes the past as a substantive mistake.

For all the unscientific folly of his reliance upon intellectual authority, Averroes was in some respects a true scientist, and a true scientist will not neglect the negative instance, the refractory residue of intractable data, the errors of the past. Averroes tried to read Aristotle more faithfully than Al-Farabi and Avicenna ever had, and Averroes must have instinctively felt that the obvious construction put upon the Aristotelian text by Al-Farabi and Avicenna could not have been exactly what Aristotle had meant. And, of course, Averroes was right. His peculiar philosophical light must have come to him when he realized that Aristotle's thought was inexpressible in Arabic. Ordinary language (as Averroes might have put it, for it is extremely doubtful that he would have been in a position to distinguish in this respect between Arabic and Greek) differentiates between "what-is-it-ness" and "being-found-ness," and even Aristotle (as indeed the *Arabic* Aristotle does) finds it necessary to express himself in terms of this distinction. But the doctrine of Aristotle makes sense if, and only if, one denies that such a distinction obtains in reality. The only way to express (in Arabic) the inexpressible (in any language but in the ambiguity of Greek) is the roundabout and negative procedure of denying Avicenna's doctrine that existence was an accident of the essence which constituted it as a substance. One must rather say that whatever is real exists of its own accord, by the very fact that it is whatever it is.

Given Averroes' objective, namely to understand Aristotle, confident that to understand him was to understand all truth, it cannot be doubted that Averroes was the most successful Aris-

165

totelian of the Arab and the Christian mediaeval world. Of course, the relatively greater historical accuracy of the doctrine of Averroes as a representation of Greek thought is precisely what made it much more, (and much more obviously), incompatible with Christian belief than Al-Farabi's and Avicenna's thought. It is hardly surprising that St. Thomas found Averroism to be the great enemy of Christian thought, whereas he judged Avicenna to be one of the most valuable guides to the interpretation of Aristotle's mind. Nevertheless, from the Christian (if not also from the Muslim) viewpoint, the doctrine of Avicenna is far from satisfactory. Its great difficulty is that its laudable effort to provide for the contingency of creatures is short-lived: its effects do not reach very far and do not last very long.

The God of Avicenna was, to be sure, Being Itself—in the sense which this expression might have had for Parmenides, Plato and Aristotle. This means: the God of Avicenna was Being Itself, first, in the sense that τό ὄν "is un-become and imperishable, whole, single, unshakable, temporally without limits, and complete." [32] But the God of Avicenna was also Being Itself in the further Greek sense that God was necessarily and essentially whatever he is, since for him to be whatever he is does not depend upon his being made to pass from possibility to actuality. Does this really safeguard the contingency of creatures? Well, if God is Necessity itself, and creatures are created by God, then creatures are created necessarily. It might be argued that God creates creatures by an act of his will, and that therefore he creates freely, and that God's free creation does not cease to be free even if he creates necessarily. This view might be given support in several

[32] Werner Jaeger, *The Theology of the Early Greek Philosophers*, (Oxford, 1967), p. 106.

ways, for instance, as would St. Thomas' later argument, by distinguishing between absolute and hypothetical necessity, so that God's "willing things apart from Himself is not absolutely necessary. Yet it can be necessary by supposition, for supposing that He wills a thing, then He is unable not to will it, as His will cannot change." [33] The difficulty is not, therefore, that the necessary creation of creatures by God would intrude upon God's freedom and sovereignity. The difficulty is that, if creatures are created necessarily, then they are not truly contingent. Yet, it was their contingency that the doctrine of Avicenna intended to safeguard.

Let us recapitulate. Before it occurred to Al-Farabi, thanks to Aristotle, that there was an intimate relation between what things are, and their aptness for "being found," that is, between their quiddity and their reality, the Muslim (and the Christian) faithful could comfortably believe in the gratuitous creation of the world by God, and in the world's consequent total dependence upon God: acceptance of this condition of the world is what lends its very name to *Islam*. If we follow the voice of reason, however —that is, the voice of Greece, of which Aristotle is the prophet— the only way to maintain this belief *reasonably* [34] would be to agree with Al-Farabi that quiddities are mere possibles until reality accrues to them. But this means, as Avicenna realized, that God is essentially necessary, and that therefore God's creation is what brings the mere possibility which is a quiddity, into the actual reality of the things which "are found" in the world. But the real difficulty begins at this very point.

---

[33] *ST*, I, 19, 3.
[34] Averroes or, at any rate, some Averroists, would find a way to maintain it, albeit unreasonably, with the so-called doctrine of the double truth.

The fact that creatures are created by God necessarily may not take away from God's freedom, but it does make creatures necessary precisely because they are created. Creatures may not be able to make themselves pass from possibility to actuality; but once they are created they are obviously no longer mere possibles. And if they are not merely possible, then they are necessary. However extraneously their reality may have accrued to them, once they are real they are necessarily whatever they are, and, therefore, their reality is necessary. Indeed, reality seems to be definable as necessity: "necessity so clearly is the very name for existence that, in the doctrine of Avicenna, to be caused, to exist is to be made to be necessary-by-another." [35] The doctrine of Avicenna, thus, is that whereas God is necessary by himself, creatures are necessary by another, namely by God. But both creature and creator are necessary just the same. It is as if Greek necessitarianism were a camel whose searching nose Al-Farabi had imprudently admitted into the tents of Arabic thought. St. Thomas, at any rate, apparently thought that Avicenna's curbs could not effectively keep the pagan beast out of the china shops of Christian truth. But, convinced as he was, like the Arabs before him, of the truth that quiddity and reality were somehow related—a truth behind which stood not merely Aristotle, but the full force of all Greek thought —he made a fresh start on the problem, with results the originality and novelty of which have been most studiously ignored by those who have profited the most from them, namely, contemporary thinkers of all persuasions, but particularly perhaps those who work in the phenomenological and existentialist fields.

[35] Gilson, *Elements,* p. 129.

THOMISTIC METAPHYSICS
AND EXISTENTIAL REALITY

It is of relatively little moment whether we determine what was
the source of the inspiration of St. Thomas' metaphysical trans-
figuration of Greek thought. Gilson has made much of the hypothesis that St. Thomas' "notion of being was born at the
moment when, for the first time, a metaphysician fully informed
of the history of the notion happened to be, at the same time,
a theologian fully conversant with [*Exodus* 3:14]." [36] I have no
doubt that St. Thomas' theological reflections had much to do
with it: it is undeniable that *ultimately* his inspiration was the
Christian faith. But St. Thomas was not the first Christian thinker
to read *Exodus* 3:14 and to reflect upon it. Why should St. Thomas
have given this text his peculiar interpretation, when the text
fits equally well (or ill) the construction (or misconstruction)
put upon it by countless Christian thinkers in the millenium of
Christian speculation before him? [37] The idea that in *Exodus*

[36] *Ibid.*, p. 132.

[37] Before St. Thomas the most common interpretations of *Exodus* 3:14
asserted that the name *Yahweh* revealed God's essential constitution as
either eternity, immutability, necessity, self-sufficiency, self-identity, unicity,
and the like. The point that all these various interpretations have in common is that *Yahweh* reveals what God is *essentially*: if God is *Qui est,*
or ὄ ὄν, without further qualification, then he is essentially whatever he
is. But it never occurred to Christian thinkers before Thomas that existence
should therefore be essentially predicated of God as well, since to them
that which was signified by *is* in the proposition was part of *what-is*
predicated. Thus, St. Hilary in the mid-fourth century explained that
*"non anim aliud proprium magis Deo quam esse intellegitur . . . quia
. . . non potuit aut poterit aliquando non esse,"* De Trinitate, I, 5, and
that *"Deus est essentialiter. Essentia eius gloriosa est sicut nomen eius,"*

169

3:14 God revealed some sort of metaphysical name is not, of course, what is original with St. Thomas: what is original with him is the specific metaphysical meaning of the name "He Who Is." Previous Christian thinkers had understood this text as they had because they thought of being as they did. To understand the same expression as St. Thomas did it was necessary first to have understood being as he had. Gilson's argument is, accordingly, not simply that St. Thomas found his philosophical *inspiration* when he read *Exodus* 3:14 in a peculiar and original manner —a contention which would be entirely plausible, though strictly a conjecture—but the rather more ambitious claim that St. Thomas discovered, for the first time in Christian history, the true meaning of the revelation cryptically contained in *Exodus* 3:14, or, in other words, that St. Thomas' doctrine concerning the meaning of *Exodus* 3:14 was not merely a plausible exegesis of a text, but a decoding of a cryptically revealed truth.[38] Evidently, this transgresses the boundaries of permissible speculation,

---

Adversus Scrutatores, XXVII. His contemporary, St. Ephraem, maintained that *"Moysi manifestavit nomen suum, cum 'Qui sum' sese appellavit, quod nomen est essentiae . . . ut uno nomine quod emisit doceret se esse solum ens, non vero alia,"* *Adversos Haereses,* LIII. St. Ambrose, like St. Hilary, gave the reason *"quia nihil tam proprium Dei quam semper esse,"* *Enarrationes in XII Psalmos Davidicos,* XLIII, 19. A specially interesting interpretation is St. Jerome's: *"Deus vero qui semper est, nec habet aliunde principium, et ipse sui origo est suaeque causa substantiae, non potest intelligi aliunde habere quod substitit,"* *In Ep. ad Ephesios,* II, 3, 14. St. Augustine's interpretation is that *"esse nomen est incommutabilitatis,"* *Sermones,* VII, 7; cf. *Enarrationes in Psalmos,* Ps. 134, 4; *De Trinitate,* I, 1, 2 and VII, 5, 10.

[38] Apart from the truth of the matter and the indications of modern exegesis, the idea of cryptic revelation which Gilson's doctrine seems to imply would be very difficult to defend theologically.

or even conjecture, and can be ascribed only to discipleship.[39]

A possibility which may not be much more likely than Gilson's, but which is at any rate legitimately conceived, is that St. Thomas may have drawn some hint, leading to his eventual solution of the problem, from the conjunction within his mind of the doctrine of Avicenna with his own reading of the Latin translation of Aristotle, (which conveyed, of course, different terminological

[39] Disciples of St. Thomas attempt to justify their discipleship, in effect, with the following argument. Although the thought of St. Thomas is the product of human reason and nothing but human reason, its truth is not human, but divine: the truth of St. Thomas' philosophy is not St. Thomas', but God's. Thus, although the philosophy of St. Thomas is not, like Christian doctrine, an object of belief, but an object of understanding and understanding alone, its rejection would be the material, practical, and moral equivalent of the rejection of Christian truth. What Christian could reject, for instance, the doctrine that God is Subsistent Being Itself, despite the fact that this concept of God was never explicitly affirmed by Christians before St. Thomas devised his metaphysics, when this doctrine affirms a truth which was, however cryptically, revealed to man from the very lips of the living God? No Christian need know that God is Subsistent Being Itself, for no Christian need understand philosophy in general or St. Thomas' thought in particular; but no Christian may deny that God is Subsistent Being Itself, for no Christian may deviate in any essential respect from the thought of St. Thomas without thereby deviating from the truth of the doctrines of the Christian faith. Thus, Thomistic discipleship grants to some philosophical thought a revelatory value which other believers would wish to reserve to *inspired* thought, in the strict sense of the term.

However, it should also be noted, first, that this doctrine of the relations of the philosophy of St. Thomas to Christian belief was not invented by the Thomists of the 20th century, but by those (mostly, as it so happens, in Roman and other Italian circles) of the mid-19th, and, second, that this doctrine derives its force and influence from its having become the official teaching of the Church, beginning with Leo XIII's encyclical *Aeterni Patris* (1879). Once an act of faith in the teaching of his encyclical is made, it is impossible not to think of St. Thomas' philosophy and theology as Thomists usually do.

171

predispositions from the Arabic versions available to Avicenna). I have particularly in mind the fact that the Latin translation of Aristotle must necessarily show a different face from the Arabic, when it uses the term *essentia*—cognate of *esse*—to designate what the Arabs had called *mahiyyah*, quiddity, a term without linguistic affinity, as we have seen, to any expressions used to refer to the (existential) reality of things. But let us go back for a moment.

As everyone knows, *quidditas* is an abstract noun of obviously technical, artificial coinage, deriving from the interrogative pronoun *quid* in the question *quid est?* There is in the Christian philosophical literature "a single example of *quidditas* earlier than the 12th century."[40] Nevertheless, the term *quidditas* did not gain currency until Arabic thought began to exert some influence in Western Christendom. It seems, therefore, that for all practical purposes *quidditas* is, in effect, modelled upon *mahiyyah* and, like the latter, is linguistically unconnected with the terms used to refer to the (existential) reality of things, (*wujud* in Arabic, *esse* in Latin). There is, however, a much older term, *essentia,* which is etymologically related to *esse;* it was coined by Roman philosophy during early Christian times as the technical equivalent of οὐσία, literally *being-ness*. And *essentia,* if an etymologically pure English equivalent were required, would have to be rendered as *being-ness:* if we find it strange to think of essence as being-ness, despite the fact that such is the literal meaning of the term, it may be because repetition and familiarity can easily dull this sense of the word. But what is *being-ness?* It depends, of course, strictly on what is meant by *being*. The term *essentia* retains with enviable fidelity most of the ambivalences of οὐσία and of the

[40] Graham, " 'Being' in linguistics and philosophy," p. 228.

172

Greek concept of τό ὄν, being. However, the nominal character of *essentia,* like that of the made-up participle of *esse,* (namely, *ens,*) tends to give a slight advantage to the quidditative aspect of the word which the Greek originals, οὐσία (*being-ness*) and especially τό εἶναι (*being,* literally, "the to-be") lacked. Only the use of the *verb,* the infinitive *esse* as a noun (as in *hoc esse*) preserved perfectly in Latin the ambiguity of the εἶναι family of philosophical terms. On the other hand, *ens* and *essentia* are cognates. They naturally join in a single root notions which *quidditas* and *esse* convey separately. It is possible that St. Thomas' metaphysical insight began with the consideration that *quidditas*—which as Al-Farabi and Avicenna had shown, was other than *esse* (though according to them, it was related to *esse* as substance is to accident)—was, after all, the same as *essentia.* That is, the light may well have come to him through the thought that *quidditas* is intrinsically related to *esse,* because *essentia,* which means the same as *quidditas,* is but the being-ness of an *ens.*

As I have admitted, this is a conjecture—a conjecture which I have indulged only because it makes little difference whether it is correct or not. Whatever its inspiration, what matters is the doctrine itself. The great insight of St. Thomas was that the contingency of created reality is, somewhat paradoxically, dependent upon the *intrinsic* character of its reality. The real dependence of the creature upon God does not consist in the former having received its necessary reality from the latter, but in its having received a reality which is not necessary, even after it has been "received." If so, the reality of its being is much more closely connected with its intelligibility that Avicenna ever realized. For the reality of a being does not *accrue* to the essence of a being.

173

The reality of a being is, rather, the act by which the being has its *essentia,* its "beingness." Without this act, the essence is nothing; for without this act there is no *ens,* and where there is no being, no *ens,* its "beingness," its *essentia,* is an abstraction that has no reality at all—not even the reality of the (really) possibly real.

Reality cannot *accrue* to the essence, because essence cannot receive reality *before* it is real. Thus, reality cannot be actually received by a reality which would be real prior to its reception of reality. After a being is real, it can be said, in a sense, to have *received* its reality; but what this means is that the reality of the *ens* is not attributable essentially or properly to anything which it can claim of its own. What a created being really "receives" is itself—that is, its whole reality, its whole self is from God: it receives its quiddity every whit as much as it receives that-by-which it appears in the world, standing outside nothingness, ready to be encountered, able to affect and be affected, apt to enter into transactions with its fellow creatures, and situated so as to take its place in the events and adventures of the world. If this means that being "receives" its *wujud,* then so be it: the point is, in any event, that its *wujud* is not the accident of the essence. It does not come to the essence from the outside—except, of course, in the metaphorical sense already mentioned, namely, in the sense that the whole being, the one and only *ens* that is real, does not have reality by virtue of anything of its own, so that its whole reality, its whole self, comes to itself, as it were, from the outside.

But the more precise way of putting this is in terms of the *intrinsic* character of the act by which the beingness of any being actually "finds" itself, that is, constitutes and makes intelligible a

174

being. In other words, the actual reality of a being is the act of its essence. This act is, of course, the act of *esse*. Thus, the act of to-be no longer means indistinctly, at one and the same time, as it did to Aristotle, to stand outside nothingness and to have a certain intelligible constitution. It no longer means both the aptitude of a thing to be "found" by another, (e.g. by a mind), and what this other would "find" if it did encounter it. After all, there are noticeable, indeed, obvious differences among the various things we "find" in the world, whereas all things "found" in the world have in common their aptitude for "being found."

But this aptitude they have in common is, of course, only our abstraction from their reality. For, as we have already seen, *esse* is the act of the *essentia* and, hence, constitutes each thing in its individuality and concreteness. Let us say, then, that the act of *esse* is limited and made actual and concrete by the *essentia,* the quiddity of an *ens,* and that *essentia* is, conversely, the concrete limitation of the act of *esse*. *Esse* is, thus, the first and, as it were, essential act of a being. Unless a being be, it is nothing; it is only because it *is* that it can be this, that or the other sort of being; it is only because it *is* that it will act in certain determinate and necessary ways; and it is only because it *is* that man will be in a position to ascertain *what* it is.

According to Gilson, St. Thomas also thought that, since essence is the concrete limitation of the act of *esse,* God has no essence. I do not believe this interpretation is correct, but since the matter is not crucial to the discussion at hand, and since in any event I have discussed it elsewhere,[41] I will not take it up here—except in one respect which may help clear up the otherwise puzzling question why St. Thomas should have re-

[41] *The Future of Belief,* pp. 180–184.

tained the Avicennian and Al-Farabian terminology, (i.e. that *esse* is "other than" essence), whence the later label commonly applied to this doctrine, namely, the real *distinction* in creatures of *esse* and *essentia*. I say this is puzzling because the doctrine of St. Thomas is not so much that *esse* and *essentia* are distinct, but that they are related. This was to some extent true already of Al-Farabi and Avicenna, as I have remarked; but it is truer still of St. Thomas, the uniqueness of whose doctrine is not in the least that *essentia* and *esse* are distinct, or even that they are conjoined, but on the contrary that they are *intrinsically* related, a truth which not even Avicenna has grasped. Part of the reason for St. Thomas' turn of expression is that common Latin usage before St. Thomas embodied precisely the same ambivalent notion of being that we have observed above in relation to Greek. Boethius' terminology comes immediately to mind: *"diversum est esse et id quod est."* [42] This does not mean, of course, what it literally says to a post-Thomistic philosopher. On the other hand, it is Boethius' usage that is normal and historically proper. St. Thomas' doctrine actually proposes a new usage, in which *esse* would be restricted to tl.e *id quo,* (that *by which* a being was a being), whereas its cognate *essentia* would be restricted to meaning *id quod* (that is, *what* a thing was). Thus, St. Thomas' doctrine of the way in which *esse* and *essentia* are related is also, in a way, a statement of why the same root, *esse,* can be used in *two distinct ways*. But it is a statement of why it can be used in two distinct *new* ways.

(May I incidentally remark upon the awkwardness of this terminology: *essentia,* being-ness, is actually the term which is logically suited to designate the act by which an *ens* is. An ideally

[42] *De Hebdomadibus,* Rule II.

176

rational and well constructed philosophical vocabulary which wanted to express the doctrine of St. Thomas should really speak of the real distinction between *essentia* and *quidditas*. Perhaps this awkwardness was the reason why St. Thomas' terminology was soon complemented with *existere*, meaning *esse*, and with *existentia*, meaning *actus essendi*, within the century following St. Thomas.[43])

In any event, beyond the aptness of Latin (despite the awkwardness just noted) to express the ambivalence of εἶναι, (that is, the twofold functions of "to be"), there may be a more powerful reason yet why St. Thomas, unlike Avicenna, never said that God had no essence, despite the fact that this is a possible conclusion to be drawn from the existential concept of being— if a certain line of thought is pursued. For, if essence is the limitation of *esse*, then God, the being *a se*, the being whose *esse* is not contingent but necessary, cannot have a limited *esse*, and hence no *essentia*. As Gilson has argued: "were we to say that God is *this*, be it essence, our proposition would entail the consequence that God is not that." [44] But Gilson is careful to point

[43] The verb *existere* was, of course, in common Latin usage from a much earlier time, functioning existentially in somewhat the same philosophical neutral sense as English *to obtain* or German *geben*. I am referring rather to the technical term which connotes precisely this: something that real things do, an act which renders them real and objective, (regardless of what they may be), but with priority to that which they may be (this priority having, of course, not a temporal sense, but merely the sense that, without this something, real things would have no reality at all, and would not be what they are, because they would be nothing at all). *Existere* and *existentia* could not have been given this meaning, of course, until the very idea of which it is the linguistic form was introduced into the Hellenic-Western tradition—an event which St. Thomas must be given principal credit for.

[44] Gilson, *Elements*, p. 135.

out also that, nevertheless, "in saying that God is neither this nor that, we implicitly affirm that there is nothing that, in His own transcendent way, God is not. To affirm that God is only being [i.e. *esse*] is only to deny of him all that which, because it is a determination of being, is a negation of it." [45]

The trouble is that, although in the doctrine of St. Thomas essence truly is the limitation of the act of *esse,* essence is not merely—or even formally—the limitation of the act of *esse.* The ontological function of *essentia,* considered from the viewpoint of the *contingency* of creatures, is, to be sure, that of limiting the act of *esse.* But this is not the only function of essence, nor indeed its essential one; it is not the function which makes essence formally definable as essence; it is, if I may so put it, what essence *does,* but not what essence *is.* For essence is also, and primarily, *quiddity,* what a thing is. And what a thing is, is what makes it intelligible and, therefore, that which makes it to be necessarily whatever it is and, therefore, that which makes it exhibit the constancy of properties and behaviour so assiduously noted and so searchingly explored by all philosophers since Greek times. There is a difference between saying that God is neither particularly this nor particularly that, because he is somehow both this and that, and saying simply that he is neither this nor that, nor indeed anything at all. Gilson notes both these affirmations, but makes no effort whatever to relate them. St. Thomas, however, never failed to keep them constantly related in his philosophical thinking and was, as we may suspect, no more than vaguely aware that they might—unthinkably—have to be divorced in the end.

I am arguing neither for the truth nor falsity of the view that

[45] *Ibid.*

God has no essence—as a matter of fact, if I had to decide the truth between Gilson and St. Thomas my every inclination would be towards Gilson. (But I speak hypothetically. St. Thomas' doctrine and Gilson's alternative when put together do not amount to Hobson's choice.) My point is rather that St. Thomas seems to have kept in mind that essence, which *functions* as the limitation of *esse,* was in the first place devised by the Greeks to account for the intelligible necessities *of things.*[46] If so, we can understand why. despite the fact that the really distinctive and novel insight of St. Thomas was not that *essentia* and *esse* are

[46] The doctrine of Gilson, that God has no essence, intends presumably to remove essence *exclusively* from the being of God. Yet, this may be not easily accomplished. "In our attempt to describe God by removing from Him what is proper to the being of creatures, we must give up essence in order to reach the open sea of pure actual existence, but we must also keep the notion of essence present to the mind so as not to leave it without any object. This we do when, to the question, where do we find God? we simply answer, beyond essence," *Elements,* p. 134. But can essence be "proper to the being of creatures"? To judge from Gilson's reasoning it can only be proper *to human thought:* it must be a category of the mind (in the Kantian sense of the term). For if we must "keep the notion of essence present to the mind so as not to leave it without any object" in the case of our thinking of the being of God, it follows that it is in the nature of our thinking of being of any sort to "keep the notion of essence present to the mind." Therefore, we have no reason whatever to assert that intelligibility is an intrinsic constituent of the reality of any being, created or not. I have no objection to this view—I will advance it myself below, though for my own reasons, (and in no event will I agree that God is pure existence any more than pure essence). But if Gilson wishes to avoid this conclusion he will have to explain how. If, on the other hand, he is willing to accept it (he has, of course, given no indication whatever that he is ready to do either), then he should be prepared also to revise the remainder of his metaphysics in a fairly radical way. For to depart from the idea that essence is an intrinsic constitutent of being as such is to depart not only from St. Thomas but also from the Greeks.

distinct, but that they are as intimately connected as any two things can ever be, St. Thomas nevertheless consistently referred to them simply as being "not the same" or as being "other than" each other, (in the case of creatures), or as being "the same," (in God). The intended or unintended, but in any event, literal connotation of this terminology is precisely that which had been historically taken from it until Gilson claimed otherwise, namely, that even in God "the essence of a thing is what that thing is necessarily and primarily as the first principle of its intelligibilty." [47]

It goes without saying that the quiddity or essence is also made to be the quiddity of the real being by the act of *esse* which it concretizes and limits, whereas *esse* is, of course, the act by which the being is, and is a being, and is therefore whatever it is. Whether or not this accounts for St. Thomas' terminology, there can be little doubt that the intelligibility of quiddity was before St. Thomas' mind constantly. Indeed, this would be the road—quite different from that taken by Avicenna—through which Greek necessitarianism would surreptitiously introduce itself into St. Thomas' thought and, thus, in the end compromise St. Thomas' philosophy as effectively as it had Avicenna's 300 years before. But to understand how this came about it is necessary first to examine a more immediate problem brought about by the very metaphysical creativity which St. Thomas exhibited to such unprecedented degree.

[47] Jacques Maritain, *Introduction to Philosophy*, (London, 1947), p. 151.

CONTINGENT REALITY
AND PROBLEMATIC EXISTENCE

Whether or not St. Thomas thought that God could be said to have an essence (though it is beyond question that if God has an essence then his essence is "the same" as his *esse*), there can be little argument that, in any case, to St. Thomas' mind creatures certainly did. For, whatever else he may or may not have been certain about, St. Thomas does not appear ever for a single moment to have doubted that being is intelligible. He was inspired, like Avicenna, to redeem the truth of Greek philosophy from its pagan necessitarianism—and the truth of Greek philosophy begins with the essential intelligibility of being. Thus, like Avicenna, he accepted without question the idea that the existential reality of *entia* is related to their definability and intelligibility. But, unlike the assumption of the Greeks, the view of St. Thomas is that this relation was not the merely logical relation of identity: it was a real relation between distinct elements of an ontologically composite, single created reality. Nor was this relation, unlike Al-Farabi and Avicenna had thought, the essence's reception of existence as an accident which accrued to it; for this would not have effectively safeguarded the contingency of created being. Thus, if existence did not accrue to essence from the outside, as it were, it must be, as we have seen, an intrinsic constituent of every created *ens*.

Yet, this supposition may well have a certain consequence which would be paradoxical and ironic, if it were upheld. For if *esse* is an element of created being, other than essence, but its act, then it is possible to argue equally well in two opposite direc-

181

tions. The first we have already seen: a being thus constituted is existentially contingent, for its reception of existence does not render it necessary—not even necessary in virtue of another. On the other hand, it might also be argued that a being whose reality, once constituted, is the reality of an act of *esse* which is the act of its own existence, (however limited this existence may be), *exists by itself* and has no further need of a creator in order to exist. Such a being would be, perhaps not necessary in the strictest sense of the Greeks, but certainly not contingent enough to remain compatible with the traditional Christian faith. It would be, as it were, genetically, but not ontologically, contingent. Even if this sort of being remained corruptible and subject to substantial annihilation, these features would not make it truly contingent existentially; for its corruptibility and its possible annihilation would be due to the limited, restricted essence which happened to have been its nature to have. That is, such a being would be existentially contingent only in the sense that it need not be; but this existential contingency would not necessarily mean that such a being was contingent *upon God* or upon any "other" for its existence: its existence would be strictly its intrinsic perfection. Its existence, while it existed, would remain with full sufficiency its own, and its alone. It might depend on God in other ways, but not for existence. It would owe its origin, perhaps, to God; but now that it existed it would owe its existence to no one but itself.[48]

[48] Underneath the professional atheism, as it might be called, of philosophers and scientists in modern times, and of those who are consciously and directly influenced by them, there is a popular atheism or a layman's atheism, as it were, which definitely transcends mere agnosticism, but which usually lacks decisiveness, fervour or militancy. This popular atheism is automatically reached when people draw, more or less

If St. Thomas did not actually anticipate this difficulty in the precise manner in which I have presented it here, he must have done so in an equivalent way. In any event, his solution was exactly like that at which, shall we say, any creative genius would have logically arrived when faced with this precise problem. Let us look at the question in some detail.

With the benefit of hindsight we can now discern that the principle of St. Thomas' solution lay in reversing the order of demonstration which had been used by the Arabs. Al-Farabi and Avicenna had, in effect, argued from their religious convictions. I have no intention of implying that this is never permissible in good scholarship, (although I do believe it is always dangerous, and requires, more than intelligence, a degree of truthfulness, integrity, honesty and self-knowledge that believers surely do not always have). The edge of my statement is, rather, that Avicenna's method reveals a very strong apologetic component in his thought: his procedure was to argue from what he believed God to be, (namely, the creator on whom creatures totally depended), to what creatures surely had to be if God was to remain the creator on whom they totally depended. Thus, since creatures depended on God, they could not have their existence in virtue of their own necessity (or, which is the same, in virtue of their own essence). Hence, the *esse* of creatures was "other than" their *essentia*.

_____

consciously, more or less logically, this very conclusion or a practical equivalent thereof: that human existence, however mysterious, is evidently as contingent as man's consciousness of himself, and that therefore it could not come to man from without—least of all from a Necessary Source. In other words, an existent owes its existence to no one but itself, because existence is not the sort of "thing" that can be owing to another—even if it had in point of fact been "received" from another.

St. Thomas would have had little scruple in arguing from his own religious beliefs. In fact, on several occasions [49] he substantially repeated, with approval, Avicenna's argument, and on at least one occasion he did so with specific reference to his source. [50] But St. Thomas' doctrine of the contingency of creatures is, as we have seen, quite unlike Avicenna's. Avicenna's argument "proves only that, in a created universe, existence must come to essences from outside and, therefore, be superadded to them." [51] I would like to think that St. Thomas was sufficiently empirically minded to have preferred arguing *to* the nature of God *from* the nature of creatures—and I have no doubt that he was, in any event, much more inclined in this direction than Avicenna, his admiration of Aristotle being at least as devout as, but his profit from its study having been probably greater than, the Arab's. But even if it had run against the grain, *the very nature of his doctrine* forced St. Thomas to argue in the first place in this manner, namely, from creatures to God—however free he may also have felt *thereafter* to argue, like Avicenna, from God to creatures. For the possible difficulty of which St. Thomas was surely not wholly unconscious, as I have explained above, was that the very existential creatureliness of creatures might be endangered if it were granted that their existence was not the accident of the essence, but its act. In the doctrine of St. Thomas *esse* might come to *ens*—not to *essentia*—from the outside. But *esse* never lay outside *essentia,* nor did it ever lie outside the being, (*ens*), once the being was. It is, as I have said, paradoxical; but if the existential contingency of *creatures* was to be retained, it

[49] For instance, *ST,* I, 44, 1; *Contra Gentiles,* II, 52.
[50] *De Veritate,* VIII, 8.
[51] Gilson, *Elements,* p. 128.

was necessary to derive their creatureliness from their existential contingency, not the other way about. Hence, St. Thomas' problem really was, in Gilson's memorable phrase: "how do we know that empirically given beings [as such, i.e. not creatures as such] are compounded of essence and existence?" [52] In other words, if creatures are really contingent and are not necessary *even after they exist,* then their contingency should be evident *in them,* in themselves, as they exist, not in the relation that they may have to God. The Christian thinker should, therefore, be able to determine the contingency of creatures from a philosophical analysis of them precisely as contingent beings; that is, from a consideration of creatures not as creatures, not as dependent upon uncreated being, but from a consideration of them simply as they are in themselves and as they are immediately known by the philosophical intellect prior to all enlightening of the philosophical intellect by faith.

Once again, the student of philosophy could entertain himself speculating on the source of St. Thomas' inspiration for the solution to this problem. Several possibilities will readily suggest themselves, not excluding Aristotle, several of whose texts in the *Posterior Analytics* could have been easily interpreted by St. Thomas (not quite accurately, but not at all implausibly), as meaning that the knowledge of what a thing is does not imply a knowledge of its existence. I have myself stated above that the doctrine of Aristotle in the *Posterior Analytics* can be easily interpreted to mean that having knowledge of a thing does not of itself imply its correspondence to the thing as it is in reality. This is hardly to be *correctly* interpreted in the sense that for Aristotle we could know essences without knowing whether they

[52] Ibid., p. 127.

exist; it means (for Aristotle) that knowledge is not necessarily true, that knowledge of a thing may really turn out to be unwarranted by the reality of a thing. But it would not be difficult to interpret it in the former sense if only one approached the text with Al-Farabi and Avicenna looking over one's shoulder. Or, at any rate, one could well be inspired by this text, if one had also read Al-Farabi and Avicenna and noted that Aristotle speaks better Arabic than Latin. The fact is, however, that this idea, that knowledge and existence do not of themselves imply each other, which seems commonplace enough to so many of us today,[53] could not have been easily entertained, at least not in its full force, by someone who, like Aristotle, assumed that things could be known only because they necessarily *were* (i.e. were what they were).

But we do know of a philosopher who did distinguish, if not exactly between *essentia* and *esse* (for these, to be precise, imply the idea that *esse* is the act of *essentia*), at least between quiddity

[53] It seems commonplace enough to those of us who have directly or indirectly retained the metaphysical formation given to Western civilization by mediaeval and modern philosophical thought. But some reflection, even at the non-technical level of common, everyday contemporary thinking, should reveal that this idea is in point of fact totally incredible and contrary to what experience tells us about itself. Any knowledge whatever, at any level whatever, even that of the simplest and least sophisticated apprehension, involves knowledge of the existence of something; what may very well happen is that we may have very little knowledge of *what* that something is. Conceivably, one might have knowledge of something simply as *something,* or as a *being,* or as a *reality,* though in point of fact most human knowledge, even of the most elementary sort implies a sufficiently complex mode of self-relation to reality to warrant the assertions (a) that we usually know, more or less precisely, what the objects of our cognition are, and (b) that the problem that we usually face is not that of learning in the most elementary way what things are, but that of perfecting our understanding of them. Cf. below, p. 256.

and that in reality which (if I may be allowed to mix Arab and Persian literary forms) constitutes the grounds of the serendipity of man in relation to being. I refer to Al-Farabi, whose remark I have quoted above: "if the existence of man coincided with his corporeal and animal nature, there would be no person who, having an exact idea of what man is, and knowing his corporeal and animal nature, could put in doubt the existence of man. But this is not at all the case, and we do doubt the existence of things, until we have a direct perception of them by sense, or a mediate one by demonstration. Thus existence is not a constitutive character of being, it is only an adventitious accident of it."

Whether St. Thomas found his inspiration in this remark of Al-Farabi or whether he was able to reason the matter out for himself without Al-Farabi's help, in either event St. Thomas did find it possible to excogitate an argument showing that empirically given being *as such* is composed of *esse* and *essentia*, existence and essence:

Whatever does not belong to the notion of an essence or quiddity comes from without and enters into composition with the essence, for no essence is intelligible without its parts. Now, every essence or quiddity can be understood without anything being known of its existing. I can know what a man or a phoenix is and still be ignorant whether it exists in reality. From this it is clear that the act of existing is other than essence or quiddity, unless, perhaps, there is a being whose quiddity is its very act of existing. And there can be only one such being, the First Being.[54]

It should be noted that the argument hinges in no wise upon the notion of creatureliness, formally so-called. An atheist might well subscribe to it in full fidelity to his belief. The argument ap-

[54] *De Ente et Essentia,* IV.

peals, rather, to the essence of essence, as it were. Granted his twofold *demonstrandum,* namely, first, that *essentia* is other than *esse,* and, second, that the latter is its act—this is the part of the doctrine that is distinctively St. Thomas'—the argument proceeds, in the first place, from the definition of essence. But note the double weight of the sentence "whatever does not belong to the notion of an essence or quiddity comes from without and enters into composition with the essence, for no essence is intelligible without its parts." In one sense this provides a preliminary premise for the argument that follows: surely if quiddity is intelligible without *esse,* then *esse* cannot be an essential part of quiddity. But since that to which this principle will be applied is nothing other than the quiddity itself, then the statement also means: it follows from the very essence of quiddity that quiddity must be intelligible by itself. Now, every quiddity is intelligible apart from *esse.* Therefore, *esse* cannot belong to *essentia* by the very nature of *essentia* and hence is "other than it." Had St. Thomas not assumed that being is intelligible precisely as being, then his doctrine of the existential contingency of being would not have been coupled with the continuation of the Greek doctrine of the essential necessity of being and, if so, the history of philosophy, and of Christianity, would have been far different from what it has in fact been. This is, of course, not a very profound observation. But it highlights, nonetheless, the importance of St. Thomas' argument. For, as we shall now proceed to analyze, it was at this very point that the seed which would eventually become the transcendence of the most basic presuppositions of Greek thought was planted in the Western mind, where it would slowly but unfailingly yield both the bitter and the sweet fruits of contemporary Western thought.

St. Thomas' argument for the composition of empirically given being by essence and existence appeals in part, as I have said, to the nature of essence as the necessary intelligibility of being. But if essence is the necessary intelligibility of being, if essence is that without which a being cannot be or be thought (for that which can be is the same as that which can be thought), then St. Thomas' argument at bottom appeals to the Greek concept of knowledge. The difficulty with this procedure is that the Greek understanding of knowledge was devised in connection with the assumption of the necessity of being—both the essential and the existential necessity, indistinctly. The use of the Greek notion of essence in connection with the notion of being which was existentially contingent, because *esse* was the act of *essentia,* had an explosive epistemological potential which in due course was bound to be set off.

St. Thomas' argument depends upon the major premise that "every essence or quiddity can be understood without anything being known of its existing." In keeping with the requirements of his objective, this observation of St. Thomas concerns empirical being as such—it does not concern empirical being insofar as it is created. This is, indeed, an empirical observation concerning empirical being as such. It is not (as is the preliminary supposition which I have noted above, which is all that Al-Farabi and Avicenna had based their arguments upon, namely the definition of essence), an *a priori* proposition about being. The example offered by St. Thomas himself to illustrate the principle serves to remove every reasonable doubt about this point. For the text of St. Thomas does *not* say: "a man or a phoenix can be merely possible, can be conceived by God, and yet not be brought into existence by him." It says: "I can *know* what a man or a phoenix is and still *be ignorant* whether it exists in reality." It concerns that which "I can know" and that which I can "be ignorant" of. Now, considered by itself, this was hardly a novel observation. Al-Farabi had said as much, and if Aristotle had not himself done so, the reason is not that he lacked all acquaintance with the experience of doubt, but that he could not very well have conceptualized this experience in terms of an (existential) reality in being other than the very (intelligible) reality of being. But everyone who has any experience with reality knows very well that despite the aptitude of reality for "being found," sometimes we can look for it without success. On the other hand, neither the common experience of any culture, nor that of Avicenna and Al-Farabi in particular, had ever before coupled this observation with either a philosophically elaborated or a common sense apprehension of the existential contingency of reality, *ens,* whose existence was the act of its essence and its knowable content. The conjunction of the two in St. Thomas would have the effect of extending the realm of possible doubt about the existence of beings from *given beings* to *being as such,* since it would subject to possible doubt the actual existence of every essence—perhaps not as such, as intelligible, but, in any event, as related to the act of *esse*—including the essence of an essentially existing God. At least, such would be the ultimate result, namely, to cast doubt even upon the existence of any God who was intelligibly constituted. The more immediate effect was simply to cast doubt upon the reality of anything whatever whose essence and whose existence were not "the same."

The reason is that an observation about empirically given being concerns *being,* to be sure, but it concerns being which is *given* in experience: St. Thomas' argument concerns *being,* but

190

it is thereby concerned with what "I can know" and what I can "be ignorant" of. Hence, this observation about being is also an observation about experience itself; in this sense it can be stated, therefore, that St. Thomas based his distinction between essence and existence, in empirically given being as such, upon a reflexive analysis of experience. I hasten to add that this is not in the least objectionable. It is, in any event, inevitable: philosophers from Parmenides to our own day have never analyzed reality except insofar as it was given in experience, and it is difficult to imagine under what conditions it would ever become possible for any philosopher to do otherwise. For it appears that there is no way, at least for man, to analyze anything unless it be somehow given to him in experience. The novelty of St. Thomas' doctrine, however, is that this was the first time in the recorded history of Hellenic-Western philosophy that any scholar began to take advantage of this very fact. And insofar as later thought has only taken increasing and ever more conscious advantage of the same fact, it is fair to state, simply as a matter of historical fact, that later Western philosophical thought, up to and including contemporary thought, continues and fulfils the philosophical creativity of St. Thomas himself (albeit, to be sure, along lines which St. Thomas would not have himself wished to take).

For what St. Thomas did was nothing less than to take advantage of the givenness of reality to experience—for that is what, by another name, is the cognoscibility of being—in order to reach a conclusion about its nature as being. The difficulty, however, is that St. Thomas, as did his modern successors until recent times, also retained the classical conception of knowledge, with which the doctrine of the existential contingency of being is ultimately incompatible. But until this incompatibility was unearthed, confusion, if not outright chaos, reigned in the Western philosophical world. For if St. Thomas meant exactly what he said in the *De Ente et Essentia* (that is, if the *empirical* reason why essence and existence are really distinct in empirically given being is the *empirical* fact that in such being essence can be known without its actual existence being *ipso facto* known), then the problematization of knowledge, specifically as posed by Descartes, would sooner or later arise. Its basis would be that provided by St. Thomas, namely, a reflexive analysis of experience itself.

St. Thomas himself did not incorporate into his system as a whole the full doctrine of *De Ente et Essentia*. The doctrine of the empirical basis of the distinction between essence and existence is a sort of loose end, asserted but once, and in an early work. What remained vividly in the forefront of St. Thomas' thought was the conclusion that in empirically given being as such (and not merely insofar as it is created) "existence is a distinct element, other than essence, and its act," or in other words, that "there are beings, or substances, given in sense experience whose structure reveals itself to the metaphysician as composed of essence and existence." [55] This means that the heart of the metaphysical "revolution" [56] wrought by St. Thomas, the potential violence of the philosophical subversion of Greek thought fomented originally (albeit, surely, unconsciously) by him, is not definable exclusively in terms of the bare concept of being according to which the contingency of creaturely existence is to be found in connection with their intrinsic possession of their own existence—but also by

[55] Gilson, *Elements,* P. 127.

[56] Gilson, *The Christian Philosophy of St. Thomas,* (London, 1957), p. 39.

the methodological fact that this concept was derived empirically rather than *a priori*. St. Thomas' thought was particularly revolutionary because it rested not upon an analysis of empirically given being, on the incorrect, self-contradictory assumption that being is not-given in experience, but upon an analysis of empirically given being *as such;* hence, it rested, *materialiter loquendo,* upon an analysis of created being, though not on the relation of createdness of creatures to their divine creator.

Thus, the heritage left by St. Thomas was from the outset as ambivalent as that of Aristotle before him—though, of course, in quite a different way. The fully developed metaphysics of St. Thomas remained Avicennian in character—by which I mean that it did not altogether successfully exclude Greek necessitarianism from the Christian world, though such necessitarianism was allowed to insinuate itself only through the concept of God. Thus, even in relation to the distinction between *essentia* and *esse,* St. Thomas' most frequent mode of argumentation is not that of *De Ente et Essentia;* rather, he usually proceeds to an understanding of created being from the nature of its relation to God. And St. Thomas' God is not less self-necessitated than Aristotle's or Avicenna's: "as the divine existence is necessary of itself, so is the divine will and the divine knowledge." [57] St. Thomas, to be sure, does qualify this doctrine, noting that there is a difference between the self-necessitation of the divine knowledge, which "has a necessary relation to the thing known," and that of God's will to the thing willed. For "his willing things apart from himself" is necessary, but "not absolutely necessary"—it is necessary only "hypothetically (*ex suppositione*)." [58] God does, however,

[57] *ST,* I, 19, 3, ad 6.
[58] *ST,* I, 19, 3.

necessarily will himself. St. Thomas' qualification, thus, only re-asserts the contingency of creatures; it does not take away in the slightest from the view that the supreme and absolute being is supremely and absolutely necessitated.

It matters little for present purposes if St. Thomas could also claim that the self-necessitation of God does not interfere with God's divine freedom, because his necessitation is *self*-necessitation. The fact, however, that the ultimate reality to which man has ultimate relations is by nature Necessity Itself would have not a few consequences in the subsequent formation of Christian prac-tice and belief. Ample justification remained in the doctrine of St. Thomas for the retention of an essentially Hellenic cultural form for the Christian *faith*. On the other hand, the concept of being which he effectively contributed to the *philosophical* tradi-tion of the Christian world, and effectively bequeathed to the development of philosophy, tended in the opposite direction: it was a concept of being empirically grounded upon a reflexive analysis of the reality given in immediate experience. After St. Thomas, the real distinction between essence and existence became a philosophical commonplace—not always in so many words, but at least as directly implicated in a concept of being which eventually became a part of modern Western culture itself. I mean: the existential concept of being. For not only phil-osophers, but everyone who speaks a modern European language knows and uses the word "existence" in the post-Thomistic sense, that is, as an act of things which is responsible for their being real, an act which things *do,* which has the effect of positing them (as some philosophers would say) *extra nihil* and *extra causas.*

Not even all philosophers who trade in the common coin of

existential being are aware of the historical and empirical origin of this, now typically Western, mode of self-relation to reality, and appear to assume that all men at all times have at least implicitly conceived the reality of being as its existence. (Some philosophers even appear to think, if one is to judge by their mode of argumentation, that all men at all times have at least implicitly conceived the reality of being in the *English* language concept of existence.) The fact is, rather, that not even within the Hellenic-Western tradition has this always been the case, and that this is a relatively recent development in the tradition considered as a whole: it is a development, however, which in a very real sense marks the conception of a world whose gestation has come to term only in recent times.

Be that as it may, after St. Thomas it was only a matter of time before someone would draw the inevitable consequences from the idea that the contingency of empirically given being (I mean, the contingency of being precisely as given by the real distinction between what-a-thing-is and the act whereby it is what-it-is) was grounded upon a characteristic of things *insofar as they were objects of knowledge.* Sooner or later some philosopher was bound to reason that, if the contingency of every being that is the object of experience is evinced by its very property as object of empirical intuition, then it follows that we can never assert that any being actually exists, simply on the grounds that we know it. Indeed, there can never be any empirical grounds for asserting that *anything* actually exists. We all know, of course, how logically and consistently Western philosophy developed thereafter, up to and including the discovery of philosophical atheism.

THOMISTIC EXISTENTIALISM
AND CARTESIAN AFTERMATH

For it follows from the premises established by St. Thomas, that if by knowledge we attain to an extramental reality which (a) does not necessarily exist and does not have within itself anything which is the sufficient reason for its existence, and which (b) cannot, simply because it is known, be necessarily known to exist (for this indeed is the basis of the previous assertion), then the existence of every being we know (or could know), the existence of anything constituted by an intelligible quiddity, is philosophically problematic. Irrespective of its perseity, extramentality and existential independence, empirically given being is known to us in virtue of its intelligibility; and its intelligibility may be essential to its constitution, but since it is "other than" its existence, and since it exists contingently, no amount of knowledge about empirically given being will reveal whether or not it exists.

In recent times, well after "the problem of knowledge" became a philosophical conundrum, Thomists have tried to avoid this difficulty, taking advantage of St. Thomas' doctrine that truth is found only in the judgment and not in simple apprehension, arguing that existence is apprehended by the judgment. Textbook writers have made short shrift of the question: simple apprehension apprehends essences, judgment apprehends existence; what one operation of the mind does not know in the first moment of knowledge, the second operation catches at later stage. The more thoughtful Thomists, like Gilson,

Maritain, Lonergan and Rahner have realized, however, that the matter is much thornier than appears at first sight.

This is why there is among sound Thomists, as Gilson has said, a strong temptation, yet also "a general reluctance to conceive the act of being (*esse*) as a distinct object of understanding." [59] If we attend to the implications of such a hypothesis we can well understand their "reluctance." If the doctrine were proposed that existence is apprehended by the judgment, (or, for that matter, by any other operation of the mind) in such a manner that *esse* became a distinct object of understanding, then the act of *esse* would be at one and the same time the act of the essence and a sort of essence in itself, a principle of intelligibility in itself, which would make essence superfluous and difficult to relate to existence.

Textbook writers avoid this difficulty by ignoring the dilemma: they feel no compunction about stressing, on the one hand, "the dynamic character of existence," insisting that "*esse* is not 'existence,' but the 'act of existing'," the "supreme actuality and force," and so on, while making existence elsewhere in their system of thought—nay, making *esse,* "which is not a substantive, but a verb"—to all intents and purposes the super-essential object of the *complex* apprehension (but *apprehension* nonetheless) of the intellect in the second, judgmental operation of the mind. As if it were not serious enough, in any case, to make of existence a sort of essence in itself which would make essence essentially superfluous, such a procedure would leave behind a created being constituted by a principle of intelligibility which was identical with its act of existence—which is precisely what a contingent being could not possibly be. No, the existential contingency of being, if coupled with the idea that being is intelligible pre-

[59] Gilson, Elements, p. 131.

cisely as being, means that *esse* cannot be intelligible in itself (except, of course, *in* God, and *to* God): "the act of existing cannot be the object of a perfect abstraction." [60] *Esse* can be in-

[60] Jacques Maritain, *Existence and the Existent,* (New York, 1948), p. 24. Gilson has, so far as I know, made no attempt to deal with the problem philosophically, presumably because his Thomistic specialization is not in the field of epistemology. Maritain, however, has tackled the problem explicitly and directly, with results which, in my opinion, carry him as far as any Thomist has ever been able to go. The principal texts of Maritain's analysis are to be found in *Existence and the Existent,* pp. 15–35, and the decisive passage runs as follows: "Existence is not an essence; it is shut off from the whole order of essence. How then can it be the object of the intellect, and its supreme object? How can we speak of the concept or the idea of existence? Ought we not to say rather that existence is not apprehended by the intellect, or apprehensible by it? that existence does not admit of conceptualization? . . . that existence is an unknowable upon which metaphysics builds without itself attaining to it? [Para.] . . . Essences are the object of the first operation of the intellect, or *simple apprehension*. It is *judgment* which the act of existence confronts. The intellect envelopes [*sic*] itself and is self-contained, is wholly present in each of its operations [N.B. But is it wholly present in each of its operations *by* the very operation *in* which it is wholly present? Maritain does not go quite this far.]; and in the initial upsurge of its activity out of the world of sense, in the first act of self-affirmation accomplished by expressing to itself any datum of experience, it apprehends and judges in the same instant. It forms its first idea (that of being) while uttering its first judgment (of existence), and utters its first judgment while forming its first idea. I say, therefore, that it thus lays hold of the treasure which properly belongs to judgment, in order to envelop it in simple apprehension itself; it visualises that treasure in an initial absolutely original idea, in a privileged idea which is not the result of the process of simple apprehension alone, but of laying hold of that which the intellect affirms from the moment it judges, namely, the act of existing. It seizes upon the eminent intelligibility or the superintelligibility which the act of judging deals with (that of existence), in order to make of it an object of thought. [Para.] Thus existence is made object; but . . . in a higher and analogical sense resulting from the objectising of a trans-objective act and referring to trans-objective subjects that exercise or are able to exercise this act. Here a concept seizes upon that which is not an essence but is an intelligible in a higher and analogical sense, a super-intelligible de-

telligible only in and through its relation to essence. But this is precisely what made philosophically, though only philosophically, problematic the existence of all contingent being as such.

---

livered up to the mind in the very operation which it performs each time that it judges, and from the moment of its first judgment. [Para.] But this concept of existence, of *to-exist* (*esse*) is not and cannot be *cut off* from the absolutely primary concept of being (*ens,* that-which is, that-which exists, that whose act is to exist). This is so because the affirmation of existence, or the judgment, which provides the content of such a concept, is itself the 'composition' of a subject with existence, i.e. the affirmation that *something exists. . . .* The concept of existence cannot be visualised completely apart, detached, isolated, separated from that of being; and it is in that concept of being and with that concept of being that it is at first conceived. Here we touch upon the original error that underlies all the modern existentialist philosophies. Ignorant of or neglecting the warning of the old scholastic wisdom, that 'the *act of existing* cannot be the object of a perfect abstraction,' these philosophies presuppose that existence can be isolated," pp. 22–24.

Maritain began with two questions: (a) "how . . . can it [existence] be the object of the intellect"? (b) "how can we speak of the concept . . . of existence." I take it that it is not the same thing to ask (a) what in the nature of existence renders it apt to be an object of knowledge despite the fact that it is totally other than essence, and (b) how is it possible for the intellect to conceive existence despite the fact that existence is not apprehended by simple apprehension but by judgment and, thus, cannot be apprehended by a concept? But because these two questions are worded somewhat equivocally by Maritain, his reply in the end answers reasonably only the second: his reply to the first is, in effect, a bare, unsupported statement that existence is not an essence but is intelligible (or super-intelligible) just the same, period. I have no quarrel with Maritain's analysis of the way in which the intellect must surely operate *if* it is to attain to the intelligibility or "super-intelligibility" of existence, and if it is going to do so not in the first but in the second operation of the mind. Indeed, I cannot but agree that Maritain's answer to this precise question, once granted its premises, is the most, if not the only, reasonable one that philosophy could provide, namely, that for all its logical features, like its compositive and divisive functions, judgment is essentially an apprehensive, cognitive act. But the question which is left unanswered is: can we maintain that existence can be the object of such, or any other apprehensive, cognitive act, (be it judgment or what-

I stress that the existence of empirically given being became only *philosophically* problematic, because, ironically enough, it is distinctive of the improperly so-called "problem of knowledge" that its problematic aspect, its ἀπορία, consists in the self-contradictory character of the *epistemological* analysis which leads to it. The problem of knowledge is the problem of how to reconcile the classical concept of knowledge with the consequences of enquiring *philosophically* into knowledge thus conceived. For, according to the concept of knowledge which underlies the entire historical development outlined above, namely, that knowledge is the mind's intentional intussusception of an extramental reality, no *real* doubt about the (existential) reality of extramental being could be entertained. Thus, as posed by Descartes the problem of knowledge was essentially this: how to establish *philosophically* the real existence of objects of knowledge about whose *real* existence neither common sense nor philosophy could entertain any doubts—for their real existence was presupposed not only by

---

ever), since existence is by its very reality totally other than essence, whereas, the latter is by definition that ontological constituent of being which makes it apt to be known? Maritain's answer simply begs the question: existence is grasped by the mind because existence is intelligible. It is indeed super-intelligible. (To be sure, if existence is not essence and is nevertheless intelligible we may as well say that it is super-intelligible in order to distinguish it from the ordinary intelligibility of essence. But, if so, why not say that existence is a *super-essence?*) Why must it be said that existence is intelligible *in itself?* Because, as Maritain has just shown there is no reason why it cannot be conceived *by the mind* despite the fact that, not being an essence, it is not the object of simple apprehension: existence must be intelligible *in itself* because it is understood *by the mind*. This is nothing but Parmenides' reasoning, all over again. The circle is thus complete. The question how *is* existence to be conceived—I do not say, how *can* existence be conceived—given the premise that it is not essence, has been left totally without reply.

common sense, but also by the philosophers' very concept of knowledge as the mind's attainment of an extramental reality.

Descartes' ingenuity is nowhere more evident than in his attempt to capitalize upon this paradoxical quality of knowledge. Descartes shared with St. Thomas the classical concept of knowledge—though he developed scarcely the same theory to account for it. This is why he never had, any more than St. Thomas ever did, any doubt that the known is in point of fact an extramental existent: the very fact that it is known means that, prior to its being known, it already was some sort of independent existent. But the effort of epistemology to demonstrate philosophically what must be assumed by the philosopher to be true in any event, is required by the fact that philosophical reflection upon the nature of the objects of knowledge (i.e. philosophical awareness of their existential contingency) leads to the conclusion that its ontological structure (i.e. its existential contingency) makes it problematic precisely as object of knowledge. Therefore —but only *therefore*—the same fact that makes the *object* of knowledge problematic, makes *knowledge* problematic as well. This point, I believe, has not been well appreciated by historians of philosophy in modern times.

The "problem of knowledge," as it unfolded between St. Thomas and Descartes, did not originate when philosophical reflection applied itself to the nature of knowledge—for instance, to the fallibility of human knowledge. On the contrary, if it was only contemporary philosophy that found it possible to make any inroads into this area, the reason is that it was only in recent times that philosophy finally did realize that it was the very *nature of knowledge* that was at stake in the problem and which, therefore, required critical attention for its own sake. The problem took its origin, rather, from philosophical reflection upon the nature of being—more precisely, upon the nature of being as intelligible in its very being, upon the nature of being as constituted by essence, upon the nature of being as object of possible knowledge—and the difficulty was that the nature of being thus understood seemed by its own inner logic to escape the very possibility of becoming known. This is why, after all, the problem of modern epistemology was not "does man actually know?" It was: "how is it possible for man to know?" It was not until Kant, at the earliest, that philosophers began to advert to the implication that if the *known* is problematic, then *knowledge* is problematic too and, hence, must be critically examined in order to solve, the "problem of knowledge."

Descartes himself, as I have mentioned, never entertained (so far as his writings indicate) any real doubt about the real extramental existence of the object of knowledge. Nevertheless, he deemed this extramental existence philosophically problematic. Hence, he thought that to solve the problem it was necessary for philosophy to entertain not a *real,* but a *methodic* doubt. Why? Because, on the assumption that knowledge does in fact intentionally unite to the mind an extramental reality whose existence is philosophically problematic, the essence of the problem is precisely this: the same empirical observations which, on the one hand, are incorporated into the classical concept of knowledge, also imply, on the other, that there can be no empirical difference, no humanly detectable distinction, between an act of knowing a quiddity which actually existed extramentally, and an act of knowing a quiddity which did not. Therefore, although the existence of the extramental could not be *really* doubted (and must be, surely, demonstrable, unless a self-contradictory scepticism were admitted), this real existence cannot be demonstrated except perhaps on the methodological hypothesis that knowledge would be possible (as William of Ockham had earlier pointed out) [61] even in the absence of an extramental existent. For, to repeat, it follows from St. Thomas' grounding of the contingent existence of empirically given being upon a reflective analysis of knowledge, that there could be no empirically noticeable difference between knowing *id quod* (that which is known), and knowing *id quo* (that by which we know that which exists extramentally), whether the *id quo* be the concept or the mental proposition.[62] Therefore, the philosophical demonstration must

[61] *In Sententiarum,* II, 25.

[62] Unlike Gilson and Maritain—I criticize transcendental Thomism separately in Appendix 2 below—the less astute among neo-Thomists appear to think that the entire problem of knowledge from Descartes onwards can be solved in favour of some sort of realism by observing that truth is found in the judgment, whereas Descartes' problem appears to concern only the objects of simple apprehension. The fact is, however, that the problem of Descartes and of later philosophy is not in reality the problem of the nature of human knowledge or even the problem of the nature of the truth of human knowledge, but the problem of the knowability of the contingently existing essences which are, supposedly, the objects of human knowledge and the reality in relation to which human knowledge can be true. But surely even the less astute philosophers will admit that if the objects of simple apprehension are not indeed apprehended, then there can be no true judgment and therefore no truth. But perhaps they should be reminded that the very name, *simple apprehension,* contrasts the first operation of the mind with the *complex apprehension* which is otherwise called by traditional logic the *judgment.* No neo-Thomistic or transcendental-Thomistic solution to the problem of knowledge can be seriously advanced which does not give place of prominence to the judgment. But the solution, as I have already suggested, cannot depend upon the simplistic expedient of essentializing the act of existence.

For both Gilson and Maritain, despite marked mutual differences on the degree to which they would allow a critical examination of knowledge, the solution to the problem of knowledge depends upon the deducibility of the knowability of things—and, thus, the deducibility of the possibility of knowledge *at all its various levels,* not judgment alone—from the actuality of knowledge: "the critical problem is . . . to be stated in these terms: 'at the various levels of elaboration of knowledge, what value is to be assigned to *percipere* and *judicare?* Granted that thought takes itself, to begin with, as warranted in its certitude about things and its being measured by an *esse* independent of itself, how are we to judge whether, how, under what conditions, and to what extent it is so warranted, both in principle and at the various moments of human knowledge?' . . . Since the intellect bears in the first place neither on itself, nor on the *ego,* but on *being,* then the very first evidence . . . for the intellect is that of the principle of identity 'discovered' in the intellectual apprehension of being or the real. . . . The reality in question is not necessarily of the actual (existential) order, even though the intellect does first grasp the principle of identity as incarnate in some example of sensible existence. Of itself that principle bears upon the whole range of being and first of all on the order of essences, on the *possible real," Les Degrés du Savoir,* pp. 142, 149.

I cannot, for reasons that should become apparent below, agree that this represents a correct, adequate epistemological approach. But I believe that this is a profound, cogent and sophisticated doctrine, devoid of facile apologetics and merely rhetorical argumentation. On the other hand, precisely because my disagreement involves the very concept of knowledge and not merely the theory of knowledge, I cannot agree to discuss the problem of knowledge in terms of the judgment rather than simple apprehension. For I cannot agree to discuss a question which I consider illegitimate. I insist that there is a prior question to be discussed, namely, whether the classical concept of knowledge is adequate and, if not, how it should be transcended and how the empirical facts should be accordingly reconceptualized. Nevertheless, I will point out that even in the traditional accounts, as the Maritainian text quoted above amply shows, knowledge *begins* with simple apprehension, and the first "certitudes" of the mind bear "first of all on the order of essences, on the *possible real."* It is, therefore, not at all relevant to the criticism of traditional epistemologies that truth may be found only in the judgment and that simple apprehension may be *completed* only by the apprehension of existence in the judgment: for if simple apprehension does not attain to its object in the first place, then there can be no truth in the judgment at a later stage. If the first operation of the mind cannot be critically relied upon to apprehend quiddities, no other level or form of knowledge whatever can be assumed to be certain or reliable.

proceed *as if* what is known were only an idea in the mind, *as if* what is known were only the representation of that which exists in reality as an in-itself—though the philosopher knows very well that in reality this is not the case, because were it otherwise, it would not occur to him to attempt the demonstration in the first place. The first *Meditation* of Descartes is devoted to nothing but this very point.[63]

For all its ingenuity, the Cartesian procedure was a fateful one. Descartes' doctrine could only lead, as it did historically lead, to the philosophy of Hume. Worse yet, it led to the paradoxical situation in which scepticism in epistemology, and solipsism in metaphysics, were the unacceptable yet unavoidable outcome of philosophy's critical enquiry upon the knowability of being. And, of course, it led to apostasy and atheism as well— aided and abetted by the intransigence of a Church which, deny- ing in constant deed its theoretical belief in the rationality of faith, time and again pitted its all too fallible but authority-in- flated judgment, against reason and even elementary common sense. It was not only that the reasonableness of belief in God was eroded as the potential scepticism of the doctrine of St. Thomas was gradually drawn out. The existential contingency of creatures whose existence was an act which intrinsically be- longed to their own intelligibility, their own essence, implied also their existential autonomy. The doctrine that "in a caused sub- stance, existence is a distinct element, other than its essence, and its act" [64] was not, of course, the only force working within Christianity pressing man to face his freedom and to put his

---

[63] In Norman Kemp Smith's translation of *Descartes' Philosophical Writings*, (London, 1952), see pp. 200–201.

[64] Gilson, *Elements*, p. 128.

creativity to work: the Christian faith itself had always served that very end, and it served that very end, in one way, through the philosophy, (St. Thomas', as it so happens), which at the appropriate historical moment it inspired.

The distinctiveness of the specifically *metaphysical* revolution wrought by St. Thomas was perhaps one of the most effective channels for the subversive Spirit of freedom and creativity to stir the waters of the faith of Christendom. That atheism and secularism have been the excesses under whose sign man has, if not once for all come of age, at least entered his childhood's end, is an unfortunate accident—but one which, like all fortuitous mishaps, can be redeemed and, in some way, turned to good account. When Christian philosophers begin to tell people, as St. Thomas did, that they exist in their own right, and give them the premises from which they will in time deduce that they, too, are creators, and that they have a decisive role to play—for better or for worse—in the shaping of themselves, and that it is better to have creatively attempted something and failed than never to have created anything at all, one has to expect that some people— perhaps even most people for a while—will not know just what to do with their discovery and will not quite manage themselves well. But *ars essendi longa, vita hominis brevis.* A little atheistic wild oats, a little experimental apostasy, may not be such a bad thing in the end, if only the Christian world learns to profit, even from them.

No doubt, scepticism, solipsism, atheism and apostasy are not desirable in themselves. Insofar as the floodgates of these were opened by Descartes, the adverse judgment upon him by later Catholic philosophers seems to me valid. But this hardly means that the history of philosophy is truthfully divided into the age of Thomistic sheep and Cartesian goats. It is not true that

"Descartes' continuity with scholasticism . . . is . . . [only] a *material* continuity" and that "in the order of *formal* and decisive characteristics he breaks with it, completely reversing its movement of thought." [65] I would say: on the contrary, the continuity of philosophy from St. Thomas to Descartes (and, of

[65] Jacques Maritain, *The Dream of Descartes,* (New York, 1944), p. 166. Gilson, likewise, since his earliest philosophical days has been of the opinion that "Descartes . . . vainly tried to solve, by means of his own famous method, philosophical problems whose only correct position and solution were inseparable from the method of St. Thomas Aquinas. In other words . . . I discovered that the only context in which the metaphysical conclusions of Descartes made sense was the metaphysics of Saint Thomas Aquinas. [Para.] . . . Since (however, it had become clear to me that, technically speaking, the metaphysics of Descartes had largely been a clumsy overhauling of scholastic metaphysics, I decided to learn metaphysics from those who had really known it, namely, [the] Schoolmen. . . . The chaotic condition of contemporary philosophy, with the ensuing moral, social, political and pedagogical chaos, is not due to any lack of philosophical insight among modern thinkers; it simply follows from the fact that we have lost our way because we have lost the knowledge of some fundamental principles which, since they are true, are the only ones on which, today as well as in Plato's own day, any philosophical knowledge worthy of the name can possibly be established. . . . The great curse of modern philosophy is the almost universally prevailing rebellion against intellectual self-discipline. Where loose thinking obtains, truth cannot possibly be grasped, whence the conclusion naturally follows that there is no truth," *God and Philosophy,* (New Haven, 1941), pp. xiii-xv.

Elsewhere Gilson has explained that the philosophy of Descartes emerged in a historical situation characterized by its abandonment of the teaching of St. Thomas: "during the Middle Ages, the exact place of philosophical speculation had been clearly defined by St. Thomas Aquinas; nothing, however, could have obliged his successors to stay there; they left it of their own accord, and they were quite free to do so, but once this had been done, they were no longer free to keep philosophy from entering upon the road to scepticism. The Renaissance at last arrived there. But man is not naturally a doubting animal; when his own folly condemns him to live in uncertainty concerning the highest and most vital of all problems, he can put up with it for a certain time; but he will soon remember that the problems are still there clamouring for solutions. Usually a young hero then arises who decides that the whole business has to be done

207

course, beyond, to our own day), is of the order of formal and decisive characteristics. The only continuity with St. Thomas and with Scholasticism that was lost by post-Cartesian philosophy, (and even that only to a degree), was material. For after Descartes every one in the Western world to our own day has philosophized in an environment whose origin in the Christian philosophy of St. Thomas is well nigh forgotten, but which remains nevertheless, with both its tares and its patrimony, an invisible spirit haunting the unconsciousness of an apostate Christian philosophical mind.

But if we can trace to St. Thomas' metaphysical creativity the introduction of the conditions which led to the problematization of knowledge, we can also trace to the same wellspring the conditions which led to the possibility of transcending the problem by transcending the classical concept of knowledge. St. Thomas' doctrine, as I have stressed, took advantage of the reflexivity of knowledge, if only slightly and haltingly. The positive gain of the last one hundred years of philosophy can be summed up in its having learned to take advantage, with ever increasing consistency and consciousness, of the reflexivity of human consciousness, arriving in the end at the conclusion that the mind is indeed essentially definable in terms of the presence of the self to itself. And this is a truth the rudiments of which were first taught to philosophy by none other than St. Thomas Aquinas himself.

---

all over again, like Descartes; he may eventually start his experiment by the same blunder that had brought on both scepticism and his own struggle to get out of it, like Descartes; so that the same old cycle will have to revolve in the same old way until philosophers are willing to learn from experience what is the true nature of philosophy," *The Unity of Philosophical Experience*, (New York, 1948), pp. 120–121.

4.

The Restoration of the
Foundations of Belief

In order to convey the interpretation of the history of Christian
consciousness as a continuous and logical development, without
breaks or radical discontinuities, (whether these should have been
introduced by natural evils or by human perversities or by intellectual failures or mistakes), I have had frequent recourse to
graphic, well-tried, easy—but thoroughly inadequate metaphors.
I have unhesitatingly referred to philosophical doctrines, to human thought, to moments of human consciousness, to realities
of human existence, to processes of understanding, to the physi-
ologies of human intellectual and affective life, as if they were
so many manipulable building blocks of knowledge, as if they
amounted to so many spiritual atoms or teaspoonfuls of truth
which are parts of a whole and can be put together to constitute
a whole. And thus I have spoken of the *foundations* of belief, and
of their *erosion,* leading to their *breakdown* and *unserviceability*
for the purpose of *erecting* upon them Christian faith, suggesting
that their *restoration* or even their *reconstruction* be undertaken,
in order to *build* upon them the new *structures* of belief.

It is now time, however, to avow that these analogies are
radically and essentially misleading insofar as they may revert to

the implication that human consciousness, including philosophical and religious consciousness, is the grasping of a reality which
"in-itself" lies outside man and is subsequently reflected inwardly
by him. At least, such a view would underlie every interpretation
of my imagery in the sense that any development of human consciousness, such as Christians might undertake in relation to
their faith, is a recasting, resetting or rebuilding of the bases of
belief in a *second, positive stage,* essentially distinct from and
indeed opposite to, the *first, negative moment* of the critical,
philosophical and theological process. But this would be
like supposing that adulthood, say, begins when the destruction
of childhood has ended, or that the construction of human nature
began only at the moment when that of his ape-like ancestors
reached its final decomposition. Yet, one of the most important
ways in which the Western mind has begun to dehellenize itself
has been precisely in its "recasting" the concept of *becoming,*
honouring more faithfully and critically than at any previous time
the observable facts, finally concluding against Plato and Aristotle
that change is not "from opposite" [1] to opposite and that it is
not "the act of that which is in potency insofar as it is in
potency." [2]

The anabolic and catabolic moments of any vital process are
not really distinct. Becoming is not the result of a process of
generation which begins as corruption ends. If we can find no
discrete boundary between the terms of any process of develop-

---

[1] "In general everything that admits of generation is generated in this
way and no other—opposites from opposites, wherever there is an opposite . . . It is a necessary law that everything which has an opposite
is generated from that opposite and from no other source," Plato,
Phaedo, 70E.

[2] Aristotle, *Physics,* III, 1 (201 a 10).

ment, the reason is not that we cannot observe empirically what is undoubtedly intelligibly true; on the contrary, the reason is that our conceptualization of the processes of nature now finds it impossible to take leave from the empirically given facts. Likewise, if any evolutionary process reveals the production of a novel form, the conclusion to be drawn is not that the novelty must somehow be reducible to an antecedent potency but, on the contrary, that the evolutionary process is creative of irreducible forms. Thus, from one viewpoint it could be said that St. Thomas Aquinas introduced into the Christian world certain philosophical forces which, in one sense, spelled the "dissolution," the "decay" of the old "foundations" of belief but which, at one and the same time can be said, from another viewpoint, to have provided the principles by which the new could be "rebuilt." For destruction and construction are, where human consciousness is concerned, strictly relative terms. The history of the consciousness of Western Christendom since St. Thomas is the history of *both* the destruction of the traditional forms of Christian belief and the reconstruction of the possibility of the new. One and the same process may be viewed from two quite different, indeed, opposite, viewpoints—both of which are true.

The breakdown of the foundations of Christian belief is only a relative breakdown. Nevertheless the reconstruction of belief has remained, so far, largely a possibility. The problem of contemporary progressive Catholic thought is, as I have suggested above, precisely the problem of whether and how to bring about the self-reconstruction of Catholic belief. This has remained so far largely a mere possibility because of the cultural schizophrenia already noted, which has divorced the Christian belief from the typical modes of contemporary experience, since both believers and non-believers have judged that belief was contingent upon the mode of experience for which traditional thought provided uniquely the philosophical foundations: the only difference between Christian believer and Christian non-believer in this respect is that the former chooses belief in preference to the mode of experience for which contemporary thought provides philosophical foundations, whereas the latter chooses the other way about.

In short, after having stressed the "destructive" aspect of St. Thomas's thought, I will now dwell on its "constructive" possibilities, how these have been in part actualized, mostly by atheists, and how they may yet be more fully realized by the believers' reconstruction of belief. But I am anxious to leave no openings for possible misinterpretation on this point. I would not for a moment wish to suggest that St. Thomas discovered some perennial truth which has been forgotten or allowed to lie fallow, and which must now be recovered and put to work, or even explicitated, applied or otherwise exploited by those who first take care to apprentice themselves to his guild. The doctrine of St. Thomas, true enough as it was, is dead. But it is not dead as a doornail. It is dead as a venerable ancestor is dead, who begat an existence which begat ours in turn, and to whom we owe our consciousness and life. Ancestors are to be neither cursed and forgotten, nor left unburied and mummified in case they may suddenly find it possible to come back to the world. They are to be gratefully and regretfully buried; they are to be truthfully and honourably remembered, and their truth and virtue is to be perpetuated, not in the vain attempt to resuscitate them, but in the conscious exercise of our own descendant but independent life.

Hence, when I say I shall now deal with St. Thomas' "constructive" side, I mean that I shall be dealing with one and the same doctrine as before, namely, the doctrine of the existential contingency of empirically given being as such—that is, as revealed by its very empirical givenness, as revealed by the observation of the empirical facts. But I shall now attempt to explain, not how this doctrine "eroded" and finally brought about the (relative) "ruin" of the traditional foundations of Christian belief, but how *this very doctrine* is the principle on which new philosophical foundations of belief have been "erected"—at least up to a point. I say, up to a point, because, as they now stand, they have yet had only *un*-belief erected upon them. To explain and support this thesis I must once again return to Greek philosophy in order to complement the epistemological remarks I have previously made.

NECESSARY REALITY AND COGNITIVE LIFE

As I have suggested, Greek philosophy was marked from the outset by a certain *religious* belief, an attitude towards reality which is quite clearly connected with the Greek (as well as more primitive) religious experience. According to this faith, the proper characteristic of the world of reality is its inexorable quality, which renders inevitable the course of natural and human events. To call it inexorable may seem like speaking of it in relation to man. Yet, if reality is truly inexorable, can it be understood to be so only in relation to man? Surely not. For if reality is inexorable, conforming not to our wishes or entreaties, heedless of whatever counter-suggestions man might make to it, then reality is such as it is because it is inexorable *in itself*. To say that it is inexorable, then, is to say that it pays no attention to man and that it is, therefore, necessary by its own intrinsic nature. In other words, reality as such is self-necessitation. Man may have the ability to *want* reality to be other than it is, but he must in the first place discover within himself the ability to *recognize* reality for the unswerving Fate it actually is. This is the root of the Greeks' pagan belief.

It could scarcely be suggested that to reject the belief that gives Greek epistemology its typical orientation and form, (a belief which the Christian tradition has always consciously dissented from, even when the logic of its Hellenic philosophical form has pressed it, above all in its real everyday life, to adopt), is to claim that the basis of Greek epistemology is a figment of the Greek imagination, an error which leads man's evolving philosophical consciousness astray and is, therefore, best forgotten and dispelled. The Greek belief in the necessary nature of reality may be mistaken; if so, it may have turned the Greek philosophical enterprise into a fundamental misinterpretation. Nonetheless, every philosophical endeavour to understand anything, no matter how baselessly and gratuitously conceived, no matter how misguided by man's prior assumptions and decisive self-dispositions, rest upon—rather, conceptualizes, and hence relates man to—the facts of reality. Thus, the philosophical mind may, as it were, misuse the facts, or use them less wisely than it might perhaps have done; but the fact that the facts have been used at all, that they have been brought to human attention, that meaning has been created out of them—this is a positive gain on which later intellectual gains will directly depend.

The Greeks invented philosophy. This means: they awoke

in the human intellect the sense of empirical reason, they taught man to take account of his experience in order to understand the world and himself. In this sense, Greek philosophy is essentially empirical. *A fortiori,* Greek epistemology is likewise empirical, that is, it is the attempt empirically to understand experience itself. This is why the contrast frequently made between the rationalism of Plato and the empiricism of Aristotle is, though legitimate so long as the terms are used in a strictly relative sense, not very useful and, indeed, somewhat misleading, if these categories are thought to designate characteristics of these philosophers in themselves.

Let us recall that an essential part of the Socratic method is the appeal to experience. Almost every argument in Plato's *Dialogues* takes its departure from its recall of certain facts, directing Socrates' listener to make certain observations about himself. Even when the topic of discussion is human experience itself, as it so frequently is, Plato's procedure remains exactly the same.

In Plato's understanding of it, knowledge in the most proper (if not also the only truly valid) sense of the term, namely, ἐπιστήμη, does not relate man to objects which pertain to the level of reality in which he abides. Therefore, knowledge in this strict sense does not, properly speaking, take place either in this world or during man's lifetime. This is why philosophical understanding, which is the closest approximation to ἐπιστήμη in this world and in our lifetime, is fittingly called, according to Socrates, a "rehearsing . . . for dying and death." [3] But if we can so much as conceive or suspect the experience of ἐπιστήμη, the reason is only that reflection, (most especially philosophical reflection), may produce a recollection, ἀνάμνησις, of the knowl-

[3] Plato, *Phaedo,* 64A.

edge once had by the soul when it had been able to contemplate its proper objects, because at that time it abided at the same level of reality at which they could be found. It would be difficult, thus, to find an epistemology in which knowledge is further removed from experience than in this. Nevertheless, Plato's theory of knowledge is empirically grounded. This is true in a twofold way.

First, Plato's arguments, even in this matter, appealed to common experience. Consider, says Plato in one of his best known arguments, "such a thing as equality." [4] This "form" or "idea" [5] is made use of in mathematics in a special way, though to some extent it is part of the experience of everyday life. We are all acquainted with "equality." Yet, this experience could not be the result of acquaintance with any concrete instance of "equals" in the world of our everyday experience and life. For "equality" cannot mean, of course, "more-or-less-like-ness." It can only mean,

[4] *Ibid.,* 74A.

[5] *Form* and *idea* have each two distinct senses in Plato, of which the more common, namely, a reality which is self-identical and therefore not found in the empirical world, is a technical, derived sense of these terms. The more primitive, non-technical sense is: that which is experienced, contemplated, or seen, that which one is acquainted with or aware of. Evidently, there is a certain opposition between these two usages, for the very good reason that Plato was straining and extending the use "of old linguistic material," in the perfectly normal "crushingly despotic" fashion (see above, p. 134) which precedes the birth of new concepts. Beginning with "form" or "idea" as that which is (empirically) seen, Plato deduced that behind this appearance there was a real "form" or "idea" which was not (empirically) seen. Thus, the same term must be used, following the typically Greek dialectical method, to signify consequently the opposite of what it meant originally. Even the very terminology used by Plato's most distinctively "idealistic" and "aprioristic" doctrine, namely, the doctrine of the "Forms," reveals its empirical basis in the pedestrian Greek meaning of "form."

"precisely the same as" or "self-same" (αὐτὸ τὸ ἴσον); the expression "more or less equal," if strictly taken, would be a contradiction in terms. Yet, do we find any actual reality in the world which is "precisely the same as" another, in even the slightest respect? No, we do not. Nor do we find anything which is self-identical, since all things given in experience are known to change. Thus, the idea of equality is not gained by acquaintance with the reality present in this world. But we are only in this world; we no longer are, (if ever we were), in the world where "equality itself," (or "the self-same") was available for contemplation. If so, Plato concludes, "recollection" is brought about by common, ordinary experiences: "was it not from seeing [approximately] equal sticks or stones or other [so-called] equal objects that we got the notion of [absolute] equality, although it is something quite distinct from them?"[6] The answer, of course, is yes. Plato's epistemological and metaphysical doctrine is, in the

---

[6] *Phaedo*, 74 B. My interpolation may be found objectionable, on the grounds that it may render Plato self-contradictory: if "equality" is "precisely the same as" or "self-same" (αὐτὸ τὸ ἴσον) then there cannot be a "more or less equal." Therefore, Plato would never say, or at any rate should not say, that "equal sticks or stones" are in reality "approximately equal." However, this interpolation does not render Plato more "self-contradictory" (if self-contradiction can be "more or less") than he already was. For his contention is precisely that "equal sticks or stones" are *not really equal,* if by "equality" we mean "equality, period." Hence, appearances are "not really real." But since we evidently think of "the real," and "the really real," or of "being," and "what truly is," it follows that there must be an absolute reality in relation to which appearances can be relative. This is but another instance of the same dialectical procedure I mentioned above, (note 5), which supports my assertion concerning the empirical basis of any possible past or future philosophy, however aprioristic and rationalistic its conclusions may be. To rise above the empirical grounds of human experience it is necessary first to stand on empirical grounds.

217

end, nothing but an interpretation of the facts of experience, an interpretation which attempts to account for that which is given in experience as such.

But Plato also depends on experience—and, specifically, his account of the nature of experience depends upon the facts of experience—in another, yet more fundamental way. Plato relies upon experience not only because he appeals to ordinary experience in order to show that knowledge in the proper sense is altogether other than ordinary experience. He quite consciously assumes [7] ordinary experience as the only form of immediate experience, as the only form of experience with which we are directly acquainted, on the basis of which ἐπιστήμη could be conceived at all. In other words, Plato assumes ordinary human experience as the only form of experience which can be itself the object of (reflexive) experience. Ordinary, everyday knowledge is the only human experience *in relation to which* it is possible to conceive the higher, truer form of knowledge which is not the approximate form of knowledge but knowledge "precisely the same as" itself. To argue, as Plato does, that "before we began to see and hear . . . we must have somewhere acquired the knowledge that there is such a thing as absolute equality," [8] is not to argue from what we knew "before" to what we know now; it

---

[7] It is fairly certain that Plato must have been conscious of this assumption. This is obscured by translation. But in Greek the words "idea" (ἰδέα), "form" (εἶδος, literally, "that which is seen"), "to see" (ὁρᾶν, aorist εἶδον), and "to know" (in the sense of "to be acquainted with," εἰδέναι, past part. εἰδός) are quite obviously related. (Contrast "to know" εἰδέναι, with "to know," in the sense of "to be certain that," πιστεύειν). In Latin the relation among these terms is paralled by *spectare*, "to see," and *species*, with the twofold meaning of "form" and "idea," ("form" as in *genus et species*; "idea" as in *species intelligibilis*).

[8] *Phaedo*, 75 B.

is not an argument *a priori*. On the contrary, it is to reason from the experience we now have, an experience we subject to empirical analysis *here and now,* to a knowledge—that is, to some sort of experience—which took place elsewhere and at another time.

It is, of course, consistent with the doctrine of the Forms to suppose, as Plato does, that to understand understanding, to know knowledge, (in the "real" sense of both "to know" and "knowledge,") it is necessary to know its ideal form, to know "knowledge itself" by an act of knowledge which is "knowing itself" (as Aristotle would later put it).[9] Plato was only the first of many philosophers who have attempted to understand the nature of immediate experience by analyzing its ideal form or its most perfect instance, (e.g., science), rather than the other way about. There is, thus, a profound inconsistency between Plato's theory of knowledge and the concept of knowledge implicit in his own foregoing empirical procedure. For, in the last analysis, the supra-empirical knowledge which he took as representing what knowledge *really* was, was conceived and described by him in strict relation to everyday experience. Plato's very attempt to demonstrate that knowledge properly so-called was other than experience, aessumed *in actu exercitu* precisely the opposite, namely, that common experience was the paradigm on which all knowledge must be conceived. This is a fact which a philosopher can, for his own reasons, deny—but a fact which no philosopher can but assume in order to philosophize. In this sense, therefore,

[9] "Therefore it must be of itself that the divine thought thinks . . . and its thinking is a thinking on thinking. . . . Since, then, thought and the object of thought are not different in the case of things that have not matter, the divine thought and its object will be the same, i.e. the thinking will be one with the object of its thought," *Metaphysics,* XII, 9 (1074 b 33–34; 1075 a 4–5).

it may be stated that *every* epistemological inquiry is a reflective analysis of experience. But not every epistemological analysis is aware that it is a reflexive analysis of experience: the philosophical story that is spun thereby is twenty-five centuries long.

To the degree that Aristotle became conscious of Plato's inconsistency, (or, at any event, of the fact that experience is the paradigm of knowledge), he was bound to revise the epistemology of Plato—though to the degree that he retained Plato's assumptions, his revision was bound to be incomplete. Aristotle's doctrines, that the mind is like "a writing tablet on which as yet nothing actually stands written" [10] prior to experience (leading directly to his novel psychology of abstraction), and that "no one can learn or understand anything in the absence of sense," [11] (leading directly to his novel psychology of sensation), are among the most distinctive aspects of his epistemological empiricism. On their account Aristotle is remembered as an empiricist, despite, the essential similarity of his concept of empirical knowledge to Plato's, and despite the basis of this concept upon the same empirical foundation on which Plato developed his philosophical thought.

COGNITIVE EXPERIENCE
AND CONSCIOUS REFLECTION

When St. Thomas based his doctrine of the existential contingency of empirically given being upon the empirical basis of an empirical analysis of knowledge he did, therefore, nothing

[10] *De Anima*, III, 4 (430 a 1).
[11] *De Anima*, III, 7 (432 a 6).

which, in a sense, had not been previously done. He did, in fact, nothing else than what any philosopher can ever do (at least at the current stage of human development), namely, to understand understanding by reflecting upon it. On the other hand, St. Thomas' analysis of empirically given being as such was not coupled with the assumption that being as such is in every respect necessary. This permitted him to support philosophically his belief in the contingency of being (a contingency, however, which he conceptualized specifically as existential, thus leaving himself free to retain the view that being was essentially necessary). Yet, the same assumption rendered self-contradictory and impossible the concept of knowledge as the intentional possession of an extramental reality. This is precisely why it served to focus philosophical attention on the fundamentally empirical nature of every enquiry into the nature of experience: it made philosophy conscious for the first time of that which philosophy had always done since its invention.

But, of course, there is a wide difference between being conscious, as man has always been, and his becoming conscious of his own consciousness—for this is the way in which consciousness evolves, namely, by becoming what it already is. Likewise, there is a very important difference between the philosophical reflection upon empirically given being as such, and the philosophical reflection which knows itself to be grounded upon an analysis of empirically given being as such. For the latter is the beginning of man's awareness that he is present to himself, not because he has made actual a potency for knowing his own knowledge, but because he has begun to realize that he has *always been* present to himself (that is, for as long as he has been human), and that therefore his nature as conscious is to be present to himself. The better to understand this we must go back for a moment.

Most philosophers, from Parmenides to Hegel, who have shared the classical concept of knowledge, have been well aware that man knows himself, and that he knows himself to be a knower, and that he knows himself only because he is a knower. These, too, are empirical facts concerning experience, and no philosopher can easily avoid them. But to share the traditional concept of experience is *ipso facto* to conceptualize man's awareness of himself as the *result* of an act of knowledge which bears upon a *prior* act of knowledge. Probably few Thomists have yielded on this point as far as has Maritain, for whom the reflexive character of knowledge is "implicit" and "preconcious" in the consciousness of being. Yet, even Maritain retains unaltered the essentials of this view:

Since the intellect bears in the first place neither on itself, nor on the *ego,* but on *being,* then the very first evidence (I mean first in the order of nature, I am not talking about the chronological order, in which, what is first in itself is often only implicit), the evidence that is *first in itself* for the intellect, is that of the principle of identity 'discovered' in the intellectual apprehension of being or the real.

We have said that the real in question is not necessarily of the actual (existential) order, even if the intellect does first grasp the principle of identity as incarnate in some example of sensible existence. Of itself that principle bears upon the whole range of being and first of all on the order of essences, on *the possible real*. At the same time, we have said that in the intelligible order itself a certain *actual reality* is given to the intellect in this first act of perception and judgment, namely, from the side of the subject: the existence of the thinking subject itself. However, it is given only in an implicit, preconscious way and in initial act, and not yet as the object of explicit knowledge.

Thus, the intellect embraces at one and the same time, in its own proper sphere, both the possible real (the object 'every being . . .' set

222

before the mind and grasped by it and signified in the enunciation of the principle of identity), and the actual real (the reality of the thinking subject, though not yet attained in final act). *Intelligible being* and *self* are given to the intellect together and from the very start. But *being* is given in the foreground and up-stage; the *self* is in the background, behind the wings as it were. It is only with the mind's second movement, in the reflex intuition that serves as the starting point for critique, that it moves to the front of the stage.[12]

Yet, for all of his concession to the intellect's embracing "at one and the same time . . . *intelligible being* and *self*," Maritain failed to learn the lesson that the history of epistemology actually teaches. And what it teaches is not that knowledge bears first of all upon the possible reality of being and, in one and the same act, albeit, implicitly, upon the actual reality of the self. For this retains the idea that man's awareness of himself requires a "second act," a "final act" which is to be distinguished from "first act" and from "initial act" as "reflex" is from "direct" knowledge. And the difficulty with retaining this idea is that it is not warranted—that it is indeed contradicted—by the facts of experience itself, as they may be ascertained by empirical reflexion upon experience itself. But it took a great deal of philosophical effort and a very long intellectual process to realize this, a process the beginning of which can first be discerned in the transition from Aquinas to Decartes.

I have already suggested the reasons why the Cartesian problem was actually created by the conditions set by St. Thomas, and why the doctrine of Decartes took advantage of those conditions. What I should stress now is that the Cartesian *cogito* is but an expression of those conditions. It is a statement of what "I can

[12] Maritain, *Les Degrés du Savoir,* pp. 149–150.

know" and what I can "be ignorant" of. Of course, since Descartes assumed the same concept of knowledge as St. Thomas did, and the same concept of the self as an object of knowledge which as such is no different from any other (it is simply a different sort of substance), it did follow logically that the knower could not know anything other than himself except because of some guarantee extrinsic to knowledge itself. The difficulties experienced by post-Cartesian philosophy have been correctly attributed by Christian philosophical thinkers to the use of the *cogito* as the original philosophical certitude. Yet, it is significant that even those who have adhered to the strictest realism and who have (with undoubted correctness) doubted the viability of every theory of knowledge which proceeds from the Cartesian *cogito* or its equivalent, and who have decried the consequences of intellectual uses to which it has been put, have in no case denied the validity of the Cartesian observation that no one who is able to think, *and who is aware of it,* can possible doubt his own existence.

As is frequently noted in histories of modern Western philosophy, the Cartesian *cogito* did imprison man within his own subjectivity, from which the efforts of the British empiricists did not succeed in liberating him. And neither Kant's nor Hegel's novel versions of the *cogito* did, for all their ingenuity, accomplish the feat more successfully—though it is only fair, on the other hand, to note that their contributions did serve to bring philosophy ever closer to a realization of the new turn it should take. But the Cartesian *cogito,* and even more Kant's reworking of it as the *Ich denke* which must "accompany all my representations" [13] and Hegel's as the for-itselfness of Spirit,[14] did constrain

[13] *Critique of Pure Reason,* B 132.

224

the philosophical tradition of the last one hundred years, beginning with Kierkegaard and Marx and leading to Dewey, Husserl, Heidegger and Sartre, to consider anew the meaning of the empirical fact that consciousness is self-positing: that whether or not extramental things exist, the mind itself cannot know itself except as existing, and that, thus, consciousness is not definable in abstraction from its subjectivity, or in abstraction from the self which is given *in* it and *to* it. But to reconsider this was, in effect, first, to put in doubt the adequacy of the very *concept* of knowledge which went back to the Greeks, and, second, to redefine knowledge on a *consciously* empirical basis.[15]

---

[14] "Spirit . . . may be defined as that which has its centre in itself. . . . It exists *in* and *with itself*. . . . Spirit is *self-contained existence*. . . . This self-contained existence of Spirit is none other than self-consciousness—consciousness of one's own being. Two things must be distinguished in consciousness; first, the fact *that I know*; secondly, *what I know*. In *self* consciousness these are merged into one; for Spirit *knows itself*," *Introduction to the Philosophy of History*, (in J. Lowenberg, ed., *Hegel Selecitons*, New York, 1929, pp. 359-360. Cf. *Phenomenology of Mind*, Preface, 5-6.

[15] John Dewey was one of the first philosophers to have suggested that the reconceptualization of knowledge (cf. *Reconstruction in Philosophy*, New York, 1920, Chapters IV and V) implied a departure from the Greek roots of Western philosophy and in particular the transcendence of the Greek "spectator theory of knowledge," that is, "the theory of knowledge . . . modeled after what was supposed to take place in the act of vision," *The Quest for Certainty*, p. 23. Many philosophers simply do not take much interest in locating their own thought within the development of the history of philosophy. However, Heidegger's historical interpretation of his own thought is topsy-turvy: he insists that he is simply recovering the earliest Greek thought, which had been forgotten ever since Plato and Aristotle (and, later, Christianity) disfigured its meaning and hid it from the sight of man. I have suggested some adverse criticism of the retrojective approach to the reading of history, whether by Heidegger or by Gilson, in "Neo-Thomism and the continuity of philosophical experience," in Gregory Baum (ed.), *The Future of Belief Debate*, (New York, 1967), pp. 211-229.

If the classical concept of knowledge has been so difficult to transcend, even after the Cartesian problem pressed philosophy to overcome it, part of the reason is its utter self-consistency once its value is conceptualized as truth, that is, as the adequation of mind to being. For this renders knowledge, the process whereby truth is had, and truth, the consequence of knowledge, mutually supporting and mutually dependent. Thus, the classical concept of knowledge cannot be doubted without doubting the only possible doctrine of truth, and the classical concept of truth cannot be doubted without doubting the only possible doctrine of knowledge.

But perhaps a yet more fundamental reason for the slow awakening of epistemology to its meta-Hellenic possibilities was that the classical concept of knowledge appears to impose itself upon philosophical reflection by the sheer weight of its *empirical* obviousness. It seems grounded upon common sense, upon common, primary and undeniable facts which anyone can experience for himself; facts which everyone has indeed always known or will infallibly realize as soon as his attention is directed to them; facts which cannot be reasonably denied and which are to be affirmed at least implicitly by anyone who, in the face of evidence, foolishly thought to deny them. The classical concept of knowledge, in other words, appears to be self-evident. It is, apparently, implicit in any man's reflection upon knowledge itself.

The empirical fact on the basis of which the classical concept of knowledge can be reflexively justified by classical epistemologists is the same empirical fact that makes the classical concept of knowledge self-evident: the apparently self-justifying quality of the classical concept of knowledge is not due to any logically fallacious circularity on the part of the philosophers, but to the fact that the classical concept of knowledge is grounded

226

upon an empirical fact which is clearly undeniable and primary. This empirical fact, this primary, undeniable and universally accessible observation, is the irreducible opposition between that being which is oneself, the *knower,* and that being which is not oneself, the *known.* As I have already suggested in the previous chapter, to be conscious is to think, or to be able to think, something like: "there it is; here I am." No spatial connotation is intended by these prepositions. We might as well say: "it is it, not I," or "I am I, not it." Nor is the emphasis to be placed on whether the priority of the meaning of the thought is on the *I* which is *not-it,* or on the *it* which is *not-I.* Nor does the most basic element of human consciousness imply any understanding of what *I* am, any more than it necessarily implies any understanding of what *it* is. I might not be able to tell whether that hand there, whose connection or lack of connection with *me* is somehow hidden from sight and from sensation, is or is not part of *me;* but what is always clear is that *it,* whether it be really my hand or someone else's, is essentially distinct from *my act* of knowing it. Thus, I may have to learn experimentally what *I* am, and precisely where *my body* ends and *other bodies* begin. But what I do not need to learn through trial and error, what I do not need to be taught, and what indeed I cannot be taught, because it is an essential part of consciousness which conditions every instance of it, is that the act itself is other than its object.[16]

This is why it makes no essential difference whether we con-

---

[16] I am not distinguishing here between *object* and *thing.* I am willing to grant to realists that "philosophical reflexion has no need to reconstitute the *thing,* starting from the *object,* as a necessary hypothesis, nor to suppress the *thing* as a superfluous or even self-contradictory hypothesis. It has rather to observe that the *thing* is given with and by the object [of knowledge], and that it is indeed absurd to want to separate them," *Les Degrés du Savoir,* pp. 180–181.

sider acts of knowing in which that which is known is a thing other than myself, or acts of knowing in which that which is known is myself. In either event, it remains true that knowledge does in every instance imply an opposition between the knower as such, "the knower in act," and the known as such, "the known in act"—even when the known is materially the same as the knower. Thus, the following proposition, which describes the basic empirical fact on which the traditional epistemologies depend, applies to both the knowledge of an-other which is in every respect other-than-I, an object substantially other-than-I, and to the knowledge of an-other which is substantially myself, and it applies indifferently to direct and to reflexive knowledge: the knower as such is other than, and indeed as a being in itself it is essentially separate from, the known as such, which is in its turn an other-than-him. In other words, the universe which knowledge reveals is to be described in terms of a dichotomy between the self and the world.

I have granted that this fact is truly primary and undeniable. I have, therefore, no intention of denying it or reason for wishing to do so. On the contrary, I will return to it in a moment, to stress it as the very first truth of a more adequate epistemology than any of the traditional ones. But first I would point out that it is extremely easy to interpret the foregoing empirical observation as implying three further positions which classical epistemologists have, indeed, with but few exceptions, commonly held.

The *first* I have already alluded to. It is the view that self-consciousness does not coincide with (other) consciousness, and that therefore self-consciousness is essentially reflexive, (I mean, that it must re-turn upon itself in order to know itself). In this view the act of knowing is always the act of knowing an-other, even when the other is materially oneself; thus, in this perspective knowledge cannot *formaliter loquendo* attain itself except reflexively. For the intellect is "measured by a thing, by an ontological 'for itself' that exists apart from it (by an existence less noble than that of knowledge), and to which the intellect has to unite itself by a submissive effort, without being able ever to exhaust it." [17] To know is to perfect oneself by acquiring the perfection of the other,[18] but this perfection need not be found in an-other which is in itself and as actually existing, actually other than oneself. For the knower is himself a being, and is what he is prior to his being a knower; he is, therefore, as much an object of knowledge (even an object of his own knowledge) as any other being actually found in the world. But to acquire what amounts to nothing other than his own perfection, but by way of knowledge, (which, as Maritain says, is nobler than that of simply being), implies that the distinction between the self and the knower pertains essentially to knowledge. Therefore, according to this view, knowledge, in order to fulfil its proper perfection, always attains to an-other, and formally speaking it can attain *to nothing but an-other*. Though the knower may be, *materialiter loquendo,* the same as the known, this is not true of the knower as such. We must, therefore, say that even in the case of self-consciousness the act or knowledge does not attain to itself except by a *re-flexion* upon itself.

This is without question the doctrine of St. Thomas, who alleges two reasons why this should be so: first, the nature of the mind as an object of knowledge and, second, the nature of the very act of knowledge of the human mind.

---

[17] *Ibid.,* p. 210.
[18] Cf. St. Thomas, *De Veritate,* II, 2.

The nature of the mind makes it impossible for it to know itself without having to apply itself to a prior act of knowledge by means of a second act of knowledge, because

in its essence the human mind is potentially understanding. Hence, it has in itself the power to understand, but not to be understood except insofar as it is made actual. . . . Therefore, the intellect knows itself not by its essence, but by its act . . . as when Socrates or Plato perceives that he has an intellectual soul because he perceives that he understands.[19]

But how does man perceive that he understands? "The mere presence of the mind is sufficient for [this]; since the mind itself is the principle of action whereby it perceives itself, it is said to know itself by its own presence." [20] However, is this doctrine to be interpreted in the sense that the mind's presence to itself in its original act of knowledge suffices for the mind to perceive that it understands? Not at all; it means, as a study of the context of St. Thomas' remark amply shows, only that no "careful and subtle enquiry" is required by the mind in order to have some awareness of itself. It means that if the mind is to know (e.g. philosophically) the *nature* of the mind, a great deal more is required of it than its simple presence in reality as active and, thus, as automatically able to reflect upon itself, without having to exercise itself in a more profound or skillful manner than it had already been able to do when it had actual knowledge of other things; on the other hand, simply to be aware of itself it needs only to be and be active.

This interpretation is confirmed by a consideration of the nature of the act of knowledge:

[19] *ST*, I, 87, 1.
[20] *Ibid.*

the human intellect . . . is not its own act of understanding; nor is its own essence the first object of its act of understanding; rather, this object [of its first act of understanding] is the nature of a material thing. Therefore, that which is first known by the human intellect is an object of this kind, and that which is known secondarily is the act by which that object is known. And through the act the intellect itself is known, the perfection of which is this act of understanding.[21]

If any shadow of a doubt remained, St. Thomas' further remark, spelling out the precise nature of the reflexivity of consciousness, should dispel it once for all:

the human intellect's act of understanding is not the act and perfection of the material nature that is understood [by it in its act of direct knowledge], as if [it were true that] the nature of the material thing [understood by the direct act of knowledge] and the act of understanding [that object of direct knowledge] could be understood by one [and the same] act, in the same way as a thing and its perfection are understood by one [and the same] act [of the intellect]. Thus, the act whereby the intellect understands a stone is other than the act by which it understands that it understands a stone, and so on.[22]

The same doctrine, conversely put, is that self-consciousness is possible only insofar as the subject objectifies itself, so that the subjectivity of consciousness does not mark it off from its more primary objectivity as being. As Maritain says,

I know myself as subject by consciousness and reflexivity, but my substance is obscure to me. . . . When a man is awake to the intuition of being he is awake at the same time to the intuition of subjectivity; he grasps, in a flash that will never be dimmed, the fact that *he is a self*, as Jean-Paul said. . . . But the intuition of subjectivity is an existential intuition which surrenders no essence to us.

[21] *ST*, I, 87, 3.
[22] *ST*, I, 87, 3, ad 2.

We know *that which* we are by our phenomena, our operations, our flow of consciousness. The more we grow accustomed to the inner life, the better we decipher the astonishing and fluid multiplicity which is thus delivered to us; the more, also, we feel that it leaves us ignorant of the essence of our self. Subjectivity as *subjectivity* is inconceptualisable; it is an unknowable abyss. It is unknowable by the mode of notion, concept or representation, or by any mode of any science whatever—introspection, psychology or philosophy. How could it be otherwise, seeing that every reality known through a concept, a notion, or a representation is known as object and not as subject? Subjectivity as such escapes by definition from that which we know about ourselves by means of notions.[23]

[23] *Existence and the Existent,* pp. 68–70. Maritain, who develops Thomism further than most other Thomists do regarding this question, adds (p. 70) that, nevertheless, subjectivity "is known in a way, or rather in certain ways" which he then proceeds to enumerate. But in the end he admits that "in none of these instances is the knowledge of subjectivity as subjectivity, however real it be, a knowledge by mode of knowledge," (p. 71). There are intimations of subjectivity, as it were, but since consciousness cannot be present to itself in and through the very act by which it is present to another, these intimations come to nothing in the end. Maritain's last word on the subject is that, in the final analysis, only God knows the subject as such: "I am present to Him in my subjectivity itself; He has no need to objectise me in order to know me. Then, and in this unique instance, man is known not as object but as subject in all the depth and all the recesses of subjectivity . . . I am not uncovered to myself. The more I know of my subjectivity, the more it remains obscure to me," (p. 77).

I should like to add that Maritain confuses the evident empirical fact that the presence of the self to itself does not uncover an essence clearly and distinctly once for all—experience rarely does, except for those philosophers who think they can know men or phoenixes without necessarily knowing whether they exist—with the interpretation that the self could not properly speaking *know* its essential self at all. I admit—indeed, I insist throughout this book—that the presence of the self to itself is future-tensional, self-creative and *eschatological: in lucem tuam* videbimus *lucem,* (*Psalms* 36). And I have no desire to suggest that the presence of the self to itself reveals the "substance" or "essence" of the soul, in the Thomistic sense of these terms—for I do not in the first place agree that there are "substances" or "essences" in the Thomistic sense of the term.

How could Maritain think otherwise, since for him the mind's reflexive awareness of its own awareness can take place only "thanks to the production of a new concept"? [24]

Second: it follows from the foregoing interpretation of the empirical fact of experience itself that the self is not merely that which is revealed to experience by the empirical facts themselves. This is why philosophers in this tradition have long assumed that the self to which the object of knowledge is opposed, is a substance in precisely the same sense as the object of knowledge is, likewise, a substance. Why, precisely, is this so? It will repay us to give close attention to the argument.

I have already said that, according to classical thought, reflection upon experience reveals that there is an opposition between the knower and the known: the one is not the other, although the other is, as such, that which faces the one—just as the one is, as such, that which relates itself to the other. It might seem, then, that knowers are definable by their opposition to being, and that being is definable by its opposition to the knower. Yet, this cannot be true, because knowers are beings, and because beings are constituted by their intrinsic intelligibility and not by their being known. Hence, the knower is, to put it precisely, a know-

---

Nevertheless, the subject knows himself as subject; he knows himself in his subjectivity. But this implies the view of consciousness and of its "reflexivity" which we are about to explore.

[24] *Les Degrés du Savoir,* p. 234. *Thanks* may not be the the the happiest expression in this context. For, as Marx and Kierkegaard first observed, in this philosophical tradition consciousness is, in effect, deemed to be self-alienating, that is, consciousness makes an-other out of itself—*fieri aliud a se* is one of John of St. Thomas' definitions of knowledge—hence, in this tradition consciousness must ultimately reject its own subjectivity, and implicitly understand itself *as a thing.*

ing *being,* and the known is a known *being.* Therefore, the opposition which is immediately revealed by reflection upon knowledge is not the opposition between the knowing being and its
object of knowledge, but between the *act* of knowledge and its
object. The fact that knowers can know themselves by re-flexion
should concern us at this point, because even in self-knowledge
there is a distinction between the act of self-knowledge and the
self of which knowledge is had. Hence, the opposition which is
immediately revealed by reflection upon knowledge is not an
ontological opposition—precisely because it is revealed by reflection.

As we shall study below, the fact that *no ontological* opposition
is revealed by reflection upon experience should give considerable
pause to anyone who had previously asserted that the basic
empirical fact of knowledge is the *entitative* opposition between
subject and object. But since, as I have suggested, philosophers
in this tradition have made use of the empirical facts without
taking sufficient account of their empirical nature, they have
found it possible to ignore (rather, they have not found it possible to notice) the obvious conclusion to which this reasoning
should lead—a conclusion which shall concern us below in
explicit detail. Instead they have drawn precisely the opposite
lesson: since the subject known by his own reflexion upon his
own experience is not made objective by its peculiar subjectivity,
it must be made subjective by its peculiar objectivity. The self
which experiences itself by re-flexion is not the objective, entitative, transcendental self; it must be merely an empirical self, an
objectification of the real self, the self-appearance of the real,
existing self which underlies substantially all empirical, accidental
acts, including the act of knowledge by which it objectifies
itself.

234

For, surely the *I* who knows and the *I* who is known are not two distinct beings. If so, the *I* who knows is distinct from the *I* who is known as the *act* of the power of knowing is distinct from the *being* who has the power to know. A knower is a being in precisely the same sense that any other being in the world is a being: he is different from other beings in the world only in that he has certain powers which not every other being in the world also possesses. Subjects are made to be subjects only by the peculiarities (i.e. the intentional faculties) which pertain to certain objects, namely, to knowing beings. Hence, the opposition between knower and known is *in the first place* an opposition between two beings, an opposition of the ontological order between one thing (knower) and another thing (known): *this* is the condition of the possibility of actual knowledge. But the condition of the possibility of knowledge is precognitive.[25] Therefore, when knowledge actually occurs, the union between knower and known is strictly of the intentional, not the ontological, order, whether we have to do with direct or reflective knowledge. But the opposition is strictly and exclusively intentional in the case of reflexive knowledge, that is, self-knowledge arrived at through knowledge of one's direct, prior knowledge. In the case of direct knowledge the opposition is, in the first place, an *ontological* dichotomy, which is thereafter intentionally transcended.[26]

[25] This is why I said above that, according to this view, the *universe* in which knowledge occurs is definable in terms of the opposition between the knower and the world.

[26] This is why the distinction between *object* and *thing* imposed itself upon this epistemological tradition—the object being simply the thing insofar as it is known. But, as noted above, the thing and the object are ontologically one, so that to know an object is to know (at least in part) the thing of which the object is an ontologically constitutive "aspect." The distinction between the object and the thing pertains strictly to the intentional order, and is said to be not real, but logical.

In conclusion, according to this reasoning, the subject is really an object before it is a subject, and its accidental subjectivity is superimposed upon its substantial, primordial objectivity. Moreover, this doctrine can be made to accord perfectly with the doctrine of the existential contingency of man by further distinguishing between the act of existence (*actus essendi*) and the act of operation (*actus operationis*) of such powers (*potentiae*) as the power of knowledge. For only the Necessary Being could know itself by its own essential self, since only he is essentially whatever he is. Man, however, is not what he is by his very essence and, therefore, as we have seen, "in its essence the human mind is [only] potentially understanding. Hence, it has in itself the power to understand, but not to be understood, except insofar as it is made actual." [27] Even Descartes, who defined the self as *res cogitans*,[28] hesitated to admit the conclusion that the self is what it is because it thinks. It was only Kant who made fully explicit the distinction between the empirical self and the transcendental self, that is, between the self which "gives" itself to itself in experience, and the substantial self which is, by this reasoning, supposed to underlie the self that empirically experiences itself.

The *third* position follows, likewise, from the interpretation of the empirical facts revealed by reflection upon experience as a distinction between reflexive and direct knowledge—in the sense that self-knowledge is essentially re-flexive, not direct. For when we are aware of ourselves, we are aware at one and the same time of two things: first, as we have seen, that the *I* who knows and the *I* who is known is one and the same; but also, second, that it

[27] *ST*, I, 87, 1.
[28] *Meditations on First Philosophy*, II.

236

is only the *I* who posits the act of knowledge that we can without hesitation or doubt distinguish from the *I* who is known—or, conversely, that the *I* who is known may not always be distinguishable *as object* from other objects in the world.[29] For instance, a self may be unable to know some of its own parts as part of itself.[30] The *real* self, therefore, cannot coincide with that immediately apparent self which appears to itself in essentially the same way as does any other self, or any other object, and which we thus call "the body that is mine," or *"my* body." [31]

This is why every classical epistemology implies a dualistic anthropology: man is composed of two elements, soul (or mind, or the like) and body. If we interpret experience in terms of reflection, (I mean, as the re-turn of the mind upon itself), then the mind, or soul, or substantial self, cannot coincide with the body, and the only thing philosophy can do once this basic stand is taken is to try to explain what the relation of the two parts of man may be. Philosophy is then constrained to explain, for instance, whether the soul is not somehow in the body,[32] and

[29] For instance, if one were to see one's anaesthetized hand, but none of its visible connections with the rest of "one's body" it would not be necessarily known as *"my* hand" simply because one was conscious and able to reflect upon one's own acts of knowledge.

[30] Avicenna, five centuries before Descartes, was one of the first philosophers to draw from the distinction between essence and existence the conclusion that it would be possible for the soul to know itself without knowing its body.

[31] The *my* emphasizes the necessary implication of analyzing man into body and soul (or mind, or the like), namely, that the body which is "mine" can be said to be part of "myself" only because it is *mine,* but despite the fact that it is a being essentially like any other being in the world of empirically given being, that is, a body.

[32] This is the more obvious conclusion, since on the above reasoning, the body seems to be more extensive than the soul (i.e. there are parts of "me" which are excluded from my necessarily and constantly self-

if so how, or else whether the body is not, on the contrary, contained by the soul.[33] Philosophy must explain, moreover, how the unitary, vital processes of man may best be described once either of these suppositions is made. This has proven, to say the least, a very difficult task.

But irrespective of the manner in which these problems may be solved, the underlying assumptions remain the same, and the division of man into a mental and a bodily self will seem, for all practical purposes, self-evident. Indeed, once certain premises are granted, the duality of man becomes self-evident in the most literal sense, for this idea is but the necessary concomitant of conceptualizing the experience of experience as a re-flexion upon oneself. If the self is not given (to itself) from the outset, then

---

identical self, the self which is always present and identical with itself). The soul knows its own limits, as it were, whereas it does not always know where *its* body ends and another body begins.

[33] Though less evident, this is the more sophisticated view. Thus, St. Thomas' definitive doctrine is not so much that man is a corporeal being which, like every corporeal being, is composed of "matter" and 'form," (*ST*, I, 75, 1), different from other corporeal beings only in that his "substantial form," unlike that of other corporeal, (and even that of other corporeal, living, sensitive) beings, is "subsistent," (*ST*, I, 75, 2), and therefore "incorruptible," (*ST*, I, 75, 6). His final doctrine is rather the more complex view that "the actual being of the human soul surpasses corporeal matter, and is not totally included in it, but yet in some way is touched upon by it. Inasmuch, then, as it surpasses the actual being of corporeal matter, having of itself the power to subsist and to act, the human soul is a spiritual substance; but inasmuch as it is touched upon by matter and shares its own actual being with matter, it is the form of the body," (*De Spiritualibus Creaturis,* II). This means: the human soul is more principally "a spiritual substance" than a "substantial form." But because it "is the lowest in the order of spiritual substances, [it] can communicate its own actual being to the human body" and thus function, for its own *proper* perfection, to be sure, as the substantial form of the body, "so that from the soul and the body, as from form and matter, a single being results," *ibid.*

the empirical self is not the ultimate, real self, and this real self cannot coincide with the body. It is, therefore, hidden from it. The only problem that remains is whether the real self is hidden from the body by being within it, in order to use it as its tool, or else hidden from the body by substantially and subsistentially comprehending the body and acting as its substantial form.

Now, I have granted the basis of the classical concept of knowledge, namely, the empirical observation of the irreducible opposition between self and non-self, the reflexive awareness that knowledge consists in transcending, first, the restriction of a subject to its own entitative perfection and, second, the restriction of an object to its own entitative perfection, in order to raise oneself to a higher level of perfection in and through the raising of the object to a more "noble" level of existence than its material one. I have granted, I repeat, that all this is truly undeniable and even an absolutely primary observation which epistemology must take as its point of departure—and yet, I have denied the adequacy of every classical epistemology which has been grounded on this observation, when this observation has been interpreted as noted above, Why? Because a more comprehensive, more adequate interpretation of the same facts has become possible in the light of the effort of the last two or three generations of philosophical research.

EPISTEMOLOGICAL THOUGHT AND EMPIRICAL FACTS

It is not altogether devoid of irony that the inadequacy of the traditional epistemologies has its source in the understandable but consequential failure of philosophers—during that first age of

our philosophical history which ran from the Greeks to Hegel—
to appreciate sufficiently, and to be sufficiently consistent with, the
real primacy and the true undeniability of the empirical fact from
which the classical concept of knowledge takes it origin. For in
large measure the difficulties of epistemology during this period
can be interpreted in terms of the recurrent failure of philosophers to abide by the empirical facts [34]—or, perhaps more
accurately, in terms of the recurrent, unconscious and implicit
denial by philosophers, at one stage or another of their epistemological elaboration, of the basic empirical fact given by reflection upon experience itself. Paradoxically, the deeper value of
the observation has been diminished, and even jeopardized, by the
traditional failure to take constantly into account something that

[34] As should appear below, where the nature of error is discussed, these
philosophical failures cannot be accounted for in terms of any intellectual
or moral aberration of the history of philosophy in the Hellenic-Western
intellectual tradition. Error always makes historical sense, and philosophical error is eminently intelligible from a historical perspective. I would
emphasize instead that, like every error and every failure, the recurrent
failure of philosophy to abide by the empirical facts, above all in connection with the philosophical study of experience itself, is clearly and
crucially *symptomatic*. (If there were such a scholarly methodological
practice as the application of psychoanalytic techniques to the therapy of
the dysfunctions of the scientific and philosophical intellect, as it were,
this failure would stand out as obtrusively as would, in the case of
psychopathological analysis, a patient's inability to remember his father's
name). And if it is symptomatic, then it stands in need of analytic
understanding as much as it requires synthetic correction. For this
philosophical failure was a perfectly "normal" one, in the sense that the
very nature of experience makes it normal for the human mind, when
it first becomes philosophically conscious, to interpret its own experience
in a manner which is warranted by the empirical facts, (cf. my illustra-
tions of Plato's "empiricism," above), but not as comprehensively, intensively
or insightfully as it will *normally* do at a subsequent stage of its *self*-de-
velopment.

almost every philosopher had, each in his own way, more or less clearly affirmed all along, but without realizing, as fully as philosophers in later times can, its importance and meaning. I refer to the fact that the undeniable and primary opposition of object and subject is indeed assertible and warranted because it is a matter of plain observation; it is a simple question of empirical fact.

The real lesson to be learned from the last century of epistemological speculation is humiliatingly simple. It seems almost incredible that it should have taken the philosophical intellect fully six centuries after St. Thomas to run into the ground the last alternative to the reformulation of the problem, and the full century since the reaction to Hegel began, in order for philosophy to learn a truth which had been on its lips from the outset: empirical facts are observed facts. Thus, to ground the theory of knowledge upon the observation of an irreducible, undeniable entitative opposition between subject and object, between knowing being and being known, is to ground it upon a *known* fact.

Therefore, the primacy of this opposition tells us not only about the nature of being, but also about the nature of knowledge. The first principle of epistemology is not, as traditional philosophical thought has assumed in the past, a statement of the *a priori* conditions of knowledge: it does not describe the pre-cognitive conditions, the conditions that must obtain before knowledge can obtain, and before it can be examined by the knower. To repeat: it is necessary to take with the utmost seriousness and consistency the proposition that the opposition between subject and object *is* an empirical fact. For this proposition means: man's relation to the world in which he exists, man's relation to the world from which he is distinct, man's relation to the world to which he does nonetheless *relate* himself, cannot be understood as any sort of transcendence of the dichotomy of object and subject, self and world. For when this opposition becomes observable, that relation—let us continue for the present to call it knowledge—has *already* occurred.

It is beyond dispute that there is a dichotomy, an opposition, between object and subject. But is this opposition the condition of the possibility of knowledge? If the opposition is itself an empirically observable fact—and if it were not, then we would not be aware of knowledge, we would not be conscious—the answer must be negative. Philosophy has not been mistaken because it has apprehended the fundamental fact, the object-subject opposition, but philosophy has been inadequate to the extent that it has failed to abide by what it has correctly apprehended. From the empirical nature of the observation that there is an object-subject opposition it follows that this opposition is, far from the antecedent of knowledge, its result. The object-subject dichotomy is not the condition of the possibility of conscious experience. On the contrary, consciousness is the condition of the possibility of the opposition of subject and object. Thus, Kant astutely divined that a "Copernican" revolution in epistemology was but the logical outcome of the history of philosophy—though he himself was unable to realize that it was not only the theory, but also the concept, of knowledge which must be turned about, after having stood upside down since Greek times. Or let us more aptly and precisely say: it is incumbent upon philosophy, in the light of its awareness of its own history, to look upon experience from a wider and deeper perspective than has been adopted in the past.

242

The concept of consciousness is not only more adequate than the concept of knowledge: it is also more comprehensive. In the unity of the concept of consciousness philosophy can understand the diversity of "operations" which in classical thought required distinctions between sense knowledge and intellectual knowledge, as well as between cognition and appetite (both sense and intellectual cognition and appetite). But even if we confine our consideration of consciousness to that aspect of it which corresponds to cognition, the concept of consciousness takes nothing away from the concept of knowledge: it takes away least of all from the empirical fact which underlies every philosophical analysis of experience. But it adds to the philosophical analysis of experience a crucial refinement, namely, taking account of the empirical fact that the empirical fact of knowledge *is* an empirical fact. "A thing cannot be known without being known:" this is neither a trivial proposition nor does it mean that we cannot know reality as it really is.[35] It is neither a postulate to be

---

[35] Maritain's epistemological research has been so predominently preoccupied with the apologetic task of refuting Descartes and the whole epistemological issue from Descartes to our own day (for the avowed sake of undermining the religious errors which have accumulated in his wake, cf. *Three Reformers,* London, 1947, pp. 53–89) that he misses altogether the lesson which idealism can teach to those who grasp its filiation to realism: "between the thing and thought . . . there is an incomparably deeper unity than between a model and a tracing [thereof]. For if things were modified or changed in any way . . . by sensation or intellection, then there would no longer be either truth or knowledge, and the epistemologist could not express himself even by wagging a finger, for in such a case only two equally impossible alternatives would remain: either to say that knowledge implies a relation to things, but a relation that deforms them (so that, consequently, they never become known); or else to say that knowledge implies no relation to things, and is an absolute deployment of thought having only itself for an object (a position

hypothetically adopted, nor a supposedly self-evident principle to be dogmatically asserted. It is an empirical fact. And its importance lies in that it is an index of what knowledge is.

A philosopher who were to ask "what is knowledge?" and who then proceeded to dismiss the empirical fact of knowledge, or to ignore it, or even to minimize it, would be as fittingly rebuffed as should be those well-meaning but annoying people who ask questions and proceed to answer them before one has fully opened one's mouth. If a philosopher can conceive knowing as a union—"in the act of knowing, things . . . and mind are not only joined, they make up strictly *one*" [36]—and if his conception is not gratuitous, but based upon a consideration of the facts as the philosopher applies his knowledge to knowledge itself, then the empirical basis of this concept of knowledge is the same irrefutable, empirical opposition between knower and known which, when construed as a (mutual) ontological independence between knower and known lies at the heart of realism. Whether

---

which would be incompatible with the fact of error and with the fact of negative ideas and which, moreover, would be self-refuting, since one cannot affirm that knowledge is this or that unless one assumes it to be something distinct from the act by which it is thought) . . . The principle according to which every relation must modify or alter its term is a sheer postulate . . . All efforts to demonstrate that principle may be reduced to the assertion that a thing cannot be known without being known— of which everybody had but little doubt," *Les Degrés du Savoir,* pp. 167– 168.

But the point is, precisely, that philosophy had long known this, and yet had failed to give it more importance that Maritain does, even today. Nevertheless, the fact that reality cannot be known without its being given in experience is a fact that epistemology must include in its calculations, for it is indicative of the most fundamental features of the nature of knowledge.

[36] *Ibid.,* p. 169.

or not the realist construction be justified, the fact remains that even realists must erect their realism on the basis of their reflection upon *empirical data*. If so, no philosopher, not even a realist, is entitled to ridicule the observation that a thing cannot be known unless it is known—for it is only because things are known that anyone can conceive knowledge, whether he does so in the classical manner or in any other way.

The so-called "naive" realism of Greek and mediaeval philosophy is perfectly understandable historically and philosophically: it would be self-contradictory to suppose that the beginning of the philosophical understanding of knowledge could have been otherwise, since philosophy could not improve upon its reflexive understanding of knowledge unless it first began to reflect upon it. A philosopher who expected philosophy to be "critical" before it was "naive" would be like the child who asked to take the second spoonful of medicine first, because he had heard that the first spoonful was the worst. However, "critical" realists are rather like children who refuse to take medicine at all. Critical realism depends upon the continued assumption, in the face of a long history that leads but to the Rome of self-contradiction, of the idea that man's knowledge of human knowledge is a self-evident given, a sort of unique, innate idea which owes nothing to experience and which is infallibly attained as soon as the philosophical mind begins to operate. The possibility that man may have to learn from the bottom up what knowledge is does not seem to have really occurred to them. And yet, if we reflect upon the matter, surely the mere fact that everyone knows does not mean that everyone knows what knowledge is; it is surely not true that an adequate concept of knowledge is a matter of mere intuitive perception of a self-evident truth by the natural and common sense of every human intellect. Thus, epistemology must not only begin with the facts: it must also keep its attention riveted on the facts; it must resist the temptation to stick to its first limited apprehension of the facts rather than to take a second and closer look at them; and, of course, it must continue forever doing so.

Nor does the fact that things cannot be known unless they are known mean that things can be known only after they have passed through the filter of knowledge, and that, therefore, they can never be known "in themselves." This would be an absurdity, a self-contradiction which can hardly be formulated, least of all upheld. What the assertion that things cannot be known unless they are known does mean is that we cannot assume that knowledge is the unification of things which, to begin with, were, each of them, an in-itself.

At least, we cannot so assume without thereby committing ourselves to certain epistemological and metaphysical consequences and, in the first place, to the epistemological position that truth is the adequation of the mind to things and to the metaphysical position that being is intelligible as such. The observation that things cannot be known unless they are known does mean, in other words, that epistemology does not only *start* empirically, but that it must also *proceed* empirically. And it does most emphatically mean—however puzzling it may be—that this very circular and self-obtrusive quality of knowledge, this very fact that the known can be known only on the basis of its being known, means that knowing can be known only on the basis of *its* being known. Knowledge is self-involving. This is its first characteristic. This characteristic can be neglected by epistemology —but only at a price. If, on the other hand, the opposition of subject and object is an empirical fact, and if we take account of its being an empirical fact, and if we continue to proceed empirically, then we will not be easily tempted to say that the opposition of object and subject is, as it were, a fact of nature, a fact anterior to knowledge which knowledge does in its peculiarly intentional way, effectively nullify. For is this not the very contradiction of the empirical fact?

Let us look at the basic empirical fact once more. The fact we can observe, if we but consider our own experience, is that *it* is it; *it* is not I, and *I* am not it. Well, then: this is what we are constrained to affirm by considering *experience.* Can we possibly say that this, which we affirm when we consider experience, and when we consider what is empirically given, is *not really* a description of experience, but of something which is *anterior to experience,* and that experience is, *on the contrary,* the overcoming of that which we experience, namely, the overcoming of opposition of self and world? Evidently, we can so affirm only if we have not really thought the matter through.

For—to put it conversely—if we wish to begin to understand knowledge by simply reporting and describing what happens when we know, then we shall be obliged to say this: the most fundamental and irreducible fact of experience, as we can observe by considering experience itself, is the opposition of object and subject. Well, then: *that* is what experience is. Experience is not something else. Experience *is* what happens when subject and object are—indeed, *become*—opposed. Knowing is the opposing of self to world and world to self. But since prior to knowledge there can be no such opposition, we can deduce, moreover, that knowledge is the *introduction* of an intentional opposition, an intentional dichotomy, into that which was originally undifferentiated, unrelated, and perhaps even physically [37] continuous and one.[38] Thus, knowledge is that within which, and in consequence of which, the opposition of subject and object can appear. Knowledge is the condition of the possibility of subjectivity appearing in the world of objects, by the subject's own self-differentiation from, by its opposing itself to, and by opposing to itself, the objectivity of the world.

Nicolas Berdyaev has expressed somewhat the same idea in a lucid paragraph which I would reproduce at length:

The dogmatic ontology of the Greek and the mediaeval philosophy could not resist the critique of reason, and it is impossible to return to the precritical forms of philosophizing. Even modern Thomism, which refuses to recognize Descartes and indeed the whole of modern philosophy, is nevertheless bound to be neo-Thomism and to pass through critical reflection. The point is that the critique of knowledge, the reflection of reason upon itself, is not the abstract theory which it claims to be, but a living experience. However strongly knowledge may contrast itself with life and doubt the possibility of knowing life, it is itself a part of life; it is generated by life and reflects its destinies. The same thing is true of epistemological thought . . . The opposition between knowledge and existence, regarded as an object standing over against the knowing subject, is not primary but secondary, and is the result of reflection. The primary fact is that knowledge itself is a reality and takes place in reality . . . If we rise to a spiritual conception of knowledge, we shall see that knowledge is an act in and through which something happens to reality. Reality is illumined through knowledge. It is not a case of someone or something cognizing being as a separate and

[37] I do not mean spatially, but "in things themselves," prior to and apart from what they may become on account of the introduction of consciousness into the world.

[38] The unity of the mind "in itself" is, however, the unity of un-relation, as I have just suggested. This is why the meaning of things "themselves" can appear only when they become related to mind, and this, of course, occurs only when they are known. Cf. below, pp. 294–298.

independent object: being cognizes itself, and through this cognition expands and is lit up from within . . . A cleavage takes place in reality, and in knowledge it expresses itself as objectivization.[39]

Jean-Paul Sartre has likewise suggested that:

Knowing is neither a relation established after the event between two beings, nor is it an activity of one of these two beings, nor is it a quality or a property or a virtue. It is the very being of the for-itself insofar as this is present to-; that is, insofar as the for-itself has to be its being by making itself not to be a certain being to which it is present. This means that the for-itself can be only in the mode of a reflection (*reflet*) causing itself to be reflected as not being a certain being . . . We shall grant to idealism that the being of the for- itself is knowledge of being, but we must add that this knowledge has being. The identity of the being of the for-itself and of knowledge does not come from the fact that knowledge is the measure of being but from the fact that the for-itself makes known to itself what it is, through the in-self; that is, from the fact that in its being it is a relation to being. Knowledge is nothing other than the presence of being to the for-itself . . . The for-itself does not exist in order subsequently to know: neither can we say that it exists only insofar as it knows or is known, for this would be to make being vanish into an infinity regulated by particular bits of knowledge. Knowing is an absolute and primitive event; it is the absolute upsurge of the for-itself in the midst of being and beyond being . . . In a word, by a radical reversal of the idealist position, knowledge is re-absorbed in being . . . From this point of view it appears necessary to abandon the idealist position entirely, and in particular it becomes possible to hold that the relation of the for-itself to the in-itself is a fundament ontological relation . . . To realism, on the other hand, we shall grant that it is being which is present to consciousness in knowledge and that the for-itself adds *nothing* to the in-itself except the very fact that *there is* in-itself . . . Knowledge puts us in the presence of the absolute, and there is a truth of knowledge. But this truth, although releasing to us, nothing more and nothing less than the absolute, remains strictly human.[40]

[39] *The Destiny of Man,* (New York, 1960), pp. 1–2.
[40] *Being and Nothingness,* (New York, 1956). pp. 174, 216–218.

But one of the earliest recorded instances of philosophical awareness that the deficiency of the traditional epistemologies lies not in the way in which they account for knowledge, but in the more basic conception of knowledge which underlies every attempt at epistemological explanation—from which follows, as I have suggested in this book, that knowledge is not to be conceived as man's transcendence of the in-itselfness of himself and his alienation from "the other" in-itself, but as his self-relation to the other—one of the earliest statements of this view must be credited, so far as I know, to Heidegger:

Perception is consumated when one *addresses* oneself to something as something and *discusses* it as such. This amounts to *interpretation* in the widest sense; and on the basis of such interpretation perception becomes an act of *making determinate*. What is thus perceived and made determinate can be expressed in propositions, and can be retained and preserved as what has thus been asserted.[41] This percep-

---

[41] As I said, this is an early statement. Heidegger's later views on the nature of language are, I believe, no longer well represented by the equivocal proposition that propositions *express*—in the specific sense of *signify*—a prior thought process. (I say equivocal, because it is possible to continue to use this term without such connotation. I have refused to forbid myself in this book the use of the term despite its usual connotations, since this term can also be used to express—that is, give form to —the idea that thought is given form creatively by its linguistic, communicative expression). On the other hand, Heidegger's own historical positioning of his concept of knowledge always was and, so far as I can determine, continues to be, a historical retrojection with considerable foundation in fact but with no more justification than could be granted, say, to his historical positioning of his own concept as a recovery of the genuine thought of St. Thomas, so badly disfigured by Duns Scotus and Descartes. For Heidegger still appears to believe that his concept of knowledge is really that of the pre-Socratics, and that "both realism and idealism have—with equal thoroughness—missed the meaning of the Greek conception of truth," *Being and Time,* (London, 1962), p. 57. It seems to me that Dewey's assessment of the historical situation of con-

tive retention of an assertion about something is itself a way of Being-in-the-world; it is not to be Interpreted as a 'procedure' by which a subject provides itself with representations of something which remain stored up 'inside' as having been thus appropriated, and with regard to which the question of how they 'agree' with actuality can occasionally rise.

When Dasein directs itself towards something and grasps it, it does not somehow first get out of an inner sphere in which it has been proximally encapsulated, but its primary kind of Being is such that it is always 'outside' [,] alongside entities which encounters and which belong to a world already discovered.[42]

In traditional epistemological thought, as Heidegger has also noted, "we are sometimes assured that we are certainly not to think of the subject's 'inside' and its 'inner sphere' as a sort of 'box' or 'cabinet'. But when one asks for the positive signification of this 'inside' of immanence in which knowing is proximally enclosed, or when one enquires how this 'Being inside' which knowing possesses has its own character of Being grounded in the kind of Being which belongs to the subject then silence reigns." [43] Thus, "the question of whether there is a world at

---

temporary thought is much more to be preferred as resting upon sound historical sense. Thus, as I use the term *reconstruction* in this book, with reference to the projective task of philosophy today (and, indeed, at all times), I intend it in a sense much closer to Dewey's (though by no means identical with it) than to Heidegger's, which I deem to be no less perverse, in its own way, than the neo-Scholastic sincerely insincere claim that "metaphysics is necessarily progressive and inventive," (Maritain, *Preface to Metaphysics,* p. 12), is in its own.

[42] *Being and Time,* p. 89.

[43] *Ibid., p.* 247. I would not exactly say "silence reigns," but "equivocation begins, and dogmatism rears its circular head." To wit: "the expressions 'in the mind,' 'outside the mind' have no more spatial significance than the word 'spirit,' which originally meant breath, or the word 'God,' which originally meant light. [N.B. More precisely, the Indo-European

Dieus derives from Sanskrit *div,* "daytime, daylight," cf. *dyaus,* "sky, day."] Just the same as when we speak of creatures existing 'outside God,' spatiality is in this case purely metaphorical. What is meant is only that sometimes the thing exists for itself—either actually or possibly—in the universe we see (and, more generally, in the order of simple existential position or effectuation) whereas at other times it exists not for itself or in this universe or in space or in the order of simple *positio extra nihil,* but rather under conditions quite other than those of thought, and as the principle or term of the act of thought; in this case we say: it exists in thought. The shallow sophism of idealism is to draw its argument from the spatial and material meaning metaphorically evoked by this 'within' and by its correlative 'without.' Yet, to forbid oneself the use of the expressions 'in consciousness' and 'outside consciousness' under the pretext that consciousness is neither a circle nor a casket, would be to reject from the outset the interiority to itself which is proper to spirit, and to condemn oneself to describe knowledge in abstraction from spirit; in other words, it would be to forbid oneself every sort of penetration into what knowledge is. This observation having been made once for all, we will pursue our objectives without allowing ourselves to be held back by words, and without fear of using forms of language which, like all metaphysical terms, connote spatiality only by way of metaphor," *Les Degrés du Savoir,* pp. 164–166.

Maritain is quite right of course, to refuse to deny himself the use of whatever metaphor either intrinsic aptness or tradition may render useful—I have claimed the very right only a few lines above. But Maritain misses the point of the criticism which can be levelled at traditional realist epistemologies, namely, that knowledge is incorrectly imagined to be the transcendence of the opposition between knower and known. It is undoubtedly true that the expressions "in the mind" and "outside the mind" as used by realism are not to be taken spatially. But has every critic of realism (or, for that matter, of idealism) always taken them so? Maritain will surely not deny—indeed, he himself has explicitly affirmed—that "there are two different *esse*'s, two levels of existence, for things: their own existence, which they enjoy in order to maintain themselves outside nothingness, and the existence which supervenes upon them in the apprehension [of them] by the soul, in order to be known," (*ibid.,* p. 166). I will without hesitation agree that "without" and "within" the mind are spatial metaphors; but Maritain will surely not deny that these spatial metaphors refer, respectively, to "the in-itselfness of the knower" and to "the otherness of the in-itselfness of the known." And insofar as this duality is an empirical fact Maritain does no wrong by

all and whether its Being can be proved, makes no sense if it is raised by Dasein as Being-in-the-world; and who else would raise it?"[44]

However, although the question "makes no sense" it is, as I have suggested above, not in the least foolish. On the contrary, it emerges in the normal course of the development of philosophical consciousness. Moreover, philosophy is in a position to conclude that the question "makes no sense"—that is, philosophy can conceptualize knowledge more adequately than this question implies—only *after* experiencing that this question "makes no sense," precisely because of the self-contradictory implication of its assumed concept of knowledge. And by "self-contradictory" I do not mean logically untenable on the grounds that it involves at one and the same time concepts with different denotation. I mean, rather, that the concept of knowledge it implies interprets empirical facts of experience as if they were not empirically given, but as if they were the facts which constituted the

---

using his spatial metaphors. But these metaphors become thoroughly misleading as soon as one forgets, I do not say their metaphorically spatial connotations, but their empirical correlate, namely, that this duality is a matter of empirical fact. The mistake begins when, on this account, the philosopher forgets that the empirical fact is an empirical fact, and supposes that the first observation on which epistemology rests is the mind's observation of the condition of the world, and its relation to mind, before any observations have been made by the mind which exists in the world. The self-encapsulating properties of this reasoning are not at all apparent to Maritain. But they have become gradually apparent in the history of philosophy as a whole. That is why from St. Thomas, Descartes follows, and from Descartes, Hume, and from Hume, Kant and Hegel, who carried the Hellenic-Western tradition to its final, impossible outcome, after which the transcending of the classical concept of knowledge was the only step remaining for philosophy to take.

[44] *Being and Time,* pp. 246–247.

cosmic state of affairs prior to experience, the state of affairs within which experience occurs.

At any rate, Heidegger's pioneer work put in relief that:

> Kant's 'Refutation of Idealism' shows . . . how what one wants to prove gets muddled with what one does prove and with the means whereby the proof is carried out. Kant calls it a 'scandal of philosophy and of human reason in general' that there is still no cogent proof for the 'Dasein of Things outside us' which will do away with any scepticism. . . . The 'scandal of philosophy' is not that this proof has yet to be given, but that *such proofs are expected and attempted again and again*. Such expectations, aims and demands arise from an ontologically inadequate way of starting with *something* of such a character that independently *of it* and 'outside' *of it* a 'world' is to be proved as present-at-hand . . . [and] if one were to conclude that since the Being-present-at-hand of things outside of us is impossible to prove, it must therefore 'be taken merely on *faith*', one would still fail to surmount this perversion of the problem. The assumption would remain that at bottom and ideally it must still be possible to carry out such a proof . . . To *have faith* in the Reality of the 'external world', whether rightly or wrongly; to 'prove' this Reality for it, whether adequately or inadequately; to *presuppose* it, whether explicitly or not—attempts such as these which have not mastered their own bases with full transparency [i.e. consciousness] presuppose a subject which is proximally *worldless* or unsure of its world [or, I may add, alienated from it by a little learning], and which must, at bottom, first assure itself of a world . . . The 'problem' of Reality in the sense of the question whether an external world is a present-at-hand and whether such a world can be proved, turns out to be an impossible one, not because its consequences lead to inextricable impasses, but because the very entity which serves as its theme, is one which, as it were, repudiates any such formulation of the question.[45]

This is why knowledge must be itself philosophically re-known, and why thinking must be philosophically re-thought: "in know-

[45] *Ibid.*, pp. 247, 249–250.

254

ing, Dasein achieves a new *status of Being* towards a world which has already been discovered in Dasein itself. This new possibility of Being can develop itself autonomously; it can become a task to be accomplished, and as scientific knowledge it can take over the guidance for Being-in-the-world. But a 'commercium' of the subject with the world does not get *created* for the first time by knowing, nor does it *arise* from some way in which the world acts upon the subject." [46]

Thus, isolation from the world, self-containedness, lack of relation to reality, self-identity, impassivity, atomicity, substantiality, perseity, in-itselfness—these are not the characteristics of the world in which knowledge occurs. Man is, to begin with, and as an existent, already in relation to reality whenever he exists, precisely because he is part of the world in which he exists. Knowledge is, indeed, posterior to being—but knowledge is not posterior to experience; hence, being is not the *a priori* condition of knowledge. Knowledge emerges in the world of being and, as it were, as the creature of being. Knowing is, therefore, a form of being, a manifestation of reality. What is peculiar to it is not that it relates one reality to another, but that it enables reality to become self-related. Knowledge is not peculiarly a relation *to* reality, but a *self-relation* to it. Man is, thus, the being who relates himself to being. Consciousness is the being of the being who not only is being, but who relates himself to being: it is man's *self*-relation to being that makes him the sort of being he essentially is, namely, the conscious being, man.

This is why, if we but reflect upon the empirical data of ordinary, everyday experience, we must arrive at the conclusion that St. Thomas' argument for the distinction between essence and existence is, for all its basis in a reflexive analysis of experience,

[46] *Ibid.,* p. 90.

vitiated by his more fundamental *a priori* premise, namely, the definition of essence as the intelligible constitution of the real as such, which in turn rests upon his (historically understandable) uncritical assumption of the classical concept of knowledge. It is barely credible that generation after generation of philosophers have accepted without murmur the assertion of St. Thomas (or any of its numerous equivalents in later philosophical speculation up to the Hegelian climax of Scholastic thought), that "every essence or quiddity can be understood without anything being known of its existing," that, for instance, "I can know what a man or a phoenix is and still be ignorant whether it exists in reality." [47]

For this assertion is nothing short of fantastic: it is precisely the opposite of what any legally sane, adult citizen can verify for himself by having recourse to no more sophisticated or authoritative testimony than that of elementary experience. For every essence or quiddity may remain misunderstood or even unknown—except in one respect, namely, in respect of its real existence. If man bears any conscious self-relation whatever to any essence or quiddity, then the object of knowledge must be known as somehow existing, as something that is *there,* as a reality other than the consciousness which, by being itself, is correlatively other-than-*it*. I may not know *what* it is, but *it* is a reality, *it* is by definition other-than-me. Thus, I can know something in reality which, as it so happens, is a man or, say, a phoenix, without knowing what man or phoenix is—but I cannot know either man or phoenix and still be ignorant whether *they,* whatever they may be, do not somehow and in some way *really* exist.

[47] *De Ente et Essentia,* IV.

It follows from this conception of cognitive consciousness as man's self-relation to reality by its objectification and by his self-differentiation from it, that man's selfhood, the subjectivity of conscious being, is not to be understood as a special sort of objectivity, that is, as the result of a derivative, secondary *actus operationis* which is the accident of a substantial being who is, as such, objective in precisely the same sense as every other substantial being. The subject is not an object, and its not-being-an-object is part of his very being. The uniqueness of man is not sufficiently well recognized if we conceive him as a rational animal with but a specific difference to be *added* to his generic animality. For man as such is, to begin with, emergent *from* the world of reality in which he exists. By being conscious he differentiates himself from the world. He cannot be a being who is, at bottom, nothing but an object, even if he is an object who thinks.

For it is thought that differentiates him—it is by thought that he differentiates himself—from the objective reality of the world. The subject is, as such, what an object as such *never* is, namely, conscious. And consciousness is not reduplicative of reality, but self-presentative, both in the sense that it presents itself to the world, and in the sense that by so doing it presents itself to itself. Consciousness is, thus, the self-presence of being, and man is being present to itself. But this is precisely what being as such is not; for, as such, being merely is. The subjectivity of conscious being is nothing less than the being of consciousness itself. Let us now contrast this with the traditional view.

The assumption of the Hellenic-Western philosophical tradition which is now embodied in the language and in many other cultural forms of our world—despite the fact that it is far from self-evident or a necessarily universal form of experiencing the world—is that every real being is a self-contained object. (I will not say that the opposite view, namely, that every real being is essentially related to every other, is self-evident either, but I will suggest that it recommends itself to everyday experience with much greater plausibility and force than the former, as long as one is free from the Greek conception of space as the matrix of existence in the world.[48])

If so, man is, likewise, an object. That is, considered from the outside or in his primordial reality, man is one being among many other beings; he is a being who is a being in precisely the same way as any other being. It is only when we consider him from within, that is, when we reflect upon our own experience (and it is the idea that this reflection is indeed a re-flexion, a re-presentation, a re-cognition, that renders self-experience the experience of that which is "within"), that we can observe that man's being is a special sort of being. From this viewpoint man's distinctiveness is his capacity for transcending his original in-himselfness, his original inwardness and encapsulation, while receiving within himself the perfection of "the other," so that in principle, "it is possible for the perfection of the whole uni-

---

[48] See Plato, *Timaeus,* 48 E-52 C, where χώρα, (i.e. place or space, literally "field, region, province, locality,") is explained as the ὑποδοχή ("receptacle") or ἐκμαγεῖον ("mould") where through the process of becoming the generation of the world of empirically given bodily things takes place. For Aristotle this is little more than a self-evident truth which can be illustrated from such non-technical accounts as that of Hesiod, who "thought, with most people, that everything is somewhere and in place," *Physics,* IV, 1 (208 b 32). But Aristotle gave credit to Plato "because, while all hold place to be something, he alone tried to say what it is,"*ibid.,* IV, 2 (209 b 16). Aristotle's doctrine of χώρα is but a elaboration, however considerable, of Platonic thought.

verse to exist in a simple, particular thing." [49] In this view a subject is simply an object who has these extraordinary capabilities. Hence, what distinguishes man is the subjectivity of his objectivity, whereas objectivity is characteristic of the objects to which the subject is opposed. Knowledge is the overcoming of the dichotomy between object and subject, in a union the peculiarity of which is its intentional—that is, subjective—nature: "the scholastics used to say that the relation from the soul that knows to the thing known is a real relation, (it posits something new in the soul), but that from the thing known to the soul that knows it is a relation of reason, which does not affect or modify the thing known in any way." [50] Thus, when knowledge takes place the object remains, supposedly, the same; the only change occurs not in (outward) reality, but in ourselves—and in our *subjective* selves.

Because in all classical epistemologies the cognitive union is subjective, the characteristics of the object precisely as known, precisely as residing in the subject, or precisely as intentional, depend upon the nature of the subject. If the subject is, for instance, spiritual (i.e. immaterial, for that is what spirituality is

[49] St. Thomas, *De Veritate*, II, 2.

[50] Maritain, *Les Degrés du Savoir*, p. 168. The latter observation is, I think, not entirely correct. It holds only if we restrict consciousness to its present-temporal condition (I mean, its condition of being out-of-the-past-into-the-present). But the fact is that in reality, as we amply realized as early as Francis Bacon, knowledge is *virtue* not only in the Socratic, moral sense of ἀρετή, but in the sense that it is *power*. For consciousness does not remain present: as it comes out of the past into the present it goes ahead of itself into the future. Thus, as man becomes conscious of the world, he transforms it. And as he becomes conscious of himself, he evolves. And as he becomes conscious of himself as evolving by the very nature of self-consciousness he begins consciously to direct the evolution of himself.

reduced to in Scholasticism), as the human soul is spiritual, then the object is rendered "actually intelligible by the abstraction of the intelligible form (*species*) from material conditions," [51] and is thus made apt to exist in the knower under immaterial conditions. However, insofar as knowledge is the reception of an object, the content of knowledge, the formal reality which is received by the mind subjectively (that is, according to the mind's own existential condition) can be in no way determined by the mind. To imagine otherwise would be to deny the reality of knowledge. This is why knowledge is, by definition, not merely the intentional acquisition or intussusception of an-other; it is the intussusception of an-other as other. That is, it is the *intentional* reception of an object. Therefore, whatever reality man may contemplate must by that very fact be supposed to be objective: to be, to be knowable, and to be objective, are one and the same thing. Reality is definable in terms of, and is identifiable with, objectivity. The reality of the self must, then, be an objective reality. Subjectivity is a specific sort of objectivity. Subjectivity is but the specific difference of objects which have cognitive capacities. It is the objectivity of those objects that have the power to know.

An epistemology which, unlike the foregoing, remained faithful to the empirical fact that we can know experience only through itself, and that we cannot know experience by any conceivable analysis of the condition of reality prior to our own experience of it, must diverge from classical epistemologies at this very point. For if we attempt to understand our own understanding by observing it empirically, its first observable feature directly contradicts the idea that the mind is, at bottom, some

[51] St. Thomas, *ST*, I, 79, 3.

sort of object. The mind does not know itself by confronting itself, or even by confronting a previous act of its own knowledge in a later, re-flexive act of knowledge. The mind is present to itself from the first moment of its consciousness. One does not have to stop, meditate, and think it over, before one is in a position to answer one's own question "am I thinking?" If one is engaged in any sort of conscious activity, say, counting the cigarettes in a package,[52] then, in order to be able to answer the question "what are you doing?" one does not have to think-back or think-again in order to know that one was engaged in some sort of conscious life. In short, one does not have to think *once more anew* in order to be conscious: there is no human knowledge, no experience which is shaped by a human, conceptual form, which is not conscious. There is no human experience that we can consciously reflect upon, which was not already conscious "before" we reflected upon it.[53] But it is equally certain

[52] Cf. Sartre, *Being and Nothingness,* p. liii.

[53] This assertion may appear at first sight to imply the impossibility of a human unconscious—a conclusion which would be scarcely tenable in view of other empirical facts concerning experience itself which inescapably lead to the interpretative postulation of the unconscious. But my statement does not actually contain this implication, since it applies to human experience that we can reflect on—i.e. it applies to conscious experience. It says nothing about the unconscious, in one direction or another. I may add, however, that the psychoanalytic idea, that through analysis we can become conscious of the unconscious, is a little imprecise. We cannot become conscious of the unconscious, precisely because it was unconscious to begin with. The non-conscious can become conscious, to be sure—e.g. ape can become man, foetus or child can become human. But when it becomes conscious it does not become conscious of its non-conscious experience, because there is none, since this is a contradiction in terms. Likewise with the unconscious: to become conscious of the unconscious is a contradiction in terms. What may happen, and what does undoubtedly happen, in psychoanalysis is that through the interpretative analysis of one's own historical experience one reorganizes one's present consciousness in

261

that consciousness *can* indeed reflect. To be conscious is not the same as to be conscious that one is conscious: to be conscious is least of all the same as to be philosophically conscious that one is conscious. But this points not to the re-flexivity (literally so-called) of consciousness; it points to the conscious character of reflection—or, which is the same thing, to the conscious character of consciousness.

The inconsistency of traditional epistemologies with the facts of experience is nowhere more readily evident than in the ambiguities that the term *reflection* has acquired. I have repeatedly criticized the conception of consciousness according to which, in order for the mind to know it knows, it is necessary for it to re-flect, that is, to turn back upon itself. This is to take the metaphor of re-flexion in its most proper, but also its least applicable, sense. We may use the term reflection and its cognates in relation to consciousness, in order to signify the fact that the mind knows that it knows. The inadequacy of the metaphor of re-flexion, however, begins as soon as one thereby supposes that one first knows and later knows that one knows. This would imply that some moments of consciousness are conscious but

---

such a manner that past conscious events are seen in a different light, (i.e., have a different role in the dynamics of one's personality), from that in which they had been originally seen. Terms like "unconscious experience" suffer from the same malady as Plato's trans-empirical "Forms," (i.e., invisible visibles), because they have been subjected to a like "crushingly despotic" regime. There are unconscious psychic processes which, like the bodily, physical effect of the world upon biologically and physiologically differentiated bodily cells constitute the condition of the possibility of experience. Let us say, then, that experience is made possible by conditions and processes which are themselves no part of consciousness and cannot become so. (This is why they are of little epistemological interest, and concern largely the psychologist and the physiologist rather than the philosopher).

that others are not. The empirical facts indicate, on the contrary, that "to know is to know that one knows . . . [and therefore that] reflection has no kind of primacy over the consciousness reflected-on." [54] In other words, the term reflection is adequate as long as it does not imply that some moments of consciousness are reflexive but others are not. For *all* consciousness is conscious; all consciousness is present to itself. On the other hand, if by reflection and reflexivity we mean precisely this, namely, the mind's presence to itself *from the outset,* then obviously consciousness is nothing but sheer reflexivity. We may please ourselves whether we use the metaphor of re-flexion or not, as long as we do not thereby distort the empirical fact. No consciousness is *re-flexive:* this is true if it means that one cannot know anything without being conscious. All consciousness is *reflective:* this is also true if it means the same thing, namely that whenever one knows anything one is already conscious.

The "re-flexive" character of knowledge is not really its capacity for turning back upon itself (least of all for turning back upon itself as it was at an earlier moment). It is, rather, its aptness for not-remaining-itself; reflexivity is the penchant of consciousness for becoming itself; it is its inclination for being-again what it already-is; it is its capacity for being ahead of itself and developing itself by itself. Reflexivity is, in short, the evolutionary character of consciousness. Well, in this sense, it is true enough that the mind "reflects." But evidently *reflexivity* is better called *transcendence.* For consciousness does not really find itself by "folding back" upon itself: it finds itself by being "beyond" itself—rather, by *having been* from the outset "beyond" itself. At any rate, in no sense does the mind need to *re*-flect in order for its subjectivity to become apparent. Subjectivity is the presence of the self to itself—a presence which cannot take place except in and through the self's self-differentiation from the known self, hence, in and through the self's self-differentiation from the known self, hence, in and through the presence of the self to the non-self. Subjectivity is not the representation to oneself of something which is the same as oneself. Subjectivity is being-with oneself, a mode of being which is possible only in relation to being-with another. And this is why the presence of the subject to itself is called *con-scious-ness*.

SUBJECTIVE EXISTENCE AND SELF-CREATIVITY

It follows from the nature of con-scious-ness that the subject or self is not distinct from other objects because it can, in addition to being the object which it itself is, also become other objects intentionally and, thus, possess within itself not only its own perfection, but potentially "the perfection of the whole universe." If subjectivity is not the specific difference of certain objects, then the situation in which knowledge occurs (and in which it can be observed) is not describable in terms of the opposition of discrete, self-contained objects. On the contrary, being is continuous and undifferentiated in its totality; reality is a universe, not a conglomeration of atomic objects. And consciousness emerges as it differentiates, abstracts, separates and opposes *things* to each other—that is, as it objectifies the world of being —and as it differentiates itself from that which is not itself.

Consciousness, then, is self-positing—that is, the essence of subjectivity is that it makes itself, precisely by differentiating itself from that which is not-subjective, but mere objectivity and in-itselfness. The self emerges in the "cleavage" of being: being emerges *as self* by facing itself and becoming present to itself. Therefore, the achievement of consciousness is not the possession of a reality from which it was originally alienated. It is rather the achievement of self-possession: it is the emergence or coming into being of a being which is present to itself. This is why it would not be in the least inexact to describe consciousness as the self's free fashioning of itself, or as the self-making and self-creation of the self by itself. Consciousness creates itself.

I will digress for a moment to emphasize the difference between being self-created and being uncreated. The suggestion that man is self-created is not infrequently resisted by believers on the hastily defensive grounds that this would grant to man a divine attribute, that it would "steal for man the very Being of the divinity of God." [55] But this is a serious confusion. God cannot be self-created. Only a creature could create itself, for despite its self-creation—indeed, because of it—it would remain created just the same. For instance, the fact that man does not come into being ready-made and having a determinate nature (but having, nonetheless, by the nature of his situation to determine his nature), does not mean that man has no nature and that man cannot be called being, *ens,* a that-which-is. For man does come into being, even if he does so by virtue of his conscious existence. He comes into being, and he is conscious, in a historical situation which precedes him—even in the crudest, most "material" mode of precedence, as well as in the most spiritual and metaphysical

[55] The quotation is retractably my own; see *The Thomist,* XXI, 2 (April, 1958), 220–229, p. 227.

mode—and which is not due to his initiative. To that situation his existence is a *response*. But his response is *creative*, in the fullest sense of the word.[56]

Hence, man is not free not to create himself. But *how* he responds to his situation, *what* he does with himself, and even the *orientation* he gives to himself—thus, the very possibilities which he opens up for himself—all this is very much the result of his conscious, if not always, alas, deliberate, mature, or wise decisions. Self-creation, therefore, does not render man self-necessitated—even uncreated being need not be so understood. But whereas God may be, if not non-necessary, certainly not contingent, man is, for all his self-creation, (and indeed, above all *because* he has a self-creative nature), contingent upon a reality which is other than his own—it makes little difference whether we call it God. But man's creatureliness does not consist in his having been provided with a certain predetermined structure which he can merely exercise in a variety of possible ways. Man is contingent in a much more radical way. He is ontologically contingent in the full (and not merely the Thomistic) sense of this expression, because not even his essence is necessary. Man is contingent because he must make himself to be whatever he

[56] Just as experience is the paradigm of all conceivable knowledge, self-creativity is the paradigm of anything that empirical reason can call *creation*. The Scriptural concept of a creative God is meaningful only in relation to whatever experience of creativity we may have. Thus, the way in which creativity is attributed by man to God is a very good indication of the level of creativity achieved by man. Perhaps this is why some cannot conceive divine creativity in terms of travail, self-exertion and triumph, but only as the supreme feat of Subsistent Legerdemain. To make something out of the void—what a spectacle to watch, if only one had been there when the cosmic curtain was raised! On the other hand, the idea that one may have to participate in the act may be a more sobering prospect than appears at first sight.

266

becomes in a situation which is, to begin with, given; and, thus, he is contingent also because this situation presses him or, rather, impels him, to create himself.[57] In that situation, however, whatever he becomes is what he makes of himself.

Perhaps I should also explain why the self-creation of man is not only truly creative, but indeed a creation of his very self. For at first hearing self-creation appears to be a contradiction. If a being creates himself, does this not imply that he already is, before he creates himself? If man exists, even if he exists only to the extent of being placed in a given historical situation, does this not imply that man already is *something,* since he *already* exists in that situation?

In reply I should explain that I have *not* suggested that every being can create itself. The foregoing objection would be valid if it referred to objects. But conscious being is not simply objective being with subjectivity superimposed upon it. I have tried to stress that in consciousness, in the process of self-creation, the creator is not an object, but a self. Likewise, what is created is not a human object, but a human self. Man's creativity is self-creative not only in that he who creates is the same as that which is created, but also in the sense that what creates and what is created is a *self.* Hence, the self which creates itself need not be there prior to its self-creation. This is possible because the self, not being an object, does not create itself by acting upon itself. It would be closer to the truth to state that it creates itself by acting upon the world. More precisely, the self makes itself present to objects as it objectifies the world. And as it does so,

---

[57] The difference between a God who presses and a God who impels is the difference between a process of cosmic evolution which is manipulated by God and a process of "creative evolution."

it becomes present to itself; and as it becomes present to itself it makes itself to be a self. For knowledge is the *self*-differentiation of the subject—or self—from the objects of the world. Consciousness can be self-creative because it makes itself come into being, not as an object, but as a subject: that is, it makes it*self* come into being through the self-differentiation of the *self* from the objective world.

We may now be in a position to understand even better than heretofore, why, and in what sense, human knowledge should not be construed as achieving the union of object and subject, or of self and world, but as the self-emergence of man in objective opposition, and in self-distinction from, the being of the world. The self-creativity of consciousness is possible, as we have seen, only because the subjectivity of the mind is strictly relative to the objectivity of the world. Therefore, although knowledge is not the subject's intentional absorption of an object, knowledge does place the subject in a certain relation to the world which he did not previously hold. This is why there is considerable plausibility, indeed a great deal of truth, in the concept of truth as objectivity, that is, as the *adequation* of the mind to being—but this is also why there is a great deal of plausibility, indeed, a considerable amount of truth, to the traditional concept of truth as the subjective possession of objectivity, that is, as the *mind's* adequation to being. The germ of truth—the double germ of truth—in this traditional idea of truth is that, in point of fact, consciousness *does* relate man to the real world. However, the essential relation of the mind to beings is not due to the subject's overcoming the transcendence of objects which in themselves are beyond him. The relation is due to the subject's transcendence of himself: it is due to the subject's presence to himself, since this presence is achieved through the subject's self-differentiation from the world, or in other words, because the subject's presence to the world is but the reflection of his presence to himself.

It is clear, then, that knowledge does not actually combine subjective conditions with objective content. If consciousness creates itself only in and through the differentiation of subject from object, it follows that the creation of the self is made possible only in and through the objectification of being. Hence, human understanding attains to a meaning which, to be sure, is not of its own making but which, on the other hand, was not precontained in the reality of the world prior to knowledge. The meaning of reality does transcend the subjectivity of mind; but reality does not *have* within itself a transcendent meaning which the mind merely transfers onto itself when certain conditions are satisfied. The meaning of reality emerges within the mind's relation to reality which consciousness achieves.

Therefore, human knowledge is truly creative, not only in the self-creative sense previously outlined, but also in the sense that consciousness is responsible for establishing *the meaning of* that which is known. But let us remember once again that knowledge is not the transposition of an objective content from reality into the subjective reality of mind. Least of all is it the transposition of an objective content from the mind into reality. The mind's creation of meaning takes place only in and through the establishment of the self's presence to reality. Therefore, quite as in the case of the self-creation of consciousness, meaning is created by consciousness, but not arbitrarily. The meaning created by consciousness is the meaning *of* reality—it is indeed the meaning of the *objective* reality that is known. And we need not hesitate to speak in this context of "objective reality" in the full import of the word. For the point is indeed that only objects properly so called *have* meaning. But by this time it should be clear that the reality of being is not identical with its objectivity. Objects have meaning precisely because they are relative to the self, a self whose subjectivity results from its differentiation from them.

Thus, there are no pre-determined categories in which we must think about reality—whether pre-determined by the nature of the mind (as Kant thought), or by the nature of reality (as all pre-Kantian philosophers thought). We may become conscious of reality and find *its* meaning in infinitely varied ways. But when we become conscious, we become conscious *of it,* and when we find it meaningful, we find the meaning *of it.* Right and wrong, true and false, adequate and inadequate: these qualities truly belong to human knowledge. But they belong to knowledge only insofar as the self becomes present to itself in and through its presence to the world. Truth and falsity thus pertain neither to subject as such nor to object as such. They pertain to the relation in which we render ourselves present to ourselves and to the world. In a word, they belong to consciousness.

This brings us to the question of the nature of objectivity, that is, the nature of being as such, since being is the *object* of consciousness. Yet, before we deal, albeit briefly, with that question, certain additional remarks about the nature of consciousness should first be made.

TEMPORAL CONSCIOUSNESS
AND MORAL LIFE

As stipulated above, I have stressed in my discussion of consciousness so far only that part of it which covers in a consistently empirical (and hopefully more comprehensive) fashion the facts which in classical thought are conceived as man's *knowledge* of the world. But let us recall that at the dawn of Hellenic-Western thought consciousness was divided into cognition and appetition, and the human spirit into intellect and will. If it is granted that man's consciousness seems in the first place to put him in possession of reality, then the empirical facts which point to his creativity and to the free emergence of his selfhood must be interpreted as pertaining to a distinct, subsequent order of his reality. But if, on the other hand, human conscious experience does not transfer reality into the mind but, on the contrary, "transfers" the mind into the reality within the world of which the mind already existed, and if consciousness does not make the world exist in man but, on the contrary, makes man *as such,* as subject, exist within the world of being and if, thus, consciousness is what makes man to be a conscious *being,* then consciousness is to be understood essentially as man's self-relation to reality, and all modes of self-relation to reality must be understood essentially as forms or varieties, or better still, as moments, of one and the same consciousness, of one and the same selfhood of man.

It is not by chance that, as the experimental psychologists of the 19th century used to say, every act of cognition is modified by "feeling tone." The fact is that consciousness has a certain property which spreads out, as it were, its self-relation to reality; this is what makes it possible (albeit incorrect) to distinguish between cognition and appetite as modes of self-relation to reality which tend in opposite direction to each other.[58] That property is none

[58] In classical philosophies cognition brings reality to man, whereas appetition brings man to reality. Thus, when "a thing in which there is good is nobler than the soul which understands its nature, the will is,

other than the temporality of consciousness, which is *unidirectional*. Cognition and appetite lie in the *same* orientation of consciousness, they tend in the same direction. This is why they are not really distinct. Let us examine what this means.

Man's consciousness of the world implies the consciousness of himself as situated in the world. Man is the being who exists *in situation*. He is the being whose being is essentially relative to that which lies beyond him; but this is true not only in what pertains to self-definition; it is also true in what pertains to self-disposition. And the difference between self-definition and self-disposition is essentially a temporal one: these are but two temporal modes of one and the same conscious existence of man.

It is not only insofar as man "knows" that he can be called transcendent. For his behaving, his self-disposing, is likewise *before* him and *beyond* him. His awareness of the world as that in which his consciousness comes into being opens up a possibility from which affective, appetitive experience takes its origin, namely, the possibility of conjuring up a different human situation. That is, the *prospect* of defining himself otherwise than as he *now* is, the *prospect* of making his situation be other than it *now* is, opens up for man the possibility of being *beyond* what he *now* is. Of course, what he now is, he cannot make to be different now: what man now is, is what man *already* is. The present can come only out of the past, and the past is *now* closed. The future, however, is open: it is yet to come out of what *now* is the case. Hence, to become aware that one exists in situation is to become aware

---

as related to such a thing, higher than the intellect. But when a thing in which there is good is below the soul [in rank] then, as related to such a thing, the intellect is superior to the will. Wherefore love of God is better than knowledge [of him]; but, on the contrary, knowledge of bodily things is better than love [of them]," St. Thomas, *ST*, 82, 3.

that one could exist differently, since awareness of being in situation is awareness of the contingency and limitation of a reality which consciousness transcends. Thus, to grasp the world as the locale of man's situation is to grasp the contingency of man's situation; but to be aware of this contingency is to be aware of the possibility of conceiving another world (or, rather, of conceiving a rearrangement of this world) which would constitute an *alternative* to one's present situation.

This means: in real life we can never witness the world speculatively, as a simple matter of fact. A purely factual world is an abstraction from the only real world of human experience, a world which integrally implies, not only our *relation* to it, but *our* relation to it. In real life the contingency of the present relations between man and world means that the world which in fact exists, is—precisely because it is not necessary—essentially comparable to other possible human situations. The comparability of the actual to some other imaginable world, a world which *might be* requires, therefore, that we grasp the actual world in terms of its being *more or less* whatever it is (in what pertains to man's relation to it). This variability, this "more-or-less," is what we call *value*. Human consciousness experiences the reality of the world as having, by its very nature, and because of its contingency and factuality, a *variable* relation to man: *world* is not merely a *fact*, it is an essentially *valuable fact*.

Thus, morality arises from "appetite". Yet morality is not a matter of desire or will. There is no opposition between value and fact. If we anticipate what our experience would be in a world different from the actual one, two possibilities logically arise. Either we would continue to experience a disparity between *what is* and *what might be*—or else we would not. In the latter case the world would be such as it *should* be. Conversely, a word not truly different (in its relations to us) from the actual world, would be a world which *might* be, but not the world which *should* be. At this level we have refined our experience to the extent that we have distinguished between the merely *logical* and the *moral* possibilities opened up by our awareness of the world. We have learned to abstract the world which might in point of *fact* come to be, from the world we *should* prefer and choose, that is, the world which we should *make be*. We have learned to differentiate between that which, as it comes to pass, will constitute a mere event, from that which in coming to pass will constitute a fulfilment—or, perhaps, a correction—of that which is already happening. The first yields the idea of the *chronometric* future, a time whose property is simply to-lie-ahead or not-yet-to-have-been; whereas the second yields the idea of the *historic* future, that is, the future as a human reality, a time-to-come which on account of its possible difference from the present offers the prospect of an *alternative situation*. The latter is the "bright future" which, as we commonly say, lies before the young, or the future we prophesy for an intelligent, industrious man—or, for that matter, that which we foretell for the wicked or the remiss. It is the future which marks not simply the forth-coming events, but the *turn* of events—whether for better or for worse. This is the future which, unlike the first, is radically un-predictable. And, unlike the first, it is the future we can *hope* for—or else dread. This is the future towards which the present reality of conscious life is radically oriented. Conversely, con-scious life thus oriented is what we call *moral*, "customary" life.

A more complex level of experience brings man to the threshold of civilized appetition, of consciously human, *ethical* moral life.

274

It is reached as human consciousness expands into the implicit recognition of itself not merely as opposed to objects, but precisely as consciousness, that is, as a public, social, cultural, historical emergence of being, as a microcosm which in its very being is related to the world. The recognition of the transcendence of consciousness, even in an implicit, lived manner, before reflection produces an explicit ethics, requires man to experience the distinction between selfhood as mine, and selfhood as an event in the world. Henceforth the self is understood not only as that which stands over and above, or against, "the rest of the world," but as a reality which occurs *within* the world. Self no longer means—as classical philosophies would unfortunately conceptualize it—a "subjective," but also an "objective" event. *I exist* is no longer the affirmation of a unique, isolated fact, but the assertion of the reality of being, even while all being is apprehended in relation to myself.

At this level of consciousness we realize that the world which *should be* does not derive its claim to come to be from the requirements of my "subjective" self—say, my needs, or my wishes—or, for that matter, from those of any other given self, or even from those of the sum of selves insofar as these, too, are "subjective" and opposable to the world. The world that should come to be should provide not merely for everybody's need and preferences, but also, as it were, for those of the whole cosmic order, *within* the total reality of which (and *not against* the reality of which) man holds his reality and selfhood. The moral contingency of the world, the possibility of its constituting a different human situation, does not depend on mere preference, or custom, or social inertia. The world that *should be* becomes at this point the world that *ought to be*: a possible future cosmic order which derives its claim to come to pass from its intrinsic nature *precisely as future,* rather than from the nature of the present, which precisely as present may be judged to be merely unsatisfactory or otherwise inadequate for man to exist in. This future would *ought to be:* that is, it has an *absolute right* to come into being.

Note that this is a right, not a necessity. But it is an absolute right: its entitlement to come into being is not derived from man's projection of it. On the other hand, this does not take away the essential *relativity to man* of the world which ought absolutely to be. For such a world ought to come into being in strict relation to man—not in the sense that its finality lies in the satisfaction of man's desires, but in the sense that such a world is intelligible only as *a world of possible human experience.* For the possible world in question is, after all, an alternative to the present human situation. And it would be absurd to conceive of an alternative to the present which could not, precisely as alternative, ever become a truly *present* situation. Therefore, the traditional Christian metaphor—that what man is morally obliged to desire is definable as "the will of God"—is inadequate, even when coupled with the belief that what God wills man to desire and do coincides with what is good and proper for man. For this way of conceptualizing the "absolute" nature of human, effective, appetitive, moral consciousness still distinguishes (and establishes a hierarchy) between the "objective" order willed by God and the "subjective" consequences for us, which follow upon the "subjective" fulfilment of the order "objectively" willed by God." [59] And the metaphor becomes absurd when, as with Kant,

[59] This is the doctrine of St. Thomas; see *ST,* I–II, 3, 1; I–II, 3, 2; I–II, 4, 1.

one not only distinguishes, but also divorces, the order of objective obligation and the order of subjective consequences for the discharge thereof.

The order of appetition, value, desire, inclination, self-projection, self-disposition and morality, is precisely the same order as that of cognition, fact, self-definition, self-consciousness and truth. The only feature of conscious life which permits one to distinguish between the two sets of abstractions I have just listed is the fact that man's *present* self-relation to reality has both a *past* and a *future*. As deriving from the past, man's present self-relation to reality can give the impression of passivity, of mere witnessing, of speculative reflection of what in fact is and cannot be otherwise than it is. But this seeming necessity is not an intrinsic constitutent of the fact. It is but the property of every present which derives from a past: it is, indeed, nothing but the very pastness of the present.

We can best understand how necessary it is—indeed how unreasonable it is—to take the "inevitability" of the past with the tragic pessimism of the Greeks, when we observe that there is neither need nor any reason whatever given to human experience to assume, with the Greeks, that as the past has been so shall the future be. And none should observe this more easily or clearly than the Christian, for whom *hope* is a theological virtue which ranks with faith. The future is no less real than the past. On the other hand, the future is as open as the past is closed; it is as free as the past is necessary; it is as apt to be created by man, as man is necessarily created by the past. Man, existing at present, can be conscious, can look at reality, only *out of* the past. But from the present he looks *to* the future. Thus, to look *at* the past is of the very nature of man. But to look *to* the past is to look backwards; it is to pervert the natural orientation of consciousness. This, too, should be most religiously held by none than by the Christian, since the Christian God is, in Karl Rahner's expression, definable as the "absolute future" of man.[60]

SOCIAL CONSCIOUSNESS
AND INDIVIDUAL EXPERIENCE

I should also acknowledge another self-imposed limitation which has qualified the remarks I have made so far concerning consciousness. Just as I preserved, as long as didactic simplicity made it expedient, the Greek fiction that consciousness can be divided into opposite realms of appetition and cognition, value and fact, I have also assumed so far the Greek idea that consciousness is an individual, personal event—even after I had rejected the primordial objectivity of the subject, making clear that the subject's very being, and not only his accidental existence, is subjective. But now I must, if only fleetingly, enter an essential qualification to my previous remarks on the nature of consciousness. Isolated, atomic consciousness is a contradiction in terms—except, of course, in the improper sense I have previously admitted, namely, that thinking is abstract, capable of morcellating reality as it will—albeit for the non-arbitrary purpose of relating itself to that reality all the better.

There is nothing wrong with abstractions. Not even primitive

[60] Karl Rahner, "Towards a Theology of Hope," *Concurrence*, I, 1 (Winter, 1969), 23–33, p. 25.

human life, least of all modern civilized life could continue for a moment if man ceased to abstract. To speak is to abstract— even to wag one's finger meaningfully (as when beckoning) is to abstract. The inexpediencies of abstractive thought (so well described by Bergson, but so mistakenly diagnosed by him) begin only when the fact that human thought is abstract is coupled with the classical concept of knowledge. For this conjunction makes it necessary to take abstractions as a representative means employed by the mind for the purpose of appropriating reality to itself. The historical disappointment of philosophy with abstraction thus construed is, therefore, understandable. But in reality the problem is not caused by abstraction, but by the concept of knowledge which interposes abstractions between reality and man. The rejection of abstractive thought, even when motivated for as intelligent a reason as was Bergson's, is a mistake: what should be rejected (or, more precisely, modified and improved) is the traditional concept of knowledge. Man abstracts so he can conduct himself in a certain manner in relation to reality, not in order to make reality amenable to imprisonment by him. Well, the individual, self-contained, substantial self is itself an abstraction which is valid only to the extent that we use it precisely as such, namely, as revealing the abstractive power of consciousness. But this abstraction becomes radically misleading if we take the abstraction as a representation of a fact.

If man can believe that, transcendentally speaking, he is not alone, it is only because he is not, in the first place, immanently, in his very humanity and consciousness, alone with himself. Not only does consciousness not possess the other; it does not even possess itself as an individual, self-sufficient being. Consciousness is a collective phenomenon—spatially collective, involving many individuals at the same time, and temporally collective, involving many individuals in historical succession over time. Consciousness does not emerge suddenly, out of nowhere, or out of the nowhen of an eternity before time. The passage from beast to man is not like the crossing of a thin line. Nor does consciousness continue to exist and somehow manage to develop itself, except because it is a collective, social, historical enterprise.

In this connection I should recall what I have suggested above concerning the relation of language to thought. If it is true that language is not the expression of thought, but the cultural form that makes thought possible by converting the objective inter-relations that life can enter into with its world, into the *conscious* experience which is man's subjective relation to the world, it should be clear that thinking is essentially as social and historical in nature as language. For the two, language and thought, are but two abstractions from one and the same single reality, namely, the consciousness of man. Likewise, man's creativity is collectively, socially and historically exercised—as the development of language amply shows.

The social and historical nature of language is the best available index to the social and historical nature of conscious thought. The Greek conception of language as conventional would lead one to believe that there is no reason why "strawberries" should not be called "oranges" and that if we but decided to do so it would be perfectly possible to speak of "jam" when we wished to designate what we now call "marmalade." This belief, if I may say so, is utter applesauce. Except, perhaps, for people who are deranged, human beings do not invent words but for a purpose—a purpose which, to be sure, need not be universal, but which is nevertheless social and, in any event, historically meaningful. Even whimsical coinages, which may at first sight appear arbitrary, are always conditioned by the situation in which they appear, and their social context is all the more real because it is purposefully limited and socially exclusive. There can be, likewise, no nonsense words. The "nonsense syllables" of experimental psychologists serve exactly the same fundamental social purpose, namely, communication and mutual interaction, as is fulfilled in ordinary, non-experimental situations, by ordinary, "meaningful" words.[61] As a matter of fact, it is the very social and historical nature of consciousness that makes conscious linguistic reformulation as difficult an undertaking as social reform.[62] This is precisely what happens in the history of scientific and philosophical consciousness. The moral lesson of this, incidentally, is that as human consciousness develops to the pont that it begins to become self-problematic, man must learn either to think cooperatively, or else he will stop thinking at all.[63]

[61] Lewis Carrol's *mimsy borogaves* is a very good example of *meaningful* nonsense.

[62] Cf. above, Ch. III, note 4.

[63] It behooves professional thinkers to initiate and lead co-operative thinking. Intellectual free-enterprise, the principle of letting the best idea survive, does not mean intellectual competition; it does not mean that every idea is a target which must prove itself by surviving every attack. This is, at best, a wasteful procedure, and I doubt it brings out the best thought more often than it succeeds in bringing thinking down to the lowest common level. Intellectual free-enterprise means free trade in thought; no ideas are to be priviliged, established or protected. It does not mean that an idea may become established only after it dethrones the previous intellectual plutocrat. And yet, intellectual criticism much too frequently amounts to nothing more profitable than intellectual gamesmanship. Cf. my "Catholic philosophy and the socialization of the intellect," *The Ecumenist*, V, 5 (May-June, 1967), 52–55.

THINGS-IN-THEMSELVES
AND PROBLEMATIC TRUTH

I have said that there is a germ of truth in the traditional concept of truth as the mind's relation to the objective world, namely,
that knowledge *does* relate man to the world, a world which in
point of fact is other than man and which exists "in itself:" the
occasion for the mistaken, traditional view of truth is the truth
that the world exists by its own existence, and that since consciousness relates itself to it, consciousness must be understood
as essentially transcendent. Indeed, I have insisted on the transcendence of consciousness strongly enough to have identified
it with human existence itself. Part of my argument has been
that if we cannot understand man's transcendence as the operation of a power which brings the "outside" world to reside
"within" man by the very existence of the act of knowledge (and
particularly the act of judging), the reason is that this interpretation does not do full justice to the real transcendence of man. For
reflection upon experience indicates, if I may so put it, not that
man is transcendent because he knows, but that he knows because he is transcendent.

Man exists, as it were, outside or beyond himself: he exists *in*
the world, not only in the sense that he is spatially surrounded by
the world, but in the more basic sense that his existence has a
real spatial location. But the real spatial location of consciousness
is not somewhere within the human body. Human consciousness
is literally located "there," that is, wherever may exist whatever
man is conscious of. One would be tempted even to say that
man exists "out there," were it not that the point is precisely

282

that the world is not *out* there, since there is not in the first place a subjective *within*. Alternatively, we might well retain the metaphors of *without* and *within*. But in that case we would have to say: since all that man is conscious of is within experience, then experience has no within; it is *all* without. But, whatever the terminology, the point is the same: the objective world does not, by means of consciousness, come to exist in man; on the contrary, by consciousness man as such exists in the objective world.

Idealists try hard, but in the end find it impossible, to understand this point—realists do not even try. Idealists apprehend the fact that we do not know, and indeed could not know, what not-knowing is and that, therefore, the reality of a knowing being cannot assimilate to itself the reality of being in-itself. But from this they mistakenly conclude that being in-itself must be mind-like, because if it is mind-like then it is in principle assimilable to mind and, thus, by knowing itself the mind may be obliquely able to know things-in-themselves. Realists, however, do not even observe that we do not, and could not, know what not-knowing is. Rather, they refuse to grant this, being under the impression that if the mind did not know what not-knowing is, it must be missing out on something good—because it would be missing out on something that is there. As long as the realists presupposes that consciousness captures—or misses —things out there, it will be impossible for the realists to realize that if the mind misses out on the experience of not-knowing, it has missed out on nothing at all. They will remain constitutionally unable to grasp that, therefore, the fact that nothing can be known except in and through experience does *not* mean that things can be known only after they have been brought *into the mind* and, thus, can never be known *in themselves*.

On the contrary, to say that nothing can be known unless it be given in experience, is to say that things can be known *in no wise* except *as they are* and *in no place* but *in themselves*. As the *locus* of man's existence, the real world is the object of man's consciousness. But if the objectivity of the real world is not its aptitude for being transferred intentionally from its physical existence and real location to a psychic existence and a mental locale, the question may be asked in what this objectivity consists —keeping in mind most especially, I repeat, that consciousness is transcendent and truly relates man to the objective world.

Just as Heidegger must be given credit for his decisive contribution to the beginning of the 20th century's philosophical reconceptualization of knowledge, (though Heidegger himself would be displeased by this description, preferring perhaps to call it the rediscovery of its long lost meaning), it is Sartre who must be recognized as having called attention to the implication of the reconceptualization of knowledge for philosophy's understanding of the object of knowledge. For the classical concept of knowledge and the classical concept of being (both in its Greek and in its Thomistic varieties) are strictly correlative.[64] It fol-

---

[64] I should put this more precisely. As suggested at length in the previous chapter, the Greek concept of knowledge and the Greek concept of being are strictly correlative and mutually consistent. Since these are the bases of Greek philosophy, Greek philosophy is in stable equilibrium; this is why for all its wanderings Greek philosophy retained a basic invariability which is not (to our good fortune) parallelled in Christian thought. Greek philosophy underwent considerable change, even development, but no evolution; it experienced crises, and even tragedy, but no revolutions. On the other hand, St. Thomas' concept of being and his concept of knowledge are, though strictly correlative, not perfectly consistent. St. Thomas' concept of knowledge is essentially the same as that of the Greeks. But his concept of being is only partly like that of the Greeks. For acording to St. Thomas being is essentially intelligible, it is intelligible as such.

lows, as Sartre was the first to suspect, that the reconceptualization of knowledge necessarily requires the reconceptualization of its object, being, as well.

However, although Sartre's work should, in my opinion, stand as a permanent contribution to the development of our Hellenic-Western philosophical tradition, it can be judged even at this early date to suffer from two inadequacies which, as I trust, will be corrected in due course. The first is the atheistic interpretation which colours his penetrating insight that, if being is existentially contingent, then its reality is not the *act* of its essence —its reality can only be its *"not-being"* the act of its essence, the *"not-being"* of being which is characteristic of conscious existence. (Sartre's unconscious dependence upon St. Thomas should be perfectly clear from this alone.) This inadequacy, however, does not concern the present discussion.[65] But the second inadequacy does directly concern the discussion at hand: I refer to Sartre's insufficient dehellenization of the concept of being, the reality

---

This makes his concept of being strictly relative to his concept of knowledge, quite as with the Greeks. But St. Thomas' also distinguished between *esse* and *essentia,* a view which, in the end, cannot be reconciled with either the Greek concept of being (as intelligible) nor with the Greek concept of knowledge (as attaining the necessity of being). This inconsistency is what made Christian philosophy after St. Thomas essentially unstable. The inconsistency affected epistemology first, but ultimately it involved metaphysics. (What an extraordinary understatement; ultimately it affected the whole of Western Christendom's life). Kant and Hegel stand as the culminating points of the negative moment of the revolutionary process which St. Thomas began. Likewise, the positive moment of the corresponding philosophical reconstruction resulted first in the reconceptualization of knowledge. Contemporary philosophy has only begun to reconceptualize being as well.

[65] In the next chapter I will try to discern the lines along which its correction might be attempted.

which is the object of consciousness and to which consciousness relates itself.

The Greeks, as we have seen, conceived being as what-is. In fact, according to them the true name of reality is being, for the very reason that reality is constituted by a certain *what;* and *what* means (or *is*) that-which-is-predicated. And, since what is predicated *is,* it follows that what is predicated must therefore be called *being.* But this was not the last word of metaphysical thought. I will recall that St. Thomas too conceived being as that-which-is; this conception of being was not altogether unlike the Greek, but it carried nevertheless a different level of meaning, because it implied not only (a) that being was constituted by a certain *what,* and (b) that since *what* is that which is predicated it must be called being, (since being is what a thing is said to be). This, I repeat, was *not* denied by St. Thomas. But St. Thomas also included in this notion of being the idea that the *what* which constitutes a being is itself constituted by its *is,* so that the *is* is a distinct element from the *what* and related to it as its act. I have previously stressed the revolutionary consequences of this for the dehellenization of epistemology; I now stress that insofar as St. Thomas' concept of being did include the Greek view that being is constituted by *what* it is, St. Thomas' metaphysics was *not* dehellenized, and that, therefore, the present criticism applies to St. Thomas' metaphysics as well as to that of the Greeks. Thus, in classical and in mediaeval and, indeed, in early modern thought, to call reality being, to say that being was being, to affirm that every being was what it was, and to state that being as such was intelligible, was one and the same thing. If reality is being, reality as such is definable by its aptitude for being known. Whatever else may be said about the constitution of being, reality is *essentially* an object of thought, that is, an intelligibility which is apt to be known, for it is indeed by its essence that being is an object of thought.[66]

But all this presupposes that an object of thought can, in addition to its existing by its own physical existence or *esse naturae*, also exist by "a very special kind of existence, which the ancients called *esse intentionale*—an existence according to which the known will be in the knower and the knower will be the known . . . in virtue of [which] the thing exists in the soul with an existence other than its own, and the soul is or becomes the thing with an existence other than *its* [i.e, the thing's] own existence." [67] For being's aptitude for being known depends upon its being so constituted that it is able to exist not only in itself, but also beyond itself. (The transcendence of knowledge, which is evident readily enough, is thus projected into being, even if

[66] St. Thomas in the middle ages, like Maritain today, would insist, of course, that Being itself is intelligible, but not necessarily "to us, (*quoad nos*)." Being itself is, however, always intelligible to God. This is why God must be said to have an essence (albeit indistinct from his to-be). God is intelligible to himself, a notion without which St. Thomas' theology of the Word would hardly be conceivable. Maritain's interpretation, which I find, unlike Gilson's, fully convincing as a statement of St. Thomas' most likely philosophical self-understanding, is given in *"Sur la doctrine de l'aséité divine," Mediaeval Studies,* V (1943), 39–50.

[67] *Les Degrés du Savoir,* p. 221. The uncritical, aprioristic character of the traditional assumption of the concept of knowledge is especially evident in Maritain's admission that this distinction between *esse physicum* and *esse intentionale* is derived, *follows,* from the concept of knowledge: "if we would conceive knowledge without absurdity, we are *forced* [italics mine] to introduce the notion of a very special kind of existence . . ." etc. Maritain assumes, of course, that knowledge is the transcendence of the subjectivity of man. It is true that to conceive knowledge in this manner, without consequent absurdity, it is necessary to posit the distinction between *esse physicum* and *esse intentionale,* if not also the full epistemological panoply of Thomism.

philosophy has, in Maritain's word, to "force" itself to do so). And in order to be known being must be so constituted, because knowledge is supposed in the first place to be the mind's possession within itself of that which is other, an other which exists originally in itself.

I may comment, however, that if, on the other hand, we do not suppose, with tradition, that the mind possesses within itself the reality which originally exists outside the mind, in itself, then we cannot very well suppose that reality is constituted by its aptitude for being known, since its aptitude for being related to knowledge, its aptitude for being related to an-other, can be nothing real in itself. In short, being in itself cannot be as such constituted by its relation to another: this would be a contradiction in terms. But let us take this up in more detail.

It is not difficult to understand why realism issued historically in idealism. The determination of realists to uphold the in-itself-ness of things may be well intended, but is somewhat misguided. The in-itselfness of being is not really recognized if one simply persists in thinking that "that which can be and that which can be thought are the same," or that "being as such is intelligible." Idealism is but an effort of realistic philosophy to be consistent with itself. If "like is . . . known by like," [68] being is knowable only because being is mind-like. As Bishop Berkeley put it:

An idea can be like nothing but an idea . . . If we look but ever so little into our thoughts, we shall find it impossible for us to conceive a likeness except only between our ideas. Again, I ask whether those supposed originals or external things, of which our ideas are the pictures or representations, be themselves perceivable or no? If they are, *then they are ideas,* and we have gained our point; but if you

[68] Aristotle, *On the Soul,* I, 2 (405 b 15).

288

say they are not I appeal to any one whether it be sense, to assert that a colour is like something which is invisible; hard or soft, like something which is intangible; and so of the rest.[69]

The assimilative concept of knowledge implies that the object of knowledge is, as such, assimilable: assimilability is its proper name. Idealism is but the effort to retain this view even after St. Thomas' distinction between essence and existence issued in the philosophy of Descartes. But perhaps we are nowadays in a position to conclude that, on the contrary, the in-it-selfness of being as such, the otherness of that which experience reveals the mind as having differentiated itself from, can have its in-itselfness fully recognized only if we do not first suppose it to be the *a priori* condition of the possibility of consciousness.

Being in itself cannot as such depend on the mind: realists do not insist sufficiently on this. They are satisfied with explaining that being does not depend on *our* mind, but they are willing, if not eager, to concede that it does, indeed, depend, I do not say simply upon Someone Else, but upon its *being known* by Someone Else's mind.[70] If God's sovereign self-necessity should demand the tribute of human recognition, it may be fair enough to God to reason as follows: if created things are created by someone's knowledge, we may as well say that it is *God* who creates them by knowing them. But this assertion may not be as respectful of the in-itselfness of being as this very theory elsewhere supposes. For it retains the idea that the *esse* of things is their *percipi,* that their being is their being known (by God), or at very least, that their being is caused by their being known by

[69] *Treatise Concerning the Principles of Human Knowledge,* I, 8.
[70] St. Thomas, *De Veritate,* I, 2.

God and that, therefore, the intelligibility of their being depends upon it being known by God. The nobility of the divine percipient may render this theory plausible in what pertains to the efficiency of the creator—for it is quite clear that *our* perception does not make things to be in-themselves. But as far as the constitution of things themselves is concerned, it makes no difference whether their *percipi* is human or divine: in either event they are constituted by their aptness to be in-another. Their in-itselfness is not, therefore, sufficiently recognized. The existentialism of St. Thomas's basic metaphysical insight is, in effect, contradicted by his insistence, and that of later Thomists, that being as such is intelligible.

Whereas other philosophers before Sartre had begun to realize that the history of philosophy clearly suggests the reconceptualization of knowledge, Sartre was the first to begin to suspect, in effect, that it also suggested the reconceptualization of being. For he has made it easy for us to reason that if the object-subject dichotomy is not anterior to consciousness, then the object-subject dichotomy cannot be superimposed upon a dichotomy of being against being. Idealism had been moving in this direction, insofar as it had insisted upon the need for philosophy to abide by its presupposition that "like is known by like." However, as philosophy has begun to surmount the pre-critical position of the problem of knowledge in terms of the *opposition* of being and thought, philosophy has thereby put itself in a position to transcend the pre-critical position of the problem of metaphysics in terms of the identification of being and thought. Hence, philosophy must now reject the supposition that *being* is the condition of the possibility of the dichotomy of object and subject effected by consciousness. It is, on the contrary, *non-being* that alone can be such a condition; for only non-being can oppose itself to being, and only non-being can be the outcome of any reality which is constituted by its self-differentiation from being itself. "I am *not*-it," and "It is *not*-I." What does this mean but that being is made to be by that which is not-being, (unfortunately Sartre calls this "nothingness"), and that "nothingness," (i.e. being-not), is that by reason of which—and that "nihilation," (i.e. the act of being-not), is that by means of which—nothingness (i.e. unreality) becomes being (i.e. reality) and becomes present to itself? Thus, nothingness *does* exist—not, of course, by not-being, but by being. Conversely, being is but *existing* nothingness, just as consciousness is but the nothingness of being conscious of itself precisely as nothingness (i.e. as being-not). It is, therefore, self-delusive to search within the order of being for either the meaning of being or for its cause.[71]

[71] For the sake of guiding the reader I will warn him at this crucial point about the direction of the road ahead. This I may best do by anticipating what I take to be inadequate in Sartre's reasoning and how it should be corrected. I must first note that Sartre's reasoning appears to me basically and logically sound in this respect: if objectivity is a property of being, then subjectivity cannot be understood in terms of being. However, Sartre assumes, with the Hellenic-Western philosophical tradition, the identity of reality and being. Hence, *non-being* is *nothing*. If the *I* becomes conscious by making itself to-be-*not-it*, then the *I* is made to be by "nihilation," (*néantisation*), that is, by the nothingness of being-not. I shall suggest in the next chapter, however, (a) that the identity of reality and being is not a self-evident fact, (b) that the opposition of object and subject reveals to man precisely the possibility of transcendent reality (i.e. reality which is other than being), and I shall in passing even suggest, (c) that since the opposition between object and subject cannot indeed be the dichotomy of being against itself, this opposition reveals to man that man's own reality, (though he is a being and nothing but being), can rise above being and aspire to being more real than being itself.

Thus, I shall suggest, in effect, first, that Sartre's atheism is the historically

291

If consciousness is not the thing's "being-with-us" but *our* "being-with-it," the in-itselfness of things can only mean, (to put it in the first place negatively), that being is *not* constituted by intelligibility, that being is not-intelligible as such. But it is at this very point that Sartre's inadequacy begins to appear. He does vividly realize that being is not intelligible. But he does not apparently grasp that the identification of being and intelligibility recognizes (to recall the Aristotelian formula) that being is in itself only potentially intelligible, its actual intelligibility being attributed to the active perfection of the mind. Hence, to deny that being is intelligible should mean not only that it cannot be defined by its *percipi,* but that it cannot be defined by *any* relation to mind. Hence, to say that being is not-intelligible, is not to define what being is, nor to define its objectivity. It is to

logical outcome of the existentialism of St. Thomas, and that if one conceives being as St. Thomas did one risks the perfectly logical conclusions drawn by Sartre: *if* by the meaning and the cause of being is meant a First Being who is Being Itself, then man, the human being, cannot successfully or reasonably search within the order of reasonably conceived being for either the meaning or the cause of being. But I shall also suggest, second, that this sort of atheism—namely, atheism in relation to the God who is First Being and Being Itself—is assimilable within a theism in which the reality of God is not conceived as being. For Sartre's assertions concerning "nothing," which he identifies with non-being, are actually applicable to a God who is conceived as non-being—but a God whose non-being-ness is not identical with the nothingness of non-reality. In other words, I shall suggest that Sartre's conclusions are essentially correct and historically justified by the history of Western philosophy, in the light of the Western transformation of Hellenic metaphysics under Christian inspiration: beyond being there is nothing but non-being, and being is strictly relative to non-being in respect of both its reality and its meaning. But to this it is necessary to *add* a crucial qualification: non-being is not the same as nothing, that is, reality is not necessarily being. This addition reconstructs Christian theism on the bases of a transformed contemporary existentialist atheism.

state that the classical concepts of knowledge and of being are not supported by the empirical facts. In this sense the statement is undeniably correct. Sartre, however, takes it also to mean that *absurdity* (i.e. non-intelligibility) is the *formal ratio* of being. But this amounts to saying that the nature of being can be defined by its refractoriness to confirm what the Greeks thought it was, namely, essentially related to mind.

Sartre's retention of a retrospectively Hellenistic bias, however negative, is thus evident. To be sure, the nature of being must be defined, by those of us who are in the Hellenic-Western tradition, in relation to our Greek origins, but not in reaction to them.[72] If the denial of the identification of being and intelligibility is interpreted as implying the definition of being as absurd, the procedure of defining being in relation to mind is retained, albeit in a negative, reactionary and inverted way. To be absurd is, after all, to be refractory to mind; it is to exclude *mind,* and to contradict it. Sartre should have realized that contradiction betrays concern. One does not fight except against that which, or against him who, one cares about—if only by hating and wishing to reject. The in-itselfness of being, hence its "objectivity," is only jeopardized by its being defined as absurd.

The positive construction to be put upon the in-itselfness of being, once it is granted that consciousness does not make being exist in us and with us, but makes us exist in being and with

[72] As I have stipulated above, the dehellenization of Christian belief means neither the rejection of our Hellenic past nor the illusion that our non-Hellenic future could be fashioned out of anything but our Hellenic past and by means of our hellenized present. The term dehellenization is not simply negative; it is not un-hellenization, but de-*hellenization.* If we wanted to put it in strictly positive terms we might describe it as "the conscious creation of the future of belief."

being, is that being as such is constituted by its own existence. Its act is not the act of its essence, it is the act of the being itself. In the world of being we do not find essences-that-exist, we find existences. We find (to give them a name which is etymologically perverse, but which modern usage understands very well), simply *facts*. Being is like Mount Everest: it is *there*, it is a *fact*. Anything that is, is essentially, and as such, a fact. It need not be, it has no meaning that constitutes it as reality—though it can have meaning if it happens to enter into relation with mind. It has no necessity of its own whatsoever; it is existentially and essentially contingent. Nothing that is need be: nothing that is need be as it is. If being is, and if it is as it is, contingency is to be assigned to its being in the same manner and for the same reason that it is to be assigned to being as it is, namely, because it need neither be nor be as it is.

Why, then, are things *as* they are? (For, evidently, the being of things is always being in a concrete, constantly changing, mutually different, unique way.) Why should things not only be, but be *as* they are, rather than otherwise? The answer, I believe, is that there is no reason *intrinsic to them* and *to their constitution* why they should be *as* they are. To suppose that they *should* be as they *in fact* are, is to go beyond the empirical facts. But perhaps the question really—and more reasonably—means: why do things *turn out* to be as they are, when evidently it is not by absurd chance that they are *as* they are? Or is it not true thata there is pattern, regularity, system, coherence, similarity and consistency in facts—for instance, in "nature"? Granted that the fatcs as such may be meaningless, and that meaning obtains only when we "put the facts in order," and provided we do not ascribe absurdity to the constitution of being itself, does it not follow that beyond existence there is, if not *whatness* at least behaviour, and that there must be something in the structure of being which accounts for the form that its behaviour takes?

There is, indeed, something that accounts for it, but it is not found precisely in the structure of being, and it is not, therefore, intrinsic to it. There is the *situation* in which being exists, the *history* (rather, the process) in which it exists, within which it changes, and to which it contributes by its behaviour. It is not by chance that Fido is a dog: it is a dog, however, not because it owns a canine structure. It is a dog because it was born of dog. If it had been born of ape, it would be ape, and if of woman, man. The world has no intelligible structure, but it has history. Things are in motion and suffused with mutual relativity. They do not happen at random, and there is a reason not only why anything is, but also why it is *as* it is. But this reason is not any inner structural constituent of its being: it is its simple situation in a world which is already in motion and, ultimately, it is the situation of the world as a whole.

The facts, however, are nothing but the facts. The world, on the other hand, is more than a collection of facts structurally related. The world is in process, and its facts are not static; they are in reality existential events. Thus, one thing comes after another, and things happen as they do, because other things have happened before them, and because other things are happening now. And the whole, moreover, is contingent, not only because it need never have come to being at all, but also because it does not follow necessarily from anything at all, and because there is no predetermined path it is constrained by necessity to follow—even after it has come into real existence. The color red might never have existed; daisies might never have evolved at all; there is no cosmic conspiracy that compels grass to be green. Of course, a cosmos without red, daisies or chlorophyll would be unimaginably different from the world that we do know. In such a world the equivalent of the electromagnetic spectrum, the equivalent of botanical intelligibility, and the equivalent of photosynthesis, (were there any of these), would nonetheless make perfect (historical) sense. Or, I should say, whatever that world were like, it would still make sense to anyone who understood it—provided he were intelligent enough to make sense out of it. It is the same with events: the burning out of the filament of this light bulb which has just gone out was not potentially contained in the original momentum and position of the atoms of the world at any given time—but doubtlessly the world would be far different if the atomic structure of tungsten were other than it is. We work with the reality we in fact have, because it has in fact come into being. We try to understand the world as it is in fact; it would be radically inadequate to imagine that what understanding does is to exorcise the gods, the necessities, which reality contains hidden within.

Hence, being as such, being in its factuality in itself, is not constituted by intelligibility—but it is intelligible nonetheless. It is not intelligible in the sense that it *has* intelligibility, actual or potential, within itself, whence it can be obtained by the mind. It is intelligible, however, in the sense that *we* can understand it. Nor need we say that it is *in itself* subject to being-understood; for its being understood is not done, as it were, in consultation with it. Being does not really "lend" itself to being understood. But nothing of this can change the fact that being is truly intelligible, because understanding does not require it to do anything in order to be understood—not even lend itself. Our understanding of being requires only that *we* relate ourselves to it: it is we, not being, who change and who are changed (by ourselves) because we understand being. To understand it is to place ourselves in a certain relation to it, to make ourselves exist in its regard: it is to abide by, with and in the facts. It is to be not simply ourselves, but to be (I mean, to have and to hold our being) *in* the reality of the world.

How can consciousness understand, if there is nothing to be understood? This is not the right question. There is indeed much in the world to be understood: there is being to be understood. But understanding being is not capturing it: it is being with-it, thereby making it be no longer by-itself. But being remains in-itself—nothing can change that. Yet, to know it is not to overcome its in-itselfness. It is, on the contrary, to fondle it, to look upon it kindly, respectfully and—literally speaking—in a friendly and benign way. No one can understand the reality of being if he does not *like it,* or if he is not at least well disposed towards it. To know the world is to realize that, for all its sharp and occasionally cutting edges, the world is essentially a comfortable locale. Thus, no one can hope to understand understanding who does not find enjoyable the company of being. But these metaphors would be radically misleading if they were taken to reflect only our *reaction* to being. They are intended rather to convey the nature of relation in which we place ourselves towards it; they do not refer to the nature of the evaluation we place upon being as it has actually been up to now and as it might, therefore, continue to be.

For, in this respect, our disposition towards being will have to discriminate between good and evil. We must tell the difference between what we decide, I do not say to encounter (for we have no individual choice about that), but to go along with, on the one hand, and on the other, what we decide to change, nullify or to do away with. The facts themselves are, of course, neither good nor bad; but our future relation to them is *either* good or evil, since it is fashioned by us according to the possibilities that we ourselves create for ourselves. But the *present* relation we establish with being is neither good nor evil. It is rather the relation we call *truth*.

What these observations have intended to convey is that truth *obtains*. There really is such a "thing" as truth; it is not a figment or an inanity. And most of the pronouncements made by common sense about truth are themselves perfectly valid and true. We have "a duty towards the truth;" there is value in "the pursuit of truth;" it is obligatory to "tell the truth;" it is only realistic to "look at the facts as they really are;" common honesty requires us to recognize (and, above all, to admit to ourselves) that "thinking does not make things so;" and he is mistaken who "allows the wish to be the father of the thought." The misconstruction of philosophy and of Western common sense begins only when we imagine therefore that the truth is not simply warranted by the facts, but also reduplicative of them; it begins when we imagine that truth amounts therefore to the correctness or adequacy of the transposition of an intelligible content into the mind—when we imagine, that is, that truth amounts to the faithful reproduction and appreciation of the facts, (and their "is" connection) by the (judgmental) activity of the intellect. What is wrong with this is not the assertion that the mind judges of things *as* they are, but the gratuitous supposition that to judge of things as they are is to reproduce and appreciate within ourselves something that was originally within things—

something by which things are as they are (this something being analyzable into what those things are, and the act by which they are what they are). For within things there appears to be nothing but themselves. It is this in-itselfness—indeed, this self-identity, if we may use this equivocal term *negatively,* to mean not a positive self-sameness, but the absence in things of anything beyond themselves—this is what is meant by the expression "being is a *fact* and *nothing* but a fact."

Truth is, thus, the meaningfulness of the facts. We might even say that truth is the meaning of the facts, provided this were not construed as if the meaning were within the facts. Truth is the mind's "making out" the meaning of the facts; it is making the facts to have meaning. Truth is not the meaning found within the facts; truth is the meaning which is put upon the facts because they are understood.

We shall consider in a moment the nature of truth in more detail. At present the question concerns, rather, that to which consciousness is related with a relation of truth, and the suggestion I wish to make is this: although the reality of the relation of truth is not given in any manner by the reality of the object of knowledge, nevertheless, the relation of truth is the relation of consciousness to its object, being.

In point of fact, if only we approach it critically, that is, without any preconceptions about the nature of the object of knowledge which would be entailed by the assumption of the classical concept of knowledge, this is not at all a difficult notion to grasp. What I am suggesting is only elementary common sense: it is only that which anyone can easily realize if only he will look at the facts, and if it is difficult to understand it, the reason is not that the suggestions I have put forth are impossible in themselves, but that most of us are accustomed to interpret experience from quite a different viewpoint. Yet, that more customary viewpoint is nothing short of preposterous and fantastic. For it is, however historically understandable, preposterous and fantastic to imagine that there should be a Thalesian divinity within things which the mind extricates and appropriates for its own use (least of all for its own use as an amulet that will transmute a fateful destiny into the smile of providential good luck). What is extravagant and incredible is the idea that the truth of human understanding is warranted, I do not say by the facts, but by the prior reality and existence of truth itself, (or its ontological equivalent), *in* the facts, if not also in the Supreme Knower whose knowledge made the facts what they are. In short, the classical epistemologies tell a very tall story, and common sense is gullible if the absurdity of the Hellenic idea of truth does not upon reflection become apparent to it: the truth cannot be that which precedes the truth.

Certain remarks Heidegger has made are an excellent illustration [73] of this very point. I would reproduce them at length:

[73] I refer to the illustration, not to the doctrine. If it is unfortunate that Sartre conceptualized the non-intelligibility of being as such as *absurdity,* it is even more unfortunate that Heidegger—though we must remember he wrote *Being and Time* long before Sartre wrote *Being and Nothingness*—conceptualized truth as "uncoveredness" and "disclosure" and "revelation." Perhaps his construction of the history of philosophy and his positioning of Greek thought in relation to the present contributed to what I take to be a serious misunderstanding. For *uncovering* (and its correlative, *covering up*) imply in the end that there is something to be uncovered. The veil is lifted and the revelation occurs simply because the unveiled is there—and this is precisely what an empirical analysis of the facts of experience forbids us to assert. Heidegger is saved from self-contradiction only because the Being which is uncovered can in fact be metaphorically construed as lending itself to being uncovered simply

Before Newton's laws were discovered, they were not 'true'; it does not follow that they were false, or even that they would become false if ontically no discoveredness were any longer possible. Just as little does this 'restriction' imply that the Being-true of 'truths' has in any way been diminished.

To say that before Newton his laws were neither true nor false, cannot signify that before him there were no such entities as have been uncovered and pointed out by those laws. Through Newton the laws became true; and with them, entities became accessible in themselves to Dasein. Once entities have been uncovered, they show themselves precisely as entities which beforehand already were. Such uncovering is the kind of Being which belongs to 'truth'. That there are 'eternal truths' will not be adequately proved until someone has succeeded in demonstrating that Dasein has been and will be for all eternity. As long as such a proof is still outstanding, this principle remains a fanciful contention which does not gain in legitimacy from having philosophers commonly 'believe' it.[74]

To sum up: we can know being in itself *as* being in itself only because we know it *in* and *at* itself, not because we make it exist in us or because it is knowable in itself. We do not know being because it is knowable: being is knowable because we know it. Only when we appreciate this truth, on the grounds that experience teaches it to us, are we in a position to deal directly with the questions of the nature of truth, and of the nature of falsity or error, which is the opposite of truth.

---

because it is rather than because of what it is. (I have granted that consciousness does relate man to the reality of being.) But Heidegger does not apparently realize fully that although truth may be in a sense the "uncovering" of Being, Being as such does not really uncover itself, or disclose itself, or reveal itself.

[74] *Being and Time*, p. 269-270.

REAL ERROR
AND RELATIVE TRUTH

The empirical basis of any concept of truth, like that of any concept of knowledge, is an observation about experience itself. But, as with knowledge, it is possible to conceive truth on the basis of empirical facts without realizing that this empirical basis is empirical, that is, given by experience, or without realizing that this "reflection" upon experience is not the result of a re-flexion upon a previous experience. Conversely, a critical philosophy of truth is at bottom nothing more than an account of the same empirical facts which have been traditionally conceptualized as "truth," and elaborated in philosophical theories of truth as "the adequation of the mind to being," but with the difference that is implied by the full philosophical consciousness of the fact that this concept has an *empirical* basis and that a philosophical theory of truth must proceed empirically, that is, that it may not cease to remain constantly and consistently in touch with the empirical facts.

I have said "full" consciousness. This is an equivocal and relative expression. Consciousness is always full, as long as it is consciousness; it always coincides with itself, and it is never less than consciousness itself. One cannot be less (or more) conscious at any given moment than what the capacity of one's consciousness both permits and demands. But because consciousness is temporal, consciousness remembers itself. Therefore, as it becomes itself consciousness recognizes that it has been less than itself. The converse of this is the experience that consciousness *now* is (at last!) itself; it is now "fully" itself; it has become "fully" conscious of itself. But it would be out of the question to imagine, simply because it has "at last!" become fully itself, that the *last* of its becoming itself has been reached, that it is not only full, but full-filled, that its capacity for being-full has come to its last end.

For one of the most elementary lessons of human experience is that only fools expect that they will never have to change their minds—though in point of fact even fools will eventually do what they did not expect they would have to do. Common prudence, even if born of no nobler mother than the mere passage of time, should teach all those of sufficient age to be mistrusted by the young that to change itself is the property of the mind.[75] To tell the truth, nowadays no one, except perhaps the self-sheltered from reality, makes the mistake of thinking otherwise.[76] We have

[75] This is somewhat obscured by the common expreession, according to which *we* change our minds. But the identity between the changer and the changed, and between these two and the process of change, and between these three and the means of change, evidently remains.

[76] Professor E. L. Mascall has ascribed to me the claim to possess an understanding of the nature of truth which is final, conclusive and irreformable, and this, according to him, renders me self-contradictory, since I assert that the truth is never final, conclusive or irreformable; see "Professor Dewart's 'The Future of Belief'," *Downside Review,* LXXXV, 281 (October, 1967), 385–394, p. 390. But this ascription is gratuitous. I do not think I have given any grounds to be suspected of presuming to exempt the truth of my own knowledge from having the properties that I attribute to all truth. I had hoped that I had always stressed sufficiently in my writings the permanently provisional —and, thus, the pro-visional—character that, as philosophers are now in a position to realize, belongs in principle to all human understanding— and therefore to their own philosophical truth—but which philosophy and all professional thinking professionally exploits. If my understanding of the nature of truth is at all correct, it will be superseded, it will be improved upon. Its very truth will contribute to its supersession; and it will be superseded precisely because it enjoyed a measure of truth.

reached the stage of self-consciousness at which it is fairly common knowledge that we are never so fully conscious of anything, least of all ourselves, that we shall not be fuller yet. Everyone knows that full consciousness is a strictly relative term, pointing to the past; but what is now full with truth will be utter vanity tomorrow. And no one but the timorous could possibly find disconsolateness or reasonable grounds for unhappiness in what is, after all, a very hopeful and reasonable fact of life.

The empirical basis which leads common thought, and thereafter philosophical thought, to speak of *truth* as soon as it has learned to speak of *knowledge,* is the observable difference between knowing and not-knowing—I do not mean between a knowing being and a non-knowing being, but between the knowing being who knows and the knowing being who does not know. More precisely, it is not only the difference between one knower who knows and another who does not, but between one and the same knower who sometimes does not know and yet can eventually know. This difference, moreover, has consequences—knowledge is virtue, as some like Socrates have said, or power, as others like Bacon have put it, or cash-value, as still others, like William James, have thought. But whatever the nature of its value, knowledge is valuable. This is why it is worthy of being pursued and loved, and why we must "devote ourselves" to it. Apart from the specific perfection which is acquired by the knower when the perfection of the other exists in him, (as St. Thomas might well have put it), the acquisition of the perfection that has been acquired is itself a perfection: it is good for the intellect to know not only on account of the nature of what it knows, but also because, since its natural end is to know, it is good for the mind to know, irrespective of what it may specifically know. Whence it follows, (if I may continue to express myself in Thomistic style), that all the sciences are good, though some, on account of the additional nobility of their object, have a correspondingly additional nobility accruing to them.

Whether or not St. Thomas might have expressed this idea in such terms, the important point is that knowledge confers upon the mind the quality of truth. This is as undeniable and irrefutable an empirical observation as is the opposition between knower and known. But what is the nature of this quality? How shall the valuable condition of the mind which evidently differentiates the knowing from the not-knowing mind be conceived? If it is assumed—very specially if it is tacitly assumed —that knowledge is the transcending of the object-subject opposition, then there is only one possible answer to this question: truth is the adequation of the mind to thing. The answer is indeed so directly implied by the concept of knowledge, that it is not really necessary for philosophy explicitly to define truth. All that is required is to define what the *term* means, stating that "to say of what is that it is, and what is not that it is not, is true." [77] Thus, it was not as a result of an inquiry, but spontaneously, that someone in the Western world whose identity we do not know, finally devised the formula which states its formal nature: truth is the adequation of the mind to things, "truth is the conformity of thing and intellect." [78]

Likewise, there can be in this tradition no real problem of

[77] Aristotle, *Metaphysics,* IV, 6 (1011 b 27).
[78] St. Thomas, *De Veritate,* I, 1. Cf. *Contra Gentiles,* I, 59; *In Metaph. Arist.,* IV, 8, 651; *In Perihermeneias,* I, 3, 7 and 13, 12.

truth. There can be at best the problem "how it happens that we think things together or apart . . . for falsity and truth are not in things . . . but in thought; while with regard to simple concepts and 'whats' falsity and truth do not exist even in thought." [79] The idea that truth is the adequation or conformity

[79] Aristotle, *Metaphysics,* VI, 4 (1027 b 26). The meaning of this doctrine, that "with regard to simple concepts . . . falsity and truth do not exist even in thought" is quite different from what approximately the same formulation conveys in the writings of St. Thomas. For Aristotle this statement does not convey an epistemological, but simply a logical, meaning. For " 'being' and 'is' mean that a statement is true," *Metaphysics* V, 7 (1017 a 32), since being is what-is (as we have studied above, Chapter III). Thus, unless something is said *to be something,* there can be no truth to what is said, because nothing is said to be. Or better: unless something is said *to be something* there can be no truth to what is *said,* because in point of fact nothing is *said* until a complete judgment is uttered. In brief, Aristotle assumes that unless speech predicates, it does not say anything, because the nature of being so requires. To predicate it is necessary to utter a complete sentence, because to predicate is to say what some thing *is;* and to say *what something is,* is to say that it *is.* The nature of the mind permits us to think merely *S,* or to utter the sound *P.* But to *say* something it is necessary to say that S *is* P. Therefore, his conclusion follows.

For St. Thomas, however, the meaning of this or a like formula could not be quite the same. Essence is really distinct from existence, and being cannot be properly identified with truth: being is only "that which precedes truth and is the basis of truth," *De Veritate,* I, 1. Therefore, if truth is found in the judgment, and not in simple apprehension, the reason has to do not with the nature of being, (as it does in Aristotle), but with the nature of knowledge. Simple apprehension does not reach being (*ens*) as such, but only its essence.

This is, of course, as we have observed above, the beginning of the problematization of reality. In relation to truth this problematization is manifested by the self-contradictory need, after St. Thomas, to grant to simple apprehension the quality of truth, despite the fact that truth cannot be found in simple apprehension: Aristotle would never have been able to formulate, least of all understand, Maritain's proposition that "to be in conformity with the real ('logically true') is the very 'ontological truth' of the senses and intellect in act . . . Simple apprehension is true only

of mind to things emerged, thus, in Western philosophical thought as a self-evident principle which serves as *the starting point* of every epistemological inquiry into truth.

Of course, within the boundaries of the assumption of this concept of truth, every question about truth, about the nature of the relation of adequation, about the process whereby it accrues to the mind, about the conditions of its presence and absence—even the misleading [80] question "what is truth?"—all these questions remain so many legitimate further inquiries. But the classical concept of truth is a parameter, and within this parameter philosophers who assume it might well discuss many things intramurally, but not what truth is. They may discuss, for instance, whether truth is found in simple apprehension or in judgment, and whether it is primarily in the mind and only secondarily in things, or vice versa. But every question of this sort may be controverted only within the assumption that, what-

---

in this way," *Les Degrés du Savoir,* p. 172n. And then Maritain adds: "but that truth is only possessed as such, when it itself is *known,* and it is known only through the judgment," *ibid.* But, evidently, "that truth" must *be* (in simple apprehension) before it can *be known* (in judgment). Thus, quite as Descartes unerringly deduced, the problem of certitude *begins* with simple apprehension: the possibility to be considered is not only that judgment may be in error, but that simple apprehension may not reach the real, that it may not have "ontological truth." If the mind does not really apprehend simply the "simple natures," (René Descartes, *Rules for the Direction of the Mind,* Rule VI), that is, the essences which are really distinct from existence in created things, there is no basis upon which the mind can thereafter judge truly that anything *is* this or that, or even that it *is.*

[80] It is misleading because, as traditionally asked, (e.g. by St. Thomas), it does not mean what it literally says; it is not a question about the essential nature of knowledge; it does not imply one does not know what truth is, but only that one does not know how to define the truth whose nature one already knows.

ever else may be said of it, truth is some sort of conformity of the mind to that which the mind knows. For, surely no cognitive perfection follows, no value accrues to the mind in act of knowing, if the act does not bring about the conformity of mind to being. Without this result, knowledge has failed: it has been attempted, but it has not come about. Though there has been, as it were, a promise of truth, the promise has not been fulfilled. The process of knowledge has aborted, and brought forth error instead of truth.

The history of modern philosophy is the history of the gradual awareness, one by one, of every last difficulty which follows from every last variation of this type of epistemology. In my remarks so far I have alluded to some of these difficulties. But now I should bring up one which somehow has not been widely noted but which, as it seems to me, is actually the supreme difficulty, the absolutely basic inadequacy, of the classical concept of truth —and, incidentally, that which has had the most tragic effects in the everyday life of Western Christendom as a whole, (but particularly, perhaps, in the life of the Church), for this inadequacy provides the philosophical justification of intolerance and dogmatism. I refer to the paradox that the traditional understanding of truth cannot admit the true reality of error. It renders the failure of knowledge unintelligible in terms of the intellectual process itself. For it makes the intellect essentially infallible. And the difficulty with this, (apart from being very hard to reconcile with any self-recognizing, honest-to-self experience), is that it is self-contradictory. This idea of error leads to the identification of truth and knowledge—and this means, in the end, a denial of the reality of truth, that is, of the distinctive value of knowledge. Ironically, the reality of truth is wedded to the reality of error.

This is not readily evident as long as we suffer from an equivocation which has been frequently introduced into many a reference to "true knowledge" and to "false knowledge." If to be in conformity with the real is the "ontological truth" of the sense and of the intellect, (that is, their entitative condition when their knowledge is true), then it follows from the very concept of truth that "all true knowledge is a knowledge that is true." [81] Thus, in most epistemological speculation since St. Thomas until well into our own age, (and, to be sure, in some before St. Thomas as well), "true knowledge" has meant not only "knowledge which is true," but also "knowledge which is truly knowledge"—while "false knowledge" has meant not only "knowledge which is false," but also "knowledge which is falsely knowledge." But if "knowledge which is true" is validly identifiable with "knowledge that is truly knowledge"—as the text I have just quoted above explicitly asserts—then one cannot identify "knowledge which is false" and "knowledge which is falsely knowledge." For if "knowledge which is truly knowledge" can be found only in "knowledge which is true," there can be in reality no "false knowledge." In other words, all knowledge that is *truly* knowledge, is *true* knowledge; and only true knowledge is truly knowledge. False knowledge, therefore, is not truly knowledge of *any* sort: it is *falsely* an act of knowledge. In this reasoning "false knowledge" is, at bottom, a contradiction in terms. And yet, since error cannot be equated with ignorance or nescience, and is too obvious a fact to be altogether denied, the concept

[81] Maritain, *Les Degrés du Savoir*, p. 172n.

of "false knowledge" must be somehow retained in a philosophical limbo despite its self-contradictory character: error is then acknowledged and deplored, it is perhaps denounced and proscribed—but it is not understood. It is sometimes even thought, it seems, than in a well-regulated and orderly world no one would ever make mistakes.

Note the implication: holding that in erroneous knowledge there can be no conformity to being, hence no truth, and therefore no knowledge properly so-called, the traditional epistemologies have not really attempted to explain the error of knowledge. They have sought to explain the *abortion* of knowledge: how did it happen that the act which of its very nature should have resulted in truth, issued instead in error, that is, failed to become truly an act of knowledge? But once the question is posed in these terms, the answer is bound to find the explanation of error in something extrinsic to knowledge itself. In this view, error is never a real quality of knowledge; it is something foreign to knowledge which somehow prevents knowledge from being truly itself.

The doctrine of St. Thomas illustrates this well. St. Thomas never once supposed that truth might be conceived except as the mind's conformity to being. The question "What is truth?" meant to him simply this: does the correspondence of being to the knowing power refer to something in the knowing power, or does it refer to something in being? [82] We need not consider here his reply, but only the assumptions that remained unquestioned: that being as such is intussusceptively related to knowledge, and that, correspondingly, truth is the conformity, the reduplicative adequation of the being of knowledge to being as

[82] *De Veritate*, I, 1.

such. This is why he found the explanation of error (insofar as he may be said to have found one) to lie in causes wholly extrinsic to knowledge itself.

For instance, falsity in sense knowledge is due to such causes as a derangement of the organ or a disturbance of the medium. And error can be in the intellect insofar as its judgment "on what is presented by sense" is conditioned by the falsity of something *outside* the intellect, namely, the falsity of sense knowledge. Thus, "sense always produces a true judgment in the intellect with respect to its own conditions, but not always with respect to the condition of things." [83] But in itself, intrinsically, the intellect cannot be deceived: "the proper object of the intellect . . . is the quiddity of a thing. Hence, just as the sensing of proper sensibles is always true, so, the intellect is always true in knowing what a thing is . . . By accident, however, falsity can occur in this knowledge of quiddities, if the intellect falsely joins and separates." [84] Likewise, in relation to opining and reasoning there can be falsity in the intellect—but only in a restricted sense. For this falsity "never occurs if a reduction to first principles is made correctly." [85] Logic may be faulty, but understanding either is, or else is not at all.

St. Thomas did not proceed to ask why these "accidents," the false composition or division of the act of judgment and the incorrect reduction to first principles, sometimes occurred and sometimes not. In other words, he did not ask how error was possible, given its monstrous character. Nevertheless, from his treatment of the question "Whether man could be deceived be-

[83] *Ibid.*, I, 11.
[84] *Ibid.*, I, 12.
[85] *Ibid.*

fore the Fall" [86] we can estimate where his doctrine might have led. His reply to this question was negative. In the absence of sin there could be in the human intellect only ignorance, not error, "the absence of some knowledge, but no false opinion." This was deduced from "the integrity of the primitive state." For "as truth is the good of the intellect, so falsehood is its evil." In itself the intellect is infallible: "as regards its proper object the intellect is ever true; and hence it is never deceived of itself." But it may be led astray "by a lower faculty," given the inner disorder of man after the Fall. Evidently, had this disorder not been introduced by sin, error would never be found in the human intellect.

I do not recall any text of St. Thomas in which he asserts that the will plays the key role in the abortion of knowledge. But in the light of the foregoing (and especially if we also remember that in the context of faith St. Thomas did assert that the will can determine the judgment to an inevident object [87]), it may be suggested that St. Thomas opened the way for Descartes' attribution of error to the imprudent precipitance of a judgment determined by man's free will. In fact, at least one well-known contemporary Thomist has thought that according to St. Thomas "there is no false judgment without sin." [88] If this statement refers to *actual* sin, it is probably an exaggeration. It would be better to say that this would be the most logical conclusion to draw from the doctrine of St. Thomas, although St. Thomas himself did not draw it. But in respect of *original* sin the assertion is wholly warranted by St. Thomas' own words.

[86] *ST*, I, 94, 4.
[87] *Ibid.*, II–II, 2, 1, ad 3.
[88] M.-D. Roland-Gosselin, *"La théorie thomiste de l'erreur,"* *Mélanges Thomistes,* (Paris, 1923), 266.

Likewise, it would be wholly incorrect to suppose that St. Thomas' doctrine of truth and error led him to the idea that "error has no rights." But it would be warranted to think that the concepts of truth as conformity, and of error as a cognitive abortion, are the conditions of the possibility of intellectual intolerance. To the degree that later ages have drawn their attitudes from, and have based their moral practice upon, philosophies of knowledge which did not, to be sure, begin with St. Thomas, but which St. Thomas perfected and codified, they have in all consistency concluded that within the community of those who believe in the truth revealed by God there is no room for error. Error is, in some sense and measure, due to sin. To countenance it is to countenance sin.

It is not difficult to understand how love of the truth can so easily beget intolerance, and why so many in the Church are frequently tempted to suppose that those who differ from them are not merely mistaken but also guilty—at least objectively speaking, however subjectively innocent they may be if they are in reality "invincibly ignorant" of the truth. In the Hellenic-Western tradition we have much too often dismissed the proximity of truth and error as an unnatural condition. Though it is at bottom simple-minded to stand for the Truth without caring as to precisely *which* truth, it is historically understandable if in our tradition we have so cared for the Truth that we have not found room for error in the natural scheme of things.

And yet, it is not so paradoxical as it might appear at first sight if, as I have suggested, any speculation about truth which does not from the outset respect the reality of error is likely in the end to fail to do justice to the reality of truth. If we reflect upon it, we may observe that experience exhibits the value of knowledge, namely, truth, not dichotomously, but as a continuously variable dimensions which has to do with the *degree* of success of the achievement of the mind. The idea that knowledge has a twofold value-disvalue, that either it is true or else it is false, is not really borne out by experience. Truth and falsity are, indeed, opposites. But this opposition is not radical. Truth and error are mutually exclusive, if at all, only at the extreme ends of the spectrum of experience. Within experience truth and error are correlative, and it is not by accident that we speak of half-truths. And most people know that one can be mistaken without being altogether mistaken. No enquiry into the nature of truth should proceed as if these facts of common experience were of little account; they should be borne in mind as we proceed.

The concept of truth originates not only in the experience of the value of consciousness, but also in the experience of the *variability* of the self-achievement or value of consciousness. Error is that form of consciousness which should be surpassed, which indeed has been surpassed, as we know whenever we experience that we are *now* in a position to think in a more adequate manner than we were at an earlier time—whereas truth is that value or quality of knowledge which increases as knowledge grows and perfects itself. Truth and error are, thus, conceived in relation to each other, and from a simply descriptive viewpoint truth might be defined as that which the exercise of the mind *tends* to, but does not definitively or necessarily achieve—whereas error is that which makes this tendency neither definitive nor necessary. The philosophical tradition has never denied that error can be conceived only in relation to truth. But philosophers have frequently assumed that truth may be adequately or truthfully understood without reference to error, and this is an assumption we must be cautioned about.

I have suggested that the traditional concept of truth is in-adequate. The precise implication of this statement on which I will now dwell is this: not every concept of truth is necessarily adequate. We can conceive truth erroneously. I remark upon this, first, because even if one understands the truth as the adequation of the mind to being, one should not assume that this concept of truth is itself infallibly true. Perhaps this view of truth is correct, but it is surely not self-evident and it cannot be reason-ably allowed to become self-validating. Surely this concept is subject to error in the same way as any other. In short, let us beware of *every* uncritical dogmatism. Our enquiry into the nature of truth must be open to the possibility that truth may not be what we have always thought it was. This is the only condition under which a critical investigation of the truth can proceed.

But there is a more important reason yet why I would stress that our traditional conception of truth can be deficient—for in-stance if we conceive truth without reference to error. Though truth and error are, as I have suggested, strictly correlative, the historical fact that we fail to appreciate one side of this correlation more readily than the other may be symptomatic: it may well tell us something about the nature of both error and truth.

It is significant that whereas the unfortunate idea that we can conceive truth absolutely has been fairly common philosophi-cal coin, few philosophers have failed to notice that we cannot conceive error without reference to truth: apparently, it is easier to mistake truth than error. But it is easier to ignore error than truth. This, as I say, is significant, because it reveals that the dimension of truth-and-error has, as it were, not only magnitude but also direction. Though consciousness exhibits truth-and-error as a continuous dimension, consciousness tends *towards* truth and *away* from error. Thus, truth is not simply the opposite of error; truth is the *vector* of consciousness. We shall have occasion to recall this below. For the moment I only wish to suggest that we should beware of misconceiving this vectorial quality of truth as its absoluteness, as its lack of relation (or lack of correlation) with error. For to do so would be to conceive truth as an essential property of knowledge, and this in turn would imply that the human mind is essentially infallible.

As we have seen, the essential infallibility of knowledge has been consciously admitted by some philosophers. I stress that we should not find this view more acceptable than its diametrical opposite, scepticism. To deny the possibility of truth because one is overwhelmed by the reality of error is not a more reasonable view, is not a stand more in accordance with the facts of experience, than the other way about. We experience the variable character of knowledge, that is, we experience both truth and error. Therefore, we must account for both truth and error, instead of attempting to reduce truth to error or error to truth. We cannot adequately understand the nature of truth except to the degree that we understand error and, of course, the other way about.

There is a pitfall at this crossroads—a shallow one, to be sure, but it is treacherous, and we should be warned about it just the same. To state that the traditional concept of truth as the conformity of the mind to being is inadequate, is not at all to suggest that the converse is true, namely, that truth is the conformity of things in themselves to the mind. It would be absurd to suppose that true knowledge could obtain by the mind's arbitrary affirmation of "what is," regardless of what things might be "in themselves:" this very supposition requires that things be "in themselves" whatever they are, independently of what we may arbitrarily affirm. No one, to my knowledge, has ever seriously suggested this self-contradiction. There can be little doubt that when knowledge is true it is perfectly possible truly to describe the relation of the mind to being as one of conformity. It is quite another thing, however, to suppose that this relation is what constitutes the truth of knowledge. Truth can consist in this conformity only if we first suppose that knowledge is the inner reduplicative possession of what in itself lies outside the mind.

Let us recall once more: knowledge cannot be the transcending of the dichotomy between object and subject, because that dichotomy takes place within knowledge. The opposition of object and subject cannot be, therefore, the precondition of knowledge. Hence, the human mind is not the power of making present to oneself things which are other than oneself. Rather, the mind is the presence of the self to itself as it becomes present to things other than itself. Therefore, the effect of consciousness is almost diametrically opposite to what traditional philosophers have thought. The mind does not make the world present to itself: on the contrary, it makes itself present to the world. But the mind renders itself present to the world only by opposing itself to the world. Hence, the self becomes present to itself in and through its presence to the world, and it becomes present to the world in and through its presence to itself. This process, this polar field, this self-sustaining function, is what we commonly refer to as human consciousness.

For the classical philosophers the mind does become present to itself—but only upon reflection. In their opinion the mind

317

first receives an object within itself, and thereafter knows its own act of knowledge, thus knowing itself as a knower of other things. I would rather say, however, that man is conscious; that is, man is present to himself whenever he is present to anything other than himself. And this is why, although we can truthfully assert that there *is* a relation of conformity of the mind to things whenever there is knowledge, this relation is not what constitutes the truth of knowledge. On the contrary, it would be closer to the truth to assert that it is truth of knowledge which is the foundation of such relation. For the attempt to understand the nature of truth must take account of the *conscious* nature of human knowledge; it must take account of the presence of the self to itself, not by reason of a subsequent act of knowledge, but in the very act by which it is conscious of anything at all. Or, again, a theory of truth must take account of consciousness not as a by-product of knowledge, but as an intrinsic constituent of it.

Now, if we take account that the mind is consciousness, that it is present to itself whenever it is present to anything else, then the reason for the inadequacy of the classical concept of truth should become immediately apparent. This concept of truth is possible only if we first make a supposition which, as it so happens, is contrary to fact. This is the supposition that we can look at the relation of the mind to being as if the mind were not present to itself when it is related to being.

Let me illustrate the point by posing a riddle. Surely anyone's definition of truth must claim to be true. Moreover, it must claim to be true according to that very definition of being. Well, take the concept of truth as the adequation of the mind to being. Is this definition true? If so, to what is the mind adequated when it thinks that truth is the adequation of the mind to being?

The Oedipus complex of modern philosophy was given to it by St. Thomas when he traumatically arrested the natural circular motion of Greek philosophy—to which this riddle could never have been put—thus preventing Christian philosophy from continuing to assume with Aristotle that being is true because it is necessary. For it was with St. Thomas that Christian philosophy provided the answer to the riddle before the sphinx of modern thought had been born. To put it plainly: it was St. Thomas' doctrine that made it possible for later times to raise the question of the truth of the traditional concept of truth. St. Thomas did so when he wrote that:

A material thing, being placed between two intellects [the human and the divine] is called true insofar as it conforms to either. It is said to be true with respect to its conformity with the divine intellect insofar as it fulfils the end to which it was ordained by the divine intellect . . . [whereas] with respect to its conformity with a human intellect, a thing is said to be true insofar as it is such as to cause a true estimate about itself . . . In a natural thing, *truth is found especially in the first, rather than in the second, sense;* for its reference to the divine intellect comes before its reference to a human intellect. Even if there were no human intellects, things could be said to be true because of their relation to the divine intellect. But if, by an impossible supposition, intellect did not exist and things did continue to exist, *then the essentials of truth would in no wise remain.*[89]

If St. Thomas had himself raised the question "why is the definition of truth a true definition?" he would have had to reply that the definition was true because it expressed the relation of conformity of the (human) mind (asserting the classical definition of truth) with that reality which was the state of affairs actually created by God, namely, the world in which the truth of things (including the truth of the definition of truth) is

[89] *De Veritate,* I, 2.

their relation to the divine intellect. In other words the definition of truth is true because God has established a world in which intellect and thing face each other, are spatially and temporarily related, can act transitively upon each other, and the intellect is endowed with intentional powers. The objective reality of truth, (which the definition of truth mirrors for us), is the relation of all these things to God—the relation, for instance, of the confrontation of intellect and thing, to God. The warrant for presupposing a pre-cognitive relation of mind to things (such as the truth of the definition of truth) is the divinely established relation of the world of God.

The failure to take account of the empirical character of truth is, thus, conditioned by the assumption that the definition of truth can be made from the viewpoint of someone who is above both the human mind and its objects. But who can *define* truth from such viewpoint? Man can *imagine* this situation; he can by abstraction *suppose* that he is above both his mind and its objects. But only a reality, God, who has actually and effectively established mind, object, and the relation between the two, can actually and effectively fill such a role. The nature of this assumption—indeed, this presumption—consisting in the attempt to understand truth from the viewpoint of God, did not rise to the surface as long as the problematic character of the classical concept of knowledge remained itself submerged. But when the Cartesian problem appeared, the assumption was unearthed. Descartes' appeal to the veracity of God was but the natural issue of the doctrine of St. Thomas.

The Hellenic-Western philosophical tradition has already walked this road once before. Why should philosophy circle back and start with St. Thomas all over again? It would seem

320

the better part of elementary common sense to take note of what the first round accomplished, and thence to proceed epistemologically only after taking account of the empirical character of the experience of truth. The philosophical understanding of the nature of truth must be reached by philosophy without resort either to the veracity of God or to the self-contradictory supposition that man can understand his own experience by looking at it from outside the object-subject relation, or by examining human experience as an alien god might—that is, by taking a field trip to the world and then returning home to write a scholarly dissertation: *Inside Darkest Creation: the Total Situation in the Universe Today, with Special Reference to the Relation Between Human Minds and Things.*[90] We must, in other words, take account of the fact that when the knowing mind is related to being by a relation of adequation (or, for that matter inadequation, a real possibility in this alternative understanding of truth), truth has already occurred and has already *been known* to occur.

Once the degree of epistemological reflexivity required in order to ground the real distinction between essence and existence upon empirical facts has been reached, the observation I have just remarked upon is in principle unavoidable: in point of curious fact, St. Thomas did not manage to avoid it altogether, although he avoided admitting it into his epistemological calculations. But St. Thomas was explicitly aware that the truth as such *is known:* truth, he thought, "may be [said to be] in the sense, or in the [simple apprehension of the] intellect . . . [in the same

---

[90] The god would have found ample inspiration for his thesis topic in Ludwig Wittgenstein, *Tractatus Logico-Philosophicus,* (London, 1961), 5, 631.

way in which it may be said to be] in anything that is true [namely, in a secondary sense of the term]; but truth is not [in the sense, or in the simple apprehension of the intellect] in the [same] way in which the known is in the knower [that is, intentionally], as is required by that which we [properly] call truth; for the perfection of the intellect is truth as known." [91] But, neglecting the empirical character of this assertion—for surely this assertion can be made only because it is a fact, not because we know what truth is before we enquire into it—St. Thomas put it to no other use than to conclude somewhat unfortunately, (and somewhat self-contradictorily, as if there could be "logical truth" without "ontological truth"), that truth is found only in the judgment.

If we take account, however, of the *experience* of truth, and of the exclusively *empirical* nature of our experience of truth, we may be in a position to note that the mind's relation of conformity to being, when it knows being truthfully, does not warrant the assumption that this conformity itself expresses the nature of truth "in itself," independently of our understanding of it, by virtue of what truth is prior to its coming into being in knowledge. For this would amount to assuming that the truth of this judgment: "truth is the conformity of the mind to being," is the mind's conformity to its own *pre-cognitive* relation to the object of knowledge. Or, to put it the other way about, the classical concept of truth presupposes that the conformity of the mind to its object (which supposedly *results* from the act of knowledge), is warranted by the relation (of opposition) which obtains between the mind and its object *prior* to knowledge. The difficulty should be obvious: this would imply that true knowl-

[91] *ST*, I, 16, 2.

edge is literally a *re*-cognition of what is; it would construe true knowledge as a cognition of things *prior to* a cognition of things. This is, to say the least, a great deal to ask. Yet, it is this very assumption that permits a philosopher such as St. Thomas to pay little more than lip service to the observation that "the perfection of the intellect is truth as known," and to ignore this observation when it comes to defining truth.

The conformity of the mind to being *can* be asserted; there is a warrant in experience for doing so. But it can be asserted self-deceptively as well as truthfully. It can be asserted from a viewpoint which supposes itself to be above or beyond experience. This is the condition of the possibility of defining truth as the conformity of the mind to being. I trust I have made sufficiently clear, however, that this definition is deficient *by its own criteria,* and is neither faithfully grounded upon experience nor able to withstand criticism. It is grounded upon an assumption which is made possible by experience, but which is nonetheless contrary to fact: it assumes that we can stand outside our immediate experience in order to judge empirically the conformity (or nonconformity) of two things foreign to us, namely mind and thing. We can, on the other hand, assert the mind's conformity to being as a matter of observation, as a matter of fact revealed by our reflection upon our own experience. But this does not imply that truth is the mind's conformity to things: it implies rather that this relation is the result of truth. If so, we still have to determine what truth is.

The classical conception of truth and the doctrine of the essential infallibility of the intellect involve each other. If either the reality of error or the empirical character of truth were acknowledged no epistemology could define truth as the conformity of the intellect to things, (and if both were maintained epistemology might even proceed to develop an alternative view of truth). For so to define truth would be to define it *a priori,* from a viewpoint external to the intellect itself.

Those who persist in defining truth as the conformity of the mind to being should not forget that this definition must itself be judged to be true. Yet, on the assumption of the classical view of truth this judgment can never be reasonably—it can only be dogmatically—made. If, on the contrary, we recognize the illegitimacy of attempting to define truth from a viewpoint other than that of experience itself, then the first constructive step is to observe that whenever we observe the conformity of the mind to being, truth has *already* come into being. The conformity in question is not a worldly or cosmic fact, a fact of nature, a fact whose truth has been itself apprehended from a third position other than those of both the mind and thing. But truth is the basis of the conformity; and truth is the achievement of knowledge. Truth pertains strictly to the order of knowledge, it is exclusively a reality of the mind; it cannot be said to be except insofar as it is the being of knowledge, the being of mind. Finally, if we also recall that knowledge produces the self-differentiation of subject from object, we are in a position to state that truth is the quality or value of the reality of man as the selfhood of consciousness emerges by self-differentiation from the world, that is, as the self constitutes itself as a self by its objectification of the reality of the world. Therefore, the mind's relation of conformity to being, which results from true knowledge, is a conformity to being precisely insofar as being is objectified by knowledge.

The conformity of the mind to being is not grounded upon the respect due, as it were, to the supposedly prior claims of being over man. The obligatory character of truth is not due to the fact that justice must be done to the world when we know it. It is due to the fact that we must do justice to ourselves when we become conscious of the world. All metaphors which indicate any sort of "submission" of the mind to reality—a submission, indeed, sometimes said to be due in humility—are radically mistaken and misleading. It is not, of course, that there would be anything shameful in such submission—any more than there would be anything meritorious in it. It is simply that the relation of consciousness to reality seems to be best understood strictly in terms of the factual situation indicated by empirical facts. This means: truth is best understood in the absence of *a priori*—I stress *a priori*—preoccupations with hierarchies of being, with veneration or *amour propre,* or with the alleged morality of the facts.[92] The facts, even the facts of experience, the empirical facts concerning the nature of man, are in themselves neither virtuous nor immoral, neither proud nor meek, neither anal-erotic nor sado-masochistic [93] but simply the facts.

The mind's conformity to being, then, is not that which we should procure on account of its value; it is not that for which we should strive or that which we should pursue. It is understandable if in this respect we have been in the past the victims of a confusion not unlike that of a doting mother who would force her child to wear eyeglasses, because a scientific survey had revealed that most geniuses had bad eyesight. But it would not be reasonable, it would not be intellectually tolerable—and, given

---

[92] I do not deny—in fact, I insist—that consciousness is moral from the outset. Cf. above, pp. 270 ff. *Consciousness* is *conscience,* as the French, Italian and Spanish languages very well know.

[93] Cf. above, Ch. II, note 24.

the economic, social and political problems created by the self-development of consciousness,[94] it would not be even biologically safe—to continue to think so.[95]

We in the 20th Century are now in a position to understand that although the mind's conformity to being has a role within the process of man's quest for truth, (that is, man's quest for creatively being himself), this role is almost precisely the opposite of what we have always taken it to be. For, in a sense, the mind's conformity to being, insofar as it manifests the truth of knowledge, is what impels the intellect to transcend its knowledge and, thus, in the last analysis, its own truth: the mind's conformity to being is there to be *overcome*. It is not to be understood, therefore, as a conformity to what *already* was, nor a conformity to what *forever* will continue to be. It is a conformity to what *is*— it is at once the sign that we have come to the truth, and the sign that the truth is yet to come. It is not a passive, but a creative relation, which began with what used to be, but which even now is being altered, re-conceptualized, re-vised and re-fashioned by the self-creative consciousness of man in order that it may become itself. To sum up: truth is that property of consciousness which renders man transcendent; it is that quality of knowledge which impels consciousness beyond itself. Truth is, therefore, that which makes human understanding dynamic and creative, searching and self-critical, restless and progressive, and ambitious to the literally ultimate degree.

[94] I have discussed this in *Christianity and Revolution,* (New York, 1963), pp. 187–199.

[95] "What is most thought-provoking? How does it show itself in our thought-provoking time? Most thought-provoking is that we are still not thinking," Martin Heidegger, *What is Called Thinking,* (New York, 1968), p. 4.

We may understand this concept of truth better if we recall the correlativity of truth and error upon which I insisted above. I then suggested that if one does not respect the reality of error one is not likely to do justice to the reality of truth. I now direct our attention to the essentially retrospective character of error. It is surely not an accident that we can never experience *being* mistaken: we can only experience *having been* mistaken. The importance of this can be obscured by a fairly common misinterpretation of the fact. We imagine that when we experience having been mistaken we but recognize the error from which we have been suffering all along. We were in error, thus, only because we had not recognized the error for what it was. Somehow the mind's act of knowledge had originally failed to establish a relation of conformity to reality. But now we know: now the mind is really true. Previously we did not really—that is truthfully— know.

The inadequacy of this view of error is apparent from its implication that it is sheer accident that error is never discovered while it is being committed. "Now we do know: previously we did not really know." But what is the difference between "knowing" and "not really knowing" except that whereas "knowing" is *always now* (it is never, not once, by way of exception, otherwise), "not really knowing" is *always* (never, ever without exception) *at an earlier time?* Can it be reasonably supposed that although one's experience of error so far has always been retrospective, perhaps the next time one will become conscious of one's mistake precisely insofar as one commits it and remains in it? It seems more reasonable to suppose instead, if we *cannot* experience being (at present) in error, but only being (at present) in the truth, that this impossibility is indicative of the nature of error and truth. The retrospective character of error points to its converse, the prospective character of truth. The truth in which we *are,* if we are aware of the real possibility of error, notwith-standing the fact that it is not being experienced at all, must be conceived as that which we *pursue.* This pursuance-avoidance, not mutual exclusion, is what describes the nature of the opposi-tion between true and false.

In other words, the experience of truth implies the possibility of error. If we do not take this proposition seriously, the experi-ence of truth can only lead to dogmatism. If, on the other hand, we pay attention to our experience of truth, we cannot but be deeply and decisively impressed by the fact that truth is never experienced as a stable condition but, on the contrary, as a process of self-organization and re-organization: we are always coming to the truth, always discovering it. We never (*pace* Heidegger) really manage to "stand in the truth." [96] We can only clamber onto it, and keep running with it in order to avoid falling into untruth. In fact, the surest way to fall into error is to *stand* in the truth.

In any event, just as consciousness is the presence of itself to itself, truth is the orientation of consciousness towards itself. That is, truth is the orientation of the mind towards that condition which it does not have, namely, truth. (This self-involving, circu-lar character of truth is responsible for the traditional alternation

[96] I maintain this criticism despite Heidegger's explanation (*Being and Time,* p. 263) that "this assertion . . . does not purport to say that ontically Dasein is introduced 'to all the truth' either always or just in every case, but rather that the disclosedness of its ownmost Being belongs to its existential condition." This is true enough. But one should also stress that truth does not belong to the existential constitution of con-sciousness all the time.

of philosophers between truth as the objective of knowledge and the subjective condition of the mind in act of knowledge.) In short, truth is that quality which consciousness must have in order to proceed towards the truth. For truth is the prospective dimension of consciousness.[97] The truth is the quality of consciousness which points or leads beyond itself. For, being a quality of consciousness, truth is the quality of that which, in order to be, must be beyond itself. Truth is but the essential property of consciousness, keeping in mind that consciousness is the *transcendence* of man. For the truth leads beyond itself above all by creating suspicion about itself, by opening up the possibility of supposing itself to be false. Conversely, error is that which we wish to avoid, that which the truth must extricate itself from. This is why in the pursuit of truth we can be held back either by retaining erroneous knowledge or by not transcending true knowledge—the two are not so very different—whereas we can be impelled forwards, towards the truth, either by transcending erroneous knowledge or by giving up the true knowledge we already have—and in practice the two amount to the same.

Heidegger has drawn attention to another inadequacy of the traditional epistemologies, recalling the etymology of the word, which points to our thinking of error as a sort of wandering, a straying from the path: "man errs. He does not merely fall into error, he lives in error always because by ex-sisting, he in-sists and is thus already in error. The error in which he lives is not just something that runs along beside him like a ditch, some-

---

[97] Whereas *freedom* is the pro-spectively self-creative reality of consciousness. Hence, the distinction between the true and the good is not a distinction between "transcendentals" of being (*passiones entis*), but between temporalities of human experience, namely, man's being-present-out-of-his-past, and his being-present-towards-the-future.

thing he occasionally falls into. No, error is part of the inner structure of *Da-sein,* in which historical man is involved." [98]

If there is no predetermined path which knowledge is required to tread, no truth predetermined by an *a priori* disposition such as a "pre-established harmony" implicit in God's creation of both the mind and its objects, then the metaphor of "error," the mind "wandering" or going "astray," is fundamentally invalid. For there is no empirical reason whatever to suppose that, prior to the truth of knowledge, there is a truth of things, constituted by God's knowledge of them, a truth which is the measure of the truth of human knowledge. But if knowledge has truth-value insofar as it is an achievement of the order of being rather than as a retracing of a path previously mapped out, then error is not a deviation from a prescribed route. It is not a failure to discover what we are pre-required to discover, but a failure of consciousness to achieve itself—to be sure, in relation to the world in which it exists and in which it is required to achieve itself—a failure which, of course, admits of wide variations in degree. Error is thus strictly relative to truth, and *vice versa*. Error is a real and intrinsic part of knowledge. Quite as Heidegger has said, man "does not merely fall into error, he lives in error."

But there is, I fear, a certain ambiguity in this expression. The least that should be added in order to clear it up, (if not also to avoid an unduly pessimistic construction of man's "life" in error), would be the qualification that man lives in error in the same way and at the same time that he "stands in the truth." There is no erroneous knowledge which does not at least point

[98] Heidegger, "The essence of truth," in Werner Brock (ed.), *Existence and Being,* (London, 1949), pp. 344–345.

in the direction, or open up the possibility, of truth. As long as consciousness is in process of development there is no error so erroneous that it may not be overcome, nor a truth so true that we may discard the possibility that in the future its relative error might come to light. Likewise, this understanding of error helps explain why there can be some *truly false* knowledge—that is, why there can be knowledge which is truly knowledge, yet not true knowledge, but false. Indeed, insofar as it is not yet achieved, is not yet fully itself, true knowledge is truly knowledge and yet is always short of the truth.

It follows that there can be no criterion of truth, if by this is meant some test or other means which could be applied to knowledge in order that the mind may be able to judge whether it is true and, if so, whether it can be confident that it will never, so long as it remains rational, find its truth to be so inadequate that it will have to re-think the matter all over again and possibly arrive at a different truth. I am not suggesting that such a criterion of truth is unattainable—I am suggesting that it is unavailable, and that even if, *per impossibile,* it were available, it would not be the intellectual bargain it is sometimes presumed to be. There can be no criterion of truth, because the certainty of human understanding must always remain, as long as it is a *reasonable* certitude, relative to the possibility of the evolution of truth. Certitude is unreasonable if it is made to consist in the judgment that, since our knowledge is true, we need not count on the possibility that our understanding may develop (except by accretion to, and explicitation of, the truth we already possess). No person has really profited by his own or by the accumulated experience of mankind if he assumes, by however indirect implication, that there are ever any circumstances in human life when

331

the possibility that one's judgment may be inadequate can be altogether discarded by a rational mind. *Nunca digas, de esta agua no beberé.* There can be no criterion of truth because the human intellect is by nature fallible—this is not an imperfection, it is but the other side of its propensity for pursuing the truth and developing its understanding. Hence, the human intellect cannot be rendered infallible with the help of intellectual gadgets, however ingenious, or by spiritual short-circuiting techniques.

It is perfectly obvious, on the other hand, if by criterion of truth is meant criterion of verisimilitude, that there is no dearth of criteria of truth. Common sense discovers not a few of these: everyone knows some signs, *however unreliable,* by which he can tell, for example, whether to buy second-hand philosophical concepts from certain men. Logic systematizes some of these means, and the reflexive study of methodology—whether, at one end of the spectrum, the scientific methodology which philosophy is concerned with, or, at the other, the life-methodology which is the subject of such varied disciplines as orthopsychiatry, psychoanalysis, personality theory and clinical psychology—applies man's understanding towards an improved understanding of the techniques whereby consciousness relates itself to reality. But precisely because no such technique can be devised except by the application of human consciousness, the criteria of truth can be no more infallible than human consciousness itself. Thus, if there actually existed an infallible criterion of truth, it would be useless; for any intellect which could discover such an infallible criterion would be infallible to begin with, and therefore would have no conceivable use for its discovery of the criterion of truth.

Error is not an abnormal, abortive issue of knowledge: it is the normal condition of its development. "To err is human" because in the normal run of human affairs it seems to be the ordinary way in which we learn and progress in the truth. The idea that unless its natural course is impeded the human intellect will uninterruptedly and without error progress from not-knowing to knowing is unrealistic and self-deceptive to the point of presumption. This unwarranted optimism, moreover, is the cause of an unwarranted pessimism in the face of the reality of error: if we imagine that the intellect is essentially infallible, we are bound to be intolerant of error. All this begins to come about when we fail to accept the facts of experience about experience itself, and proceed instead to define the truth in terms of what, presumably, it ought to be, rather than in terms of what it in fact can be *experienced* to be.

If, on the contrary, we are resolved to ascertain the nature of truth from what we observe about it, we are likely to admit that error has a most important and valuable role in the emergence of truth. The creative, developmental character of human knowledge means that the quality of its possible achievement is proportional to the quality of its possible failure. We cannot reasonably expect human knowledge to progress without making mistakes. What we may reasonably (though by no means infallibly) expect is that if we keep making mistakes we will in the end make some progress in the pursuit of truth. Conversely, we can forbid ourselves the possibility of error only by denying ourselves the cultivation of truth. Thus, it is better—I mean, it is more natural, more in accordance with the nature of human knowledge—to err than to remain ignorant, to err than to allow the truth to stagnate, to err than to forgo the development of consciousness, to err than to risk the neglect of truth. The implications of this view for such practical questions as the nature and extent of intellectual freedom, and its relevance to philosophical and theological enquiry into every other form of human self-understanding, may be easily surmised. But of all these implications one is particularly important and will be dealt with here at greater length. For all the suggestions I have made so far can be summed up in one: man's self-understanding has evolved. But human nature is definable by man's self-understanding. Therefore, human nature has evolved. What does this mean in relation to our enquiry into the foundations of belief?

EVOLVING CONSCIOUSNESS
AND EVOLUTIONARY TRUTH

Like every other form of professional human thought, philosophy contributes to the development of human self-understanding. But philosophy contributes to such development essentially by reflecting, articulating and intensifying the self-understanding that man already has. Philosophy is creative, and philosophical thought must show leadership and initiative. But philosophy can do so only because it is a reflection upon human experience. The significance of any valid philosophical reflection on the nature of man's self-understanding is given in the first place not by whatever originality and novelty it may exhibit as a defloration of virgin truths, but on the contrary by whatever success it may have in articulating and bringing up to reflective consciousness that which everyone, or almost everyone, already knows. Philosophical innovations are to a very large extent the result of our telling ourselves what we already know, so that we will not have to occupy ourselves with it any longer, and thus be in a position to go beyond what we already know. Thus, if the philosophical reflections on the nature of man's self-understanding offered above are valid, their significance lies not in their being a discovery of a truth no one suspected, but in their description of changes in the nature of human experience that have been *already* brought about by man himself.

The nature of man has changed, because human experience has changed. Human experience is typically not the same today as it was a thousand years or two ago, just as the experience of civilized man over the last ten thousand years has been vastly different from that of primitive, pre-agricultural man. Man has evolved—he has never stopped evolving. The restoration of belief cannot be undertaken except in and through awareness of its evolutionary context. But this does not mean: Christianity must reconcile *Genesis* with the Darwinian reconstruction of the apperance of man half to a million years ago or so. It means: Christianity must be relevant to the level of human consciousness achieved by man half to a million years after he appeared on earth, and it must already begin to plan for a mankind which can begin to foresee itself, if not quite another half to a million years hence, at least several hundred years into the time to come. The evolution that really counts is not that which happened a long time ago, and is now over and done with, and which we need remember only because if we did not we would misapprehend ourselves: apart from that we can forget about the evolutionary process that brought man down from the trees. The evolution that must count in human calculation henceforth is rather that evolution which may make it possible for man to climb to the stars.

This evolutionary age is only beginning, and we cannot yet tell very much about it. But we can tell even now that it is a truly different evolutionary process from that of the past, and we can point to some of the ways in which it is different from that of the past. We can tell, in other words, in what essential respects the current human evolutionary processes are already apparent, as they have continued from the dawn of man to our own mid-morning day. The philosopher's contribution to this topic is especially relevant, since one of these essential aspects is clearly of the epistemic order, namely the heightening of man's self-understanding. Man has been conscious as long as he has been man; but with accelerating speed in modern times—say, the last five centuries or so—he has become increasingly conscious of his consciousness. Therefore, man has learned to re-define himself. But his re-definition of himself is not a substitute for his previous definition of himself, as if he had now learned to define himself correctly after having failed to do so correctly the first time. Man has not simply defined himself a second time: he has re-defined himself for the first time. The evolutionary importance of man's learning to re-define himself is aptly to be compared, in logarithmic ratio, I would estimate, with the invention of agriculture, or the foundation of the city. If so, its consequences can be assessed only on a comparable logarithmic scale.

The Hellenic-Western intellectual tradition has always been aware of the importance of man's self-understanding. What we have not realized before recent times is that the development of man's self-understanding is not to be interpreted as the gradual uncovering of a reality, man, which antedates man's progress in discovering it; nor therefore, that, the significance of man's self-understanding is that a truer knowledge of what man is facilitates better applications of theory to life. What man has begun to realize is that, since understanding is to be understood in relation to itself, the nature of man can be adequately defined only in terms of human understanding, and if so, in terms of a development in man's self-understanding brought about by the development of his understanding of himself. This is why, as I have suggested, the evolution of man's self-understanding is identical with the evolution of the nature of man.[99] The novelty of the latest evolutionary development of man is that human evolution is now beginning to pass into a self-directed stage.

For all that, to say that human nature has been affected by the development of man's self-understanding is not to say that man has evolved beyond humanity. It would be clearly incorrect to suppose, for instance, that contemporary man is related to the

[99] I do not imagine that many sophisticated persons will need the following explanation, but I have in fact met some who do, and I would rather, if possible, not leave room for even unreasonable misunderstanding. The fact that some Greek philosophers, and not a few mediaeval ones, held doctrines of universal emanation, applying them even to the origin of different species, does not remotely mean that the Greek or mediaeval philosophers developed the concept of evolutionary process. No one can do so as long as he thinks that species are definable by genus and difference. The Greeks and the mediaevals did think in terms of substantial becoming and of species, and therefore in time developed doctrines of the origin of species. But they could scarcely have developed doctrines of the transformation of species, since such doctrines assume that species are not essentially definable, intelligible realities, but only *historically* definable ones. Even today evolution, even biological evolution, can be tolerated and accepted by neo-Thomists, but not incorporated into their systems; and, as is well known, human evolution in the strict sense of the term is frequently not even tolerated by these philosophers, who admit only the evolution of the body, but not that of the soul. That is, they admit prehuman evolution, but the origin of man in his full and actual humanity is due, in each and every instance and not merely *in principiis,* directly and immediately to the personal and separate intervention of God, who infuses a human soul into every fertilized human egg (possibly at the very instant when ovum and spermatozoon become linked).

man of early civilization as *homo sapiens* is related to the early hominid species. To be sure, the most likely supposition we can make today is that, if only human germ plasm lasts long enough, man will in time evolve to the point that he must be considered specifically different from that which we today call man. Man's evolution beyond anything which now could be reasonably called humanity is at least a distinct possibility, if not indeed a likelihood. But it would be out of the question to imagine that the day of the new trans-human species has arrived or is near. On the other hand, the development of man's self-understanding to date cannot be construed as an accidental change which does not touch the basic, supposedly rock-like substance of human nature. Even if man has not evolved beyond humanity we should not misunderstand the magnitude, the evolutionary nature, of the change that has occurred.

It is true that underneath all the historical changes which human memory has recorded we can find a continuity in human experience and a community of human history which some thinkers would interpret as an underlying constancy indistinguishable from human nature in the Greek and mediaeval sense of the word. Well, it is true that any man living today is capable of identifying himself, on the whole, with the human characters portrayed by, say, the Greek dramatists. We can read the earliest records of civilized man and find—or reconstruct—much of the same experiences and feelings, the same aspirations and vicissitudes, the same anxieties and hopes, the same fears and virtues, the same loves and hates, that are familiar to everyone today. Contemporary man can, however indirectly, communicate with primitive man, and up to a point could enter into society with him. As it so happens, a few, scattered human groups have

338

survived to our own day, retaining modes of experience, self-organization, self-relation to the world, and self-understanding which are most probably unchanged from what they were in palaeolithic days. Yet we have no difficulty in recognizing the essential humanity of, say, the Australian aborigines, which is probably the most primitive society extant today. Does this not point to a common nature which has not changed, and which underlies the otherwise spectacular changes of strictly accidental forms that separate, say, an Australian bushman hunter from his antipodal American astronaut?

I think not. We can speak of communication and common life between a 20th Century Western man and his primitive contemporaries, or between a 20th Century time traveller marooned in the palaeolithic and the natives of the times, only in a somewhat equivocal sense of these terms: we may be able, given enough time, inclination and anthropological and sociological *savoir faire,* to live in a palaeolithic society, but a palaeolithic man could not learn to live in ours. The palaeolithic man *could* have become one of us, had he but been born and brought up among us; but as it so happens he did not. He is now formed, and in this sense he is forever alienated from us. The fact that a certain degree of communication and common life would be possible, would only show that, as I have already mentioned, the evolution of man has not yet reached the degree which it may one day reach, when communication and society with any level of *homo sapiens* shall have become altogether impossible. But, as best we can determine today, this change, if ever it comes, will not necessarily take place suddenly or sharply; it is not likely that there will ever be a given generation which shall have crossed the threshold of a new species, leaving their parents

339

behind. Nonetheless, the development of man's self-understanding *contributes* to the process of the evolution of human nature: it can be understood only in terms of its evolutionary role. The fact that man is evolving and that, therefore, his nature is already different from what it has been at given stages of the past, is not gainsaid by the equally clear fact that the evolution of human nature has not reached its end. Conversely, the fact that human evolution has not reached its final end must not be misunderstood to mean that it is not taking place at all.

Nor should the importance of the contribution of the development of man's self-understanding towards the evolution of human nature be underrated, simply because human evolution is not mutational in character. The difference between man and ape would be insufficiently appreciated if, on the grounds provided by comparative anatomy, physiology, embryology and histology, one were to stress the constant primateness of both types, noting that the only "only" real difference between man and ape is that man has an additional pair of chromosomes. For this mere, microscopic detail makes all the difference in the world. The sort of approach to the understanding of human nature—as indeed to the understanding of the nature of anything—for which "rationality" is more important than chromosomes, has become integral part of our philosophical tradition, because it originated in the idea of defining by proximate genus and specific difference. The conception of man as a *rational animal* has embodied a certain methodological bias that ultimately makes it impossible to define man in terms of what is empirically ascertainable about, and truly distinctive of him, namely, his relation to himself. I have remarked on this above, but now we are in a position to grasp this consequence: the very continuity of human development, a continuity which is so evident that anyone should be able to take it for granted without being suspected of having failed to observe it, shows that for all its common elements throughout its history, human experience changes in *only* one crucial respect, namely, in its experience of itself. But if the "only" human experience that has changed is the experience of experience, the course of human evolution has been affected in a decisive way.

It is for this reason that it is legitimate to contrast "contemporary experience" with the experience of man during earlier historical ages, even if it is true that the change in question does not appear to make much difference to the life of every human being who has been born in the 20th Century, or even to the life of every member of those very few human societies which so reckon time that they call the present Century the 20th. It is possible to state truthfully that the atomic age was introduced in 1944 at Alamogordo, New Mexico, though it is equally true that people became aware only much later that on a certain day in the past the first man-made nuclear explosion had been set off. Likewise, when man, who has long been a conscious being (and indeed up to a point conscious that he was a conscious being) begins to realize the implications of his being conscious for his understanding of what consciousness is, the development in question must be understood as contributing irreversibly to the process of man's evolutionary transformation—even if in many outward respects human life goes on as before. This is an event of evolutionary significance, which in due course will affect the *whole* of human existence. Therefore, those who believe that human nature has remained essentially unchanged, evidently deceive themselves. For what has changed in human history is "merely" that which is essential to man—even if the change is as yet only incipient, even if its effects are noticeable only in random symptoms (like the emergence of new human problems), and even if it has not yet had enough cumulative consequences to amount to a transformation of the species as a whole.

The continuity of human experience must indeed be stressed. Those who see in this continuity evidence of an unchanging substratum do not do full justice to it. An appreciation of the actual basis of continuity of human consciousness suggests the very opposite. The fact that every human age to date has been bound to every other in common *experiences,* does not mean that human *experience* remains constant. For the real, important and essential historical continuity of man is given by this: that the evolutionary development of human consciousness is not the transformation of consciousness into something other than consciousness, nor is it a development which is due to an agency other than that of human consciousness itself. For man, who has always been conscious, and who has never supposed himself to be anything but conscious, has become sufficiently aware of his own consciousness to be able to define himself to himself in terms of his consciousness. Though man has always been a conscious being, for a long time (after an even longer period when he was unable to define himself at all) he became able to define himself only as a rational animal. When he became able to define himself as a conscious being, however, he did not cease to be a conscious being, nor did he cease to be what he had been when he thought of himself as a rational animal, or what he had been when he did not think of himself very often at all. The "only" change has been in his definition of himself to himself. But for the sort of being

342

whose nature makes it possible for him to define himself to himself, this can be scarcely deemed to be an "accidental" change. The continuity of human nature must indeed be emphasized and fully understood. Were it not for that continuity, man would not be man. Were it not for that continuity, man would not evolve.

"All" that has happened, then, is that the self-defining being learned to define himself as self-defining. Man's discovery of consciousness, man's awareness of man's self-defining (and, therefore, self-problematic) nature, is thus the discovery of nothing new: surely the continuity of the development of human nature could not be more strongly underscored than by this affirmation. Man has discovered not only what he has always been, but also what (in a way) he has always *known* himself to be, namely, a conscious being. The sum total of man's evolution to date since he became man is given by a development which consists in "no more" than this, namely, that his consciousness has continued to develop in accordance with the nature of consciousness itself, as originally constituted and as still operative today.

I have already suggested that a measure of the continuity of the development of human experience is given by the fact that in its development so far consciousness has become nothing other than itself. I should now stress that another measure of the same continuity is given by the fact that this development has been brought about by no agency outside consciousness itself. The importance of this would be overlooked if one failed to keep in mind that man is consciousness, and effectively reverted to the idea that he is essentially definable as a rational animal. If man, when he becomes conscious of his own consciousness, is evolutionarily affected in his very nature, then consciousness is not only evolving, but self-evolving. Thus, the "only" change that has taken place in human nature is that man, who has always been conscious, who has always been evolving and, indeed, self-evolving, has now become consciously self-evolving. Or, at very least, he has now become aware that he has long been engaged in self-evolution, and that he may thus now engage consciously and deliberately in self-evolution. For the first time man can now do and be what he has always done and been. Does he do this, and is he this, in a *new* way? If by this is meant that human consciousness evolves, then the answer is yes. But, of course, man has always been conscious since he became man. To become conscious through the exercise of consciousness is, in this sense, scarcely new to man. Thus, Julian Huxley's insight, that in man "evolution [is] . . . becoming conscious of itself," [100] also implies that in consciousness evolution is becoming self-evolving: man is an evolutionary process which, having by its own nature become conscious of itself as evolving, can now consciously direct his own evolution.

This is why, as I have suggested, the continuity of human experience indicates a more comprehensive truth than is realized by those who take it as the sign of a constant least common denominator of intelligibility: it also helps explain why the very evolution of human consciousness is sometimes mistaken for the absence of evolution. For the evolution *of man* takes place on an incomparably greater scale—indeed, not so much on a greater scale as along an entirely new dimension—than did the evolution *to man*. Curiously, the pre-evolutionary view of man as the apex of earthly creation may well retain more validity than biologists

[100] Introduction to Pierre Teilhard de Chardin, *The Phenomenon of Man*, (London, 1959), p. 20.

have usually supposed. In a very real sense the process of zoological evolution on earth may have reached its end with the
emergence of man, and it may now be a closed period in the
history of our world: "we are now on the way to the establishment of a Psychozoic Kingdom where brain overshadows brawn
and rationality overshadows natural instinct."[101] But whether
it is open or closed, evolution has not ceased. In either event it
proceeds, perhaps more intensively than ever, along a new, different dimension: "in Man evolution is interiorised and made
purposeful."[102]

The stage of human evolution at which man, or at least mankind's Hellenic-Western vanguard, has already arrived, a stage
which is characterized not so much by man's particular achievements as by the general achievement of his having opened up new
possibilities for himself—this stage is for Christianity not a

[101] Harlow Shapley, *The View From a Distant Star*, (New York, 1967),
p. 159.

[102] Pierre Teilhard de Chardin, *The Future of Man*, (London, 1964),
p. 212. Elsewhere in the same work Teilhard remarked that "until the
coming of man the pattern of the Tree of Life was always that of a fan,
a spread of morphological radiations diverging more and more, each
radiation culminating in a new 'knot' and breaking into a fan of its
own. [Para.] But at the human level a radical change, seemingly due
to the spiritual phenomenon of Reflection, overtook this law of development. It is generally accepted that what distinguishes man psychologically
from other living creatures is the power acquired by his consciousness of
turning in upon itself. The animal knows, it has been said; but only man,
among animals, knows that he knows. . . . But what has perhaps not
been sufficiently noted is that, still by virtue of this power of Reflection,
living hominised elements become capable . . . of drawing close to one
another, of communicating, finally of uniting. . . . In time, with the
Reflexion of the individual upon himself, there comes an Inflexion, then
a clustering together of the living shoots, soon to be followed . . . by the
spread of the living complex thus constituted over the whole surface of
the globe . . . [thus giving] birth to the Noosphere," *ibid*, pp. 158–159.

danger, but an opportunity, and it hurls at religious belief a challenge, not a threat. The contemporary period of human development, a period which is definable neither, obviously, as the final achievement of man's moral maturity nor, hopefully, as the onset of his biological senectude, but simply as the end of the adolescence of man, opens up the possibility of bringing about the universalization of the Universalist Faith in unsuspected forms, to unprecendented degrees, and in more deeply spiritual ways than has been possible at any previous time in its history. Mankind's mid-20th Century arrival at the threshold of the first planetary system of cultures, the first civilization of the human race as such, creates, I do not say merely in the history of the Christian Church, but in that of *homo sapiens,* the possibility of a truly catholic religion in the literal and widest sense of the word.

But if it is true that human experience has evolved, and that man's redefinition of himself in terms of his own consciousness is what opens up this very possibility, it follows with the strictest logic that the universalization of Universalism must begin with the reconstruction of Christian belief on the same foundations upon which man stands when he redefines himself. And, in the first place, this must be done regarding the essential object of Christian belief, namely, the God whose truest name is love, that is, self-gift.

5.

The Reconstruction
of Theistic Belief

RECONSTRUCTION VERSUS TRANSCENDENCE
IN PHILOSOPHY TODAY

The philosophical developments I have discussed so far, the shift in the foundations of all human experience as man heightens his consciousness of his consciousness, have historically resulted in Christian disbelief—and not merely disbelief in this or that doctrine, or disbelief in the doctrines of any given Christian denomination, or disbelief in any given religion, but disbelief of every religious sort, beginning with disbelief in God. This did not come about suddenly. In the process which led to this radical religious disbelief we may distinguish three stages, which correspond closely to the stages in the development of the history of philosophy from St. Thomas to our own day.

The first stage was agnosticism. The existence of God could not be proved. But, obviously, it could not be disproved either; and so the most reasonable position was that of scepticism. Like the existence of every extramental reality, the existence of God was problematic; and in the absence of a solution to the basic

347

epistemological question—supposedly, the question how to pass from immanent experience to transcendent reality—the solution to the problem of the existence of the First Transcendent Reality could not possibly have been worked out. The final attempt to do so, namely, Kant's, was grounded upon a yet more fundamentally Hellenic notion than the concept of knowledge as transcendent of the object-subject opposition, namely the dichotomy of intellect and will. But this new tack did not avoid the rocky shore of scepticism either. Belief that rests upon will is, by definition, irrational. And irrational belief may be, by definition, immune to attacks by unbelievers, but it pays for this dubious advantage in the coin of subjectivism: arbitrary choices may need no justification other than one's own satisfaction, but they cannot reasonably claim to be true, or to be valid in relation to the object of belief.

The second stage was anti-theism, of which pantheistic anti-theism such as Hegel's,[1] and atheistic anti-theism such as Ludwig Feuerbach's, Karl Marx's and Friedriech Nietzsche's are the principal varieties. Anti-theism issued from agnosticism out of

[1] I assume here the most common, traditional interpretations of the nature and meaning of Hegel's thought. It is possible, as several recent scholars have maintained, that Hegel has been well nigh universally misunderstood. I am not concerned, however, with the Hegel of *Historie,* but with the Hegel of *Geschichte,* whether or not the two coincide, and even if the historically effective Hegel was created by the misunderstanding of his thought from the outset. I may add that I am not *a priori* well disposed to any historical interpretation which in any way supposes that contemporaries misunderstand what any given philosopher actually thinks. On the contrary, frequently contemporaries—and most especially younger contemporaries—understand any philosopher's thought much better than he himself does. For any man's thought sooner or later reaches its climax and then its end. Consciousness is ahead of itself, but it never can quite catch up with itself.

the realization that religious belief in a God whose existence was problematic was not a harmless anodyne, but a disease of human consciousness. For religious belief may be unreasonable, and may be dismissed; but the phenomenon of religious consciousness is a fact, and must be grappled with. Man's search for reassurance and consolation is a necessity given by consciousness itself and by the nature of the situation *vis-à-vis* reality in which everyone finds himself. This is normal enough. But to fulfil these needs through the projection of man's own consciousness into a transcendent realm of reality beyond all reality, and thereafter to expect redemption from the human condition through the agency of such reality, is to become self-alienated. Belief in a transcendent reality amounts to the pathological development of human consciousness. And worse for consciousness than to lack fulfilment is to be deluded by a pseudo-fulfilment. More tragic for man than to be at loss and disconsolate, is to have foreclosed his future self-realization through the pseudo-fulfilment of religious belief.

This second stage was, thus, only the logical conclusion of agnosticism, which had been but a half-way house to this position. But anti-theism may be bracketed with agnosticism by virtue of certain common assumptions. Anti-theism culminated the long process which had begun with the problematization of knowledge and the ascription of existence to every being as its own primary and intrinsic act. The first moment of this process served to make disbelief in God a reasonable possibility: the second moment served to make it a moral imperative. But the philosophical foundations concerning the nature of knowledge which underlay both these conclusions were, though undermined and tottering, still not fully supplanted by those which were finally developed consciously and positively only in the 20th century. On these new foundations has now been set the third level of Christian disbelief, when positive atheism in its several varieties has taken its turn upon the philosophical stage.

The foundation of positive atheism is phenomenological ontology in its various forms. Phenomenological ontologies can be contrasted with both realistic and idealistic metaphysics, in the first place, by their epistemological basis, which transcends the Hellenic presuppositions of both realism and idealism. But the historical successor of realistic and idealistic metaphysics has been nonetheless *ontology,* that is, a doctrine of being in which it is assumed, quite as in the traditional metaphysics, that the proper name of reality is being. Phenomenological ontologies agree with metaphysics that there can be no reality other than being, that anything to which man can relate himself is being, and, in a word, that reality can be identified *with* being because it can be identified *as* being. However remarkable may be the differences between phenomenological and metaphysical ontologies in their final conclusions concerning the nature of being, these differences result exclusively from the adoption of alternative epistemological positions; phenomenological ontologies diverge from the doctrine of reality found in both realistic and idealist metaphysics, but only insofar as their prior epistemological divergence compels them to develop along different lines their doctrine on nature of reality, that is, being.

I should explain that although it is historically warranted contemporary terminology is a little confusing—but it is highly revealing nonetheless. Following the critique of knowledge developed by and since Kant, modern thought fairly generally (that is, with the exception of few philosophical circles besides Thomistin) has accepted the view that metaphysical knowledge is a delusion. When more recent thinkers like Heidegger and Sartre developed an alternative to the classical concept of knowledge, they re-opened the possibility of a philosophical analysis *of being,* that is, a metaphysics or ontology. Though Heidegger resumed for the most part the use of the name *metaphysics* to refer to this study, most other philosophers, especially those who have followed Sartre, have rejected it, partly because of its historical associations with uncritical thought, partly because of its etymological inadequacy. This is why they frequently refer to the study of being as *ontology.* But since the term ontology is historically synonymous with metaphysics, having been originally (though only in relatively recent times) devised to designate nothing other than metaphysics, it was necessary to distinguish between metaphysical ontologies (i.e. those developed in connection with either realism or idealism) and non-metaphysical, specifically phenomenological, or even empirical, ontologies. But the retention of the name *ontology* is revealing. For all its epistemological dehellenization, which carries it very far indeed towards dehellenization in the study of reality, the metaphysical dehellenization of phenomenological ontology is far from complete. Phenomenological ontology is ontology in precisely the same sense as metaphysical ontology is ontology, namely, in its identification of reality *with* and *as* being.

When the study of being is undertaken as a function of a concept of knowledge of the same general form which, as I have suggested in the previous chapter, is the logical development from Greek epistemology, philosophy must develop a concept of being of the same corresponding general form—such as that which I have suggested above. In such an ontology there can be no room for a First Being, for a Supreme Being, for an Ultimate

Reality which transcends the order of empirically given being. For in this sort of ontology, of which Sartre's is the type, being is absurd, superfluous and essentially relative to possible human experience. A First Being or a Supreme Being would be a contradiction in terms. To assert so much as the conceivability of a Being that would make meaningful that which is essentially absurd, of a Being who would be the sufficient reason of that which is essentially contingent, or of a Being who would transcend the order of reality which finds its proper function in being negated by experience as the self-differentiates itself from the world—this is nothing but the self-alienation of thought. Hence, in this universe of discourse—at least in its purest form —atheism is not simply a doctrine of the non-existence of God, but a doctrine which transcends the problem of the existence or non-existence of God.

In Heidegger this reasoning is put in a relatively primitive form. In his philosophy the practical equivalent of that which in Sartre's later ontology would become the absurdity of being is adumbrated, but under a quite different guise. Heidegger's name for it is the historical hiddenness of the very being of that being whose essence is to reveal itself:

Only the tired latecomers with their supercilious wit imagine that they can dispose of the historical power of appearance by declaring it to be 'subjective' hence very dubious. The Greeks experienced it differently. They were perpetually compelled to wrest being from appearance and preserve it against appearance. (The essence of being is un-concealment.) [2]

Solely in the enduring struggle between being and appearance did they wrest being from the essent, did they carry the essent to

[2] It should be remembered that according to Heidegger the essence of *truth* is "un-concealment."

352

permanence and unconcealment: the gods and the state, the temples and the tragedy, the games and philosophies; all this in the midst of appearance, beset by appearance, but also taking it seriously, knowing of its power. It was in the Sophists and in Plato[3] that appearance was declared to be mere appearance and thus degraded. At the same time being, as *idea,* was exalted to supra sensory realm. A chasm, *chorismos,* was created between the merely apparent essent here below and real being somewhere on high. In that chasm Christianity settled down, at the same time reinterpreting the lower as the created and the higher as the creator. . . . Nietzsche was right in saying that Christianity is Platonism for the people.[4]

But the result is the same. The historical hiddenness of the to-be of being[5] is not to be dispelled by the absurd supposition of someone like St. Thomas, who deemed that being could be more knowable in itself than it could be knowable to us. The essence of being is appearing. Being can be nothing but that which appears. A Being that would transcend appearance is a contradiction in terms. Whatever is hidden from man is either hidden because man does not see it, or else because it *is* not. Beyond being —I mean, beyond being which is, and, (which is the same), beyond being which appears—there can be only nothing. The un-reality of this nothing is effective upon being, and is responsible for its being experienced (for instance, in the form of Dread), as the background of being and as the source of the contingency of being—that is, the source of its *lack* of sufficient reason for being in itself—precisely because there is no Being behind nothingness, no Being to nullify the nothingness of noth-

[3] There is no need for Heidegger to mention Aristotle also, since Aristotelianism is but Platonism squared.

[4] *Introduction to Metaphysics,* (Garden City, 1961), pp. 89–90.

[5] Or, in the terminology of the foregoing translation, the being of the "essent."

ing, and thus no Being to take away from being that which is most truly itself.

If the interpretation of St. Thomas I have suggested above is at all correct, then it is not the slightest exaggeration to state that this doctrine is the fairly direct (though distant) outcome of the Thomistic revolution which, in order to preserve the contingency of creatures, made creatures existentially self-sufficient. This self-sufficiency remained compatible with theism only as long as creatures remained essentially necessary—that is, only as long as existence was the act of an essence which was really distinct from it, yet necessary in itself as the principle of intelligibility of *ens*. But it was this very conjunction which, at first, made knowledge problematic and, ultimately, led to the conclusion that intelligibility could not be the necessary constituent of being, but only its outcome. Thus, when being (*ens*) became definable in terms of its existence alone, the complete self-sufficiency of being (*ens*) became assured. This was, to be sure, no longer the self-sufficiency of a necessary being: it was the self-sufficiency of the totally contingent, the superfluous, the gratuitous, the absurd. In an ontology of such being the concept of God can have no place, even as the symptom of disease: God is a historical mistake, the overcoming of which is complete only when he is forgotten and no longer problematic. The only consistent atheism is silence about God.

As early as David Hume philosophy had already concluded that "whatever *is* may *not be*." [6] St. Thomas would have agreed

[6] "It seems to me, that the only objects of the abstract science of demonstration are quantity and number, and that all attempts to extend this more perfect species of knowledge beyond these bounds are mere sophistry and illusion. . . . All other enquiries of men regard only matters of fact and existence; and these are evidently incapable of demonstration. What-

that this principle is true when it refers to empirically given being, but not if it should refer to being as such: *it* could not be true of being as such because it could not be true of Being Itself, for whom to-be is necessary and essential, since in him to-be is "the same as" its essence and substance. As long as philosophy found it possible uncritically to begin its speculative task with belief in God, and to proceed thence to understand created being in relation to Being Itself, this qualification remained reasonable. And yet, it was St. Thomas himself, by a stroke of the other edge of his philosophical revolution, who made it impossible for philosophy to begin uncritically with belief in a God in relation to whose prior being the being of empirically given being should be thereafter understood. St. Thomas, in other words, taught the philosophical tradition of the Hellenic-Western world its radical empiricism. Philosophy since Hume has gradually worked out the implications of the contingency of being: "whatever *is* may *not be*." The death— rather the annihilation—of the Necesary Being, Being Itself, was but the principal negative implication to be extricated from it once the epistemological quandary of Hume was resolved in modern times.

I have asked: Can theism be erected on the very foundations of atheism? But I have put it badly. If this question means: Can belief in the traditional Christian God, that is, God as traditionally conceived by Christians, find support in the fundamental

---

ever *is* may *not be*. No negation of a fact can involve a contradiction. The non-existence of any being, without exception, is as clear and distinct an idea as its existence. The proposition, which affirms it not to be, however false, is no less conceivable and intelligible, than that which affirms it to be," *Enquiry Concerning Human Understanding*, XII, 3.

epistemological and ontological concepts that can be developed in this, the latest stage in the history of Western-Hellenic thought? the answer is clearly no. Contemporary thought is perfectly consistent. Its atheistic conclusion is formally and materially valid on its own premises, and there is no question of attempting to catch its logical mistake. The traditional Christian concept is simply not viable, and the growing awareness of this on the part of believer and non-believer alike is not likely to be reversed. It is probably only a matter of time—though in the evolutionary scale time usually stretches out unforeseeably long—before the point becomes self-evident to almost everyone —at which time Christendom as a whole will begin to wonder how it ever could have thought otherwise. The question would be vain, thus, if it entertained the hope of turning back, or turning aside, the stream of philosophical thought.

The question that may be asked, however—the question the philosopher must by his very vocation ask—is whether positive atheism, for all its conscientious avoidance of anti-theism does not remain too closely related to, whether it does not in fact retain some key assumptions of, traditional theism—and, if so, whether positive atheism may not be valid in relation to the traditional concept of God as the reality which corresponds to religious experience, but not necessarily precludes the evolution of human consciousness in relation to the very concept of God. The human intellect has developed itself to the point where it has found it necessary to redefine itself, its consciousness and the object of its consciousness. Does it not seem *prima facie* likely that man should also redefine the object of belief? In the light of this hypothesis, the question I have asked is legitimate. It means: does the interpretation of religious experience, on the assumption of the philosophical foundations of contemporary

Hellenic-Western thought, not require us to reconceptualize the reality which has been traditionally conceived as the Supreme Being, God?

This possibility has not occurred to non-believing philosophers of contemporary Western Christendom. The reason why it has not is probably the still limited awareness, even on the part of the most advanced contemporary philosophers, of the historical, evolutionary nature of consciousness in general, and therefore, of philosophical consciousness as well. Incredibly, the lesson first taught by Hegel, that philosophy is not a timeless enquiry, but exists only within history itself and must, therefore, proceed in awareness of its own history—this has been most imperfectly learned by all modern thought, but also, perhaps least understandably among professional thinkers, by philosophers themselves. One has come to expect this from Scholastics, who have, by definition, a vested interest in the past, and whose peculiar form of Christian religious belief require them to think that time should have stopped before it went too far, and that now there is nothing left but to turn back the madly whirling clock. One is astonished, however, to find that even a Heidegger thinks that the clock itself was badly assembled at the Greek factory; one is so astonished that only amusement remains to greet Sartre's yet more radical pessimism, suggesting that there should not have been a clock in the first place. When human beings hanker after the Golden Age of childhood so badly that they begin to wish they had never been born it is time to try the hypothesis which no philosopher has, seemingly, tried before: that time moves forward, in one direction only, and that it can never move either too fast or too slow. Reality is historical. Evolution—let us face the fact—appears to be the rule of life.

The consolation of philosophy today is that, dismal though its receptivity to its own historical nature may have been so far, science has on the whole performed even more badly. Science still believes itself largely to proceed as if its task were to decypher the timeless structure of the world, despite the fact that its most revolutionary modern concepts, like those of relativity and quantum mechanics, have resulted from the reinterpretation of prior scientific thought in the light of the historical development of scientific thought. Psychoanalysis is to date one of the most thoroughgoing and consistent applications of the methodological insight which came with awareness of the historical character of human consciousness, since it is a technique for effecting certain changes in man's *present* consciousneses, (in anticipation of a *future* condition, that is mental health), which are rendered possible by the present mastery over a remembered and analyzed *past*.

Well, like any other form of the self-heightening of consciousness, philosophy must understand its task as the reorganization of present experience, with an eye towards a projected future mode of consciousness, by means of its interpretation of the past. The task of philosophy today is not, as Heidegger appears to think, the "de-struction" (i.e., the "dismantling") of metaphysics, so that its original pre-Socratic materials, so badly put together by Plato and Aristotle—and so mistakenly compounded by later philosophical thought, with mistake piled upon mistake, and self-deception upon self-deception—might be re-constructed, but this time in the correct way (that is, in the way in which they should have been put together the first time). I rather think that philosophy was originally put together as well as, under the circumstances, it could have been. The history of philosophy is not the history, as the *Greeks* might have said, of one damned philosophical thing after another—it is the history of the progress of human thought. And the achievement of every stage of progress is, by definition, the achievement of that which had not been achieved before. It is understandable if, in the first blush of man's conscious discovery of progress, man believed that progress reveals nothing so clearly as the mistakes of the past. It takes considerably more reflection to begin to realize that, on the contrary, by the very fact that progress is progressive, every progress reveals essentially and above all the truth of the past.

But, of course, when progress reveals the truth of the past and knows itself to be a progression *from* the past, it is bound by that very fact to think of the past as inadequate. For, indeed, insofar as progress has been made, the truth of the past is revealed as no longer adequate. The task to which philosophy is called today is, therefore, not the dismantling and re-construction, but the transcending of metaphysics—and not merely the transcending of Greek metaphysics, which is but the beginning of metaphysical evolution, but the transcending of every metaphysics, and even the transcending of its ghost, which still haunts phenomenological ontologies themselves.[7]

For phenomenological ontologies, as I have said, retain the Hellenic idea that reality is reducible to being. The answer to the question I have proposed: whether belief can find conscious,

---

[7] Throughout this book, and in the first place in its title, I have retained the architectural metaphors to which Heidegger resorts here. However, I have explained (above, pp. 209 ff.) why the meaning of my metaphors is intended in diametrical opposition to Heidegger's. I trust that I have kept this intention, and that I have at all times retained full awareness of the temporal (i.e. the undirectional, vectorial, *from-to*), rather than the spatial (i.e. multidimensional, simultaneous, *A-B*), relations involved in the history of philosophical thought.

reflective, philosophical warrant in the mode of thought which has become possible in philosophy and throughout contemporary Western culture by the evolution of Hellenic-Western philosophical thought—the answer to this question depends on whether the retention of the reducibility of reality to begin is warranted, or whether, on the contrary, philosophy should not proceed to the next [8] stage of dehellenization.

Philosophy need not be ontological in its essential nature, if being is not the name of reality as such. The philosophical foundations of the contemporary stage of philosophical development may be the proper stand for a Christian belief in which God cannot be conceived as the Supreme Being, because he is not to be thought of as being at all. In this chapter we shall consider in some detail how this hypothesis is suggested by the history of philosophy—how, indeed, it suggests itself, to begin with, by the very history of Christian belief—before we enquire whether the best empirical evidence which we can unearth today does not recommend it for its own sake; after this we shall study the consequences of this hypothesis for the understanding of the nature of religion and of belief. But first I will briefly explain what this hypothesis is.

It is understandable if philosophy has not become conscious of the possibility of criticizing, and departing from, the Greek assumption which reduces reality to being, even while philosophy was willy-nilly opening up this very possibility by the exercise of philosophical thought. The beginning of modern philosophy was characterized, not surprisingly, by the rejection of the past. With Kant, metaphysics reached the paradoxical conclusion that metaphysics was invalid. This conclusion was reached, however, by

[8] I would not say final, for that remains to be seen.

metaphysical thought (i.e. by thought that assumed the reality of things-in-themselves and of Transcendental Reality in itself): man could not know philosophically what pre-philosophically he seemed to be certain of. Thus, the paradox was double, if not treble, for metaphysics reached metaphysically the conclusion that metaphysics was invalid, but nevertheless unavoidable. However, this negativity and this self-contradiction point to the imperfection, not to the total falsity, of Kant's critique of metaphysics. With the advantage of longer hindsight we can now begin to understand that Kant's achievement was not the liberation of reason from the burden of an inveterate fallacy, but the disclosure of the possibility that it might reach new heights. The lesson to be learned from him is not that metaphysical thought, which ought never to have been born, should at least mercifully annihilate itself. It is that metaphysics, which is the seed of later thought, can transcend itself if reason continues to develop itself. To enter a post-metaphysical age in philosophy—I suppose the purist would rightly insist on calling it a *meta-metaphysical* age—is not, as Heidegger thinks, to return to a forgotten truth: it is to pass through the truth of metaphysics into a philosopical truth beyond metaphysical thought.

I have already alluded to the impact that the critique of metaphysics has historically had on the metaphysical concept of God. But the development of man's self-understanding, his growing consciousness of his own consciousness, is to be interpreted, in the suggestion with which I concluded the last chapter, as the typical mode of the new direction taken by human evolution since man became man. If the meta-metaphysical stage of philosophy is the result of neither the valid nor the invalid rejection of metaphysics, but the outcome of the creative evolution of

Hellenic-Western thought, we would be ill-advised to suppose either of two things: either that the metaphysical concept of God was the irreformable, final philosophical truth about God, which must now be recovered and preserved, or else that it was the basic philosophical mistake about man, an error which must now be exorcised once for all. If we recognize that philosophical thought truly and creatively develops, the present period in the history of philosophy may be envisaged as a transitional zone beyond which may well lie a new level of progress in the history of religious thought. For the impasse of theism and atheism makes a great deal of historical sense, and must be envisaged as broadening the horizons of philosophical speculation about God. What justifies this hopeful estimate?

Modern atheistic thought is built upon the premise that metaphysical knowledge is a delusion. If the concept of being may not be extended beyond that order of reality which is open to everyday, common empirical understanding, belief in God is unreasonable and must be explained away in terms of empirically accessible realities—for instance, socio-economic forces, abnormal psychological mechanisms, or the projective nature of human consciousness. Now, modern theistic thought (at least in its Catholic variety) holds, of course, opposite views concerning the reality of God. But not infrequently the extremes meet. Modern Catholic theism grants the formal validity of the atheistic conclusion drawn from the critique of metaphysics, and opposes atheism not as an unwarranted development of valid premises provided by the genuine progress achieved in philosophy in post-mediaeval times, but as the logically valid consequence of an original miscarriage of philosophy which it traces at least as far back as Descartes. Theism has taken is stand on the validity of metaphysics, on the apparent assumption that the metaphysical concept of God cannot be improved upon. This means: Catholic theism is in agreement with modern atheism in one crucial respect, namely, in the supposition that if any concept of God is philosophically valid, it must be the metaphysical concept of God. Conversely, because its response to atheism has been reactionary, Catholic philosophy has willingly, if not eagerly, wedded itself to the serviceability, if not also to the fading beauty, of the metaphysical concept of God. In return, the bondage of its vow, if not also the logic of its position, has compelled it to cut itself off from modern thought, persuading itself that after St. Thomas a tragic and well-nigh total perversion of philosophy has taken place.

This reaction to atheism has been not only humanly understandable: it has had some merit of its own. Catholic theistic thought has been guilty of reaction, but it has cleaved to the fundamental facts of religious phenomena. But perhaps now it is time to do better than this. If we recognize not only that the theistic tradition has retained, albeit imperfectly, what is valid in religious experience, but also that the mainstream of philosophy has, for all its inadequacies, run logically and creatively, the possibility that naturally suggests itself is that a *meta-metaphysical* concept of God might be developed. For it should be possible to understand philosophically that which, at first "physically," and later metaphysically, has been traditionally called God, not only while avoiding the pre-critical inadequacies of metaphysics, (which phenomenological ontologists have already done), but also transcending the ontological reduction of reality; I mean, the unwarranted reduction of reality to that reality, being, which is given in empirically given being as such.

The foregoing position of the problem would be misinterpreted if it were construed apologetically. My question is not: Can the traditional concept of God—or, for that matter, any concept of God—be saved from the attacks of modern thought, by transcending, if necessary, the reduction of reality to being? My suggestion is, in the first place, that the choice open to us today is not necessarily the exclusive alternative between traditional theism and *its* positive atheism; and, second, that the inadequacies of both traditional theism and its atheism positively point towards an interpretation of the data of religious experience in terms of a reality which accounts for both (a) what traditional theism with historical warrant has interpreted as Supreme Being and particularly as Being Itself, and (b) what positive atheism with its own historical warrant has interpreted as the actual and positive absence from the reality of human consciousness, and as the absolute nothingness of any reality in relation to the reality of man, of any reality which could be in any way reasonably referred to as Supreme Being or as Being Itself.

On the other hand, there are not only positive indications to lead the philosopher of religion to the idea that the analysis of experience may require that the ontological reduction of reality be transcended. There are negative indications as well. There are not only the indications given by the history of philosophical consciousness; the history of Christian belief itself also suggests that the dichotomy between traditional theism and its atheism should be transcended—and it even hints, however inconclusively, that this may involve transcending the concept of being which would identify being with reality. In this sense an "apologetic" position of the problem would be legitimate. The nature of this "apologetic," however, would not be to defend the Christian faith

364

from external attacks, but to "defend" the Christian faith from its own internal inadequacies. Let us now consider, from this negative "apologetic" viewpoint quite improperly so-called, how the problem of God can present itself to contemporary Catholic philosophical thought, before we study, in the remaining sections of this chapter, how the problem appears to it from a positive philosophical viewpoint.

TRANSCENDENCE AND IMMANENCE IN BEING ITSELF

The classical Christian concept of God found it necessary, given its Hellenic philosophical foundations, to endow God with contradictory relations to creation—or, at any rate, with contradictory attributes which made him at one and the same time related and unrelated to the created world. The opposition between God's transcendence and God's immanence produced in the first place insoluble academic problems—at least in the sense that contradictions are rightly said to have remained unresolved and to have retained their problematic character if they have been justified on no better grounds than their supposed mysterious reconciliation within God's knowledge of himself. To say that only God knows the answer to a problem is not usually taken to mean only that *we* do not know it; it is also meant to imply that the problem was posed in the first place by God himself. But when philosophy reasons in this manner, philosophy should take good care that it is not deluding itself. Philosophy is not the attempt to reconstruct God's own thought about himself; it is not an effort to reproduce in the human intellect God's own prior philosophical, theological or scientific thought. Hence, philosophical (or other) intellectual problems can be posed strictly from a human viewpoint. If only God knows the answer to a problem then no one knows it, for what this really means is that our questioning has gone astray.

But the consequences have been worse yet. The opposition between God's transcendence and his immanence has made increasingly painful the inadequacies of the concept of God for the real-life needs of the Church—inadequacies which are to a considerable extent responsible for modern Christendom's unbelief. In one of its most candid and honest pages, Vatican II acknowledged not only, as the Church had previously done, that on account of moral shortcomings "believers themselves frequently bear some responsibility for [atheism]" but that they do so also on account of the inadequacies of the mode in which faith may be held—inadequacies which, presumably, derive for the most part from the underdevelopment of Christian belief and from the severance of Christian faith and contemporary life, to which atheism can be an understandable reaction: "for, taken as a whole, atheism is not a spontaneous development but stems from a variety of causes, including a critical reaction against religious beliefs, and in some places even against the Christian religion in particular. Hence believers can have more than a little to do with the birth of atheism. To the extent that they neglect their own training in the faith, or teach erroneous doctrine, or are deficient in their religious, moral, or social life, they must be said to conceal rather than reveal the authentic face of God and religion." [9] (I imagine this doctrine is to be apprehended in

[9] *Pastoral Constitution on the Church and the Modern World,* (*Gaudium et Spes*), sect. 19. In Walter M. Abbott and Joseph Gallagher, (eds.), *The Documents of Vatican II,* (New York, 1966), p. 217.

strict relation to the Council's teaching on the nature of the Church in *Lumen Gentium* as "the People of God,"[10] and that therefore in the foregoing paragraph where "believers" are mentioned it would be legitimate to substitute "the Church.")

I have already referred to Western Christianity's division against itself, its schizophrenic apostasy from its own religious sources, a crucial historical process so well analyzed by Arnold Toynbee.[11] This process is the best illustration of how the unavoidable and normal inadequacies of an originally adequate, inspiring, progressive concept of God have been allowed, through lack of redevelopment, to degenerate to a scandalous point. And yet, Christians generally, and the magisterium least of all, have never (until recently) felt bound to accept much responsibility for the inner division and apostasy of the Western world. And whatever acknowledgment of exclusively *moral* scandal there has been, has been blunted by frequent insistence on the yet greater moral guilt of those who have taken scandal, and on their prior moral failures, which predispose them towards the sin of unbelief.

Of course, the unqualified moral innocence of unbelieving Christendom would not be easy to demonstrate; on the other hand, the increased moral sensibility of man as he has undergone cultural development is not gainsaid by whether or not he abides by the morality of which he becomes increasingly conscious as he becomes increasingly civilized. Nor does the Christian dismissal of unbelief recognize the largely intellectual

[10] *Dogmatic Constitution on the Church, (Lumen Gentium)*, Ch. II; in Abbott and Gallagher, *Documents*, pp. 24–37.

[11] Cf. especially *An Historian's Approach to Religion*, (London, 1965), pp. 128–141, 165–169, 180–187, 208–251.

character of some of the causes of unbelief, such as the shift in the foundations of religious thought which I have described above, which lends unbelief precisely the same degree of truth which is taken away from traditional theism. And even some of the modern world's moral reasons for disbelief have been not infrequently valid—for instance, when it has rebelled against inhumanities perpetrated (with obvious and undoubted sincerity) on behalf of God. For the cynically anti-human Christian has never deceived anyone who is reasonably perceptive; the well-meaning one, however, the faithful believer in an inadequately conceived God who, in effect, exacts human sacrifice—this is the Christian belief in relation to which the truthful man feels bound to assert disbelief in order to witness to the truth.

In any event, the inadequacies of the traditional concept of God are borne out not so much by that part of Christendom that has ceased to believe, as by that which continues to do so. For believing Christendom too, has further divided itself against itself. The preservation of orthodoxy in its traditional form has severed faith from ordinary, everyday life. Thus, we confess the true God, both immanent and transcendent. But in real life we find it very difficult—often impossible—to live the contradiction, to "hold on to both ends of the chain," confident that the two are joined, out of our sight, in God himself. Impaled on a dilemma whose nature and reality we do not always recognize, we instinctively opt for the "safer" extreme. And so, our contemporary belief typically bears, *in effect,* only upon a transcendent God. We continue, in a sense, to "believe" in, (that is, mindlessly to affirm), an immanent God, and to do so sincerely—but only ineffectively. We "confess" it, but we do not *mean* what we confess.

What I have in mind is *not* that by sin we deny practically our theoretical belief in God, or that out of moral weakness we fail to live up to the moral requirements of what we actually believe. We do this too, of course; but I am now referring to the gap between what we have simply admitted to be true, and the truth we have engrafted into our experience, our creativity and our collective life. That there is in reality such a gap is the only conclusion to be drawn from the history of the Church since the beginning of the modern world, particularly from the Church's abdication of its responsibility to provide effective leadership to a mankind but recently embarked upon the task of consciously creating its own history. For each different way—and there have been many—in which Christians have held the world in contempt is a living rejection of the immanence of God. Not only our readiness, until very recent times, to convict the world of sin, sometimes prematurely and usually with indecent haste, but also our consignment of the world to perdition on account of whatever true, real and unrepented sin it may have borne: what have these amounted to, but to a living act of faith in the *absolute* absence of God from the world?

The classical concept of God has become unviable: this concept can no longer enter fully and integrally into the life of believers themselves. And it is cold comfort to warm ourselves with the thought that, retaining the classical view, we have avoided every naturalism, every scientism, every rationalism and every pantheism, since we have not effectively avoided also every supernaturalism. Worse yet, we have not even feared it as a grave danger: we have tended to assume that it is impossible to err on the side of God. But the contemporary difficulties of the Christian faith suggest otherwise. Let us attempt to trace the difficulty to its root.

The heart of the Christian Gospel was Jesus' proclamation that

Israel's messianic hope had been realized in him: he, Jesus, was the Christ. But Jesus maintained that his advent had not merely realized the Jewish hope; it had also transcended it. He was indeed the expected King, but his kingship was not of the sort that had been expected: it was "not of this world," [12] nor was it of Israel alone. It was a spiritual and catholic kingship. Therefore, the Christian Kingdom of God was not merely the morally ideal way of life anticipated by Judaism, but a new way of life not previously available to man. It was not simply a better way, the right way, in which ordinary human existence could be exercised: it was a *new* way to be. This is why the Gospel proclaimed a New Covenant, a new age in man's relations with God. In this new age God offered to man the possibility of existing at a level of existence other (and indeed nobler and more perfect) than that which man *already* had. Hence, the "spiritual" Kingdom of God was no mere continuation of "fleshly" human life with but its evils and imperfections removed. It was a new life, a passing "out of death into life." [13] To have entered into it was truly to have been "born again." [14] By baptism into the new Israel the Christian became a "spiritual man," [15] one who had "died to the . . . world" [16] and "risen with Christ" [17] to the "eternal life." [18] Like St. Paul, every Christian could say: "with Christ I am nailed to the cross. And I live, now not I; but Christ liveth in me." [19]

[12] *John*, 18:36.
[13] *1 John*, 3:14.
[14] *John*, 3:3.
[15] *1 Cor.*, 2:15.
[16] *Colossians*, 2:20.
[17] *Colossians*, 3:1.
[18] *Romans*, 6:23.
[19] *Galatians*, 2:20.

But the "new life" was offered to man only through the saving events, the "mysteries" of the Incarnation and Redemption. The Christian Gospel of the "new life" supposed, in the first place, that the King instituted by the Christ Jesus differed from that expected by Israel only because the Christ of the Gospel was not merely a Christ. Jesus was no mere champion sent by God; he was the epiphany of God. Clearly, then, the Gospel implied a new self-revelation of God. In the New Testament God was not only the creator and protector of man but, more fundamentally, self-gift or self-communication: *Deus caritas est.*[20] The Incarnation and the Redemption meant that God had literally given himself to man.

This affirmation had a twofold weight. God *gave* himself to us. And what he gave to us was *himself.* If so, when God revealed himself to us as self-communication or self-gift by manifesting himself to us in Jesus, he revealed not simply what he was *for us,* but also what he was *for himself.* This is why the doctrine of the Incarnation and Redemption implied the doctrine of the Trinity: the different ways or "modes" in which God relates himself *to us* are the truly distinct—and even, in Hellenistic terms, separately "subsistent"—ways in which he is related *to himself.* This must be true if the God who comes to man in the Incarnation is "true God," for if he is "true God" then no part of his divinity is held back from man (which in turn is the reason why we must confess not only that there are three divine "persons," but also that there are "only" three persons in the divine nature of God). In brief, God's gift of himself is identical with his offer of the possibility of a *"new* life" over and beyond

---

[20] *1* John, 4:16. Given contemporary English usage, χάρις and *caritas* are not as well translated by either "charity" or "love" as by "self-gift."

the life we *already* had. But why is it the possibility of a "new life?"

The existence every man *already* has when he is called by the Gospel is in a very real sense a gift *from* God. In fact, existence means, for the Christian, most fundamentally this: God's original and gratuitous gift of being to being, God's uncaused gift to being of *itself*. But this gift from God is not God himself: it is being, existence. It is not God's gift of himself; it is God's gift of being. The difference between the "new life" and the "old" is not that only the former is a gift from God, whereas the latter is a "natural" endowment, a gift from an original source other than God. Rather, existence means gift *from* God, and gift *from* God means existence: the two terms are convertible. On the other hand—and this is where the theology of "Christian secularity" sometimes goes astray—the identity of existence and grace does not mean that *every* moment of existence necessarily entails *every* gift from God. The temporal, historical character of existence warns us that it need not be so. In other words, there is a difference between the "new life" and the "old", and this difference is: the "old" life is *already* had when the "new" is given.

This is precisely what opens up the possibility that the "new life" be not merely a gift *from* God, (which indeed it is) but God's yet more gratuitous gift of *himself*. But the real difference between [the gift of] existence and the gift [of grace] is not that the latter is more gratuitous than the first. The real difference is that the first is the gratuitous gift of existence, the gift of *one's* own reality, whereas the latter is the gratuitous gift of *God's* own reality, of God's own "self." God's gift of himself and his offer of a "new life," are identical. But since this gift and this offer are *from* God, his gift of *himself* is of the same order as the gift of man's own self; that is, it is *of the order of existence*. The gift of a new existence means that henceforth God *lives* within man. Therefore, when man *receives* God within himself he accepts God's offer to participate in the life of God himself.

Evidently, God cannot create a being without giving it being. We can assert this not because we discern an *a priori* metaphysical law which forbids God to create unless he gave being: it is simply that to create and to *give* being are the same. Thus, God need not create being—but if he does create being, being is given to it. Therefore, if man is a being, he *already* exists as soon as he exists; the gift of existence is a gift from God insofar as it is the present (to man) of man's present out of the past. It cannot be God's present to man of man's future, for the future can be present to man only insofar as his consciousness has created itself by that self-projection called freedom. Conversely, to *have* existence is not the same as to have *received* it. I mean: every being can *have* existence, but only man can *accept* it, since only man is present to himself.

In other words, the gift of that sort of existence which man *already* has when he is called by the Gospel is a gift from God that can only be *given:* it cannot be strictly speaking *received.* Thus, God can create man without giving him more than being; God need not give himself to man, even after man already exists. But if, on the other hand, God does give himself to man, then the gift is, in a true sense, the gift of a new mode of *existence.* But because man *already exists* when this new existence is offered to him, this mode of existence must be received, accepted—or else God cannot give himself to man. In other words, the new gift of "life" cannot be *given* in the same way in which the old can, namely, without prior consultation, as it were, with the recipient of the gift. For in this case, the recipient, by definition, *already* exists: hence, the new existence can only be *offered* "without prior consultation". (The creation of man in a historical situation defined *for* him—not *by* him—as freedom, is the event in which the "offer" is made.) But to be actually *given,* and not merely offered, the new existence must be *accepted* or *received*: that is, man must make *himself* freely, and he must make himself *free.*

In the idea that the root meaning of all existence is that of a gift from God, that there is no meaning to existence except that of being a gift from God, but that the existence man already has when called by the Gospel is (though truly given) a gift that cannot be actually received (for being does not already exist before it is given existence)—in this idea we find the reason why, for the Christian faith, being as such does not acquire a necessary relation to God through creation, but remains always, even after it exists, totally contingent and historically factual. Man, though he is conscious of existence, and though he is existence aware of itself, cannot, simply as conscious being, *receive* existence from God unless God gives himself to him. But because he is present to himself man can *recognize* that existence is a gift he holds from God: this recognition is, by another name, the experience of the contingency of being as such. It is man's recognition that he holds existence gratuitously, without reason—"superfluously," if you wish—and that he truly holds it, having never had the opportunity to turn it down before it was given to him.

In brief, if "existence" is essentially the same as "gift from God," the gift offered by God to a conscious being which already exists, is literally, not metaphorically, the offer of a new level of existence.[21] Conversely, this new mode of existence is, precisely as "new", (as obtaining over and beyond the mode of existence

[21] Until I attempt below to show otherwise I shall continue to assume here, with traditional philosophical thought, that reality is reducible to being; therefore, I refer here to this offer from God as "the offer of a new level of existence." But it should be clear that this is a "crushingly despotic" use of language, not unlike that of Plato when he speaks, in effect, of visible things which are invisible. Thus, I have thrown the entire burden of the distinction between the "old life" and the "new" upon the concept of various "levels" at which "life" supposedly obtains. But it is perfectly clear that there cannot be two levels of existence: to exist is for consciousness to be one. Man does not really exist at two different levels of existence—except, of course, in the strictly metaphorical sense of these terms. But what is the reality of which this is a metaphor?

As long as we continue to suppose that reality is reducible to being no answer to this question is possible—except perhaps in terms of meta-metaphors. On the other hand, if such a supposition is not made, it follows that the "life" of "grace" is not a "life" or an "existence" at all (i.e. it is not a mode of *being*). It is, however, a *reality*, and therefore it affects man's innermost being and total existence. The offer of grace is the offer of a reality beyond being—and this is why it cannot be taken away by death or, conversely, why its absence would give death the power to take away man's reality. It is perfectly understandable if, therefore, Christians have imagined that the Christian promise is that of an "eternal life," and that after death there is a "life to come"—throwing thus the entire burden of the distinction between biological and religious "life" on the *eternity* and the *futurity* of the "life" in which we hope. There is no harm, of course, in these metaphors. But we have scarcely taken these expressions traditionally as metaphors. Yet, as I have said, it is difficult to imagine how else they could have been taken while retaining their truth, since we have also assumed that the only way to be real was to be. On the other hand, if this assumption is transcended, it follows that the Christian hope is not in a future or eternal life, but in a reality beyond being which is already given to (and accepted by) him in this (i.e., in the only) world, and in time, and before death. Conversely, one of the best indications that reality is not convertible with being is man's spontaneous refusal to believe that the end of his existence, death, is the end of his reality. This makes a great deal of sense. What does not make sense is to interpret this empirical datum in the self-contradictory terms of the "immortality of the soul" or of a "life after death."

375

already held by man), definable as participation in the life of God himself.

This is possible only if God gives himself to us in his true reality: the "new man" lives, as such, by the life of God *himself,* by a life gratuitously communicated to him by God himself. And since the "new man" lives, as such, by the life of *another* living in him, his "new life" is *not a substitute* for the "old life." [22]

[22] Except in the sense that, insofar as it is accepted, insofar as it is God's present to man as man exists (at present) towards the future—or, in other words, insofar as it concerns the moral orientation of human consciousness —the "new life" must indeed *replace* the old. Moreover, if it is true, as suggested above, (note 21), that the new "life" is not actually a life, but a mode of reality, then the "new life" does not substitute for life after death any more than it does for life before death. Were it such a substitute, it would be, both in "this" life and in the "next" a pseudo-life, an *ersatz*-life. In other words, the "new life" can be literally understood neither as an additional life above our present life, nor as a continuation of life after death, nor as the transmutation of one mode of existence into another. In this sense the death of man's "natural" (i.e. biological) life is truly final; it is the total and irrevocable termination of existence. But this is precisely why the most ancient and purest Christian tradition has always preferred to refer to the substance of the Christian hope not as the "immortality" of the soul or even that of the person, (even in the doctrine of St. Thomas the immortality of the soul does not take away the mortality of the human person, cf. *ST,* I, 75, 5 ad 2), but as the "resurrection of the dead." Since the introduction into Christian philosophy of the doctrine that the substance of the Christian hope is grounded upon the natural incorruptibility of the soul (*ST,* I, 75, 6), (which obviously and directly implies the denial of the *totality* of the loss of existence at death), Christian belief has inclined ever more pronouncedly to the attitude that death is not really and truly the utter loss of human life; the undercurrent is most frequently felt that death does not really touch the existence of man, but is like an unpleasant portal through which human existence passes on its way from one life-station to another.

In this connection Arthur Gibson has written that "theists are often guilty of a regrettable confusion of the orders of nature and grace, amounting to a proclamation that man is naturally immortal, or to a practical activity which presupposes this untenable contention. . . . The evanes-

Hence, the Christian loves—or should love—his neighbour for the love of God. This does not mean that he must love his neighbour in order to deserve God's love; this would be the legalization of charity. It means that God's self-gift to man creates the *obligation,* and confers the efficient *power,* for man to rise to the historical occasion created by the events of the Incarnation and Redemption; this is the invitation and the challenge, this is man's vocation, to imitate God through man's free decision to define himself, (that is, to reveal himself to himself in actual, conscious existence), as self-communication and self-gift.

Needless to say, the Christian faith I have rendered here in fidelity, as I trust, to the spirit of the Gospel, but in philosophical concepts which correspond to and reflect the contemporary level of human self-awareness, could have been rendered during the formative centuries of Christian dogma, or even during the

---

cence of mortality has often been betrayed by theists who have taken an illicit leap into eternity before the end of time, before the death of the individual and before the genuine eschaton. The most somber of these illicit leaps has been the Nirvana-mentality; but there have been all manner of shadings, down to and including a certain sort of Christian angelism and exaggerated supernaturalism, all the more pernicious because it so seductively responds to the twin simultaneous demands of the heart of Western man: the preservation of individuality and the guarantee of security and a safe haven, even in the midst of the waves of temporality and mortality. [The challenge of certain atheists] to take death seriously can only be salutary for the theist. This theist—this convinced believer in an anterior personal Creator who guarantees eternity for the creature; especially this Christian theist, with his firm persuasion that this anterior Creator by his ingress into human history, his grappling at close quarters with death in the Crucifixion, and his triumphal resurrection, has trailblazed immortality for all mortal flesh—must not interpolate this ultimate certitude as a palliative to the terrors and the challenge of genuine mortality," *The Faith of the Atheist,* (New York, 1968), pp. 86, 93.

Scholastic period, only in a Hellenic conceptual form. This was, of course, not only legitimate (and, in any event, unavoidable) but also most advantageous for the Christian faith. But this historical development also contained potential difficulties which, as they appeared, should have been disarmed. Unfortunately, circumstances conspired and, in the end, the difficulties were compounded instead.

As has been implied above, every conceptualization of the Christian belief in the "new life" must be relative to a prior conceptualization of the "old." Gentile Christianity, being as a whole culturally Hellenistic, could not have conceived the "old" existence, the life that man already has when he is called to "conversion" and "rebirth," except as a "natural" one. And this, of course, had corresponding consequences for its understanding of the nature of the "new life."

To the Greek mind *nature* accounts intelligibly for the actions of a natural being because nature is a principle of inner necessitation. For every being acts strictly in accordance with what it is —and a being is what its essence determines it to be. But what a being is essentially, is that which it is necessarily in order to be intelligible—we have seen how, following Parmenides, intelligibility must be acknowledged to be identical with existence or, after St. Thomas, identical with the possibility of existence. Nature, therefore, accounts exhaustively for a being's operations, since a being's essence accounts for what it is necessarily as intelligible. Free human actions, for instance, are both intelligible and possible only because they are *natural* operations. They are free not because they are unnecessitated, (this would make them unintelligible and hence impossible), but because they are *self*-necessitated. Human freedom is no more than the indifference of the will towards alternative means to one and the same necessary end.[23]

But this implies that free human actions can proceed *only* from human nature: they can be attributed only to that which (by definition) can be the only intrinsic principle of human operations—namely, human nature. Conversely, any principle other than nature could be the source of human operations only as an extrinsic principle of necessitation—and this would be (by definition) a source of *violence*. In short, human behaviour is either necessitated naturally, from within—in which case it is free— or else it is necessitated from without—in which case it is coerced.

It is instructive to note that the age which formulated the problem of grace and freedom was preceded by a period during which Christian speculation was bent upon maintaining a truer and more radical idea of human freedom than that of the contemporary pagan philosophy. However, this effort was conceptualized in terms of maintaining the autonomy of man's *nature*. Christian thought easily apprehended its fundamental opposition to the Greek philosophical attitude, particularly that of the Stoics and Epicureans, towards the human situation. Hence it was bound to emphasize the utter reality and power of man's freedom, and the benevolence of a God who did not subject man to Fate. Christians admitted that there was a Providence, quite

[23] This is why St. Thomas deduced human freedom—rather, the freedom of the will's arbitration among indifferent means towards a necessary end (*ST*, I, 82, 2)—from the *necessity* of nature towards its end, (*ST*, 82, 1). Note, moreover, that in this philosophical perspective it is necessary to *deduce* human freedom (and increasingly so as, in the history of subsequent philosophy, the impossibility of doing so becomes gradually apparent); human freedom is not acknowledged and emphasized as the empirical fact it in fact is.

as the Stoics said. But Pro-vidence, πρόνοια, was not the fore-see-ing power that frustrated man's freedom; it was not the cosmic principle of natural necessitation, indifferent to man and human striving, to which man must, however unhappily, intelligently submit under pain of greater unhappiness still. Providence was God's wise, benevolent, loving and helpful guidance of his creation towards its final achievement.

But when this doctrine, not illogically, issued in the conclusions attributed to Pelagius, it was necessary, on the contrary, to emphasize that the life of grace, (implying, for instance, a pre-ordination to a finality that man could not merit or achieve by nature), could not be brought about by the efficiency of the operations posited by human nature as such: otherwise the life of grace would have been indistinguishable from the natural state of human perfection to which Stoic and Epicurean philosophy naturally led through intellectual. and moral ἄσκησις. But to emphasize this, once the Greek conception of nature was assumed, was in effect to emphasize that in a very real sense Providence *was* a sort of Fate. Man, therefore, was in a sense truly predestined. Having accepted the terms in which the problem naturally posed itself to Christianity's Hellenic mind, Christian thought doomed itself to assert thereafter that *somehow* man was both free and predestined, that God was *somehow* the cause of Fate and nevertheless the friend of man. The *somehow* has never been satisfactorily explained. This obscurity would not have been too unfortunate if it had been truly possible for Christian thought successfully to believe with equal firmness both ends of the antinomy. But the process was far from complete when St. Augustine wrote his last anti-Pelagian word.

If it is true, as I have suggested, that one can understand the "new life" of Christian belief only in relation to one's prior understanding of the "old," then the assumption that the "old" life was a "natural" one potentially contained more than the foregoing problem of the opposition between grace and freedom. It also implied that any reconciliation of the two should be based upon a reinterpretation of the "new life" as functioning in essentially the same way as nature did, albeit without actually forming integral part of nature. The "new life" was not a substitute for nature—on the other hand, it was not unnatural. Conversely, it was non-natural—but nonetheless it was somewhat like nature. Its nature, as it were, was that of a nature which was not natural. Hence, it was a sort of second nature, a nature over and above human nature. It was, in the Scholastic expression devised *ad hoc,* man's *super-nature.* The "new life" communicated by God was a *super-natural* life.

The supernatural life of grace was, therefore, truly a sort of nature. It was, to be sure, a *super*-nature. It was, for all that, a super-*nature.* Therefore, to the extent that the life of grace became a super-*natural* life, it was no longer identical with man's participation in the life of God living within him. It would have been unthinkable for Christianity, of course, to go so far as to deny that man did so participate. The tradition of faith was much too conscious that this was the very soul of Christian theistic belief. But perhaps it was possible to say that the "new life" was not itself such participation: it was the *means* whereby such participation could obtain. A distinction obviously suggested itself: on the one hand, "uncreated Grace," which was the life of God himself insofar as it included the act by which he gave himself to man; on the other, "created grace," which was a God-created reality, a second nature, (both in the sense that it presupposed nature, and in the sense that it was a "habit" rather than a substantial nature), a super-nature which so modified man's substantial nature that he could achieve, through its efficiency, what he could not achieve by nature alone.

The traditional belief that by grace man participated in the divine nature was thus retained, but considerably weakened. In his meaningful religious experience the Christian no longer sought God himself—at least not in this life. He sought grace, an insubstantial ectoplasm flowing from above, a spiritual coin issued by God *ex opere operato* and certified as legal moral tender by the decrees of Providence, and thereafter circulated among believers through the spiritual treasury of the Church. Man's acceptance of supernatural life no longer meant literally that "I live, now not I; but Christ liveth in me." It did not convey that man had risen to a new level of *existence*. It simply meant that a certain quality—given from God, but not itself God—now qualified inwardly (but proceeding from without) the powers of nature with a perfection which was not due to nature but which enabled nature, precisely as thus super-naturally perfected, to attain a super-natural end.

Moreover, since this occurred only through the *means* of grace, "participation in the life of God" now referred to a God who was not immediately present to man. It was indeed thought that an *immediate* participation would be dangerously near to pantheism —as it would be, of course, on the continued assumption of the Hellenic concepts of nature and being. In any event, in the *effective* belief of Christians, (to the degree that their belief was formed by this doctrine), God himself was not present to man, immediately or otherwise: the presence of God was still affirmed, but it did not necessarily have a meaningful role in Christian religious experience. The operative role was filled exclusively by the transcendence of God. But this meant that God's transcendence was automatically reinterpreted as well, and rendered discontinuous with, and actually opposed to, the immanence of God. For transcendence no longer meant the incommensurability of God with the being in which he lives and to which he is present. It was the incommensurability of two essentially separate realities, creator and creature; it was the infinite distance between created being and uncreated Being. God's immanence was confessed, but no longer effectively believed in.

As Christianity's sense of God's immanence became numbed, as the Christian God receded into the infinity beyond the world he had created, and as the experience of his presence was no longer facilitated by the immediately meaningful teaching of the Church or by the everyday institutions and practices of believers, (and it should be noted that even the sacrament most directly concerned with the Real Presence tended to give less emphasis to the presence itself than to the metaphysical mechanism whereby that presence could be harmonized with a Hellenic understanding of nature)—as these things came to pass the Christian God became increasingly unbelievable. For, at the limiting case, a strictly transcendent God is utterly unreasonable, whereas, at the other extreme, a strictly immanent God is not positively absurd. In this way, to most science and philosophy belief in the Christian God became synonymous with superstitious credulity; and to many among the dispossessed, (or to many among those thinkers who cared more for the humble and poor than for logical consistency or for thought itself), institutional religion became the opium of the people. No doubt, these and like judgments of the modern world have been precipitate and undiscriminating. But it may be equally precipitate and undiscriminating to suppose that they have been altogether wrong.

What lesson can be learned from the foregoing historical development? If one remains bound to the fundamental Hellenic concepts which put the process in motion in the first place the answer is, of course, none. At least, none that the traditional Church has not known for more than a century, like contempt for the modern world, isolation from reality, and patience unto an increasingly distant future conversion of man. On the other hand, if nature is not understood as that which determines a being to act in accordance with its inner, immutable, constitutive principle of intelligibility but, on the contrary, as that which emerges from the contingent history it undergoes (or the contingent history it creates, in the case of man), then the level of existence to which man is called by the Gospel need no longer be understood as super-natural. If so, the Christian God need not have a supernatural character which alienates him from man, and the Christian faith may again become directly relevant to real, everyday, present life. Existence at that level of fellowship with God to which the Gospel calls is not superimposed upon an independently evolving history of creation: it is existence at the same level as that in which, as a matter of fact, creation evolves historically, but under the concrete, contingent, historical condition brought about by God's free decision to be present to creation and to take part in its history by making *its* history *his* home. Grace is, then, an historical fact: it is the irruption of God into man's history. Rather, it is the emergence of human history within the reality of God; it is the definitive and actual event of God's presence to man.

384

This implies that God does not reconcile in his private life the opposed transcendence and immanence of his cryptic public announcements. But from this a conclusion follows which should liberate us once for all from a metaphysical God, because it demonstrates that metaphysics leads us away from the transcendent reality of the immanent God. For the foregoing understanding of the matter means that God must be conceived as that which, though other than being, is revealed *by* and *within* being only because he is present *to* being. The historicity of grace means that the "natural" order does not actually exist in the reality of the actual world, the only world that *does* exist. But if, having reached this point by transcending the Hellenic idea of nature, we were to proceed without transcending the Hellenic assumption of the convertibility of *reality* and *being,* the conclusion would be inevitably reached that nothing which exists in reality is other than God—a conclusion which would contradict even more radically than atheism the experience of the contingency of being *as such* already noted above.

But why should we choose between pantheism and atheism? Why must we reject either a transcendent or an immanent God, after assuming as a fixed point the gratuitous Greek identification of reality and being? Why not reject the assumption? Why not retain instead the transcendence of an immanent God and the immanence of a transcendent God? For is it not much easier and logical to transcend the *confusion* of reality and being than to retain the metaphysical assumptions of Hellenic thought? Or must we say that the absolutely fixed point of departure of a Christian philosophy of God is the metaphysical Law that reality as such is definable as that which *is*? Would not the acceptance of this self-imposed "Law" imply the ultimate reduction of all reality to that type of reality which is our own, namely, the reality of that which *is*? Is not this "Law" then, the most fundamental form of anthropomorphism—and hence, the one that must be decisively rejected?

In short, let an empirical approach be taken to the facts of human existence, and it immediately follows that the very experience of being reveals that being does not exhaust the possibilities open to our experience. To say that we believe in that which transcends human transcendence, that we can make sense of the contingency and reality of our existence, is to say, in effect, that we have glimpsed the limits of being and discovered that reality is found not only *within* being but also *beyond*. What leads primitive religions to imagine that God must *be* is the fact that God is indeed *in* and *within* being. What leads traditional Christianity to conclude that God *cannot* not be, is Greek philosophy. What might lead progressive Christianity to transcend what believers have imagined and concluded in the past, is the awareness that what it imagines and concludes is better understood if it does not suppose what Greek philosophy assumed to be necessarily true.

Being exists, and God is present to it. God creates being, which exists by itself. But he creates it in his presence. Moreover, within the totality of being God brings forth the being to which he gives the power effectively to define itself, the power indeed truly to create itself—for this being is no longer simply being in relation to another, whether God or man, but being which is present to itself and, hence, being which exists in and for itself. To this being God is freely present in a correlative way, namely, by giving himself to it in his very reality—hence, by offering himself to man with such real and utter gratuity that

386

he actually creates the possibility of being unaccepted and positively rejected by man.

Correspondingly, then, God is found *in* being, (and *only* in being); but he is found in being only as that which is *other* than being. It is indeed his presence *in* being that leads us *beyond* being. There is, therefore, no infinite gap separating God from man. But there is an openness to being, and in this opening God stands. Likewise, we must say that there is no distance between God and man: on the contrary, the God of the Gospel has come into the world in his true and utter reality, leaving nothing behind and, evidently, planning to stay. The Christian God is not elsewhere: he is always *here* and, therefore, he is always faithful, always he who abides, always *Yahweh,* he who will always be before us, he who remains present here and now with us.

Therefore, the transcendence of the genuinely immanent God means (negatively) this: if the God whom we find always *here* is not to vanish into thin air, if he is not to become an idol, if he is not to be reduced to the totality of being, and if he is not to be explained away as the becoming of the world or the projection of man—in a word, if the God who is actually *here* within being is to be the God of Christian tradition, it follows that he is not to be conceived as being.

To be sure, a whole *problematik* issues from this. But if the foregoing observations are correct this affirmation is not itself problematic; it is an empirically derived principle of investigation. The history of Christian speculation about God suggests that the starting point of its quest should no longer be the supposition that although we do not experience God he must be nonetheless Being. It should rather be the empirical observation that we do experience what primitive religions call God, although evidently we do not experience him as being at all. The trends of development in both the believing and the non-believing segments of Christianity converge and reinforce each other, unbeknownst to both.

To conclude: the concept of God as supernal power and supernal reality is as primitive and as inadequate for the present stage of human evolution as would be the ethnocentric concept of the race of Man as a society of those who share one's own culture. Neither of these concepts has been yet quite transcended by man. We have made considerable progress in our awareness that there are "men" who, culturally speaking, are "not part of us," but the society of the human race is as of now a *desideratum* rather than a fact.[24] Likewise, the history of religious thought shows considerable progress in the development of the concept of God. The question is whether it should not be developed further yet—specifically, as every sign indicates, in the direction which is defined by the progression from "physics" to metaphysics, but which leads beyond metaphysical thought.

[24] It is, as a matter of fact, much more than a mere *desideratum*. It is an imperative—and not only a moral imperative, though it is that too, but a biological imperative. Hence, it is (hypothetically) inevitable: it must be brought about if Man is to survive and if human consciousness is to continue to evolve. Conversely, if it is not brought about by man's own initiative, (and we may be sure no clap of thunder from heaven will coerce man into doing it), then we shall know that man is about to fail the test of life and that consciousness has finally exhausted itself and, ceasing to be self-creative, is about to die. It is in this sense that I agree with Toynbee's statement that it has become "already unquestionable that the social unification of Mankind [is] going to come to pass. The question that still [remains] open [is] not what [is] going to happen but merely how an inevitable consummation [is] going to be reached," *An Historian's Approach to Religion,* p. 145. I am satisfied that Toynbee is not a historical determinist, but it would be well to explain that "inevitable consummations" may in point of fact never come to pass.

Metaphysical thought was made possible by awareness of the inadequacies of "physical" thought. Primitive religions conceived God as a reality of the same order as every other which falls under man's experience. Greek "physics" did not depart substantially from this, though it created the conditions of the possibility of doing so. Apart from the possible claims of Far Eastern thought, it was the privilege of Athens to be on hand at that moment in the history of man when metaphysics was born, the moment when man's accumulating, evolving religious experience was enriched by the concept of God as a reality which transcended the order of being of which we had common experience and of which we ourselves formed part. But this transformation of the concept of God was made possible only by a corresponding expansion in the concept of being: whatever man could relate himself to was an object of knowledge, and knowability constituted reality as such. Being, therefore, was the name of reality, because being was that in which intelligibility and reality were identified. The degrees of knowledge reflected the degrees of reality, that is, the levels of being.

As is well known, once it was assumed that knowability and reality were the same, two principal problems arose: what is the relation among the degrees of being, and how can the intellect pass from knowledge of empirically given being to knowledge of transcendental being.[25] The exploration of these two problems

[25] These two questions are intertwined. It is clear that in metaphysical thought *being* does not mean exactly the same thing when it is predicated of God as when it is predicated of other beings. However, it is equally clear that the term must mean somewhat the same thing, otherwise it would mean nothing intelligible when applied to God. The question whether this procedure is valid is most important. Once granted that there are degrees of being, the doctrine of *analogy* is the only explanation which accounts for our knowledge of transcendent being on the basis of our immediate experience of empirical being alone: if God is subsistent Being

spins the thread that runs through the history of metaphysics. Now, the progress made by human consciousness as it applied itself to these questions is difficult to exaggerate. Man's attempt to understand his religious experience probably took much longer strides between, say, Plato and St. Thomas, than in the previous five to ten thousand years of agricultural civilization. Neverthe-

---

Itself, there can be little doubt that being is predicated of him and of empirically given being only proportionally. But does not the concept of God as subsistent Being Itself presuppose the analogy of Being? If so, we are involved in a vicious circle, unless perhaps the analogicity of the metaphysical concept of being were empirically grounded, that is, derived exclusively from our understanding of empirically given being.

It is a tribute to the perspicacity of Jacques Maritain that he was the first among neo-Thomists to have realized that this was an implicit requirement of metaphysics, and hence the first to have asserted that there is a metaphysical "intuition of being" as analogous, that the experience of being reveals being immediately and empirically as "intrinsically polyvalent," that is, as analogical: "the intuition of being is also the intuition of its transcendental character and analogical value," *Preface to Metaphysics,* p. 44. But the difficulty with this doctrine is exactly the same as that of the earlier doctrine of analogy, namely, that its undoubted apologetic advantages fail to be supported by empirically grounded evidence. In the last analysis, Maritain's doctrine of analogy simply reiterates the traditional gratuitous assertion that there *are* degrees of being. Moreover, if being could be experienced by the human intellect as intrinsically analogical, the existence of God would be quite as self-evident as that of created beings: God would be empirically given (at least to metaphysicians) in precisely the same way as any other being. (Of course, some Thomists go so far as to accept this conclusion, and more than one of them has been heard to affirm: "I do not believe in God, I *know* that God exists.")

We shall have occasion below, in connection with the question of the validity of metaphysics, to recall these difficulties of the doctrine of analogy. What is relevant at present is that metaphysical thought can be defined with reference to the doctrine of the analogical degrees of being. For this is the foundation of the metaphysical concept of God. I mean: this is the foundation of the theism of metaphysical ontologies—just as its denial is the foundation of the phenomenological ontologies' atheism.

less, these advances were made within the parameters of meta-physics.[26] But metaphysics eventually surpassed the order of inward transformation and in due course began to edge towards the threshold of evolution beyond itself.

Philosophy is now entering a meta-metaphysical stage or, per-haps more accurately, it is now concluding the first stage of a new age which liquidates both its physical and ontological phases (the latter term comprising both metaphysical and non-meta-physical ontologies). Conversely, a metaphysical concept of God, like a metaphysical, positive atheism, is possible today only inso-far as it is supposed that metaphysics (or ontology) has survived. But this is possible only if the logic of the history of philosophy is first denied, and if some sort of re-turn of consciousness to the past is deemed imperative. Once this judgment is made it matters little whether the re-turn envisage going back only to pre-Kantian, Cartesian or Humean thought, or farther back to mediaeval

[26] This is why, despite the historical multiplicity of specifically variable metaphysical doctrines, it is legitimate to speak in the singular of the metaphysical concept of God. I have tried to make clear that the in-adequacy of Thomism, and of every subsequent form of Scholasticism up to and including neo- and transcendental Thomism, and of every non-Scholastic, post-Cartesian theism, stems from a single essential cause, namely the fact that St. Thomas' metaphysical, and essentially Hellenic, concept of God is out of phase with St. Thomas' metaphysical, but es-sentially meta-Hellenic, concept of existentially contingent being as empirically given in our apprehension of created reality. In other words, St. Thomas' metaphysical revolution is at odds with his metaphysical traditionalism. To be sure, it was St. Thomas' re-definition of created, empirically given being that enabled him to define God as subsistent Being Itself. But, whereas the definition of empirically given being as constituted by really distinct essence and existence amounted to a re-definition of creature, the definition of God as subsistent Being Itself amounted, on the contrary, to a reaffirmation and reinforcing of the already well-advanced hellenization of the Christian concept of God.

thought, or all the way back to pre-Socratic thought. For the root of the inadequacy of the metaphysical concept of God is the "physical" concept of God; it is the ascription of being to God, a doctrine which metaphysics assumes uncritically and thereafter attempts to rationalize and modify, but not to transcend.

Metaphysics is, thus, not only historically, but also essentially and substantially, related to physics. In this respect Heidegger is perfectly correct: "from the very first 'physics' has determined the essence and the history of metaphysics. Even in the doctrines of being as pure act (Thomas Aquinas), as absolute concept (Hegel), as eternal recurrence of the identical will to power (Nietzsche), metaphysics has remained unalterably 'physics'." [27] But the fundamental relation of metaphysics to physics is not given by the fact that metaphysics is in some way beyond-physics, but by the fact that in a yet more important way metaphysics is *not* beyond-physics at all. For we must remember this: the distinctiveness of metaphysical thought was not that it conceived God as being, but that it conceived being as *both* appearance and reality—hence as having degrees, levels or worlds. Its peculiarity is that it envisaged being as analogous or as "polyvalent." Only because metaphysics conceived being in this wise, it followed that God was transcendent precisely as being, whether because he was the First Form, or the Thought of Thoughts, or the First Cause, or the One, or Subsistent Being Itself.

Thus, the concept of God as being originates with ante-metaphysical thought, and a metaphysical God is little more than a

[27] *Introduction to Metaphysics,* p. 14. Heidegger believes, however, that his own "enquiry into being as such is of a different nature and origin," (*ibid.,* p. 15). But since Heidegger identifies reality *as* being, it may be retorted that the difference is only of degree.

physical God from which all limitations have been removed apophatically, a God who is being in basically the same way as empirically given being (that is, by existing), but who is nevertheless gratuitously *said*—he is hardly *experienced*—to be different from empirically given being precisely as being. For example, the question "whether God exists or not" is made fundamentally possible by the assumption of an essential aspect of the *physical* concept of God, namely, that God is being, that God is (at least in part) like empirically given being, that the concept of being means "somewhat the same thing" when applied to God and when applied to man. This concept of God is thereafter complemented with negation and supereminence, as may be required by philosophy's progressive discovery of its deficiencies and contradictions. Hence, like "physics," metaphysics conceives God as being, but unlike "physics" it conceives God as, for instance, being *a se,* and as Subsistent Being Itself.

It is, therefore, highly relevant to any contemporary enquiry about God that when we today raise the question of God our investigation is historically continuous not only with classical Greek and biblical Hebrew thought but with primitive Greek and primitive Hebrew thought—and indeed with the religious thought of mankind since earliest times. A re-formulation of the problem of God which sprang from an adequate critique of *meta*-physics would have to reject also the *pre*-metaphysical assumption of metaphysics, namely, that God is being or else nothing at all. It is illegitimate to ask "whether God exists," (or "whether there is an objective, and not merely a subjective, reality which corresponds to our religious experience,") because we cannot reasonably assume that religious experience is adequately conceptualized *a priori,* that is, in terms of a God who may or may not exist (or of a reality which may be either objective or subjective). The question of God must be so put as to allow the possibility of conceiving God *a posteriori*. That is, a philosophical enquiry into God of the critical calibre which has become possible for philosophy today, should not merely refrain from asking whether an actually existing reality corresponds to the concept of God, as if the real problem were not the mystery of the nature of a reality (usually called God) about whose actual reality there can be scarcely any reasonable doubt, but as if it were simply whether there is an extramental substance to an idea which almost anybody is reasonably clear about. Contemporary Christian philosophy must also refrain from assuming *any* concept of God—though, on the other hand, it must remember that the concept of God has a history, and that it emerged in history as an evolving interpretation of religious experience. Thus, the question of the foundations of belief in God today is for philosophy: should ontology be "rehabilitated," [28] or should it be transcended? Granted that the concept of being

[28] This is the thesis of Richard Hinners, *Ideology and Analysis: a Rehabilitation of Metaphysical Ontology* (New York, 1966). Although I believe that "rehabilitation" is not enough, and that only transcendence is adequate to the historical needs exhibited by the contemporary stage of the history of Hellenic-Western thought, I am very happy to grant to Professor Hinners that the transcendence of metaphysics does rehabilitate, though not precisely metaphysics, at least its truth. I mean: it rehabilitates the truth of metaphysics in the same sense as the transcendence of metaphysics may be said to "re-construct" historically the tradition of Hellenic-Western philosophical thought. If it is a question merely of the adequacy of different metaphors, then our differences are slight. I am not at all certain, however, whether Professor Hinners and I do not prefer different metaphors because we place substantially different emphases on the degree to which truth and philosophy evolve. Thus, if my *architectural* metaphors appear to me, as metaphors, slightly more adequate than his, which hinge upon *apparel, possession,* and *aptitude,* the reason is that

must be "dismantled," [29] do we proceed to re-construct, re-fashion and re-new—and even re-habilitate—the traditional belief in some sort of Supreme Being, or do we not rather proceed to re-develop the traditional belief into belief in a reality beyond being itself?

Given the conditions under which these questions have been raised, it is almost redundant to explain that the direction of the investigation is defined by two points. First: the reality to which religious experience relates must be empirically accessible; that is, it must be, if not actually given in experience, at least revealed in the experience of that which is given in experience; it must be somehow empirically signifiable. To accept this is no more than to accept the general validity of the critique of metaphysical knowledge. Second: if the critique of metaphysics is valid, a transcendent being is a contradiction in terms and, therefore, metaphysical theism is invalid. But this does not imply that the reality to which religious experience relates is not a transcendent reality, if the common assumption of atheism and metaphysical

---

mine are much more obviously *metaphors*. I am free to speak of "re-building" the "foundations" because I know that there is no question of going back to the past to gather our intellectual materials and put them anew in a different way. We do not re-build *with* the past: we re-build the past. The past which we rebuild is not the past that *existed* in the past; it is the past that *exists* in us at present, in our historical situation which is from-the-past even as it exists at present today. There can be no question of a historical continuity that is given by the permanence of "materials" over a period of time. Re-habilitation, on the other hand, even if we take the term with no more than minimal aptness, is a re-furnishing with new possessions; it is a process which re-novates abilities and authorities; it is a re-clothing, hence, a re-tention, of the old bones, with but a new set of muscles and skin.

[29] I hope I have left no room for misunderstanding how my views on this point differ from Heidegger's, despite our cognate terminologies.

theism—that there is no empirical reality other than being—is questioned. For the reality which answers to religious experience may be transcendent, even if it is not being. In other words, the possibility to be explored is that the reality of God may be transcendent precisely because it transcends being.

If we put together these two considerations, the meaning of the question begins to emerge. The problem really is: whether the analysis of religious experience reveals a reality which transcends being as such.

BEING AND NON-BEING
IN REALITY AND THOUGHT

There is another question, however, which must be disposed of before it becomes expedient to deal directly with the meta-metaphysical concept of God. The metaphysical concept of God is made possible by some form of the concept of being. But, if we are not to exclude the possibility that the reality of God may be other than being, must we not *ipso facto* admit the possibility that there may be a reality which is actually non-being? And yet, can this supposition be seriously considered? Is it actually possible to entertain even the hypothesis that there may be a reality other than being, a reality which is non-being? How could this be, when it appears that "the mind boggles at this suggestion"? [30] We seem to have an apparently natural, inborn, ineradicable inclination to doubt the good sense of such an idea; I confess I count myself among those who spontaneously experience this

[30] J. Edgar Bruns, " 'In God nature can do anything'," *The Basilian Teacher,* X, 8 (December, 1966), 437–439, p. 438.

difficulty. What could be seriously meant by the suggestion that reality is not necessarily being, that reality may be other than being, that it may be indeed non-being? There are real difficulties manifested by these questions. Let us begin by attempting to clarify the terminology here employed.

I have used throughout this essay the term *reality* in a sense which, as the context should have revealed, is not that of Scholastics generally, or of St. Thomas in particular, where *res* "expresses the quiddity or essence of the being," [31] even if this usage appears to have etymology on its side. I use the term rather in the contemporary, everyday sense, which is distinctly affected by the existentialistic consequences of St. Thomas' ascription of contingency to the distinction between essence and existence. Thus, by reality in today's ordinary language we usually mean that which transcends consciousness, that which is other than oneself.

Of course, common usage is subject to metaphysical influence and therefore we today commonly identify *reality* and *being*. Whether or not this identification is to be upheld is a question that will occupy our attention for a while. But at present I only seek to establish that the sense in which I use the term *reality* is not semantically peculiar to me, although the suggestions that I may offer here by way of *interpretation* of that reality may well differ from that which is put upon it both by philosophers and common sense. By *being,* on the other hand, I mean that-which-is, *ens*—although according to context, and by reason of the grammatical characteristics of English (which have their counterpart in like ambiguities in other modern European languages) *being* (*essendum*) will also have to be used in order to refer to the

[31] *De Veritate*, I, 1.

act of being, the act by which being *is,* even if the bastard noun *to-be* (*esse*) and its more legitimate equivalents may sometimes be used also to mean that by which being *is,* and *is* whatever it is. In other words, a being is a reality which *is.*

Common sense will add that there is no reality which *is not.* But common sense so believes only because its language perpetuates a certain metaphysical interpretation of reality. The fact remains that even common sense recognizes these two distinct terms. Common usage may say that being is "the same as" reality: this may be true or false, but it is in any event a statement of what reality is, and it implies that reality is made real by a certain act, namely, the act of being. This, I repeat, may be true or false—but it is in either event an interpretation, not a fact of experience and, moreover, it is philosophically conditioned; it is not a primary empirical fact.

No doubt, the fact that there is no empirically given reality which is not being does lend plausibility to the common view. Nonetheless, it is not an empirical fact that reality—even empirically given reality—is essentially describable as *being,* that is, as being constituted, precisely as reality, by an act which it posits intrinsically within itself, namely, the act of to-be. The empirical fact is simply that reality is a fact, that experience is essentially describable, in Husserl's expression, as "experience of." Experience always, without exception, and by its very nature, exhibits the duality of *self* and *other.* The reality, the otherness of the other, is not open to doubt or question: whether its otherness lies in *being,* that is, in *existing,* is, of course, another matter, about which nothing can be said conclusively at this point.

It may be wondered, then, how *reality* is distinct from *object* and *objectivity.* The answer is that *object* may indeed mean the same as *reality,* as long as it means simply that which transcends consciousness, that is, without the epistemological connotation that the in-itselfness of an object is precisely that which is transcended by knowledge. But this is precisely why I do not use *object* and *objectivity* to mean *reality*. Common usage, interpreting reality to be "the same as" being, takes the term *object* to mean a thing-in-itself. Hence, *object* cannot be identified with *reality* unless one first assumes that reality means "the same as" being. Otherwise, if the question is left open whether there can be a reality which is other than being, one must define *object* as a *real being,* not as a *real reality.* Conversely, *being* must be defined as an *objective reality.* Whether there are realities which are other than objective realities remains, of course, also an open question. For this is but the converse of the very question we have already asked, namely, whether there can be a reality which is other than being.

I have no doubt that reality is the object of man's self-relation, in the sense that reality is that *to which* consciousness relates itself. But, unless one reverted to the identification of reality and being, it would be equivocal on this account to say that reality as such is the object of consciousness, even in the case of a reality which were other than being, (if there be such thing). Hence, the essential characteristic of reality cannot be "objectivity" (i.e. being-in-itself-ness, aptness to *lack relation* to another). On the contrary, the essential characteristic of reality is its aptitude for being related. No doubt, it is also true that objective reality, (i.e. being), is related: but being is related because it *is real,* not necessarily because it *is.* Thus, reality is whatever the self can have real relations towards.[32] Being, on the other hand, is the object of thought: it is that which is empirically given as such.

---

[32] This includes, of course, relations towards oneself. If the self were not really present to itself, it would have no "sense of reality." It might

To repeat, being is real; but whether the real is necessarily being is another matter which is yet to be discussed. And no reality other than being is objectively given: that much is empirically certain. Nonetheless, what is experienced immediately, in the first place, and as a matter of fact, is the reality of being. That the reality of that which is given in experience is being—that is, an act, or something that being *does* and which is other than the reality itself—this, I repeat, may be true or false, but is in no event given in the experience of reality as such. It is not even given in the experience of the reality of being as such.

Now, granted the linguistic structure of classical and modern European tongues, (which is in this respect the same as that of most Indo-European languages), whatever can be affirmed can be also logically denied. Thus, we speak of *non-reality,* or unreality, to signify that which is not real even if, of course, there is nothing in reality which is not real. Un-reality is thus not an empirical, but a logical concept; [33] that is, it is a concept which

---

be real, but it would not be conscious of reality, it would not be a self. Thus, the self is real, and the self exists. But its reality is not necessarily the same as its existing. The problem of "immortality" improperly so-called—for in point of fact it is, of course, the problem of *mortality*—is really the problem whether the self can be real even when (I do not say after, which would prejudicially contradict the empirical posing of the question) it ceases to exist. The answer to this question is not obvious, one way or another. But it seems to me that philosophy must begin by asking the question as it is posed by the empirical facts. If the question is correctly posed as I have just suggested, it may be possible, reasonably and in the fullness of Christian hope, to maintain at one and the same time that death ends human existence finally and once for all, but that nevertheless the real, existing human self finds its final and ultimate reality only beyond existence, at death.

[33] I except the so-called "experience of unreality," equivocally so-called. For the "unreality" which is the subject of the "experience of unreality" is real enough.

is made possible by the mind's ability to reflect upon itself. For we have never experienced anything which was non-real; to say that we had would be a contradiction in terms. But granted that we have experienced and conceived *reality,* the logical properties of the mind, which are but the consequences of its reflexivity, (i.e. its presence to itself), make it automatically possible, if its linguistic form is Indo-European, to conceive *non-reality.* Likewise, anyone whose thought is of an Indo-European linguistic form is able to think *non-being,* or *un-being* as soon as he is able to think *being.*

Moreover, anyone in this position who also assumes the identity of being and reality will automatically assume also that non-reality, un-reality, that-which-is-not-real, non-being, un-being, and that-which-is-not, signify one and all precisely the same thing, namely, *nothing, no-thing.* But the possibility that we are entertaining here is whether there may not be a reality which is other than being, a reality whose reality is not given by an act of to-be. It is necessary, therefore, to leave also open the possibility of distinguishing semantically between non-reality and non-being. This is not difficult to do: let us use the term *non-being* to mean the absence of being, not necessarily the absence of reality. *Nothing, nothingness, un-reality* and *non-reality* may be retained, of course, to signify the absence of reality. *Non-being,* thus, does not mean *nothing.* It means: that which *is not* being. But should there be a real reality other than being, though it would not be being, it would not be *nothing;* it would be *something* real, albeit, *no being* at all. Perhaps we are now in a position to consider the first difficulty that spontaneously arises once a certain linguistic background is supposed.

If anything truly *is* non-being, is it not thereby affirmed to *be?*

401

It would seem so, for if it is indeed affirmed to be (something or other) it is affirmed to *be;* hence, it is being. Therefore, whatever in reality can be the object of an affirmation must be being. Non-being could be only an imaginary or logical being; it would be only the idea created by the negation of being, posited after the manner of a positive reality. But "real non-being" is a contradiction in terms. If anything *is* real, this argument would run, it is thereby conceivable only as being. *Reality* and *real being* are synonyms, and any attempt to distinguish between them is self-defeating.

There are difficulties in connection with the reality of non-being, but the foregoing is not among the more serious of these. Reality and being are neither obviously nor necessarily synonymous. It is true that (in our Indo-European linguistic systems) being must be predicated of every reality; but this does not entail the equivalence of being and reality, since the being which anything has, simply because it is the subject of an affirmation, is not the same as the being of reality. As Aristotle said, "it is not because we think truly that you are pale, that you [really] are pale; it is because you are [really] pale that we who state so, possess the truth." [34] Likewise, as Aristotle knew, it is not because we truly predicate of every subject of predication a predicate which attributes to it *being-something* that the subject *is* whatever is truly predicated of it, and that, therefore, every subject of predication is in reality *being*. (As we shall consider below, however, metaphysicians do at least implicitly argue that if we do predicate truly in terms being-something, or in terms of simply *being,* the reason for this can only be that in reality all that is real is being. This is, of course, quite another matter.)

[34] *Metaphysics,* IX, 10 (1051 b 7–8).

In other words, the being of an affirmation is the being of the consciousness that makes the affirmation. A reality is not necessarily of the order of real being simply because affirmations about it are made in terms of being. When it is said that some reality *is* not being, the "is" of this affirmation does not signify the being of the reality of which the affirmation is made: it signifies the reality of the affirmation that *is* made. All that this affirmative "is" tells us of the reality itself is that it *is* the subject of our affirmation. But it does not tell us that the subject of our affirmation actually *is*. Otherwise, anything whatever of which affirmations were actually made would thereby actually exist. As everyone knows, however, to affirm for instance, that "winged horses are difficult to tame" does not bring Pegasus any closer to reality than he was before the affirmation was made.

Hence, the affirmation that some reality is not a being, or that reality may be non-being, is not self-refuting. This affirmation *is* an affirmation, and the reality of which the affirmation is made, namely, non-being, *is* affirmed to be such-and-such. But the reality of this affirmation does not entail the existence of the subject of affirmation. Thus, if there should "be" any reality of which it could be properly said that it was non-being, the fact that an affirmation *was* made about it, and that this affirmation must *be* made in terms of *being,* would not mean that the reality was really being.

In the Hellenic Christian *philosophical* tradition, however, the difficulty has not remained at this semantic level. For philosophers have not affirmed the identity of reality and being because they have been unaware of the danger of making an invalid transition from *being-predicated* or *being-thought* to *being-real.* However, to the foregoing considerations philosophers have added an epistemological supposition which changes the problem from a semantic to a metaphysical one. Although the being of an affirmation is other than the being of that which is affirmed, the former is *representative* of the latter. For, as Parmenides said, "it is the same thing that can be thought and can be." Since language signifies thought, and thought reduplicates reality inwardly and intentionally, the being of predication signifies directly the being of thought—but the being of thought reduplicates the being of reality and, therefore, the being of predication ultimately signifies, (through the mediation of thought), the being which in reality exists. For the mind reflects reality as it is: it could scarcely reflect it as it is not. Therefore, when the predicating mind reflects reality as being, it reflects reality as it is, that is, as being.

Metaphysicians might well insist, thus, not only upon the distinction between their position and that of common sense, but even upon a certain opposition between the two. For after Aquinas they would insist that reality is reducible to being, not because the terms are synonymous but, on the contrary, despite the fact that they are not. According to them, the reducibility of reality to being is not a commonplace: it is a profound metaphysical truth which the intellect can arrive at only after long study and arduous reflection. It is an insight which lies at the heart of the metaphysical Principle of Identity, the import of which is not simply that reality is self-identical, but that reality is self-identical despite the real distinction between *what*-it-is and the-act-by-which-it-*is* what it is, (namely, the act of being). The Principle of Identity is not tautologous, nor, despite Hegel, is it reducible to the absolute lack of difference between anything and itself:

no sooner do we possess the intuition of intelligible extra-mental being, than it divides, so to speak under our eyes, into two conceptual objects. On the one side there is being as simply existing or capable of existence, as simply given to the mind, or, if you prefer, as a 'thing' . . . [as] a simple existent actually given. On one side, then, there is being given *to* the mind. On the other side, in another concept which is still being, but under a different aspect, being is perceived as involving certain exigencies and certain laws, or, if you prefer, as recognized, admitted, affirmed *by* the mind.[35]

The existential value of the Principle of Identity is perhaps most clearly brought out when the Principle is expressed in the formula "being is being." For the grammatical identity of the subject and the predicate of this proposition puts in relief the idea that nonetheless the two terms have different metaphysical meanings which can be identified insofar as the coupla "is" identifies or marks as *being* that very difference between what is given by the subject and what is affirmed by the predicate:

Being is being, this means . . . [not only] 'Each thing is what it is' . . . it also means, and in this case the predication and affirmation concern the act of existence, 'what exists exists.' This is no tautology, it implies an entire metaphysic. What is posited outside its causes exercises an activity, an energy which is existence itself. To exist is to *maintain oneself and to be maintained* outside nothingness; *esse* is an act, a perfection, a splendid flower in which objects affirm themselves.[36]

The understanding of reality as existential being does not, therefore, involve a trivial redundancy. The question arises, however: on what grounds may this interpretative understanding of reality be justified? St. Thomas' statement of the matter has yet to be improved upon:

Now, as Avicenna says, that which the intellect first conceives as, in a way, the most evident, and to which it reduces all its concepts is

[35] Maritain, *Preface to Metaphysics,* pp. 91–92.
[36] *Ibid.,* pp. 93–94.

405

being [*ens*]. Consequently [*unde oportet*], all the other conceptions of the intellect are had by additions to being [*ens*]. But nothing can be added to being as though it were not included in being—in the way that a difference is added to a genus or an accident to a subject —for every reality is essentially a being (*qua quaelibet natura essentialiter est ens*).[37]

Nothing can be added to being which is not reducible to being: the explanation is, according to St. Thomas, that to be a being is of the very nature of the reality of anything which can be conceived as real—because to be conceived as real it must be conceived as being. In other words, real being is really being. Reality is to be interpreted as being, that is, constituted as reality by an act of existence (*esse*), an act which is not simply added to what the reality already is, since it is indeed the act by which the reality is real. Every reality, everything of which anything can be thought or said, every object of thought or subject or predication, every extramental thing which we in any way know, is constituted as an in-itself, and as the source of truth, and as warranting affirmations about it, by an act (namely, an act of *esse*), a perfection which is "the highest intrinsic principle of their very being."[38] Thus, the key metaphysical doctrine involved in the identification of reality and being is that *esse* is the act "in virtue of which the essence is a 'being'."[39]

This is far removed from the common sense idea that the word "reality" really means the same as the word "being." Metaphysicians do not superficially argue that every reality must be being, because the terms "being" and "reality" are synonymous. On the contrary, they show that, semantics to the contrary, the

[37] *De Veritate*, I, 1.
[38] Gilson, *Elements*, p. 130.
[39] *Ibid.*, p. 131

terms are really to be identified; that metaphysical enquiry dictates the *interpretation* of reality in terms of being. One might go so far as to assert that the classical metaphysical doctrine is, indeed, that, the case of God excepted, reality does *not* mean the same as being. Created being is real only because it exists: its reality follows upon its to-be, without which it is totally unreal. This is why existence is not merely conceptually or lexically distinct from the thing that exists, but *really* distinct from the latter. Being is constituted *in reality* by an essence's reception of an act of *to-be*.

Let us say, then, that, unlike common sense, metaphysics does not merely identify reality *with* being: it identifies reality *as* being. And it identifies reality *with* being only because it identifies reality *as* being. Metaphysics asserts that every reality is, precisely as reality, a being (*ens*), a composite of essence and existence in which the elements are "really distinct" if the being is created, but "the same" in the case of God—who is, therefore, not composite in himself, though it is necessary for us to conceive him as composed of logically distinct essence and to-be.

On the other hand, we should not overlook the connection between the semantic identification of reality *with* being and the metaphysical interpretation of reality *as* being. For the bases of the two are one and the same, namely, the fact that in thinking and in predication nothing can be added to being which is not reducible to being. St. Thomas' identification of reality *as* being is not the same as that of common sense, but it begins with the same observation as does that of common sense, namely, that "the intellect" (i.e. the Indo-European intellect) "reduces all its concepts to being" and, therefore, (understandably enough), cannot add anything to being, (that is, cannot possibly predicate anything of being), without finding that the addition, the predicate, is itself reducible to being.

This impossibility is an empirical fact. We can observe it as an event. But I should remark at this point, before I elaborate upon this criticism below, that this is an empirical fact concerning experience itself. Thus, the doctrine of St. Thomas, like the fallacy of common sense, is based upon a reflexive analysis of empirical knowledge. This is not only valid procedure: it is even unavoidable. Unfortunately, however, St. Thomas' reflexive analysis of experience is pre-critical, that is, it is an analysis of experience that fails to recognize that it is reflexive, and that, therefore, the distinctions between object and subject, betwen "being given to the mind" and "being affirmed by the mind," are themselves the outcome of knowledge and not the pre-conditions of it.

The Thomistic argument assumes that a concept, considered not in its entitative reality as a modification of the mind, but in its objectivity, (that is, in respect of its contents, or in its reduplicative or presentative reality), is identical with "the thing itself, inasmuch as it comes immediately into intellectual knowledge, or [in other words, the concept is the same as] the object known, inasmuch as it is an object." [40] Therefore, in St. Thomas' argument, if the intellect reduces all its concepts to being, and can think of nothing which is not conceivable as being, the reason must be that reality is reducible to being. Were it otherwise the intellect should be able to conceive realities which were not reducible to being.

Now, this argument is either circular, and the reducibility of all concepts to being is justified by the conclusion which follows

[40] Jacques Maritain, *Formal Logic,* (New York, 1946), p. 18.

therefrom, namely, the reducibility of all reality to being, or else St. Thomas had an independent reason for believing that the intellect reduces all its concepts to being. I have already indicated why it cannot be maintained that the argument is circular, namely, that the Thomistic principle of identity is not tautologous, and that it makes sense only if the Thomistic concept of being is an interpretation of reality rather than a synonym for it. St. Thomas' argument rests upon the reducibility of all concepts to being as a matter of observable fact. The root of St. Thomas' metaphysics is a psychological, linguistic fact—namely the fact that all (Indo-European) predication attributes *being* or *being-something* to a subject—which St. Thomas evidently assumed to be indicative of a natural, necessary property of human thought, and, therefore, to be also indicative of the reducibility of reality to being in reality itself. For, if every reality were not essentially being, why should all "human" (i.e., Indo-European) thought attribute *being* and *being-something,* and nothing but *being* and *being-something,* to every subject of predication—unless perhaps it were supposed that thought were not warranted in its certitude about reality? Conversely, if the mind truly attains reality, then its mode of thinking reflects not the properties of thought, but the nature of reality. Therefore, if there is *any* real being, then there is no reality whatever which is not essentially being.

It is historically understandable if St. Thomas thought that *our* way of thinking is *the* human way of thinking. The fact seems to be, however, there is not a single way for man to relate himself to reality, and that no way to do so is necessary, primary, natural or privileged. All are mutually transformable and none can reasonably claim unique validity without descending to circularity—as ethnocentric arguments frequently do. But what St. Thomas could not have very well known is fairly easily accessible to most well-educated persons today. The cultivation of linguistics and of cultural anthropology in recent decades has put us in a favourable position for understanding the world of human experience outside the Indo-European linguistic family well enough to realize that our way of thinking about reality in terms of being is far from universal and, indeed, is almost confined to cultures which share the Indo-European heritage.

Our philosophical tradition has been cast in concepts which are exclusively Indo-European—and indeed, predominantly Greco-Roman. In this way of thinking concepts are reducible to being because thought has a linguistic form which can be described in terms of these two syntactic rules: (a) every complete sentence attributes to a subject a predicate, the essential element of which is a verb; and (b) the verb "to be" is ambivalent, having both a copulative and an existential function. The conjunction of these two rules means that every complete thought is reducible to the form *S is P*. For the exclusively verbal character of the sentence means that every Greco-Roman thought envisages every reality as a subject of action; hence, everything which is attributable to the subject of predication must be attributable to it as its act. As Maritain says, existence is "an activity . . . an energy"; and neo-Thomists constantly remind us that the "dynamism" of to-be is not well conveyed by the substantive "existence," and urge us to copy the violence of the Latin use of *esse* in the position of a noun, by saying not only "act of existing" but also "to-be." When to this is added the ambivalence of the verb "to be," the result is that every Greco-Roman or like Indo-European thought envisages reality as the subject of an act of *existing,* and that every attribute of that subject is reducible to an act of being—whether being pure and simple, or being in one or more categorical modalities. We have already studied this above,[41] and I need but allude to it again in this new context. In other words, the two rules taken together amount to the reducibility of all concepts to being. Existential metaphysics is the philosophical extrication, elaboration and interpretation of the implications contained in the typically Indo-European mode of human self-relation to reality: "every reality is essentially a being" because being is that-which-is, and all (Indo-European) thought and all (Indo-European) predication attributes being (*esse*) or else being-something (*essentia*) to a subject of thought or predication which is itself being, (*ens*).

I emphasize once again the difference between this metaphysical way of thinking and that of common sense. Metaphysicians like St. Thomas do not frequently confuse the *is* of an affirmation with the *is* of the reality of which the affirmation is made. The reducibility of reality to being is not due to mere semantic confusion, but to a much more serious philosophical confusion. (And I use the word *confusion* with premeditation.) For metaphysicians *con-fuse* reality and being. According to whether they identify being with intelligibility or with existence, they confuse reality with either essence or else with existence. Thoroughgoing essentialists like Plato and Aristotle do the first; thoroughgoing existentialists like Heidegger and Sartre do the second. St. Thomas stands half-way between the two, leading the history of philosophy in its passage from one to the other extreme. For him reality is neither essence nor existence but *ens;* and *esse*

[41] Cf. above, pp. 139–150.

makes *ens* to be real (i.e. real as contingently actual in creatures, necessarily actual in God), whereas *essentia,* by limiting the *esse* of creatures makes them also to be real (i.e., real as necessarily intelligible hypothetically) or else, without limiting the *esse* of God, but being identical with it, makes him likewise to be real, (i.e. real as necessarily intelligible absolutely).

St. Thomas' confusion is compounded by the conceptualization of the grounds for this very *con-fusion* as a *distinction* (i.e. other-ness) between *essentia* and *esse.* For this supposedly *real* distinc-tion is of a peculiarly real, not to say paradoxically real, sort. We have to do here with distinct "elements," the distinction between which implies not merely non-separation, but also the constitu-tion of the one and only, uniquely real being within which the real distinction occurs. The act of *esse* makes the essence to be, whereas the essence is the limitation of the act of *esse,* an act with-out which there is no reality at all. Thus, this doctrine asserts not merely that *esse* is the act of essence, distinct and (in a sense) anterior to essence, but also, and indeed primarily and basically, that by this act the reality of the only actual reality is constituted, namely the reality of being, *(ens).* As Gilson himself says: St. Thomas' "distinction between essence and existence ought never to be thought of apart from that other thesis which *provides it with a basis,* rather than completes it, the intimate union of essence and existence in the concrete existing thing." [42] It is symptomatic that it took a contemporary historian of philosophy

[42] *The Christian Philosophy of St. Thomas Aquinas,* p. 38 (italics mine). And, again, "by transcending the plane of the ontology of essence common to both [Avicenna and Averroes] St. Thomas nullifies their dispute. By lifting himself to this level he sees *at one glance what dis-tinguishes essence and existence and what unites them in the real,"* ibid., p. 40, (italics mine).

to state explicitly this "thesis," and that St. Thomas merely assumed tacitly what Gilson has now—quite correctly, to be sure —found to be the "basis" of St. Thomas' peculiar metaphysical outlook.

Thus, what is usually called the real distinction might as well, nay, better, be called *the real unity* of essence and existence. For the "real distinction" is not only a distinction without separation: it is a real distinction between realities neither of which is real insofar as it is distinct, but only insofar as, together with each other, they make up one real being. Likewise, it is said not to be a "merely logical" distinction, although it is a distinction which cannot be made for itself by reality (for if it were made *by* reality then the real distinction would be a real separation and, if so, the thing would no longer be), and although it can be made *only by the mind* as it thinks about the reality in which the two make one. The transition is thus made from the observation of the linguistic, psychological fact that everything must be *conceived* as a form of being, to the idea that everything must be affirmed to *be* reducible to a form of being. For every predicate is reducible to what-a-subject-is, while existence itself is assimilable to predication. This assimilability is implicit in the existential-copulative ambivalence of most Indo-European verbs "to be."

This pattern of self-relation to reality, however, is rarely found outside the Indo-European cultural family; the researches of linguistic scholars have given us a wealth of evidence on this score. I wish briefly to illustrate this with the instance of Chinese, a language which has a rich literature and a sophisticated philosophical tradition.

In classical Chinese the reducibility of all reality to being is hardly expressible in an intelligible proposition, least of all is it an obvious truth.[43] But the syntax of Chinese thinking diverges sharply from that to which European thinking is accustomed. First: in addition to verbal sentences Chinese has nominal or

[43] Most of my information about Chinese syntax and the philosophical implications it suggests I owe to Angus Graham's "'Being' in Western philosophy," to which I have referred above, and to his "'Being' in Classical Chinese," in John W. M. Verhaar, (ed.) *The Verb "To Be" and its Synonyms: Philosophical and Grammatical Studies,* (New York, 1967), pp. 1–39. (This is the separately published Part I, of *Foundations of Language: Supplementary Series,* vol. 1.) A more general study drawing on a multiplicity of non-Indo-European languages is Ernst Locker, *"Etre et avoir: leurs expressions dans les langues,"* Anthropos, 49 (1954), 481–510. This valuable paper shows, (p. 485), that "there are two [linguistic] means to express, in the most natural way, the notion of existence pure and simple: [first, the means which I call] the null-means (*le moyen zero*) [that is] (the mention of the being suffices to indicate its existence) and [second] the use of an invariable particle [such as Chinese *yu*]. Every tendency that would assimilate the notion of pure existence to the notion of activity [as is the case when the element indicating existence is variable, concerning especially person, number, gender and time, as in the Indo-European languages] alienates language from reality. It is noteworthy that the Indo-European languages, though they generalize the idea of activity, nevertheless exhibit the need to restrict the usage of the verb[s of the Sanskrit root] es-, and in this manner to underline its exceptional character."

I remark once again, however, that there would be a remnant of glossocentrism in the assumption that what is expressed in non-Indo-European languages in forms which are translatable into Indo-European verbs of the root *es-*, is really "existence." This would be as equivocal as the assertion by a Chinese philosopher that Indo-European languages express "indeedness" by introducing, instead of the invariable particle *yeh,* a complicated structure in the sentence in which "what is" and "what is indeed" are joined by the peculiar, inflected part of speech known (by the natives) as "the verb to be." As a statement of equivalent, mutually translatable modes of self-relation to reality this hypothetical Chinese scholar's statement would be as irreproachable as Professor Locker's. But it is important to insist that the Chinese "indeedness" must not be thought to be *really* "beingness," any more than the Western "beingness" must be thought to be *really* "indeedness." Likewise, the fact that the typical Indo-European predicative pattern "alienates language [or, rather,

determinative sentences. And even verbal sentences do not always have a *verb,* in our sense of the term. For in Chinese the distinction between the verb and the adjective is blurred and, according to some sinologists, perhaps even non-existent. For instance, the verb does not necessarily have a subject, and its function is not always that of attributing an act. Sometimes its role is not unlike that of qualifying an object. Second: in Chinese the functions of predication and existence are separated. In fact, they are separated and divorced: assertions can be made not only in sentences of non-verbal form, but even within the category of verbal sentences there is no verb corresponding to Indo-European "to be", that is, a verb which combines predicative and existential functions. Thus, to-be-predicated cannot be assimilated to being, since if I may so put it, in Chinese "to be something" is not *"to be* it".

Obviously, from the Greco-Roman viewpoint the last proposition is a non-sensical self-contradiction. Nonetheless, it expresses a fact of Chinese mental life. In Chinese the affirmation that *S is P* does not imply that *P* accrues to *S* as its actuality, least of all as an actuality reducible to the actuality of existence or to-be (in either a substantial or an accidental mode). In brief in Chinese to say that "S is P" does not imply that "S *is* P", or that "P is 'what S *is*'." This hardly makes sense in any modern European language—unless one first refuses to identify reality and being and, hence, does not insist that when we say (and think) "S is P," it must be supposed that in reality "S *is* P" under pain of

---

thought] from reality" is not to be taken as an indication of a radical deficiency in these languages. This alienation is to be understood as a matter of historical fact: it is the alienation between *subject* and *object* in Greek philosophy, it is the alienation between *essence* and *existence* in St. Thomas, it is the alienation between *human being* and *transcendent reality* in contemporary thought.

scepticism. It may well be perfectly true, of course, that "S is P." But this does not imply that in reality P is "what S *is*." Were we to adopt, as the Hellenic-Western tradition has customarily adopted, such an interpretation of reality, we would thereby fail to realize, as the Hellenic-Western philosophical tradition has customarily failed to realize, that language relates man to reality not because the *structure* of language passively *reflects* the structure of reality, but because the *function* of language is actively to *situate* man in the reality of the world.

As for existence itself, in Chinese it is not thought of as the act of a subject, but as a fact or event which is relative to an *object*. The existential sentence in Chinese is usually composed of an impersonal verb, *yu,* and an object. It would be not altogether unwarranted, though it would be nonetheless somewhat equivocal, to translate the verb *yu* by the English verb "to have" or by its Indo-European equivalents, since *yu* is also used *with a subject* to signify the act of possessing. If this translation rule is adopted, then it would be correct to assert that in Chinese one does not say "Something is" but "Has something." But it must be kept in mind that the "has" is impersonal, that there is *nothing* which "has" it. The Chinese way of envisaging (what *we* call) existential reality as the object of an event (in the world) rather than as a subject of an act (of being), becomes clearer yet when we consider that non-existence can be signified in emphatic form in Chinese by a verbal sentence which *does* have a subject, namely, "the world," (literally, "[everything] under the sky"). Instead of saying, for instance, "winged horses do not exist," the Chinese would say "the world [i.e. 'under the sky'] has no winged horses."

But even this does not convey the idea fully. For, finally, the *ob-jective* and *event-ful* nature of the Chinese way of experiencing existence, as contrasted with the *sub-jective* and *per-fective* Indo-European form, is further emphasized by the fact that the existential verb *yu* is not negated by the addition of a preposition, particle, or other qualifier, but by the use of a different verb, *wu,* with opposite meaning. It would be warranted, therefore, to translate the negative existential verb as "to lack." But if we keep in mind the previous observations, the contrast between, say, "the world lacks winged horses," which has a literal counterpart in English, and the positive Chinese affirmation of the existence of real horses, which does not, helps make clear why every translation of the latter affirmation in terms of being, or indeed, in terms of any verb reducible to being, would amount to restructuring the Chinese mode of self-relation to existential reality.

One of the characteristics of the Chinese mode of experience of existential reality is that "being" and "non-being" (as *we* would put it) are, though opposed, not contradictory. Being and non-being are mutually relative and not mutually exclusive. We should not find it surprising, therefore, to learn that the doctrine of the reality of non-being (as we would have to say in English) has long been familiar to many Chinese classical philosophers, particularly the Taoists. In a formula which would be thoroughly misleading without the background sketched by the foregoing remarks, the third-century philosopher Ho Yen defined *Tao* in these terms: "The Tao is only that in which there is not anything that there is." [44]

[44] Quoted in Graham, " 'Being' in Western philosophy," p. 100. The idea suggested by this text may be clearer from the explanation of Fung Yu-lan that *"Tao* is manifested in all things, and therefore when these things are born and grow, we may say in one way that it is *Tao* that brings this about, yet in another way we may say that all things do these

Tao is usually translated as "the Way," that is, "road" or "path," which is the root meaning of the word. But this is not primarily a metaphorical way of saying "the right way of life," or "the adequate method to achieve oneself." In philosophy *Tao* refers to the inner, self-revealing "life" or reality within the universe and within everything in the world, in relation to which meaning and purpose, intelligibility and fulfilment, can be found in reality. (It is interesting to note that Chinese translators of Christian literature regularly use *Tao* to translate *Logos*.[45]) The rationale of the metaphorical use of *Tao* to designate, in effect, the ultimate reality, may become apparent if we keep in mind that in Chinese thinking reality is not necessarily being. As Wan Pi, another third-century Taoist explained: "The Tao is a term for Nothing. Since there is nothing it does not pass through, and nothing which does not follow it, it is called by metaphor the Tao,"[46] that is, the Way. It is clear that in this formula *Nothing,* (or, in my terminology, *non-being*), does not mean the

---

things by themselves. 'What do I do? What do I not do? Things are transformed of themselves,' *History of Chinese Philosophy,* vol. I, p. 224. (The quotation by Fung Yu-lan is from Lao-tzu, Ch. 25). Likewise, "Tao invariably takes no action, and yet there is nothing left undone," Lao-tzu Ch. 37, in Wing-tsit Chan, *A Source Book in Chinese Philosophy,* (Princeton, 1963), p. 158. Note the relevance of this viewpoint to the study of the question whether creatures could, at one and the same time, be contingent upon a reality other than themselves and other than the whole totality of being, and yet not be caused or made (even out of nothing) by such a reality (with the further consequence that such a reality does not become necessary simply because its creatures are contingent upon it). The matter will be considered in more detail below.

[45] R. O. Hall, (retired) Bishop of Hong-Kong (Church of England), in a private communication.

[46] Quoted in Graham, " 'Being' in Western philosophy," p. 100.

absence of negation of reality: it means the absence or negation of an *existing* reality; it means the absence of being, (*ens*).[47]

I do not wish to suggest that the Indo-Chinese conceptual structure, unlike the Indo-European, reflects with unique accuracy the nature of reality. The Chinese language exhibits its own weak-

[47] "Objects can be said to be Being (*yu*), but *Tao* is not an object, and so may be spoken of as Non-being (*wu*). At the same time, however, *Tao* is what has brought the universe into being, and hence in one way it may also be said to be Being. For this reason *Tao* is spoken of as both Being and Non-Being. Non-being refers to its essence; Being to its function," Fung Yu-lan, p. 178. However, it may be well to add two comments. First, the opposition between *yu* and *wu* is not a dialectical opposition; in fact, it is no opposition at all. The opposition arises only in translation. In Chinese there is mere complementarity. Therefore, the foregoing statement of Fung Yu-lan should not be interpreted in Hegelian terms. Second, Professor Fung appears to some extent to have succumbed to the suggestion implicit in all traditional Hellenic-Western philosophical thought, namely, that the Hellenic "way of being" is the only philosophical "way of truth," and that every other philosophical tradition is only the "way of mortal opinion." Professor Fung shows a slight tendency to give priority to the categories of Western thought over those of Chinese. The distinction between "essence" and "function," it seems to me, disfigures the doctrine slightly, since one of the points which it attempts to convey is that the *Tao* is made known to man, precisely *in that in which it* (the *Tao*) *is not.* That is, we become conscious of the *Tao* only *in relation to something else:* "we look at it and do not hear it; its name is The Inaudible. We touch it and do not find it; its name is The Subtle [formless]. These three cannot be further inquired into, and hence merge into one. Going up high, it is not bright, and coming down low, it is not dark. Infinite and boundless, it cannot be given any name; it reverts to nothingness. This is called shape without shape, form without object. It is The Vague and Elusive. Meet it and you will not see its head. Follow it and you will not see its back. Hold on to the *Tao* of old in order to master the things of the present. From this one may know the primeval beginning [of the universe]. This is called the bond of *Tao*," Lao-tzu, Ch. 14, in Wing-tsit Chan, *Source Book*, p. 146.

nesses and creates its own philosophical problems.[48] But even an elementary acquaintance with the syntax of Chinese thought supports the suggestion that it is perfectly possible to conceive a reality which is relative to being but which is other than being—a reality, therefore, which is not a transcendent being but which transcends being, and which can thus be immanent in being while remaining distinct from being, precisely because it is other than being. The Chinese have difficulty in thinking of reality otherwise, and have to learn Western philosophy before the baffling intricacies of Western languages, which identify reality and being, begin to make sense to them.

If the foregoing reasoning is correct, then it appears that reality is to be identified neither *with* being nor *as* being. Reality does not mean the same as being; this has never been in philosophical doubt. But neither is the reality of the real to be explained in terms of being, whether in terms of essence, or of existence, or of the composition of being by essence and existence. As a Hindu Catholic student of comparative religion has put it:

The identification of God with Being cannot be considered a universally recognized axiom . . . [However,] Christianity has so far committed itself to such an identification of God and Being that any denial of the equation appears to question the very essence of Christianity. The history of human thought seems [to Christians] to show that man has no other alternative than to choose between divinizing Being or ontologizing the Divinity . . . [But what contemporary Christian philosophy must do] is first ask whether it is possible to de-divinize Being without doing harm to God and sec-

[48] "The present study does not encourage one to take it for granted that Chinese is either better or worse than English as an instrument of thought; each language has its own sources of confusion, some of which are exposed by translation into the other," Graham, "'Being' in Western philosophy," p. 112.

ond, whether it is possible to de-ontologize God without doing harm to Being . . . [For although] from Aristotle in Europe and from the Upanishads in India . . . if God exists he cannot but identify himself with Being . . . such an identification breaks down nowadays . . . The peaceful symbiosis between God and Being that from Aristotle on has constituted the spine of Western culture is no longer possible.[49]

Now, although reality is to be identified neither *with* being nor *as* being, it is true that reality may exist—evidently, every reality which is being *does* exist. It is another question whether its existence is correctly to be described as its act. Every such reality will exhibit the properties which have been traditionally conceptualized as contingency; but it is clear that the contingency of being thus understood could not be relative to the necessity of any reality which did not exist, since the reality which is being is whatever it is, (even contingent), not because it is real but because it is.

Thus, whatever *is*, (I mean, whatever *exists*), is contingent. This scarcely entails that whatever is not, whatever does not exist, is necessary. For, in the first place, that-which-is-not may mean either "un-reality" or "reality other than being." But, more important, any real reality which does not exist, will be non-contingent precisely because its reality is not describable as the factual event we call being or existing. The necessary is, after all, that which must *be,* that which cannot *be.* If there is a reality other than being, it is not possible to attribute to it *either* contingency or necessity, since of it cannot be said either that it may be or that it cannot be. We might say that such a reality was non-contingent; that would be perfectly true. For

[49] Raymond Panikkar, "The God of Being and the 'Being' of God: an exploration," *Harvard Divinity Bulletin,* Spring, 1968, pp. 12–16.

that matter, we might also say that it was non-necessary; that too would be perfectly true. But to say that it was non-contingent would not mean that it was necessary; and to say that it was non-necessary would not mean that it was contingent. Its non-contingency and non-necessity would be merely the logical equivalent of its non-being. Being, on the other hand, is essentially contingent. It is, but it does not have to be. Necessary being is, thus, a contradition in terms—like uncreated being, or like unreal reality. Hume's perceptive formula was "whatever *is* may *not be*." To that observation we may now add: that whose reality is not being, neither may nor must be.

But this complicates the problem. Granted that reality is not identifiable *as* being, and that the contingency of being is not relative to the necessity of reality as such, it follows that reality as such cannot be the "ground of being" or its antecedent, conditioning cause, or indeed, anything which in any way pertains to the order of being. If so, the question arises: what is the relation of reality and being? Granted that reality is not necessarily being, but that all that exists is real, does it not follow that reality is what metaphysics wrongly calls being, and that meta-metaphysics is essentially but a metaphysics which gives reality its true name?

The answer is: decidedly no. The concept of reality is not a substitute for the metaphysical concept of being. A philosophy of reality is not a metaphysics of being in disguise, or a metaphysics of being translated into the language of non-being. The idea that reality is not necessarily being, and that there may be a reality other than being, does not mean that reality, (rather than being), is that to which "the intellect reduces all its concepts." The inadequacy of metaphysics is not due to its concern with being (rather than with reality), and therefore it cannot be remedied by its undertaking to concern itself with reality (rather than with being). The inadequacy of metaphysics comes from its being insufficiently critical; that is, from its basis in a concept of knowledge which does not take account of the empirical nature of empirical facts. Hence, once the reducibility of reality to being is consciously or unconsciously assumed, we have entered the uncritical path of metaphysics, having thereby presupposed that in the unity of the concept of being can be reconciled the variety of degrees of reality (i.e. the degrees of being). But, likewise, to suppose that reality, by that or by any other name, would reconcile in the unity of the concept the variety of realities—for instance, real being and reality other than being, or empirical and trans-empirical reality—would be to enter upon the same metaphysical path, with but the difference that one's conceptual shoes would have been resoled. The doctrine of the degrees of being is hardly transcended if it is simply replaced by the doctrine of the degrees of reality.

Hence, the relation between reality and being is not, in the first place, that of genus and species. There is no specific difference between reality and being. But the reason for this is not, as St. Thomas might have put it, that nothing can be added to reality as thought it were not included in reality. The reason is that the logical relations among concepts cannot be taken as reflective indices of relations in reality. The relation of reality to being can be ascertained only empirically. We cannot tell from the examination of the concepts what this relation might be.

Nor is the relation of reality and being a transcendental relation. There is no analogy of reality, and whatever is real is said to be real in the same sense as every other reality. There may well be differences among realities—indeed, some realities exist and others may not. But they are not different because they are only partly the same. They are different because their realities are respectively what they are. Thus, the reality of being is nothing other than its reality as being: the reality of being is nothing other than its own being in itself. Similarly, if there is any reality other than being, its reality is not definable in terms of something more real than either its own reality or that of other realities. This is why it is true, in a sense, that transcendent reality is undefinable: [50] it does not have anything in common with the

---

[50] However, it would be unwarranted and most unfortunate if we were to conclude from this that man's knowledge of transcendent reality is negative, or least of all that it is negatively negative (i.e. *per viam remotionis et supereminentiae*). The more adequate conclusion would be that man's knowledge of transcendent reality is *relative*. The reality which transcends being can be conceived only in relation to being. "God is a reality beyond being:" this is not to conceive God as being, but it is to conceive God in relation to being. Moreover, the reason why God must be conceived in relation to being is not that he is not accessible to human experience, or that there is some filter in human consciousness which limits man to such relative knowledge. The reason is that the reality in question, as we shall consider shortly, is a reality which, in its own reality and in-itselfness, is relative to being.

On the other hand, it is not to be denied that human knowledge is limited—the fact is, after all, perfectly obvious. The point is rather that human knowledge is not limited in the sense that there is another level of possible consciousness which could know, or which does know, what man cannot by nature know. For if our concept of knowledge is empirically grounded, then the recognition of the limitations of human knowledge does not imply the supposition of another, more perfect type of knowledge which would fulfill the essence of cognition as we discover it in man, but from which all limitations and imperfections would be removed with but a stroke of the wand of (*mirabile dictu!*) *a human affirmation to that effect*. In this sense, therefore, it must be said that whatever man cannot *by nature* know and what he cannot, therefore, ever expect reasonably to know, is simply not knowable. To say anything else is to talk in metaphysical riddles. Naturally, if reality is not confined

reality of being, the reality of that which is. It follows that the mode of self-relation which consciousness can have to transcendent reality cannot be the same as that which it has to being. But the nature of this mode of consciousness will, like the nature of the relation between transcendent reality and being, have to be determined empirically and hence will be considered, together with the latter question, only after the investigation has proceeded from the abstract possibility of a reality other than being (which is what we have been discussing so far) to the question of whether the reality of such a reality is to be concretely asserted on the basis of the indications given by the empirical facts.

REALITY AND PRESENCE
IN GOD AND MAN

We have now determined that the question which the development of philosophical thought as well as the history of Christian dogma has led to in our time is this: What does the analysis of religious experience reveal about the nature of reality? And, specifically, does it reveal a reality which transcends being?

By religious experience I mean in this context nothing recondite or extraordinary. I have in mind no special experience or experiences which are distinctive by their peculiar object or content. Religious experience may indeed take extraordinary forms, (that is, peculiarly religious forms). But these are clearly derivative

----

to being, there is no question but that man is finite. My affirmation does not mean that man knows infinitely; it means that man cannot define the transcendence of the reality which is other than being in relation to its understanding of itself by itself. It means, therefore, that it cannot be defined at all.

and elaborate. Religious experience in its essential and fundamental form is nothing but ordinary, everyday experience, insofar as it is the origin of religious belief—or, rather, it is that aspect
of ordinary, everyday experience which is the origin of religious
belief. For all consciousness places man "in situation" or "in
perspective;" that is, consciousness situates man in relation to
reality. All consciousness puts man in touch with reality: but it
puts him in touch with his own self-presence (and with his own
freedom) at the same time. Thus, man's self-relation to reality
is open-ended. Reality is disclosed to consciousness as that which
man has to make up his mind about. The fundamental making
up one's mind about reality, the self-relation to reality which is
not merely speculative but decisive, not merely oriented from the
past to the present but also from the present to the future, is the
element from which all religious belief grows: "being present to
oneself, self-awareness is . . . in the last analysis religious, [it]
is inescapably a religious act. . . . Human existence does not
leave man the choice to be *not*-religious: he is forced by his own
being to be religious or irreligious, . . . and in both cases it is
a question of a religiously relevant action. To stand before oneself is to stand before God." [51] I stress that the precise nature of
the religious predicament in which consciousness naturally and
normally places man is not necessarily reflected upon or, least
of all, necessarily philosophically analyzed. But if we should
reflect upon it and analyze it philosophically we should observe
that the heart of this elemental religious experience is the awareness that being as such, being in its existential reality, is a matter
of *fact*. How does this awareness come about?

[51] Edward Schillebeeckx, "Faith functioning in human self-understanding," in T. P. Burke (ed.) *The Word in History*, (New York, 1966), p. 49.

We have seen that conscious experience reveals being to itself, and itself to itself. This implies: consciousness reveals being to itself as being *already there*. Consciousness of being is consciousness of that which one cannot question—except, of course, after one accepts it. The reality of being is there: its otherness makes it undeniable and irrefutable. It has the quality of admitting no argument or doubt unless one accepts *it* and, thus, can begin to argue *with* it or to wonder *about* it. Consciousness reveals the reality of being as an unquestionable *fact*.

The *cogito* is but a reflective exposition of the same truth: experience shows that reality in its otherness is posited by experience itself. Consciousness cannot be consciousness without being "consciousness of."[52] Hence, it is a fact that I exist, that things exist, that there is a world in which I am and from which I am separated by my consciousness of it—and, thus, by the self-hood or reality of my very self. Well, what exists is always *already* in ex-

[52] All this is implicit, but only implicit, in Descartes' *cogito*. Descartes was in no position to realize the import of his analysis of experience, since he assumed that knowledge was the transcending of the pre-cognitive object-subject dichotomy, and that therefore that which is immediately displayed as "other" by consciousness is immanent *in* experience, and may or may not be duplicated by that which transcends experience. If we do not make this assumption, then that which appears in immediate consciousness is not representative of reality, but is reality itself.
I should take this opportunity to explain the principal reason why, in a book which capitalizes on Edmund Husserl's doctrine of "intentionality," I have made only the vaguest allusion to his work. The reason is that the thought of Husserl is thoroughly ambiguous, and the use which later philosophy has made of his phenomenology is not at all what he appears to have meant by it. In my submission, Husserl was at bottom an idealist—but he was an idealist so *outré* that he surpassed idealism despite himself. My inclusion of reference to Husserl's thought in this volume would have introduced an unnecessary complication in a matter which is not simple in itself.

istence: it is never found except as being *already there*. What I might or might not do with it, or about it, or because of it, remains to be seen. But no such eventualities will come to pass unless they proceed from what is *already* a fact. Man has to "contend" with the facts because the open possibilities of the future begin with the closed factuality of the past. That which exists has been, as it were, already decided about—not in every way, of course, but precisely as existing. Therefore, any further decisions in relation to it must begin with existence precisely as a fact. Freedom and creativity imply that man's future is grounded upon his present self-apprehension in relation to his past. Being is present to consciousness, in the first place, simply as a matter of fact.

Note, however, that the factuality of being is ambivalent. So far I have stressed only that a fact is indisputable, that it is what it is irrespective of anyone's wishes or imagination. *Fact* is, therefore, that which originates, orients and directs every human attempt to find meaning. We may, of course, stray from the facts, but scarcely because we suppose this to be the road that leads to meaning and truth. To ignore the facts one must first deceive oneself. The fact that this self-deception about the facts is possible is indicative of the nature of the mind. But the fact that we do not ever imagine that to ignore the facts is the way to truth is indicative of how we conceive the nature of facts.

Thus, the very need of the mind to abide by the facts implies that facts are not meaningful in themselves and precisely as facts. As the common expression has it, the facts are "only the facts," and it is not in vain that we frequently refer to the "bare facts." A fact is "nothing but a fact." It may call for interpretation, but does not of itself constitute its own interpretation. Its meaning is not set once for all simply because it exists. And it matters little whether only one interpretation can be true, or whether alternative interpretations can be related within the catholicity of truth: in either event the facts as such are "only facts." Thus, if something is said to happen "as a matter of fact," we imply that we need not search behind it for a cause or explanation why it *had* to happen. The point is that although it *did* happen, it did *not* have to happen. Every explanation of what happens is *posterior* to the event. This is why explanations must fit the facts, not the other way about. The facts as such stand by themselves, without explanation or justification: they are that for which explanation and justification is sought.

The factuality of being should not be confused with *contingency* in the traditional sense of this term: it does not mean that being derives its indisputability from a *raison d'être* which, since it does not possess it from itself, it must receive from another and, ultimately, from a being which is not contingent, but *a se.* If we were to observe, as for instance St. Thomas does, simply the paucity of self-explanation which accompanies factual existence, neglecting the obtrusive, self-assertive quality of whatever is a fact, then we would conceive empirically given being as contingent, in the simple sense that it *need not be.* But, if the contingent is simply that which *need not* be, then we would also have to say, as St. Thomas does, that "nothing is so contingent that it does not possess some necessity in itself." [53] This would be to understand contingency in strict relation to necessity: the contingent *need-not* be. And this conception of the contingency of empirically given being as the absence of necessity presupposes an absolute necessity in relation to which being exists and is a relative necessity.

We may, of course, retain the term contingency—I shall con-

[53] *ST,* I, 86, 3.

tinue to use it here—provided we do not also retain its relativity to a prior "necessity." If we wish to avoid the *a priori* assumption of an absolute necessity and yet retain the term "contingency," we must stress that it means *absolute contingency*. As empirically given, existence is merely a fact—but it is indeed indisputably a fact. On empirical grounds we are entitled to assert that being is, even if it only *happens* to be. It would be misleading simply to assert that it *need not* be—though evidently it is the fact that it is only a fact that permits us to say that it need not be. But every assertion that it *need not* be must be complemented with the assertion that *nevertheless* it is. Of course, "whatever *is* may *not be.*" Perhaps it might never have come into being—but now it *has* come into being. It already is, and nothing can be done to alter this. And it may cease to be. But if it were annihilated, its disappearance would not in the slightest diminish (on the contrary, it would confirm) the fact that once it *had* been.

Hence, the point of affirming the contingency of being is quite the opposite of what metaphysicians have thought, and in this respect atheistic thought must be credited with a true, deep and valuable insight: if existence is a mere fact, there is no need for a sufficient antecedent reason to account for anything that exists. Indeed, there cannot be such a reason. For to argue that there must be a sufficient reason for that which is merely an actual fact, is to suppose that what is actual is more than a fact, that it contains "some necessity." But to suppose this is to go beyond what the facts of experience reveal to us about being. Thus, if we restrict ourselves to the facts, we must forestall every overt or surreptitious introduction of necessity into the contingency of being.

430

We may not suppose, for instance, that being is contingent only insofar as it is created. For the facts simply tell us that being is contingent—not that there is an exception to this rule, and that, therefore, being may be either contingent or necessary. If we remain consistently empirical, by "being" we can only mean the sort of reality which is revealed in experience—and this reality is as such factual. Therefore, it is not enough to say that *some* being is contingent; we must say that being *as such* is absolutely contingent, and that the expression "necessary being" is a contradiction in terms. Whatever exists, exists contingently—that is, it is a matter of fact.

I stress that this is to be asserted as a matter of fact. The principle that "whatever exists, exists contingently" is not an *a priori* proposition. It does not mean that its universal application results from the prior necessity of the rule. Absolute contingency is universally predicable of being simply because it pertains to being as such—any qualification added to this would reintroduce an *a priori* assumption into our reasoning. For instance, if we were to say something like "the being of which we have common or direct experience *does* exist contingently, but the question must be left open whether another order of being escapes this contingency," then the doctrine of the degrees of being would have been reintroduced into our thinking under the disguise of the distinction between actual and possible being. What is a fact may be asserted universally without the implication that it is more than a matter of fact.[54]

Likewise, the factuality of being may be asserted universally without the implication that some antecedent necessity, (for in-

[54] Thus, the critique of metaphysics is also the critique of the methodological principle *ab esse ad posse valet consequentia.*

stance, some metaphysical law of knowledge), requires its assertion. The ambivalence of the factual applies to the fact of consciousness. Man is bound to assert what the facts indicate: to say that the facts are indisputable is to say that we may not dispute them. But it is also true that what is true is not necessarily asserted. The obligation to assert what is true does not come from an antecedent necessity: it is created by the fact that we happened to discover the truth—and this happening is an event, a contingent fact. In sum, conscious existence is no exception to the factuality of being. It tells us nothing new about being. It tells us, however, something very puzzling about man himself: it creates a problem which religious reflection, whether primitive or civilized, whether commonsensical or philosophical, whether superstitious or rational, tries to solve.

Man's understanding of being as absolutely contingent creates a problem for consciousness. For man spontaneously understands his own consciousness as the presence of being to itself: man's concept of being is relative to the being which he understands himself to be. Therefore, to be conscious is more or less clearly to understand oneself as absolutely contingent in one's very human existence—and to become increasingly conscious of this is to become increasingly problematic to oneself. But this involves man in a paradox. It is nothing less human than consciousness that makes either cowards or heroes of us all. It is nothing less present than the self-presence of consciousness that makes man aware of his imperfect past and his indefinite future. It is nothing less real than conscious existence that makes man problematic unto himself. Let us now consider the nature of this paradox, and how classical theism and modern atheism have respectively dealt with it.

Man becomes self-problematic because he finds it difficult to reconcile his self-consciousness as being with his being an absolutely contingent fact. Why is this difficult? Evidently, because he can conceive a condition other than absolute contingency which would appear more suitable for him as a self-conscious being. This alternative is suggested to him by his consciousness of being as such. For man is aware that, for all the factuality of being and its total lack of meaning in itself, being can be seen by man in a meaningful light insofar as it is interpreted and understood by man. In fact, it *has* to be seen so: man seems unable to stop himself from making sense out of things. This is, to be sure, a strictly relative meaning: it does not imply that being in itself is essentially affected by man's consciousness of it. We have seen above that knowledge is not the conveyance of an intelligible burden from reality to the mind, and that truth emerges in the attempt of consciousness to relate itself to the world of reality in which it comes into being, exists and makes itself. The reality of being is not meaningful in itself, but man can, as it were, lead a meaningful life with being. Like marriage, it is a question of adjusting to reality, of getting along with it. (After all, being conscious cannot be anything much different from what happens in ordinary human life.) Human consciousness is in a very real sense man's marriage to reality: man can, he must, make sense of reality in relation to himself. But this is enough to suggest to him that his own absolute contingency—and, therefore, his own lack of meaning in himself—might be, as it were, made up for, or improved upon.

For consciousness of being does amount to a sort of improvement upon being. Let us recall the text from St. Thomas I have already quoted above:

The perfection of each individual thing considered in itself is imperfect . . . In order that there might be some remedy for this imperfection, another kind of perfection is to be found in created things. It consists in this, that the perfection belonging to one thing is found in another. This is the perfection of a knower insofar as he knows; for something is known by a knower by reason of the fact that the thing known is, in some fashion, in the possession of the knower . . . In this way it is possible for the perfection of the entire universe to exist in one thing.[55]

The implication that the "remedy" for the imperfection of being is a sojourn in the higher regions of mental existence is, of course, to be rejected, for reasons already dealt with. St. Thomas' observation is correct, however, insofar as consciousness brings light *to* being and bestows itself upon that which is other than itself. Consciousness is self-gift. Though being may lack meaning in itself, man can make it meaningful. Should not man, who is not simply being, but being present to itself, enjoy at least a comparable advantage? It seems that a being cannot very well become aware of its being, as man does, without envisaging the possibility that, despite his absolute contingency, his existence might escape meaninglessness.

The trouble is that the very possibility envisaged as a result of self-consciousness appears to be taken away by the consciousness of oneself as being. The fact that consciousness interprets being and makes it meaningful does not make consciousness to be more than an absolutely contingent fact. The self-problematization of man is indeed paradoxical: the very awareness by which man makes being meaningful, which awakens in him the aspiration to meaningful existence, also makes him aware that he is being—and that, therefore, he lacks meaningful existence in

[55] *De Veritate*, II, 2.

himself. Man makes being meaningful, and yet he has no meaning in himself. He seems unable to do for himself as such what he can do for being as such, despite the fact that he is nothing but being aware of itself.

In recent times various forms of atheistic humanism have attempted to solve this very problem, noting that man not only interprets being, but can interpret himself as the interpreter of being. I will consider this again below, but I want to remark at this point that, in my opinion, this does not quite solve the problem. It is true that man can give meaning to himself as he understands himself. But this is not enough to solve the problem of man's self-problematizing consciousness, because this meaning he gives to himself is, by definition, of the same order as that which he gives to other beings: it is the meaning given by the objectification of being.

No doubt, man can understand himself as an object, just as he understands every other being as an object. But this does not give meaning to man as a conscious existent—any more than his objectification of every other being affects that being in any essential way in its actual existence. Man may successfully speculate about himself, philosophically and otherwise—but the success of human speculation is scarcely to be identified with the success of human life. Indeed, human objective self-understanding may even have a dehumanizing effect. The frequent mechanization of human existence in civilized society amply demonstrates that it is possible for man to lose himself in his own objective meaning. Thus, man can disregard the absolute contingency of being in itself and take account, for his own purposes, merely of the meaningfulness of being in relation to man. But in his own case the opposite is true. Man can set aside the relative meaning that he can give to himself when he understands himself (for instance, philosophically or scientifically) as an object among a world of objects, as a being in the world of being. But he cannot very well abstract from his own existence if he wishes to understand himself as he really is. He can hardly disregard, therefore, the absolute contingency of *his* actual existence. It is *that* actual, concrete existence which must be meaningful if man is to be meaningful at all. And it is this sort of meaningfulness that man seems unable to give to himself.

The traditional concept of God as being originates in the supposition that there may well be a supra-human consciousness which might do for man what man can do for another but not for himself. It is not surprising if the more primitive religions pay for this service by saddling themselves with the concept of a God who is exactly as arbitrary, pragmatic and exploitative in relation to man, as man is, and rightly so, in relation to being: as the world of being is man's possession, man seems to be God's. The more advanced religions mollify this to some degree or another. But in every case the operative reasoning is that what one being cannot do, a more perfect could do—and, at the end of this trend of thought, that an infinitely perfect being could do it perfectly. For instance, once a self-subsistent source of meaning is supposed, as is done in the doctrine of St. Thomas, it can give meaning not only to man but to being, and human experience can be understood as merely recovering the meaning put into being by God.[56] In any event, both the physical and the metaphysical solutions to the self-problematization of man involve the *a priori* introduction of something at least partly like man himself, (namely, something of the order of conscious being), to do

[56] *De Veritate,* I, 2.

what man could envisage his own consciousness as doing, if only he were not hampered by limiting circumstances beyond his control.

Perhaps the principal contribution of Kant to religious speculation was to show that this sort of procedure involves an uncritical use of human reason. But the inestimable contribution of atheism has been to show that it also involves a self-negating contradiction, a self-alienation, of human consciousness. Atheism has challenged philosophical thought to take seriously the absolute contingency of man, and to follow it through to its ultimate consequences. For it has taught us that the height of man's contingent actuality, of man's emergence from nothingness, is not to be measured, as may be that of other beings, by the possibility that he might revert to nothingness: it is to be measured by the possibility that his emergence from nothingness might turn out to be meaningless, by the possibility that man's conscious and creative effort to be might turn out to have been expended in vain.

The truth of this insight must be admitted. We must beware of every *arrière pensée,* every suspicion that the humble recognition of our contingency could be used as the means to avoid facing our self-problematization as we become conscious of our contingency. Throwing ourselves on the mercy of God, as it were, is not likely to change the nature of existence. On the other hand, I am not so certain that atheism does not assume, however subtly, another form of the same gnostic idea I have just described.

It is tempting to solve the problem by declaring man absurd, to account for his inability to find meaning in the factuality of conscious existence by conceiving human consciousness as absurdity become conscious of itself. According to this view, man's self-interpretation as the interpreter of being would seem to yield meaning, if only he recognizes that being is absurd. Yet, this involves what Schubert Ogden has called a "strange witness." [57] The idea that conscious existence is definitively and absolutely absurd is itself an interpretation of man which would define his essential meaning. "If all our actions are in principle absurd," Ogden has argued against Camus, "the act of heroically resisting this absurdity must also be absurd." [58] I would prefer, however, to put it more broadly: if being human is absurd, man's self-definition as absurd must also be absurd. Ultimate meaning cannot be found in ultimate absurdity, as if absurdity accepted ceased to be absurd. In the last analysis, existence stands as a more indisputable and stubborn fact than any conscious attempt to explain it away. Even interpreters of being are what they are only because they exist.

The common inadequacy of atheism and classical theism as solutions to the self-problematic character of man stems from the idea that if there is a meaning to existence, it must be found within being, within existence itself. The history of philosophy shows how man has run down, one by one, the various ways in which this meaning could be found in being, until only the final, atheistic alternative remained: that it could not be found because it did not exist. But even this still assumes that *if* there were a meaning of existence it would be found in being. However, if this assumption is recognized and avoided, then the history of philosophy holds a different lesson: the meaning of existence cannot indeed be found in being, because it does not exist in being. It may, however, be found elsewhere.

[57] Schubert Ogden, *The Reality of God,* (New York, 1966), pp. 120 ff.
[58] *Ibid.,* p. 41.

That it is, in fact, found elsewhere is borne out by experience. The self-problematization of man does not imply only man's awareness of the absolute contingency of being. It also implies his awareness that reality transcends being.

The consciousness of being, though revealing only being as the object of experience, places man in a position to question the ultimacy and exclusiveness of being. Consciousness of being as such bestows upon man the capacity to deny and reject being, even while he knows that he himself is involved in this rejection. For instance, consciousness creates in man the possibility of choosing not to exist at all rather than to exist in certain ways. It makes little difference whether we consider a hero's choice to die for a morally worthwhile reason, or a fool's choice to give up his life for a pittance or a whim. In every case, the implication is that existence can be judged by man—indeed, it cannot but be judged by man—once he becomes conscious of it. To the degree that a being becomes conscious of its being, its existence loses its automatic character and demands instead a conscious *effort,* as it were—and the rejection of existence witnesses to this no less forcefully than does the affirmative choice. Even the choice to drift with existence, or to avoid the encounter with life, implies the self-same requirement of consciousness as it brings man face to face with himself. In the moral order this is reflected in the fact that no one can abdicate his conscience in favour of someone else's judgment unless he *judge* that someone else's judgment is for some reason to be preferred over his own. All this implies that existence has been put by man into a certain perspective. Its awesome character has been put, as it were, in its proper place. Existence is tamed by thought; it is domesticated by the consideration that, when all is said and done, existence is simply a matter of fact. Thus, if we should ask, with Leibniz, "why is

439

there something rather than nothing?"[59] we are bound to reply: "only because a sufficient reason of being exists." But if we ask, "why should not there be nothing rather than being?" the only reply permitted by empirical reason is: "Why not, indeed? Is being as such not absolutely contingent? If it is, there is no reason why there should not be nothing rather than anything."

But to give this reply is to transcend the assumption that being exhausts reality, that existence marks the totality beyond which only nothing is found. Is not the point, if we reflect upon it, fairly evident: that the absoluteness of the contingency of being reveals, (at least by indirection), that being is not, as it were, the most important, the most significant, the noblest thing in the world? There are "things" higher than being. What does it profit a man to gain the world (of being)? For all its value and dignity, all being and all existence, including human existence itself, can be counted for nothing and given up—without regret. As the Gospel tradition reminds us, man should not so love existence, even his own, that he would not stand ready, I do not say to accept, but even to seek and to embrace death. If we understand this, and are able thus to subtract ourselves from any bondage or debt in which we might be held by being on account of our having been born into being, and if we can, thus, thereafter exist freely, as the result of conscious choice, the reason is that we can understand ourselves in the light of that which transcends being in every way.

I have said that the contingency of being reveals this at least by indirection, because our awareness of the contingency of being

[59] G. W. F. Leibniz, *The Principles of Nature and Grace, Based on Reason,* VII, in Philip P. Wiener, (ed) *Leibniz Selections,* (New York, 1951), p. 527.

does not alter the fact that it is being, not that which transcends being, which is the *object* of human thought. If we can so easily misconceive what our religious experience reveals, the reason is that being is and remains always the *object* of conscious experience. That which transcends being is revealed only *in* being, and *within* the experience of being, in the sense that our experience of being, and only our experience of being, reveals in us the capacity to judge being (whether rightly or not) and to dispose of it (whether for good or for ill). Though conscious being is conscious of being, and though it is conscious of no object but being, in the consciousness of its object, namely, being, it can become conscious of that which is not an object, namely, that which transcends being. It is in this sense that man's consciousness of being is not bound by being: consciousness is not enclosed by that which it itself is, or by that object which it is conscious of. Consciousness transcends not only itself: it transcends itself precisely as being; it transcends being as such. Thus, since being remains the object of consciousness even after the the disclosure of the reality which transcends it, every conceptualization of that which transcends being is necessarily relative to being: the very concepts I have used constantly here, "the reality of non-being," "a reality other than being," and "a reality which transcends being," are the most obvious instances of this.

Nevertheless, our experience of being reveals that which transcends being, though it reveals it in relation to being. This is why the disclosure of that which transcends being is at the same time also the disclosure of man's deepest reality to himself. In this sense, awareness of the reality which transcends being may be said to be that which reveals to man the meaning of existence. But this formula is somewhat equivocal: what religious experience really reveals is that the meaning of existence is not to be found within existence itself, but beyond. And when human experience reveals this, human experience has become *religious* belief. Moreover, it is the experience of *belief:* since being remains the object of experience, this revelation has the peculiar quality of faith. The affirmation of the meaningfulness of existence requires belief because it is the affirmation that existence is meaningful only in relation to that which transcends existence —and the affirmation of that which transcends existence requires belief, because it is the affirmation of that in relation to which man understands himself as having a meaningfulness which he does not have in himself.

For these reasons, among the various ways in which we may conceptualize positively that reality which transcends being, "presence" seems to me particularly apt.[60] Presence signifies that

[60] Some of my critics appear to me to have misinterpreted my previous conclusions to this effect. I have not suggested that whereas the existence of a transcendent being is not demonstrable, the existence of a transcendent presence may be. Since in the context of my views transcendent presence means a reality other than being which is nonetheless related to human experience in man's consciousness of empirically given being, the attempt to demonstrate the *existence* of such a presence would be self-contradictory. What I have proposed is that belief in God is reasonable and well-grounded in experience if it means not belief in a reality which *exists* in the presence of man yet cannot be experienced, but in a reality which is present to man in his experience of existing being. I have suggested, therefore, that God is better conceived as a reality which is *present to* being than as a reality which *is* being, that God's reality should be conceived in terms of *real presence* rather than in terms of *real being*. (The theology of the Eucharist is but one area of theological research where this philosophical approach may prove useful.)

The objection of Michael Novak, (see "Belief and Mr. Dewart," *Commonweal*, LXXV, 17 [February 3, 1967], 485–488), that this would make God indistinguishable from a yellow elephant which for all its unreality is present to a deranged mind, does not seem to me well taken. It is true, of course, that the yellow elephants of hallucinations and delusions are not real

which in its very otherness is related to one. We say, for instance, that someone is of good presence if his bearing seems striking to us. A foreign power is present in the former colony if, despite the latter's newly acquired independence, it still helps fashion its culture and policies. And another human being is genuinely present to us, and not merely as a matter of geographical location, if he makes us come alive, if he brings out our best—or, for that matter, our worst—self, if he contributes significantly, for good or for ill, to the emergence of our selves.[61] But, as we have just seen, is this not what God does for man, namely, to reveal him to himself in a dimension which would otherwise remain altogether closed to him? But I seem to have put it backwards. I should rather say: it appears from the foregoing reflections that being reveals itself most meaningfully to itself, and consciousness becomes most fully itself, when the presence of being to itself takes place in the presence of an order of reality which transcends being itself.

Religious experience, then, does not reveal a transcendent being: what it reveals is that being exists in the presence of a reality which transcends it. To conceptualize in the contradictory terms of "transcendent being" the belief made possible by the awareness of absolute contingency may well have been unavoidable at

---

and yet are present to human consciousness. But surely this does not take away the possibility that there may be a transcendent reality other than being which would be present to man: it does not imply that God has as little reality as a delusory yellow elephant. What it *does* imply is that in one *negative* respect God is very much like a delusory yellow elephant: neither is an *objective* reality, that is, neither is a real *being*. This scarcely means that God is unreal: it does mean, however, that his reality may be neither the objective reality of real being, nor the subjective reality of immanent consciousness. Cf. below, pp. 466–471.

[61] Cf. Gabriel Marcel, *The Mystery of Being*, (London, 1950), vol. I, p. 205.

a certain level of the evolution of human consciousness. But to conceive it in terms of "transcendent presence to being" may be more adequate today.

It is little to be doubted that we do experience being as the reality of the world and of ourselves. But to go beyond this empirical fact and invest being with a transcendental character is gratuitously and *a priori* to impose upon any possible transcendental reality a preconception which may be harmless only as long as it is not pursued to its bitter end. For atheism, which is in part a protest against the prejudicial con-fusion of being and reality, is also in part a consequence of it. As we invest being as such with a transcendental character we close ourselves off to the possibility of experiencing any reality other than that of the world and of ourselves. Metaphysics has had, in effect, the un-bargained-for result of placing God beyond all possible experience. But, like the luminiferous aether, a metaphysical God ultimately became superfluous and had to be either discarded or else irrationally believed in. In this as in other respects, the traces of the great contributions of Greek, mediaeval and modern philosophy to human thought can be found within the most progressive, but also within the most anti-Christian, aspects of contemporary thought.

EXPERIENCE AND MEANING
IN RELIGIOUS BELIEF

It should be clear from the foregoing why God—if we continue to use this name for transcendent reality—is, in traditional terminology, both transcendent and immanent. He is immanent in being. He is present to man as that which manifests itself in and through being. It is not by chance that no one has ever seen God in himself: for God is not visible (or intelligible, or relatable to) in himself. Consciousness can relate itself to God, can see God and can understand God, only in and through being. This does not mean that man's relation to God only in and through being *could* take place in a different manner, but *happens* to occur in this particular way because God arbitrarily has chosen to manifest himself in this roundabout way. It means, rather, that God is accessible in this manner only because the nature of the reality of God so requires. God's "mysteriousness" is not an accident; it is intrinsic to the essence of God. This mysteriousness is not the concomitant of his distance from man, or of his immensity, or of his transcendence. On the contrary, it is the concomitant of his immanence. What makes God invisible, unintelligible and mysterious is the fact that he is a reality encountered *in being* which is *other than* being itself. Being can, as it were, tell man about more than being itself. But this reality can be heard only when it speaks with the voice of being: it cannot be told about except as that which is found in being, within the reality of being itself.

But what I have just described as the immanence of God could also be put in terms of transcendence. That which is in being cannot be being: it is other than being. That whose mysteriousness and hiddenness is hidden in being and can be manifested only through being, must evidently transcend being. Only that which is not-being can be in being. The creative wisdom of Greek and Christian metaphysics is nowhere more evident than in its ability to have dimly discerned that being can be understood, (I mean, can be the object of man's self-relation), only in relation to something other than itself. The historically understandable, but decisive misapprehension of Greek metaphysics was to imagine that this other was actually being itself, so that being (τὸ ὄν) should be explained by the beingness (οὐσία) of being itself. The counterpart in Christian metaphysics was to imagine that the other was indeed being itself, but that being (*ens*) should be explained by the to-be (*esse*) of Being Itself. The simpler truth is that neither the beingness of being nor the to-be of being are a reality other than being itself. The reality of being, (whether its *essentia* or its *esse* or its *entitas*), cannot be really other than real being itself. Thus, the reality in relation to which being is being, and in relation to which it is real, and in relation to which it is intelligible, and in relation to which it is actual, is a reality which transcends being itself.

It should be similarly clear from the preceding section that the self-givenness of transcendent reality does not break down the processes of "nature," (i.e., the complex of mutual relations within the world of being), any more than it disrupts the free self-creativity of man. For God does not enter into the world of being as would a transcendent being, namely, from some incomprehensible, self-contradictory, eternal region outside the world. God is *in* the world of being, outside which there is only nothing, only un-reality, only un-being. But the being of the world is not necessitated by God's relation to it precisely because the being of the world is not enclosed or hemmed in by a Being which transcends it. The being of creation is free in its very being —and this is why the self-givenness of God towards it, in its evolution and history, is not an interference, or even an intervention in the affairs of the world. It is a participation in them, a participation which does not govern, but inspires, which does not press but attracts, which does not propel but fuel, which does not guide but lets be. So much the more so when it is the case of being present to itself, in whom indetermination is not simply spatial, dynamic and kinematic, as it were, but temporal, actual and historical. The self-givenness of transcendent reality does not pre-destine man, who does not have a destiny in the first place, since he creates himself. But the free self-creation of man can embody either the acceptance or the rejection of God's offer of himself. In fact, without either such acceptance or rejection there can be no self-giving of the transcendental reality at all. The self-gift of God is given only in and through the acceptance or rejection of it. Without human freedom it would be idle and self-contradictory to speak of God's grace.

These conclusions, I have said, follow fairly evidently from the foregoing remarks. What may not be sufficiently clear is a question already broached but not previously dealt with in sufficient detail. Let us grant that the analysis of experience reveals how consciousness of the factuality of being witnesses, manifests, through the absolute contingency of being—through the fact that there might be nothing in reality at all—a reality beyond being in relation to which existing being can be, I do not simply say found, but made meaningful and truthful by man.

I trust I have sufficiently clearly excluded the possibility of both fideistic and rationalistic misinterpretations of my remarks. I do not mean that unless we posit such a transcendent reality we cannot find meaning in human existence and that, therefore, *si* vis *rationem, para fidem.* Nor do I mean that the reality of a transcendent reality can be deduced from the absolute contingency of being, and that, therefore, *si vis* rationem, *para fidem:* what major premise could possibly connect both God and creature unless it uncritically imagined that the viewpoint of man can be external to the relationship of God and creature? No, if we are led to *belief* in a transcendent reality despite the fact that all empirically given reality is being, (and definitely nothing but being), the reason is that human reality, I do not say will not, but *cannot* be meaningless, despite the fact that it is meaningless in itself—because meaning is for it not an available product, a ready-made merchandise, but an objective to be realized and a reality to be found. Despite the absence of meaning in the being of his mind, and despite the absence of meaning within himself as an in-itself, man cannot not be meaningful in himself, because he cannot remain meaningless to himself. To be either meaningful or meaningless man must search for meaning: to be conscious of himself is for man to understand himself as oriented towards meaning and as made meaningful by this very orientation towards that which he lacks insofar as he does not *already* have it, but which he has insofar as he already *searches* for it.

Ubi ratio, ibi fides. Man *eventually* believes, because he *already* understands. Well, then, the problem that emerges from this is: since the analysis of experience reveals a reality that transcends being, and since the object of experience is being, does not the analysis of experience reveal a transempirical reality—a reality which would be, therefore, metaphysical? Have we in a roundabout or surreptitious way returned to metaphysics and to the degrees of being (or of reality)? How can any consciousness of reality other than being be said to be empirical, if only being is empirically given? What is the order of experience from which *faith* follows—and does it not leave experience behind when it *follows* experience? In short, what is to believe, and in what sense, if any, can belief be empirical?

Bare allusion will now suffice, I trust, to recall to mind the concept of knowledge traditionally assumed by Christian thought.

Man is related to reality, first, cognitively, by intentionally transposing it to himself and, second, affectively, by intentionally transposing himself onto it. Cognition is becoming the other as other, and truth is the adequation of the knowing mind to the essential-existential reality which is its object. Well, if one assumes this, one cannot very well avoid conceptualizing religious belief in the traditional terms of Catholic theology. For it is a perfectly obvious matter of experience that the object of Christian belief does not lend itself to immediate intussusception in the same way that the object of ordinary cognitive operations does. God may be being, but he does not appear as empirically given being does: "neither faith nor opinion can be of things seen either by the senses or by the intellect." [62] Faith must be, therefore, understood in opposition to empirical knowledge; indeed, strictly speaking, belief cannot be called a form of understanding, although it has "something in common with science and understanding," [63] namely, certitude. Faith is not *thinking* in the full sense of the term, but may be so called insofar as thinking may denote that incomplete intellectual activity "which precedes the intellect's arrival at the stage of [proper] perfection that comes with the certitude of sight." [64] In this tradition, then, faith is but a substitute for knowledge, made available to us in the absence of the possibility of real knowledge. It "must needs reside in the intellect," [65] but it is not knowledge, since it is that act which the intellect performs in the absence of the evident reality which it affirms.[66]

How can the intellect assent to any truth it does not see? The

[62] St. Thomas, *ST,* II–II, 1, 4.
[63] *ST,* II–II, 2, 1.
[64] *Ibid.*
[65] *ST,* II–II, 4, 2.
[66] *ST,* II–II, 4, 1.

answer is that although the intellect cannot determine itself in the absence of evidence, "the intellect of the believer is determined to one object [rather than to another] . . . by the will, wherefore [the] assent [of faith] . . . is an act of the intellect as determined to one object by the will." [67] But if the intellect gives its assent under the constraint of the will despite a lack of evidence for the truth to which assent is given, does it not follow that the act of faith is irrational and arbitrary? Not really, according to this view. Faith is not arbitrary, for the will is itself moved by grace: "faith, as regards the assent which is the chief act of faith, is from God moving man inwardly by grace." [68] Nor is it irrational, since the truths proposed for our assent rest upon the infallible authority of God, who is neither deceptive nor deceived: "nothing can come under faith, save in so far as it stands under the First Truth, under which nothing false can stand." [69]

I should incidentally note that although this reply usually satisfies most doubts on the subject, if one should go further and ask what assurance can be had that the truth of certain propositions has been guaranteed by God, the answer takes one far into the field of the reliability of tradition and, ultimately, into the remote, dark, apologetic area of the testimony and credibility of Jesus, the Apostles, the Evangelists and the hierarchical church. I am not suggesting that the credibility of Jesus is irrelevant to belief in the witness and person of the Christ: it would be fatuous to imagine that Christian belief has little to do with what one thinks of him. The point is that if we agree to follow this path,

[67] *ST*, II–II, 2, 2.
[68] *ST*, II–II, 6, 1.
[69] *ST*, II–II, 1, 3.

the original question concerning the nature of faith is naturally dissolved into the quite different question concerning the validity of Christian doctrine. In this confusion may lie the origin of the curious assumption, so frequently made by Christian thinkers, that the traditional concept of faith should be above criticism, since it appears to them that to question the validity of the long-held Christian concept of faith is to question the validity of the Christian truth.

The disadvantages and problems, both theoretical and practical, of the traditional Catholic understanding of the nature of faith are many and well known. The history of Christianity since the end of the middle ages itemizes their compendious catalogue. But most of these difficulties can be summed up in few words: the widening chasm between belief and knowledge, the self-compounding alienation between reason and religion, the accelerating divergence between Church and world. For the traditional idea of faith tends of its very nature to separate faith from human experience. It did so in principle when it made faith an imperfect act of knowledge: the normal development of human consciousness took care of the rest, since of its very nature it was impelled ever to transcend itself in its quest for truth. Christianity's insistence upon belief thus understood was not self-contradictory as long as human intellectual progress was, though real, not yet conscious of itself. But as consciousness gradually discovered its self-perfecting nature, faith, as traditionally understood, became unviable on its own terms. Christianity's retention of the traditional forms of its faith, even unto the traditional concept of supernatural faith, became thus by its own inner logic, despite continued lip service to the faith in reason which it took to be a "natural revelation" to the Greeks, a bar to reason and intellectual progress. Christian belief ceased to lead the intellectual development of Western Christian man; and the intellectual development of Western Christian man frequently led him away from Christian belief.

The isolation of the Church follows a similar pattern. The authority of a revealing God cannot be authoritative except to him who already believes. Anyone who claims that what he proposes ought to be believed not, to be sure, because of his personal authority, but because his teaching authority derives from God is asking in effect that *his* word be taken for the truth of the claim that what he proposes is the truth proposed by God. Many people in Christendom who are ready to believe in God and who would have no difficulty believing in God, find it impossible to do so if *first* they must believe in spokesmen for God.

I should explain that in my opinion this popular reasoning, which is not altogether mistaken, is not altogether sound either. Belief must necessarily have a social and historical dimension, and man's religious development cannot take place in splendid isolation. We cannot reasonably expect private revelations for each or for any individual, any more than we can reasonably expect that scientific, philosophical or other truth will disclose itself to each man privately and individually. Philosophy and science can be practiced and cultivated and advanced only when there is a philosophical and scientific community in which the philosophical and scientific tradition is vested, a philosophical and scientific community to which the individual's contribution can be made. In a very real sense, likewise, Christian belief must be belief *in the Church,* and no apology need be made for the fact. For Christians the *Church* has always been as much an object of belief as God himself; (I say the Church, not the papacy or the hierarchy or any other part of the Church).

On the other hand, the identification of the authority of the Church with the authority of the magisterium becomes scandalous once human consciousness reaches a certain level of development. The nature of the authority of the teaching office of the Church cannot be adequately understood in the simplistic terms of the past: that there is a divine guarantee for the truth of what the magisterium thinks, regardless of what the Church as a whole may think. For man no longer learns, in any sphere whatever, by being told authoritatively what the truth is. This is not to his shame, but to his credit. To persist, I do not say in leading believers, cooperatively and in dialogue, in the development of belief, but in telling them authoritatively what to believe, has become countervailing. The present level of human evolution continues to require that man's belief in God takes place in and through belief in and with the Church. But the claim of either the magisterium, or even the Church as a whole, to speak "authoritatively" in the traditional meaning of this term (I do not mean warrantedly, but with a commanding claim to obedience and "religious assent"), is no longer valid. The Church itself has changed,[70] and this is no longer the way in which it can generate and nurture Christian belief: the Church is no longer the believer's Mother image but the believer's Fatherland.

[70] The magisterium itself has contributed to this change. The *effective* (as contrasted with the *intended*) teaching of papal documents for some time in the recent past, beginning with John XXIII, (who was aware of it, but did not seem to mind) and continuing with Paul VI (who does not seem fully aware of it, but who probably does mind), has been that the magisterium is *not* authoritative in the sense that it discloses and declares with unique reliability a truth which by its very promulgation has a claim to the believer's assent. I have no doubt that *Humanae Vitae,* for example, was a courageous, sincere and conscientious act of Paul VI. But its effective teaching, which was scarcely on the subject of contraception, but on the nature and limitations of the magisterium, has so far been not quite the same as that which he presumably intended to communicate.

The extremes to which the separation of faith and experience has been allowed to go in Christianity is in no way more evident than in the very expressions to which I have had to resort in order to describe its inadequacies. There is in none of the languages of the Western Christian world any ready-made expression to designate the experiential character of faith. Thus, I have spoken of the separation of faith *and* experience, two distinct things which presumably should not be far apart but which are nonetheless quite different things. What I really mean, however, is that the traditional Catholic concept of faith tends of its very nature to separate ordinary experience from religious experience or faith.

Consider, likewise, another implication of the traditional notion of faith. If faith is assent to a truth revealed by God, an assent given on the basis of God's authority rather than on the basis of our vision of the truth, then the formulation of the truths of human faith lies outside the realm of human experience. Thus, the truth of faith is a divine truth, for it is the truth of divine concepts, and the truth of faith is identical with the truth of divine revelation. Religious truth is not a human truth about God, but is the truth of God himself transplanted into a human mind which can but mindlessly hold it, nodding to itself that, whatever it may mean, the truth it holds within itself is divinely guaranteed. But surely this is not true. And surely this can only destroy in the end the faith which is part of human experience.

It is, to be sure, an intrinsic part of the Christian tradition that faith is a gratuitous gift from God. But this does not mean that whereas it is the role of God to propose truths to man, the role of the human intellect is that of assenting—or failing to assent

—to the propositions formulated by God about himself, propositions which he thereafter communicates to us, suitably translated into a human language. This would be an oversimple view of revelation. To put the objection in a correspondingly oversimple manner: it is difficult to suppose that God's mother-tongues are Hebrew and Greek. But it would be more difficult yet, since God's native speech cannot be that of any human tongue, to suppose that he has devised his own celestial language in which he thinks and speaks to himself.

The empirical fact is that every truth that man can possibly assent to, has, by definition, a human experiential content and a human cultural form. No concept of the nature of faith which is reasonably to be proposed today can abstract from all consciousness of this fact. To understand what faith is, is to understand how it functions in human experience. Conversely, we can remedy this undesirable situation by seeking—as we have to put it —the "integration of faith and experience." Yet, this expression is doubly misleading. There can be no question of rendering two things into one; first, because unless we suppose the traditional interpretation of knowledge, belief and experience are not dichotomous modes of thought; nor, scholastics to the contrary, do faith and experience each have "its own domain." [71] But also, second, the expression is misleading because the integration of faith and experience does not mean their congealment into an undifferentiated whole. How could experience ever be anything other than experience, or faith anything other than faith?

The answer is that although faith is of the order of experience, (since it is a mode of consciousness, a mode of self-relation to reality), faith is not an experience alongside every other experi-

[71] Maritain, *Le Paysan de la Garonne*, p. 209.

ence. The experience we call belief stands out from every other experience because it is the experience that makes meaningful every other experience. Indeed, faith is nothing but that meaningfulness itself. Therefore, to integrate faith and experience is nothing else than to experience meaningfully and, therefore, truthfully. That is, to believe is to derive meaning from experience, and, therefore, also truth; to believe is to derive understanding and wisdom from the mere knowledge of the reality of the world of facts: "the fundamental problem to be solved . . . is that of making sense of our experience in the new setting [of contemporary human existence, a setting definable by] the unique historical possibility of a totally humanised and controlled world." [72] Thus, to make sense out of everyday experience is the Christian vocation "which the very humanization we have brought about demands of us. If the world is to be one of increasingly human control, the problem is that of finding an intellectual basis upon which to understand the meanings which the world offers us. This is the first priority—not the imposition of Christianity . . . but the discovery of a new kind of intelligibility." [73]

These formulae could all too easily be given a "naturalistic" and "secularistic" sense, in the traditional Catholic acception of these terms. Yet, this view need not imply that faith (that is, religious experience) is reducible to non-religious, secular or "natural" experience. Quite the contrary, the point is that *ordinary* human experience is insufficient unless it extend itself into a new, extraordinary dimension. When it so extends itself, experience

[72] Brian Wicker, *Toward a Contemporary Christianity*, (Notre Dame, 1967), pp. 261, 260.
[73] Ibid., pp. 261–262.

becomes *religious* experience or faith. Thus, the apparent opposition between belief and experience means this: precisely because experience is immanent in the being of man, experience has a transcendent dimension, namely, faith. But faith transcends experience only because faith is the transcendence *of experience.* Faith does not transcend experience by ceasing to be experience. Faith is, as it were, the real, ultimate meaning of that which *already* exists, namely, human experience.

But in this context *ultimacy* should not carry the Hellenic connotation of *finality.* It conveys only that experience as such already exists, but that unless we were to understand it "speculatively," (as in the tradition that began with the pre-Socratics and extended to Hegel), we must understand it as participation in reality and not as a reduplication of it. But if experience is participation in being and, therefore, man's self-constitution as being, it follows that the experience which *already* exists clamours for a meaningfulness which it can find only *beyond itself*—that is, a meaningfulness which it can find, not beyond experience *tout court,* but only beyond experience insofar as experience *already* is.

If this is not readily evident, and if its importance for an understanding of the nature of the experience of religious belief has not been widely recognized, the reason may have to do with our deeply-seated disposition, of obvious Hellenic provenance, to analyze human experience into the two irreducibly distinct modes of affectivity and cognition, corresponding to two distinct orders of "faculties" directed to essentially diverse "objects" of intention, the good and the true. But these distinctions are not only unnecessary: they cannot be validated through an *empirical* analysis of experience itself. What does emerge from such an analysis, as we have seen, is that experience is not exhausted by what it is *at present,* by what it already is. Once it is, experience must *project* itself and envisage what it *not yet* is. I mean: though experience always is *now,* insofar as it is conscious and grasps its own *presence* it can look to its present as revealing what it *has been* (for to be *now* is to be *already,* and to be *already* is to *have been*). But by the same token, it can look to its present as revealing what it may *yet become* (for to be *now* is, of course, *not-yet*-to-be that which it *may yet become*).

Man is not a thinking *and* willing substance. The "projectivity" of consciousness is not to be understood in terms of the exclusively moral, affective existence of man: it is a dimension of every *present* experience, it is a constitutive part of *every* mode in which man is. (Conversely, it is not to be understood, as Sartre would have it, as a paradoxical attribute of human freedom—as if the openness of a *totally* indeterminate future which we must indeed *create* were a condemnation willy-nilly to choose freedom without becoming free—for if contemporary philosophical thought were to readmit the Greek postulate of the reality of Fate, a reality whose dreadfulness consisted in lying ahead, in the future, inexorably waiting to ensnare approaching man, contemporary philosophy might as well do so openly and revert to Scholasticism.) No, man's conscious experience is always present—but it can be present only because it projects itself into the future out of the past. Man is, therefore, the being who comes into being, the being who emerges as such through self-differentiation. He is, therefore, being conscious of itself, being present to itself. Well, faith is precisely the transcendent, projective dimension of the presence of human consciousness to itself.

This is why, as Schillebeeckx has put it in the text already quoted: "to stand before oneself is to stand before God." Evidently, this proposition could be thoroughly misunderstood. It could be taken in a Feuerbachian sense. I imagine Schillebeeckx intends it rather in the sense I have explained above: to be conscious, to stand before oneself, is to exist in a human situation in which experience must orient itself towards that which experience does not reveal as its object. But, of course, insofar as experience does reveal, by its essential constitution and its existential situation, its need to transcend being, it also reveals, in this oblique, roundabout way, that which is other than being. The obliqueness or indirectness of this experience, the relativity to being of that which is other than being, is what gives this experience its peculiar character of *belief*.

Could it be supposed, therefore, that the supernatural condition of the Christian faith implies that any lack of integration between the Christian faith and contemporary experience is to be remedied by an adjustment of experience *to faith,* not vice versa? It would be very easy for the believer to allow himself to be wafted away by piety beyond the earth of truth. If one leaves enough facts out of account, if one omits enough human experience, and if one rejects enough human intellectual progress, then one can solve many a contemporary Christian problem with a formula such as "we must serve God and not man," or "the Christian must not kneel down before the world." But the trouble with appeals to these or like principles is that they ignore the irrelevance (in this context) of complying with anyone's demands for homage, or with anyone's wishes, solicitations or commands. To argue in this matter from divine sovereignty is to forget that the function of the mind is to think: its role is not to please God before pleasing itself (or, for that matter, the other way about). Indeed, given the opportunities enjoyed by the Christian faith today, it is almost physically impossible to maintain that the faithful believer must—I do not say creatively transform his own experience in order to bring about his own self-transformation into that which (by virtue of his faith) he feels obliged to project for the *future,* (for that is precisely what he actually ought to do)—but that he must suppose the reality of *present* experience to be other than it actually is, if this is the only way in which faith can remain what it has been *in the past.* Naturally, if one were determined to retain any given form of religious consciousness come what may, it would make sense to suppose that the validity and adequacy, the truth, of any experience to the contrary, must be *a priori* denied. This, after all, is but the essence of dogmatism.

Does this conception of faith as the transcendent, future-tensional, truth-orientational, projective dimension of experience not make it an essentially "natural" mode of consciousness? If "natural" is contrasted to "super-natural" the answer is clearly and definitely yes. Belief is as "natural" to man as experience itself is: man is by nature a religious animal, and without religious belief of one sort or another, primitive or elaborate, conscious or unconscious, theistic or atheistic, right or wrong, his experience would be less than human. If on the other hand, the question means: does the understanding of belief as a "natural" mode of human consciousness take away the possibility of its being given by grace, then the answer is, decidedly no. The first characteristic of belief revealed by an analysis of the phenomenon of religious belief is that faith does in a very real sense "come from God", at least in the sense that it does not originate within ourselves. To put it more precisely: faith has an essentially transcendent quality, not only in the sense previously noted, but also in the sense that its essential and primary function is to embody man's reaction to a situation which is not of his own doing. Faith originates in man's experience of himself when he suddenly discovers himself to be already existing, and already existing in an on-going world. Everyone grasps more or less clearly that neither his own existence nor that of the world is the result of any initiative of his. Belief is not the outcome of concluding, from this experience, that Someone created man and the world, and that, therefore, one should pay attention to Him. But belief does begin with a commitment to uphold this experience and to live in function of it. It implies, therefore, a commitment to uphold the view that the initiative which brings the world of being into being and into reality lies elsewhere than in being. And least of all in ourselves.

Thus, since we apprehend the existence of being primarily and immediately in ourselves, for we are conscious of existing, we may conclude that it is consciousness, the presence of being to itself, which defines human existence as essentially religious. Faith is not self-understanding—but neither is it God-guessing. Faith is made possible only by self-understanding in the presence of that which transcends oneself—I mean, in the presence of that which transcends oneself not only as does the reality of being, but as does the reality which is other than being. Let us say, then, that faith is the manifestation of self-understanding in the presence of a reality that transcends the transcendence of the consciousness of man.

I need hardly stipulate that man's response to his religious situation is not always and necessarily positive belief. The real possibility of unbelief is implicit in the very situation in which the possibility of belief is also given. Thus, belief is, like unbelief,

461

a fundamental option which embodies and symbolizes the exercise of man's free existence. But man's situation is necessarily religious; that is, it is a situation which requires him to make a free decision of an absolutely fundamental sort in relation to the transcendent. And this religious decision must be *either* belief or unbelief.

From this conception of faith it follows that faith cannot be adequate unless it is "integrated" with everyday experience—I mean, unless it fulfills its essential role of making experience meaningful. If one's belief in God does not enhance the meaningfulness of the world in which one actually and presently exists, one's faith is somehow twisted—and if its vice is not corrected it may eventually become perverse. If to believe one has to pretend that the world does not exist, or that truth has gone out of style, or that the past is yet to come back, or that the future can look after itself, then one can be fairly certain that one's faith is no longer really Christian, and that it may indeed be no faith at all—except, perhaps, faith in oneself or, worse yet, a faith in faith itself.

The believer has to make sense out of common experience, not because he would be warranted to adopt common experience as the standard to which his belief must conform, but because common experience is the foundation of religious belief. Faith exists for the sake of experience, not the other way about. And belief is, for human consciousness, that which makes the difference between experiencing and experiencing meaningfully. Hence, the relations of faith and experience should be ruled in accordance with the idea that faith is but the transcendent dimension of man's experience of reality, rather than the idea that faith is the imperfect knowledge of a transcendental, trans-empirical realm of transcendental being.

If this analysis is correct, it also follows that there is a most intimate connection between truth and belief that the traditional conception of faith fails to understand and exploit. For in that interpretation of faith as the substitute for knowledge in the absence of evidence, belief is a decidedly inferior order of intellectual activity: it is required only because of the alienation of man from God. If, on the contrary, religious belief is the culminating form of human experience, the reason is that faith is the mode of intellectual existence which is made possible to man by the immediate and real presence of God. Faith perfects ordinary experience by transforming it and opening up for it the possibility of an additional dimension. For, as I have suggested, faith lends to human knowledge the dimension of truth. But perhaps this should be put the other way about: the analysis of human experience indicates that the quest for truth is to be undertaken in faith. Man does not believe in order that eventually he may cease to believe and begin to understand. Rather, man's understanding must be oriented towards the truth. Faith provides this orientation; and so, in the light of faith man may progress in his understanding of the truth. For there is no truth which does not solicit from man the self-commitment of faith. The pursuit of truth must be a pursuit in faith. Thus, faith is concerned with the transformation of facts into truth: in this sense, faith is that which renders experience true and fully human. Conversely, experience seeks to perfect itself and to lead towards the truth. But it achieves this only by extending itself into that form of experience which we call religious experience or belief.

In connection with the relation of faith to the truth of consciousness I would append a concluding remark. I have suggested that faith is not an assent to truths proposed by God. This implies that God does not in the first place propose truths to man. Yet, it is part of the Christian tradition that God reveals truths to man. There is, however, a difference between proposing and revealing truths, and it is not necessary to imagine that God's revelation is the divine purveyance of eternal truths translated into the language of men. If truth is not the adequation of mind to being, truth is not revealed by transmitting an intelligible message through propositional communication lines. Truth can be communicated, but only through interaction, that is, through the creation of a common consciousness between God and man. Thus, there is no religious reason to doubt the empirical truth that every religious truth is cast in strictly human concepts, and that it is put in strictly human terms and propositions. Nevertheless, God can be said to reveal truth to man, insofar as his presence to man affects decisively the individual and collective evolutionary history of human consciousness. God communicates with man, and man with God, in the creation of a common consciousness, a common existence, a common life and a common history. But, if so, God cannot be properly speaking said to reveal truths to man: he can only reveal himself. And he reveals himself in and through human concepts whose truth is ever inconclusive, ever growing, ever evolving, since these concepts share in the nature of all human conscious life.

In this light, the question of the inerrancy of Scripture can be briefly dealt with before bringing this discussion to a close. It is understandable if previous Christian ages have thought that Scripture was inerrant, because its truth was revealed by God, who can neither deceive nor be deceived. Now, no one could seriously propose that an omniscient God can make mistakes. And it is true enough that, insofar as it is the product of man's consciousness evolving in the presence of a God who is active in history, Scripture carries the revelation of God. But it may be somewhat inadequate to think of God as someone who makes use of a medium of communication that is in itself subject to truth or falsity, as propositions are, but who is at the same time so proficient at formulating them that he could make no mistakes. Thus, belief in the teaching of Scripture as true, insofar as God reveals himself in that teaching, need not imply the validity of the propositions stated in the Bible on the grounds that God is its "Author"—unless perhaps the divine authorship of Scripture were understood in an impossibly literal way.

Apart from any question raised by the nature of the medium of revelation, it is even more important to note that the truth of God's revelation cannot be understood as the truth of an eternal fact: it is a truth *for us,* and therefore our understanding of it enters vitally into its very being. To the degree that we become aware that beyond the adequation of the mind to reality truth requires the ever more intense presence of itself to itself, inerrancy should become totally inadequate as a category expressing the relation between the truth of revelation and man's belief. Truth is not the adequacy of a representation, but the adequacy of self-existence, the adequacy of the presence of oneself to being, or of oneself to another, or of oneself to oneself. Thus, the ultimate truth is not the correct representation, the faithful reproduction, of ultimate facts. The ultimate truth, the divine revealed truth, is the truth that confers life decisively. It is the truth that saves. It is the truth that is also the way and the life.

OBJECTIVITY AND SUBJECTIVITY
IN RELIGIOUS TRUTH

I have repeatedly suggested in these pages that the concepts of truth and of reality, the foundations of all religious belief, have evolved as markedly and profoundly as any other aspect of human experience and life. But man's self-understanding depends closely upon his understanding of truth and reality. Therefore, man's self-understanding is evolutionarily affected when he learns to think of truth not as a quality which accrues to the act of knowledge or as the result of playing a fair game with reality, but as the inner orientation of man's self-creativity within the world of reality. We have now discussed some of the consequences that this development has had for theistic belief, and for the believer's reflective understanding of the nature of belief. But it is not only belief, and the concept of belief, that are affected by the development of man's self-understanding. For there is nothing to the understanding of which man's self-understanding is irrelevant, since the empirical nature of man's understanding means that he cannot understand anything without his being present to himself, nor in any other way than as present to himself. This is why, as Bernard Lonergan has put it, "an understanding of . . . understanding [leads] to a basic understanding of all that can be understood." [74] Man's presence to reality occurs in and through his presence to himself and, therefore, whatsoever he understands, he understands in relation to himself.

[74] *Insight: a Study of Human Understanding*, (London, 1958), p. xxviii.

Thus, as man's self-understanding progresses, all his religious concepts require periodic redevelopment and all the doctrines and other forms of his faith stand in need of reinterpretation and renewal, in order merely to preserve—all the more so if he is to enhance—the meaningful function that religious truth has in relation to human life. Indeed, in the light of the changes which man historically and collectively brings about in his self-and world-conception, the very concept of religion must be reinterpreted.

The traditional Christian concept of religion relies so closely on the identification of reality with being, and of being with objectivity, that the reality of God is indistinguishable from his objectivity. Whatever else God may be, he is an objective reality, that is, a real being. His reality must be the reality of something that exists objectively, that is, something that exists in-itself, independently of, and prior to, our knowledge of it; a reality which as such is essentially external to our own reality, although through the exercise of our spiritual powers we are able to know it and love it. Thus, in this way of thinking, the reality of God, (his essential otherness and distinction from man's own self), is inseparably wedded to the divine existence, (to God's original alienation from man as a thing in itself), and, therefore, to the idea that God comes into man's consciousness from without. The idea that God is encountered by man within himself, within the reality of his own self-consciousness, would appear to this style of thinking, at best, as a poetic metaphor. The hard fact would be that if God is real, independent of man's own reality and thought, man can be related to God only as he finds God outside himself. Only if God and man are first isolated is it possible for a God-man relation subsequently to develop. Just as intellect and will overcome the dichotomy of man and being, religion overcomes the natural, necessary, real and entitative opposition between God and man. I need hardly illustrate how this idea of God as an objective reality, and of religion as the conquest of God's objectivity and the remedy for man's un-Godly subjectivity, colours the whole of the religious life of the Christian world.

Much of the force of this idea comes from a consideration of the only alternative to thinking of God as some sort of objective reality which suggests itself once the traditional epistemological premises are assumed, namely, the alternative of thinking of him as some sort of subjective modification of man's own reality. If so, it would be necessary to explain God away, say, as a symbol of man's transcendent desires, or else as a symptom of his neuroses, or at best as a projection of man's own creativity, freedom and transcendence. Most believers would agree, however, that such a God would, for all his usefulness as a convenient fiction, have no reality other than that of man's own subjectivity: to believe in such a God would be to believe in nothing but man. A *real* God—it is thought—must therefore be the opposite of this: if God is real he must have objective reality. For to have real reality and to have *objective* reality is the same. Though God may differ from every other object of human apprehension, he is the same as every other object in one respect, namely, in his objectivity. A real God must be objective in the same sense as every other reality is objective, that is, he would have to stand outside the subjectivity of man. It is for this reason that the relations with man into which God enters are subsequent to, and are, as it were, a remedy for, the imperfection of an original separation from man. God's reality is essentially to be found outside man. Religion is the means of bridging the natural and normal alienation between a transcendent God and man.

The objectivity of God appears, thus, as self-evident to many believers. If we reflect upon it, however, we may have to concede that, if we find it impossible to think of God except as an objective reality, the reason is not to be found in the nature of religious experience—which, if anything, would tend in the opposite direction—or even in the specifically divine notes of the concept of God. On the contrary, it is only if we first assume that any reality which is not subjective must needs be objective that we consequently find ourselves compelled to suppose that if God is real then he must be an objective being. This—let us suppose—may be true or false: but it is not in either event self-evident. The idea that reality is either subjective or objective is part of a certain concept of the nature of human consciousness, a concept the historical emergence of which is perfectly understandable, but nevertheless a concept which should not escape critical reflection, and which indeed upon such examination as that conducted above may be found to need substantial modification.

It is true enough that man's belief in God is valid only if it refers to a reality which transcends man's own: faith is a commitment to conceive oneself, to find meaning in oneself, and to exist consciously, in the light of a reality that transcends one's own transcendence. Belief is reasonable only if the reality of God is a truth which neither wishing nor imagining—nor even being—can either procure or take away. But this need not imply that God is an object, a thing-in-itself whose specific distinctiveness is divinity or infinity. For if neither objectivity nor subjectivity adequately describe man's self-relation to the world of empirical objects, least of all do they do so in relation to the ultimate reality of God. We may think of God rather as present to man in and through man's presence to himself. God reveals himself to man by revealing man to himself. To put it negatively: God is that without which man cannot find meaning in his presence to himself. But it may be better to put it positively: as man discovers himself, God becomes evident to him—with corresponding gradualness—as that which defines the direction of man's self-creation and as the ground of man's self-concept and self-projection. Hence, it is not only true, as I suggested above, that God must be a reality which transcends man's transcendence: it is also true, in a way, that God has no reality outside human experience. It is not only that he does not "exist," but also that his reality is not like that of a reality which comes to man from without himself.

From one viewpoint this statement is not very important: since human experience does not have an outside, the statement is but a rejection of a certain epistemology. But from another viewpoint it is important: it means that God is not a being; it means that he may be found *in* being, but only as *other than* being; it means that he may be found only as present *to* being and as manifesting himself in the reality *of* being. But as other-than-being he is not to be sought outside ourselves.

The concept of religion which follows from these principles can be easily surmised. Religion does not mediate between God and man, and even revealed religion does not descend from above, as a Jacob's ladder whereby to traverse the void to heaven from earth. Religion is, on the contrary, the symbol of our encounter with the reality of God—that is, religion is the embodiment of our self-disposition and self-relation towards God. Religion is the conceptual, cultural form of the experience of reality as such. It is not the means to attain to God; it is not the means to become united with a reality from which we were separated at the outset. It is the evolving expression of our evolving consciousness of God. Religion is the ever developing, ever growing meaning of the reality of man, in his self-creating existence in the presence of God.

6.

The Meaning
of Religious Belief

If Christianity were indefinitely to persist in maintaining, in effect, that human consciousness can historically progress in every respect except religiously, Christianity would eventually render itself altogether incredible. It would become all the less credible because it was Christianity itself that, in the first instance, awakened man to consciousness of historical progress. Christianity would not but destroy its credibility if it continued to tell man, as it has for a century or more, that it did not really mean what it had been from the outset effectively preaching as God's Word. Of course, some Christians believe that the Church would, on the contrary, destroy its credibility if it were to acknowledge that to have retained its Hellenic forms, and particularly its Hellenic foundations, over the last century or two, had been in point of fact a mistake. Yet, this position may be dictated by an unhealthy fear rather than by a reasoning one, and by a profound misunderstanding of the nature of error and truth. For the Gospel preached by the Church nowhere contains as an article of belief the doctrine that Greek philosophy (or even Thomistic philosophy) is eternally valid, and that the Hellenic foundations of belief are the indispensable *preambula* to the

472

Christian faith. Nor is Christianity, therefore, married to the Greek (or the Thomistic) philosophy of truth. For the Church to admit honestly, humbly, sincerely and candidly that it was a mistake to have thought so—for a relatively short while—would of itself probably earn only respect and admiration. To uphold the traditional Hellenic forms simply because they were adequate in the past is to take for self-consistency what may be only stubbornness and fear.

In other words, Christianity may well have to learn to abide by the consequences of its own revolutionary ferment upon the human race. The Christian Church will have to take the results of having promised man, I do not say, Heaven, but God himself. One cannot let the Gospel loose in the world and expect that nothing drastic will happen. One cannot tell people that God lives among them and becomes one of them, and that the truth shall make them free, and that death has no sting, and that the *eschaton* of time is at hand and to be hoped for—one cannot, in a word, preach Christ crucified and yet reasonably expect that the world will go on much the same as before. The introduction of the Gospel into the history of man was an evolutionary event. I do not see how anything that anyone should at this late date do, could possibly change that historical fact.

No, man evolved into man—and presumably this did not occur while God was busy elsewhere. And man did not cease to evolve when he evolved into man. Man has evolved, indeed, even since he became civilized. Are we to believe that man has not evolved since he became Christian? He has evolved in modern times, in the last century, and possibly even in our own generation's time. Man has never ceased to evolve, and possibly never will for as long as he is man. And man's religion must evolve with man.

Otherwise, religion would cease to be an evolutionary force within man, and this would mean that something had gone wrong with the evolution of man.

The evolution of man has proceeded along the dimension of consciousness. As man has reached certain levels of self-consciousness his nature has gradually changed, and he has increasingly found that he cannot adequately continue to relate himself to reality in the same ways which at earlier times may have been entirely appropriate. Thus, the very nature of the religious situation in which man exists changes as man himself evolves, and the new wine of his religious belief cannot be put into the old skins of traditional forms.

THE QUEST FOR SALVATION

Atheism is not only an intrinsic possibility, opened to man by the very nature of his religious situation; it is also an intelligent, albeit inadequate reaction, only partially correct, to the evolution of consciousness. It has been influential and even in a sense progressive, although it is only partially correct, in the absence of any other suggestion that the evolution of religious belief, beginning with the reconceptualization of God, should have been consciously undertaken by man. If atheism should be overcome, it is not because man should fear being alone: if he were in fact alone all he could intelligently do, given his nature, would be to adjust to the fact. Marxist atheism is in this respect highly consistent—even if its consistency is unfortunate in other respects—for it does not bewail the absence of God and instead dedicates itself to the construction of the future of man. Other atheisms are not so worthy of admiration in this particular respect. If God has no reality it is a little childish to lament his nothingness, to indulge the experience of forlorness, or to wish that things were otherwise. On the other hand, all atheisms are commonly somewhat closer to the mark when they taunt believers with unacknowledged cowardice. A mature person, a person who has taken advantage of the possibilities open to him by the cultural evolution of man to date, should not believe because he is incapable of unbelief—and least of all because he could not otherwise lead a creative and moral life. If, despite the real and avowed possibility of his unbelief, a man stands in belief, understanding belief as an act of fundamental self-conception, ultimate self-disposition and decisive self-projection beyond himself, religion would not be for him a qualification imposed upon human existence from above: religion would be the meaning of his life, vivifying him from within. For such a person to believe would not be really distinct from thinking or from his being what and who he was. To believe in God would not imply submission to a Supreme Being, but self-relation to the reality beyond all being which manifested itself *in* being. The unfathomable mystery which manifests itself *in* being would, at one and the same time, be required for the understanding of being, and require being in order to be understood. Transcendent reality can be believed in only because being can be empirically known. In brief, man is not alone. But man is on his own. The transcendent reality whose company man keeps does not take away any of his responsibilities. On the contrary, man acquires responsibility because he exists in the presence of God.

True and valid religious belief, sufficient unto salvation, is neither natural nor rational, if this means that human nature and reason, sufficient unto themselves according to their intrinsic necessities, are also sufficient to transcend their intrinsic necessities and rape the inner necessities of God. I have no doubt that the traditional Christian distaste for naturalism and rationalism is perfectly well taken—but I stress that their diametric opposite, supernaturalism and obscurantism, hobble human development with comparable efficiency, and that diametric opposition to naturalism and rationalism commit one to an acceptance of the pessimistic, closed, Greek concept of nature, and of the uncritical, circular, Greek concept of reason. But true and valid religious belief is natural and rational if nature is freedom, given to man by the situation in which he exists in the presence of God, and if reason is his means of self-orientation towards the future, of self-projection towards God and of self-disposition in favour of all reality. In this sense, the Christian faith in God coincides perfectly with faith in nature and with faith in reason. (I presuppose here, of course, that reality is not to be identified with being, nor reason with the intussusception of that-which-is.)

Religious belief leads to "salvation." But what precisely is it to be "saved"? This question underlies every religious enquiry. If the answer were simple or clear religious reflection would lack its motive power. (I do not mean, of course, that religious reflection is necessarily a form of self-seeking, at least intelligent self-seeking. It is true, on the other hand, that it can become self-seeking—for instance if it were to conceive salvation as survival over disasters which one must avoid at all costs, even, if necessary, as a privileged individual whose happy fate need not be shared by anyone else.)

Perhaps the beginning of wisdom is the thought that it is not easy to know what a man must do to be "saved." The answer to

476

the perennial problem of self-problematic man is not self-evident above all because the problem is not that of finding an elusive, or presently unavailable, means to an otherwise clearly delimited, and obviously all valuable, end. The problem is indeed almost precisely the opposite. For we may be certain that, regardless of the nature of whatever future we may project ourselves towards with ultimate and total self-commitment, the means to achieve it are perfectly clear and available to everyone: the means can only be the exercise of our free, creative existence in the presence of God. But the problem is that it is not so very easy to give a concrete shape to the central, final project of our total life. Nor must we suppose that the concrete form of this project must be the same for everyone: to each life or creative freedom corresponds a vocation, (which is itself subject to evolution throughout life), which is not definable from the outset and which can be understood only to the extent that it is realized, and which must therefore be undertaken not under the sign of certainty, (rational or religious), but only under the sign of faith, hope and love.

Evidently, then, "salvation" is not a question of finding out in what may consist one's ultimate "safety," one's ultimate rescue from an inhospitable situation or from a dangerous or frustrating world. On the contrary, it is rather a question of finding out what is a truly worthwhile risk. It is, (if I may be forgiven a capitalistic, but instructive, metaphor [1]), a question of finding out what constitutes a wise investment of one's existence. The traditional metaphor, "salvation," was understandably applicable at that level of human development when man naturally and concretely perceived his situation within reality as fraught with dangers lurking beyond the range of his effective control. This

---

[1] Which derives some authority from *Matthew*, 25: 14–27.

is not quite so true today—at least, we can glimpse the threshold of a world when the danger of the human situation will have been, by and large, taken away, and when the world shall have become a fairly safe place for every man. This is in some respects already true: the hostility of the situation of man today, at least in the more advanced cultures, does not come from without as much as from within, not so much from external forces as from evil possibilities inherent to man. We no longer need fear hunger, pestilence, disease, poverty and abject ignorance: though we have not nearly eradicated these, it is not because we do not know how. The major blocks in the way of universal health and prosperity belong strictly to the order of human self-organization. But we are threatened by disorder in this very respect: what we may fear is self-destruction, genocide, boredom, despair, moral overcommitment,[2] cultural demoralization, institutionalized anarchy, and self-induced hallucinations on a national if not also global scale. Perhaps, then, we should move away from the question of "salvation" and ask ourselves instead: how can man find ultimate meaning in conscious existence freely undertaken? How can I best discharge the final and total responsibility in which I am placed by being conscious that I exist? In what way should I definitively orient myself, as I discover that the definitiveness of human temporality is given by the termination of life in death?

[2] One of the gravest threats to contemporary international political stability (and, hence, to the survival of man) derives from the obsolescence of political institutions which make it perfectly possible for an extremely small number of men to make irrevocable decisions that affect the human race as a whole and commit on a moment's toss the very existence of man, without providing at the same time nearly enough safeguards against the possibility, if not indeed the likelihood, that the corresponding selective processes may be so biased that they would frequently place men in political situations which are above their intellectual and moral depth.

It is almost as easy to be carried away by realism as by piety. It is indispensable to recall at this point that it would be the worse part of realism—one scarcely needs faith to be persuaded of this —to forget that, whatever the future may hold, there is much wrong with man today. I mean, not only with individuals, but with the human race. There is an absurd, ridiculous disparity between the abstract and the concrete possibilities open to man, between what man can dream of and what he can actually bring about. Christian optimism would be imprudent, it would indeed be unrealistic and foolhardy, if it imagined (as Marxist utopianism inveterately does) that this disparity could be overcome without the elevation of man towards the transcendent reality of God. Progress will not remedy the generic condition of man unless it be progress in man's relation to God.

The perfection of human nature *may* be achieved; it will not be *inevitably* achieved. Man is invited, challenged to progress. Progress is normal and natural to him insofar as he is impelled to evolve by the actual situation in which he exists—for instance, by his nature as conscious, which automatically leads him to become conscious of himself precisely as conscious, and hence to create himself consciously and in awareness that the very possibilities that will be opened to him in the future depend upon what he does with himself today. But progress obtains through man's free self-creation: it is, therefore, far from assured. Human existence can, quite possibly, ultimately fail. But even if the adventure of man ends in disaster, the Christian can be certain that it will not end in tragedy. For the possibility of its success was as real and as indeterminate as that of its failure. Heaven and Hell do not await man. Heaven and Hell are created by man's arrival at them.

Hence, the "restoration" of man to his "proper" condition is to be achieved only through the creation of a world made in the divine presence and decisively guided by the historical agency of God. But this is scarcely a *re*-storation, and man's attainment of it is not proper to him. It is not a restoration, because the evolution of man is not a return, but an ascent, to God. And it is not proper to him, because it is not an ascent to his own. For God does not belong to man—not only because man never possessed him, but also because man may yet fail in his attempt to ascend to God. Human nature is not ready-made; it is on the way, evolving towards a goal which can be truly realized, but which was not pre-set from the first. The goal itself is creatively determined within man's evolutionary history in the presence of a historically active God.

THE MANNER OF WORSHIP

If God truly is, and if in man's good conscience and faithfulness God must be conceived as a historical presence which sets in the human soul an instinct for the future, a dissatisfaction with the present, and a foundation in the past; and if God is so utterly real that he is, in his utter and total reality no further away than the nearest particle of being anywhere and at any time; and if God is not a personal, Supreme Being who is in Heaven beyond the world—if all these things are true, and if all the traditional devotions can find no substance in them, what can be, then, the meaning of belief today? Can a divinity, a God such as that of whom I have written here be, for example, *interested* in man? Is this the sort of God, let us say, to whom a man could *pray*? The answers depend upon what the questions really mean.

What is to take interest? If to take interest is to experience solicitude, to wonder what will happen, to wish that one might help someone avoid or remedy mishaps, then it is very doubtful that God has any interest in the world or in man. For whatever else God may be, we can be certain of one thing: he is not a man. The only thing we may be sure he cannot be is a conscious being who rises sufficiently above being to have his being in the knowing of being, but who in the end is being nonetheless. Such a God would be possible if God were Supreme Being. In this case every problem concerning God's "interest" in man could be easily solved by saying that God's interest in man is to be analogically understood. But a God thus interested in man would be self-contradictory unless he were subsistent Humanity Itself. On the other hand, if to have interest in the world is to have an investment in it, to be affected by what man does, to be self-involved in, and self-committed to, the history of creation—then God must be clearly interested in man and in the world. For a God who is the reality beyond being manifests himself, invests himself and commits himself in being, and is especially manifested by, invested in, and committed to the being which is present to himself, since such a presence manifests, invests and commits being to itself. Man's creatureliness, his essential relation to God, is definable in terms of the presence of being to itself in consciousness. Just as being vitally interests itself, and totally invests itself, and irrevocably commits itself to man in the evolution of consciousness, so God vitally interests himself, totally invests himself, and irrevocably commits himself to the whole world of created being—and he does so in a climactic, reflective manner to the climax of reflective being, man.

As we have seen, God does not create necessarily. Indeed, if to create is to fashion or to make something out of nothing in accordance with one's own Ideas or Exemplars, that is, by projecting oneself into reality beyond oneself, then God does not create at all: being does not flow from God. For to say that being comes "from nothing" is to say that it does *not come from* anything at all, not even God. But God is responsible for being: it is in this sense that if there were no divine reality then there would be no world. God neither exists in himself at a moment of his eternity while he creates the world, nor does he create eternally an effect that follows temporally—for in this final, efficient, material and formal casual sense he does not create at all. But God invests himself, commits himself, interests himself, and in this sense—which is in no way aetiological—he *gives* himself to the world. Therefore, to be "interested" in the world is the very essence of God. The very "life" of God is put by him at stake in the world. To interpret this, however, in terms of God's feelings for being, or his tenderheartedness towards man or his watchfulness over the predetermined course of the world, would be misleadingly to misconceive God as a superconsciousness quantitatively infinite, but essentially of the same nature as man.

Prayer cannot be, therefore, man's endeavour to interact with God's consciousness of man. But if God's self-investment in the world and in man is what makes him present to being, for it makes being to be in reality and in relation to reality itself, then the responsibility of man towards reality cannot be discharged except insofar as he renders present to his own consciousness, by his own conscious existence, the presence of God. Man does not invent or discover prayer. Man's being is prayerful. And insofar as man is "naturally" prayerful it is true that man "owes" by his very nature worship to God. But as man is conscious and becomes conscious of himself, his prayerfulness becomes conscious of itself: man is not only prayerful, but he prays —and, like every other development of man's consciousness, there is no pre-established guarantee that his development will be from the outset what it can reasonably become only at a later stage.

It is understandable if when man first began to pray he imagined that he was talking *to* God, not realizing that God was present to him before *he* became aware of the presence of God, not realizing that he could not very well talk *to* God if God was not an objective reality whose otherness was alienated from the reality which was man's own. A more adequate, though still misleading—if not incomprehensible—metaphor which becomes possible at a later stage is that of *listening* to God, that is, being consciously aware of what has always been there, becoming conscious of that which has never been absent, but whose very presence is the condition of the possibility of one's presence to oneself. It would be still better to say, however, that prayer is worship, and that worshipfulness is neither obedient awe nor respectful submissiveness, but the manifestation of man's self-relation to reality under the sign of man's self-creativity in the presence of God. Prayer in this sense is, thus, the response of man's responsibility, and it is made possible by the prior, creative responsibility of God. Prayer is not the attempt to reach God and influence him, but, on the contrary, the conscious resolution to be consciously reached by transcendent reality and to be influenced by the ultimate responsibility of God. Worship is the conscious presence of consciousness to the real presence of God.

THE STYLE OF THE CHURCH

The institutional implications and the practical consequences of any possible conscious development of Christian belief along the lines which simple extrapolation from the foregoing reflections would suggest are difficult to draw in any concrete detail—partly because these implications would not, in the concrete, be necessitated by their premises. They would have to be worked out in the same way as every other facet of human life, that is, creatively, freely and in interaction with the whole of creation and with God. Nonetheless, there is such a thing as logic, and they would be right who foresaw in the eventuality of Christianity's reconstruction of the foundations of belief along the lines indicated by the historical development of Western philosophy a radical change in the character of religious belief and its place in human life.

For I should imagine that any consciously undertaken development of Christian belief would work in the direction of heightening the religious self-consciousness of man—and that this would be destructive of the traditional style of Christian belief. This is why even the semi-conscious reconstruction inspired by Pope John and Vatican II which we call "renewal" threatens, (or promises, according to one's viewpoint), a new style of Christian life. It would not be altogether mistaken to describe the new style already in vigour as more commitment and less devotion, more spirit and less superstition, more autonomy and less authority, more society and less herd, more concern and less worry, more spontaneity and less guilt, more creativity and less rote, more joy and less fear, more humour and less pomposity, more thought and less talk. Being a Christian is much more human and natural today than it appears to have been for a very long time. Well, it is difficult to suppose that the further evolution of Christian belief will reverse this trend.

I discard the possibility that the institutional Church will altogether disappear. Like every other socio-historical, cultural reality, man's faith—however "supernatural"—must be embodied in institutions; and if no institutions exist to give cultural forms to human experience, or if institutions decay or disappear, new institutions are created by him who might very well be described as the institutional animal, man. Indeed, the institutional Church is likely to be stronger, more cohesive, (but also more spiritual, less inflexibly structured), in the near future than at any previous time. The spiritualization of the concept of God, the autonomy of religious profession, the exaltation of freedom and creativity, the integration of religion and life, the historification of revelation, the defatalization of reality, the secularization of the sacred, the sacralization of the secular, the "de-divinization of Being" and the "de-ontologization of God" —if these ever do take place, the role of the community of believers in the formation, strengthening, creation and evolution of Christian belief will be magnified many times over. The Church would then become a significant and obvious object of belief, and then faith, hope and love of God would be indistinguishable from faith, hope and love of the Church. For God would be manifest above all in the common life and common consciousness of believers as that reality in relation to which common consciousness was real and true—but a reality nonetheless which was other than its reality and its truth. Just as being is the only way in which being can be real, the Church would be the only way to ascend to God.

Hence, I also discard the possibility that *ecclesial* institutions will remain substantially unaltered: the traditional forms of Church structure are far too inadequate to the new needs of the Church. The likelihood of eventual *radical* change in this respect is deducible not so much from the conscious efforts of many insufficiently progressive elements in the Church who wish to refashion (while invariably retaining) all the traditional structures, for their reforms are usually unstable and please no one in the end. It is deducible, rather, from the very strength and intransigence of reactionaries, from the outrance and the self-encapsulation of too many officials in the Church, and from the ineffectualness of the very efforts to retain the situation of the past. If enough ecclesial institutions become irrelevant to the life of the Church, reform will not be needed: the institutions will be by-passed. Thus, radical changes are not likely to come either through revolution from without or through evolution of the institutions from within, but through the marginalization of many (or perhaps most) of the traditional structures of the Church and the creation of novel ones to take their place.

Of all the traditional ecclesial institutions the one whose marginalization is most devoutly to be hoped for is that of the *clergy*. It is perhaps symbolic of the advanced stage of clericalist degeneration of the Catholic Church that in order to prevent misunderstanding and avoid giving offence I feel compelled immediately to explain what should be obvious: when I hope for the dissolution of the clergy I have in mind neither the hierarchy as such, nor the ministry of orders, nor religious profession. When I say *clergy* I mean *clergy*: a sociological and juridical reality embodied in manners, mores, attitudes and other formal and informal institutions which make up the clerical cultural complex which has long constituted the sociological heart of the Catholic Church, and which, to a rapidly diminishing but still decisive degree, still does so today. Clerkship has in itself nothing to do with sacred orders or with ministerial charismata or with hiearchical authority, and least of all with the nature of the Church. But for Catholic Christianity it is difficult to realize this today and to remember that clergy means clergy, not priesthood, ministry, or Church, precisely because in the past priesthood and hierarchy—and indeed Church—have been, with all the good will in the world, largely absorbed by and made subservient to that which originally stemmed from them and had been instituted to serve them, namely, clerkship. For although the juridical and sociological institution of clerkship may have had a useful function at certain points in the past, its value was dissipated long ago and its retention has become increasingly scandalous both within and without the Church. Hence, the reason why the clergy *as such* must disappear is that the good of priesthood, hierarchy and Church so require. Conversely, to retain the clerical society regardless of the needs of today's Church would amount to a perversion of priesthood, hierarchy and Church. It is not, however, every priest who is conscious of this, and it is a rare bishop who is aware of so much as the possibility that clericalism may be a serious threat to the institution of the Church.

Of course, "priests with a sense of Christian values have always disowned the clerical mentality, that frame of mind so naturally developed in the Catholic enclave, but the problem has been widespread nonetheless." [3] What is wanting today, however,

[3] Eugene Kennedy, "The dissolution of clerical culture," *The Critic,* XXVII, 1, (August-September, 1968), p. 13.

is a collective, institutional decision to disown clericalism as a whole, and this is a much more difficult achievement. It would take an extraordinary amount of insight and not a little genuine devotion to the Church for the clergy collectively to declericalize itself—even when pressed to do so by a historical situation which defines the only alternative to this as the ruin of the Church. On the other hand, it is encouraging that so *very* many priests, and even some bishops, have in the past few, short years clearly and spontaneously realized the self-development required of them by the needs of the historical situation of the Church, and have not hesitated to give up the ways and attitudes of clerkship they may have previously had. Indeed, they have frequently been eager to do so. For the priest who discovers—if he did not always know—that his vocation is to priesthood, not clerkship, usually finds that clerkship is—or becomes—distasteful to him. But, conversely, the priesthood has become distasteful to many priests because clerical culture has crumbled in recent times (to an extent they would have thought impossible but shortly before). Thus, the crisis of identity of today's Catholic priest is experienced not only by those who find it difficult, (for a variety of inward and external reasons), to exercise the declericalized priesthood that they wish to exercise—but also, at the other extreme, by those who find it difficult to exercise a priesthood which, despite their wishes, has become considerably declericalized. Perhaps the task of the first will be eased in the future, and the problem of the second will disappear of its own accord as the historical processes already at work in the Church proceed to reach their logical term.

If ever (as I think is quite likely) the Church becomes entirely declericalized, then the Church will have truly become what it has not effectively been at any previous time, possibly not even in the primitive Church, namely, the sociologically *catholic* spiritual corporation, the "one-throughout" spiritual body, or the *integrated* society of those who profess Christian belief. To the degree that the Church, (like man), is already such a spiritual body, the future of the Church is (like man's) in its own hands: what the Church will be like in the future depends strictly upon what Christians decide today.

Finally, speaking more generally, let us remember that the prospects which the present stage of human evolution open up for the Christian faith are without a doubt almost unlimited. But not even the future of the Church is fated. Christian belief may yet become the leading cultural force contributing to the conscious self-creation of the human *world,* the foundations of which may yet be laid over the next thousand years or two. On the other hand, it is also perfectly possible that the Church may become even more self-involuted and isolated than it has been in its recent past, nursing its grudges, indulging its melancholy hostilities and hoping that time will soon begin to flow in reverse. Or it may become anything between these two extremes. The point is that whatever the Church becomes, it will become what it makes of itself.

Again, if the new forms of the Church will be creatively determined, extrapolation may be of very limited usefulness. Nevertheless, the changes which the Church is likely to undergo (say, within a generation or so) could be subsumed under two headings. First, the diminution of all institutional forms which rest upon a juridical basis and of all rigid structures and, conversely, the growing importance of institutions grounded upon social relations and of those which have flexible structures.

489

Superimposed upon this there may well be a more general trend towards more formal and more numerous structures, but each less influential and powerful than heretofore. It would not be incorrect to refer to these two trends respectively as the *socialization* and the *democratization* of the Church. Like human culture as a whole, Christianity in the future may become more of a do-it-yourself affair than at any previous time.

The Meta-Metaphysical Concepts of Essence, Existence, Being, Reality, Man and God

The thesis of this book has been that Christian belief today is best set down upon the intellectual foundations of a meta-metaphysical understanding of *reality* and *truth*. It may be useful to sum up briefly, however unsystematically, the meaning of the basic concepts of a meta-metaphysical approach to the philosophical mode of man's self-relation to reality.

Essence, what a thing is, or the intelligibility of being, is not an intrinsic constituent of being. It is the relation of being to consciousness. But this relation is established by consciousness through *its* relation to being, namely, truth. Essence is, thus, correlative with truth. It is what a thing is as intelligible. It is, —likewise, the meaning of being. But it is not a constituent of being or of the reality of being. Nor is it the meaning of being in- and for-itself. It is the meaning of being for-us. Being has no meaning in- and for-itself.

Existence is not the act exercised by being. It is an event, a fact. Existence does not constitute being: existence is being, that is, it is the reality of being. Existence is not distinct from being itself in any way. We may as well speak of existence as of being. Therefore, existence is unintelligible in itself, just as being is unintelligible in itself. On the other hand, being can be understood, and its essence can be ascertained; likewise, existence can be understood, and its essence can be ascertained. The essence of any existing being can be ascertained by consciousness, because being exists historically. Likewise, the essence of being as such, of existence as such, can be ascertained by consciousness in relation to the historical situation of being as such, namely, its relation to reality as such. The only difference is that when human consciousness ascertains the meaning of existence as such, it must extend experience into the dimension of belief, since reality as such is manifested empirically in being as that which is beyond being, but which is not being itself.

Being is, of course, that which *exists*. It is better, for the sake of clarity, to say that being *exists,* rather than being *is.* For both *being* and *being-something* have to do with predication. Thus there *is* a reality which is other than being, although such a reality does not and cannot, of course, *exist.* Only being exists. It follows that essences do not exist. For they are not being (since they are not a constituent of being). Essences are essences *of* being. But neither being nor essence should on this account be confused with reality, which does not, *as such,* exist. (Note, however, that nothingness does not exist either—but for an entirely different reason, namely, because it has no reality). For although only that which is real can exist, reality does not necessarily exist. It follows that being is real only when, if and because it exists. Being is, therefore, objective reality. Being is real, and its essence is to exist. Being is objective reality because it is the object of human understanding, since man becomes conscious by objectifying being, that is, by differentiating himself from it.

Reality, therefore, in which, (and in relation to which), man is, (and is conscious), is neither essence nor existence nor being

492

—though being, essence and existence are real (which is why reality may both exist and be intelligible). But reality remains: it is *that in relation to which* absolute contingencies can be absolutely contingent upon. In other words, the reality of being is not distinct from the being of real being; but reality as such is not being. Reality as such is that in which being can be real: reality is that in which existence can be and essence can be understood. A being must be real if it really is and if it can be really understood. Reality is, thus, that which anything must "have"—rather, must be-had-by, or better, must be-with in order to be real. This is true of all being; it is true of consciousness in the same way as it is true of the object of consciousness. All real being is related to reality. Consciousness, however, is self-related to reality. This does not make of reality an absolute, that to which all things are related and which is related to none. For reality is, on the contrary, that without which there would be nothing to be related to it. Reality is rather—if I may so put it—absolutely related. That is, its relativity to being is an integral part of it. Reality is relative by itself and not merely (as being and consciousness are) relative only by virtue of the relations into which it actually enters. Thus, the essence of reality is self-diffusiveness, self-communication. Reality is essentially not only self-gift, but, as it were, self-exporting self-gift.

Man's reality is peculiar. He exists; he is a fact; he is a contingent fact; he is nothing but a contingent fact. But he is a contingent fact that is present to itself, a contingent fact whose contingency makes him self-problematic. This self-problematization, however, is like the generation of an inner life: a being who is self-problematic is by that very fact oriented by nature towards truth. This truth is not a reality outside himself. Truth is the very orientation of the contingent being who is present to itself and who, therefore, must search for meaning. The search for meaning is wrongheaded, however, if it proceeds in the direction of objects, on the understandable misunderstanding (but misunderstanding nevertheless) that in a real (even if only partial or secondary) manner the truth is elsewhere than in consciousness. The truth is rather the very projective character of conscious existence; it is but the child generated by consciousness out of being. The procession from being through consciousness towards truth is evolution, history and time. Thus, since human existence is conscious of itself, human existence is temporal—that is, it evolves historically. In other words, it exhibits a feedback effect upon existence itself; and when existence faces itself it acquires meaning. That is, it acquires *its own* meaning. Its contingent existence has then had issue: without ceasing to exist or to be contingent it has become meaningful to itself. Temporality, therefore, is the interface between existence and meaning. From this it follows that although the reality of man is an existing reality, existence does not have a hold on man. Other beings may cease to exist: only man can die. Indeed, the best index of man's dignity is that only he ceases to exist by dying. Thus, the reality of man is, though existing, not merely existing—because man can die. This is why every existing reality conscious of its existence will project itself beyond existence. In this manner man conquers existence; existence does not conquer him unless, perhaps, he should deliver himself to mere existence. That would be, of course, the worst error man could commit. Now, it is not particularly sad in itself, but it is a real fact, that man can err. Moreover, man can mistake the nature of error and thus mistake himself for an infallible existent (which would be, of course, a contradiction in terms).

The fact that man can err must be taken into account by him; it must become part of man's consciousness of himself. It must be taken into account above all as he tries to understand the nature of error itself. Philosophy helps man understand all the various ways in which he errs. (The acquisition of this wisdom is no small feat.) Religion is the other side of philosophy; it helps man understand the verious ways in which he can project himself towards the truth. (The acquisition of *this* wisdom is a veritable gift.)

God is, to speak properly, not "ultimate" reality, since he is not the reality which exists "after" immediate reality: he is the reality *in relation to which* any other reality is real. God is reality as such. Thus, whatever is true of any being is true because it is real (and not only because it *is*). On the other hand, reality *as such* does not exist, and therefore, the reality of any given being, or the reality of being as such is not the same as reality as such. Of course, reality exists *as* being, and being as such is real. But existing reality is not reality as such; it is being. Thus, being is real because God is real, but God does not exist simply because being exists. Likewise, the relation of God and being, as best we can ascertain from an empirical examination of being, can be described in the following terms. Being is being because it is; it has reality because it exists, and to exist, (I do not say to come into being), it needs neither help nor impulse, neither support nor energy, neither extrinsic influence nor intrinsic activity; if it exists it is already existing, and to keep on existing it has to do nothing, nor nothing be done to it. The temporality of being is not without being itself, and there is outside being no yesterday or no tomorrow which being needs to uphold itself in. All an existent has to do is to exist; if it does, its past is there already and its tomorrow should automatically come. And if it does not come, it is only because something happened to it (of the same order as that which enabled it to come into being); and so it ceased to exist. When this happens, the reason is not that it failed to exercise existence or to be supported in it. On the other hand, if anything that exists is real and is not nothing, then, despite the fact that *its* reality is identical with itself, it has a reason for being real, namely, its relation to reality as such. But I stress that the reason for being real is a *historical* reason, and that the relation of being to reality as such is a historical relation. For being as such is a fact; thus, it lacks a sufficient reason for its existence and reality, since it neither exists necessarily nor is intelligibly necessary (e.g. has no immutable essence to constitute it) *even after* it exists. But the reality of existing being in relation to God is a *historical* fact. The creativity of God does not make it necessary simply because it does make it a fact. The reality of God cannot, therefore, be deduced from the existence or intelligibility of anything, but the reality of God is nevertheless that in relation to which being exists and can be understood. This may shed some light upon, and hopefully dispel, the radically mistaken idea that whereas God is absolute reality, human and all other created realities are relative to the reality of God. (But if we begin, however innocently and even unavoidably, by misunderstanding the nature of *our* relation to reality, imagining that we spy it, seize it, consume it, and then hunger for more, it cannot be reasonably expected but that we will misunderstand in turn reality's relation to us, imagining that it expelled us, that it is alien to us, that it rejects us—and that it does all this, to boot, without malice, strictly out of its inner intelligible truth.) The opposite would be closer to the truth. God is relative to creatures precisely because his reality is that which makes all being real. He is, if I may so put it, subsistent Relativity. It is only man's reality (and that of other creatures, though unfortunately for them they do not know it) that can *lack* relation. Only man can be consciously un-related. Only man is capable of refusing to relate himself—for instance, refusing to give himself. Thus, the contingency of man is what renders him apt to alienate himself from God; and the ground of this possibility is being, since only beings as such can be contingent. Consider: if man fails to relate himself to God, whose misfortune is it? We have persisted over an astoundingly large number of centuries in telling ourselves that the loss is really God's—because God needs man in order to love himself all the more. Well, two wrongs do not make right; two solitudes do not good company make. Absoluteness is the actuality of neither God nor man: but it is the real, peculiar possibility of conscious, free, self-creative being. Evidently, this possibility ought not to be realized; to-be-absolutely is the essence of sin. In God absoluteness is not even a possibility. For if God were absolute then creation would be necessarily absolute, not by choice but by nature, and man would be evil, not by freedom but by necessity. (The Greeks did believe that God was absolute, and that is why they also believed in the evil of reality and in tragedy and Fate. But at least they avowed this belief, and they practiced it consistently, and never told themselves anything but the truth which they did believe.) Consequently, to "love" God is not quite the same as to conceive kind thoughts about him, to wish him well, or to treat him as we would he treated us, so that, for instance, if he visited the world (and told us in time to make the preparations) we would declare a holy day in his honour and gratefully

497

put on a great feast for his pleasure and that of his cortège. To love God is to live in function of the awareness of his substantial presence in the world: it is to stake one's future on the belief that man is not, never has been and, above all, never will be, alone in or even with the world. For *Yahweh,* as we believe, will never withdraw himself or his presence from the world of being, and thus will always remain related to us. To love God is to embody in one's existence and self-disposition the belief that God is so far from being an absolute reality that he can be defined indeed as absolute relativity itself.

APPENDIX 2.

On Transcendental Thomism

There can be little doubt that in what pertains to the development of Catholic theological opinion, and even in relation to the development of Catholic dogma itself, the most influential variety of Catholic philosophical thought in the twentieth century has been that movement which most frequently calls itself "transcendental Thomism," the school of Joseph Maréchal, its founder, and André Marc, Johannes Lotz, Karl Rahner, Emerich Coreth and Bernard Lonergan, to single out its most distinguished figures. To their efforts the only alternative worth mentioning has been offered by "neo-Thomism," sometimes also called "traditional Thomism," though its adherents prefer the simple term "Thomism." This is, whatever its name, the Thomism articulated mainly by Jacques Maritain and Etienne Gilson.

But the contest between these two groups has been uneven. Neo-Thomism—I state this strictly as a matter of fact—has suffered from theological sterility. Neo-Thomists are simply not very concerned with the advancement of theology. However much and however valuably Gilson and Maritain may have reworked, explicitated or even developed St. Thomas' philosophy, St. Thomas' theology they have merely repeated and reproduced. On the other hand, the contributions of transcendental Thomists to the growth of Catholic theology during the last thirty years or so are too well known to require listing here. Suffice it to note that there is hardly a well-known European Catholic theologian who does not, more or less directly, more or less systematically, avail himself of the philosophical premises, concepts and approaches of transcendental Thomism. And almost every progressive theological element incorporated into the teaching of Vatican II originated, more or less directly, with the same philosophical school.

There would seem to be, therefore, considerable plausibility to the opinion which has been increasingly voiced in North America as the tide of transcendental Thomism has somewhat belatedly reached our shores: that the contemporary Catholic philosopher could safely ignore the neo-Thomism of the traditionalist mold, but that he must come to terms (or at least to grips) with transcendental Thomism. But the plausibility, I believe, is only superficial. In reality, I suggest, it would be only a slight exaggeration to affirm that the very opposite would be closer to the truth. The Catholic philosopher today must *contend* with neo-Thomism. Transcendental Thomism he must rather invite to rise above itself, to transcend itself into a meta-metaphysical, ex-transcendental, non-Thomistic, Catholic philosophical project.

The least important reason—though hardly one to be scorned —why neo-Thomism cannot be ignored hinges upon the very fact that Thomism has not contributed very much to the progress of recent Catholic theology. Because neo-Thomism is innocent of all theological innovation, and because (though admitting some sort of development in philosophy) it assumes the perennial validity of the unchanged, unreconstructed, original theological *Weltanschauung* of St. Thomas, it has emerged as the philosophical ideology of post-conciliar traditionalism. It might have been tactically wise—let us for the sake of the argument say—to ignore a few misguided academics who had inspired only the reactionary *caveats* attached by way of ineffectual concession to most of the documents of Vatican II; but it is scarcely possible to pretend that the neo-Thomism which still provides the intellectual background of, for instance, post-conciliar papal teaching, does not really exist. Neo-Thomism may be a theological paper tiger, but it is a paper tiger armed with canonical teeth.

But it is hardly a question of ecclesiastico-political life among the People of God. There is a compelling historical reason why traditionalists generally, and those in ecclesiastical power in particular, should be naturally inclined, both spontaneously and upon reflection, to assume the concepts of truth and of reality which orthodox neo-Thomism defends. The neo-Thomistic historical claim to a unique and exclusive relationship with Catholic belief cannot be easily dismissed. Transcendental Thomism is, in a sense, a historical aberration. When Thomism takes a "transcendental turn" it abrogates its title to Thomism. For to the degree that it becomes transcendental its systematic contents falsify its historical claim. This is why unlike neo-Thomism, which can take its Thomism for granted and concern itself instead with retaining the purity of Thomistic doctrine, transcendental Thomism has to explain and justify its Thomistic quality. Its Thomism does not rest on its unquestionable continuity with the historical positions struck by St. Thomas; it depends upon the premises that the truth of Catholic philosophy must by definition be Thomistic.

Both neo-Thomists and transcendental Thomists believe that the contributions of modern philosophical thought can be regained for Thomism because, as it were, *anima* (*philosophi*) *naturaliter Thomistica*. Both assume the twofold premise provided by *Aeterni Patris:* Catholic philosophical thought must be in some sense Thomistic, because the thought of St. Thomas enshrines certain fundamental truths which, precisely because they are true, are indispensably required as the foundations of Christian belief and are as eternally valid as Christian doctrine itself. Both agree, thus, that whatever truth may be found in modern philosophy is in principle assimilable by Thomism. The great divergence between neo-Thomism and transcendental Thomism begins, however, with their diametrically opposite ways of translating this principle into action.

It is not without significance that neo-Thomism has never actually found it possible to adopt any concept, any attitude, any suggestion from contemporary thought, and that its professed openness to all truth wherever it may be found has never issued in its actual discovery of any truth in modern thought which it had not, as it invariably turns out, previously learned—possibly in even purer form—from St. Thomas himself. For neo-Thomists judge whether any given modern doctrine is true from its reducibility to the principles of St. Thomas. Understandably, they instinctively suspect the opposite procedure followed by transcendental Thomism, namely, to judge that since certain doctrines proposed by modern philosophers are at least partly acceptable as an advancement of the truth—for instance, Kant's transcendental method—these doctrines must therefore be at least implicitly Thomistic. I say understandably, because I agree with neo-Thomists that truth does not usefully serve as the criterion of historical Thomism, least of all on the prior premise that Thomism is essentially true. For this procedure presupposes a prior decision about the truth of philosophical doctrines independent of their reducibility to Thomism. Whoever proceeds in this way has failed in practice to abide by his protestations of commitment to historical Thomism.

To sum up: there is not much point in dwelling on the charge that neo-Thomism is retrograde and that it has failed to learn anything of substance from post-mediaeval philosophy. For neo-Thomism is established, whereas transcendental Thomism is not. Moreover, it is established for a historically sound and indeed perfectly valid historical reason: as long as the basic premises of *Aeterni Patris* are assumed, neo-Thomism is historically warranted as the uniquely valid approach for contemporary Catholic philosophical thought—just as traditionalism is historically warranted as the uniquely valid form of Catholic belief as long as the basic principles of traditional Thomism are assumed.

I insist, moreover, that the principles of traditional Thomism descend to neo-Thomism, unadulterated and pristine, from the doctrines of St. Thomas himself. Even if it were true that the transcendental method is but an explicitation of the philosophical *Denkform* of St. Thomas, it would not be easy to deny that transcendental Thomism has accepted its epistemological *Problematik* from Descartes, not from St. Thomas; it has learned its transcendentalism from Kant, not from Aquinas; it has been taught to trade in dialectics and polarities by Hegel, not by the Angelic Doctor; it has acquired its phenomenological techniques from Husserl, not from the mediaeval thinker; it has grasped the significance of the presence of the questioner to his own question in the light of Heidegger, not in that of the Common Doctor of the Church. Thus, all my sympathy with transcendental Thomism and with progressivism, and all my disagreement with neo-Thomism and with traditionalism, are not enough to dissuade me: the neo-Thomistic historical evaluation of transcendental Thomism is essentially correct. Transcendental Thomism compromises with doctrines which from Descartes and Kant onwards have repeatedly proven their incompatibility—as Vatican I clearly taught—not only with St. Thomas but even with the most basic doctrines of the Christian faith as it has been traditionally understood since mediaeval times. I need scarcely explain that I also agree with transcendental Thomism's evaluation of neo-Thomism as hopelessly outdated. This partial agreement and partial disagreement with both groups explains why I am not a Thomist of any stirps, believing instead that a Catholic philosophical approach adequate to the needs of Christianity today must lie beyond both transcendental and neo-Thomism—believing, likewise, that the division between traditionalism and progressivism is to be fruitfully resolved only by circumventing that common ground where their conflict has so far been fought.

I should now offer some evidence, however sketchy, in support of the judgment that transcendental Thomism cannot lay a historically valid claim to the name of Thomism. The philosophical doctrine of Karl Rahner provides an apt instance of this at an altogether crucial point, namely, in relation to the concept of knowledge:

Thus for the Thomistic metaphysics of knowledge the problem does not lie in bridging the gap between knowing and object by a "bridge" of some kind: such a "gap" is merely a pseudo-problem. Rather the problem is how the known, which is identical with the knower, can stand over against the knower as other, and how there can be a knowledge which receives another as such. It is not a question of "bridging" a gap, but of understanding how the gap is possible at all. If being is being-present-to-self, then in such a concept of knowledge it is perhaps easy to see further how a being could know another in its being-present-to-itself insofar as it apprehends itself as the creative ground of this other.[1]

Though I am tempted to cavil at certain points, my partiality towards this view of knowledge should be evident from what I have written on the subject elsewhere in this book. But my disagreement with the historical judgment that this concept of knowledge can be remotely attributed to St. Thomas also follows from what I have explained above concerning St. Thomas' philosophy of knowledge. The text and the context of St. Thomas' own words clearly indicates that in his estimation the problem of knowledge is precisely that of bridging a gap. This is not, of course, a physical gap, but a metaphysical one. It is the gap created by the fact that "the specific act of existence of one thing is distinct from the specific act of existence of another." And since this means that "the imperfection of each individual thing considered in itself is imperfect," there must be "some remedy for this imperfection," namely, an order of being in which "the perfection belonging to one thing [may be] found [intentionally] in another." This *remedium* is *cognitio*. Knowledge is the knower's intentional acquisition of the formal perfection of the known, 'for something is known by a knower by reason of the fact that the thing known is, in some fashion, in the possession of the knower, (*ipsum cognitum aliquo modo est apud cognoscentem*)." [2]

Likewise, the idea that St. Thomas might have remotely agreed

[1] Karl Rahner, *Spirit in the World*, (New York, 1968), p. 75.
[2] *De Veritate*, II, 2.

505

that "being is being-present-to-self" (I would myself prefer to say not that being, but that the being of consciousness, is being-present-to-self), or even the idea that this is implicit in the doctrine of St. Thomas, cannot lie in peaceful juxtaposition with St. Thomas' doctrine that "the act whereby the intellect understands a stone is other than the act whereby it understands that it understands a stone, and so on." [3] Thus, although I concur with Rahner when he remarks that "because we know the world objectively, [in knowledge] we are always already present to ourselves in a complete return," [4] it seems to me historically inaccurate to assert that:

However little it is expressed explicitly by Thomas . . . his whole metaphysical enquiry poses its questions from out of man's situation, and simultaneously places man in question. For although the basis upon which Thomas places all his philosophizing from the outset is the world, yet it is precisely the world into which the spirit of man—in turning to the phantasm—has already entered. For strictly speaking, the first-known, the first thing encountering man, is not the world in its "spiritless" existence, but the world—itself—as transformed by the light of the spirit, the world in which man sees himself. The world as known is always the world of man, is essentially a concept complementary to man.[5]

Because Rahner assumes the foregoing philosophical concept of the nature of man's self-relation to reality he is entitled to state theologically that:

Dogmatic theology today has to be theological anthropology . . . The question of man . . . must be looked upon . . . as the whole of dogmatic theology. . . . As soon as man is understood as that being

[3] *ST*, I, 87, 3, ad 2.
[4] *Spirit in the World*, p. 407.
[5] *Ibid.*, p. 406.

which has absolute transcendence toward God (and it is surely obvious that he is such) then anthropocentricity and theocentricity in theology are not contradictories but strictly one and the same thing seen from two different aspects, and each aspect is unintelligible without the other. That theology should be anthropocentric does not contradict its being most rigorously theocentric: it is, however, opposed to the view that man is merely one particular topic in theology among others, for example, the angels or the material world.[6]

Very true—but the suggestion that St. Thomas might have found this conception of theology acceptable (or, most probably, even orthodox) appears to me ruled out by *ST*, I, 1, 7. The fact, I believe, is that Rahner learned to think of human existence as *in-der-Welt-sein* from Heidegger and from Heidegger alone— who, we may be sure, did not learn it from St. Thomas. Rahner's doctrine of the nature of human consciousness and of its object is neither implicit nor in any other way potentially contained in the doctrine of St. Thomas. For St. Thomas the *primum cognitum* is simply being—that is, being in its "spiritless" condition—and definitely not being as "transformed by the light of the spirit" of man. So far as I can determine, if any view on the nature of consciousness is, if not actually implicit in the doctrine of St. Thomas, perhaps potentially so, it is the doctrine which Maritain has developed in *The Degrees of Knowledge* and in *Existence and the Existence,* which we have studied in this book.

It could not be denied, on the other hand, that there is a sensibly smooth, almost tangible continuity between St. Thomas and later philosophical thought up to our own and Heidegger's day. I have in this book attempted to show how this continuity obtains at the very crucial points where breaks are most com-

[6] "Theology and Anthropology," in T. Patrick Burke (ed.), *The Word in History,* (New York, 1966), p. 1.

monly asserted by neo-Thomists. I have tried to demonstrate, in the first place, that St. Thomas' analysis of empirically given being depends for its conclusion upon a property of human consciousness, namely, its presence to itself, without which St. Thomas' empirical observations would not have been possible —so that St. Thomas' existential metaphysics rests, in effect, upon a reflexive analysis of being as phenomenally given. I have stressed the historical importance of this event as marking the first time that a philosopher had, in effect, taken advantage of the self-positing nature of human consciousness in order to study the nature of human consciousness. I have tried to show, moreover, that although in the doctrine of St. Thomas knowledge cannot be considered problematic, as Gilson and Maritain systematically maintain even in our day, there was, nonetheless, an inner tension in St. Thomas' doctrine which would eventually lead to the problematization of knowledge in epistemology and, indeed, to the idealization of being in metaphysics. But this scarcely means that scepticism and idealism, and even less the atheism which follows upon this dialectical development at a later date or, for that matter, Heidegger's phenomenology or Rahner's transcendental Thomism, are but implicitly contained in St. Thomas' thought, from which they were to be explicitated in good time as the inner logic of Thomism was allowed to bloom. Gilson and Maritain have extended and amplified the philosophy of St. Thomas without experiencing, evidently, the slightest constraint to draw transcendental conclusions from St. Thomas, even in the light of later thought, and Heidegger has developed the transcendental method of Kant and the phenomenology of Husserl without the slightest constraint, apparently, to extend and amplify Thomism. On the other hand, precisely because philosophy is whatever philosophers do, and because philosophy does not have an antecedent nature which philosophers merely strive to extricate from the mind of God and concretize in participant modes—each philosopher in his own way —philosophy has a historical reality and its nature is historically produced. The historical development, the evolution of philosophy is, for all of philosophy's creativity, and despite the emergence of real philosophical novelty in its midst, truly and intrinsically conditioned by its historical antecedents—and yet, not reducible to the explicitation of the implicit or even to the actualization of its potency as such. Thus, whatever truth modern philosophy may hold has been rendered possible by many philosophers, though signally by a very few of them, among whom St. Thomas holds a historically crucial place. (Correspondingly, not a few aberrations of the modern mind have also been conditioned by precisely the same historical protagonists of philosophical thought.)

I conclude that transcendental Thomism deceives itself when it believes itself to be Thomism. This self-deception lessens its relevance to the needs of the contemporary Catholic Church:

While not denying the tremendous value of the achievements of transcendental Thomism or its importance for an up-dating of philosophical and theological reflection in the Church, of its "pseudo-Thomism" one is tempted to say with Blondel: this is an impracticable task, an illusory project, an intervention that merely hinders progress. What is needed from a Christian point of view, is not primarily a dialogue between mediaeval Thomism and contemporary transcendental philosophy, but, philosophically, a contribution to the explicitation of man's self-understanding today in terms and categories in which he can recognize himself; and, theologically—as in the days of St. Thomas—an encounter of the Christian message with

509

man's self-understanding as it voices itself in his philosophy. That is what St. Thomas did in his time against many odds. That is also what should be done frankly and clearly in our day. And we are in a better position to do so than Aquinas. Metz has shown quite convincingly, that the anthropocentric form of thought, as it emerged since the Renaissance, is fundamentally the result of the Christian world view. . . . If this is true, if the transcendental method or, more broadly, the anthropocentric form of thought is fundamentally Christian there is no need to show with artificially elaborate explanations that it is also Thomistic.[7]

The question whether transcendental Thomism is really Thomism is, therefore, not a quixotic one, nor does it concern mere academic subtleties: "the importance of a book like Rahner's *Spirit in the World* is diminished or at least less evident by this procedure." [8] Indeed, the inaccuracy of the historical self-defini-

[7] Bernard A. M. Nachbar, "Is it Thomism?", *Continuum*, VI, 2 (Summer, 1968), p. 234. Moreover, as Richard Hinners has said, "to urge interpretations of [for example] the moral philosophy and theology of Aquinas which would make his position [more] 'appropriate for our time' [than the older neo-Thomism] could of course be done: that would add one more member to the long line of the 'successors' of St. Thomas, stretching from Suarez, John of St. Thomas, and Cajetan down to Maritain, Gilson, Maréchal, Rahner, Lonergan, Coreth, and Metz. Many of these 'successors' may now appear 'degenerate' and to have had their day, but do not all still remain 'true' because the principles, method or basic concepts of their work are the eternal truths of Thomism? To call some of them 'degenerate' is merely to point out that others are up-to-date and I believe it is not difficult to draw the unhappy conclusion from this notion of Thomism that even a Rahner or a von Balthasar will soon be numbered among the 'degenerate successors' of St. Thomas. . . . As long as Catholic theology, and especially philosophy, persists in attempting more or less successfully to account for and appropriate contemporary concepts and experiences by fitting them into a fundamentally hellenist and even Thomist mold, then the future of theism is indeed bleak in that it will become increasingly irrelevant," *Continuum*, V, 1 (Winter-Spring, 1967), 146–147.

[8] *Ibid.*, p. 233.

tion of transcendental Thomism has had serious adverse consequences for its systematic positions in both epistemology and metaphysics. This brings us to the two yet more basic criticisms that, apart from historical considerations, could be levelled at transcendental Thomism.

Transcendental Thomism is, in the last analysis, metaphysically inadequate. For, as Schubert Ogden has with customary felicity put it, "transcendental Thomism is precisely that—adjectivally transcendental and substantively Thomism," that is, "the material axioms of this metaphysics, and so its conclusions as well, are one and all of *pre-*, rather than post-critical origin." [9] Transcendental Thomism holds "tenaciously to an objectivist metaphysics which has, no doubt, historical value but which is simply not suited to express the modern and contemporary forms of thought." [10] I will now attempt to illustrate this with reference to the work of another well known transcendental Thomist, Bernard Lonergan.

As earlier with Rahner, I will omit from consideration all that I consider valuable and original in the work of Lonergan and direct my attention only to aspects which I evaluate adversely. Lonergan's philosophical doctrine of God is one of these. According to Lonergan God is the "primary intelligible," which entails, if he exists, that "the primary intelligible would be also the primary truth." [11] But "the primary intelligible would be also the primary being; and the primary being would be spiritual in the full sense of the identity of the intelligent and the intelligible." God, the primary being, "would be without any defect

[9] "The challenge to Protestant thought," *Continuum*, VI, 2 (Summer, 1968), p. 239.
[10] Nachbar, p. 233.
[11] This and subsequent quotations from Lonergan refer to *Insight*, pp. 658-661.

or lack of imperfection," and the "completely perfect primary being also is the primary good." Likewise, "the primary intelligible is self-explanatory" and "unconditional," and "it cannot be contingent." Thus, "if it exists, it exists of necessity." There is, of course, "only one primary being," and it "is simple" and "timeless." God, the primary being and the primary intelligible "is the omnipotent efficient cause"; he is "the omniscient exemplary cause"; he is "free" and "without any increment or change in its reality."

If this is not a faithful re-statement, howbeit refined and perhaps critically modified in a certain nuances, of the essentials of St. Thomas' tract *De Deo Uno,* then, as is entirely possible, I have misunderstood the author's intention. It goes without saying that Lonergan's metaphysics of God is not necessarily inadequate simply because it substantially repeats St. Thomas'. The point of my assertion is rather (a) that for all the post-Thomistic factors that enter into the composition of the metaphysics of Lonergan's transcendental Thomism, its Thomistic foundation remains unaffected, (b) that an evaluation of the philosophical contribution of Lonergan must begin with a critique of its Thomistic foundations, and, therefore, (c) that for all the important differences between Lonergan's Thomism and that of Gilson and Maritain—differences which concern only doctrines which are subsequent to the common epistemological and metaphysical foundations of both schools in St. Thomas' thought—the most basic epistemological and metaphysical foundations of Lonergan's thought are precisely the same as those of Gilson and Maritain, for they are those of St. Thomas himself.

From this it follows that, to the very extent that my criticism of St. Thomas, Gilson and Maritain should be valid, the same criticism should be fundamentally valid in relation to Lonergan as well. But I wish to stress once again that the differences I have so lightly passed over are extremely important, as is the fact that the flaws in Lonergan's philosophy do not nullify the value and originality of his theology—whereas Gilson and Maritain have little theology which their metaphysics could either detract from or enhance. On the other hand, it is not accidental that among Lonergan's theological contributions one of the most valuable is quite obviously related to that aspect of his philosophy which is least distinctively Thomistic, namely, his doctrine of the nature of consciousness. For I have in mind, of course, Lonergan's pioneering, original Christological work on the consciousness of Christ. This is a topic which few neo-Thomists have so much as found problematic, least of all constructively speculated about.

Finally, it must be added that the metaphysical inadequacy of transcendental Thomism rests upon a yet more basic, if much less evident inadequacy in that very order in which it otherwise excels, namely, epistemology. For transcendental Thomism holds "so tenaciously to an objectivist metaphysics" only because it first compromises at a fundamental level with pre-critical realism. All its profit from modern thought does not avail it to get to the root of the matter, namely, to the concept of knowledge, the classical understanding of which it continues in certain essential respects uncritically to assume. This is why "transcendental reflection entails a rejection or 'retorsion' of any counterposition to the objectivity or intentional character of knowledge. Knowledge is validated because it is intentional and because it is intentional it can validate itself." [12] I will attempt briefly to document this, first, in relation to Lonergan and, next, in relation to Coreth.

[12] Richard Hinners, "Teleology and 'Archaeology'," *Continuum*, VI, 2 (Summer, 1968), p. 222.

APPENDIX 2.

The substantial value of Lonergan's concept of consciousness
could not very well be gainsaid by someone who has exhibited
the views on the nature of consciousness I have in this book. I
may refer to the passage of *Insight* that deals most directly with
the issue:

Consciousness is not to be thought of as some sort of inward look.
People are apt to think of knowing by imagining a man taking a look
at something and, further, they are apt to think of consciousness by
imagining themselves looking at themselves. Not merely do they
indulge in such imaginative opinions but are also likely to justify
them by argument. Knowing, they will say, is knowing something;
it is being confronted by an object; it is the strange, mysterious, irreducible presence of one thing to another. Hence, though knowing
is not exclusively a matter of ocular vision, still it is radically that
sort of thing. It is gazing, intuiting, contemplating. Whatever words
you care to employ, consciousness is a knowing and so it is some
sort of inward looking.
    Now while consciousness is a factor in knowing, and while
knowing is an activity to which a problem of objectivity is annexed,
still it is one thing to give an account of the activity and it is something else to tackle the problem of objectivity.[13]

The negative remarks of this text could scarcely be more apt.
And yet, the assumption appears to have been explicitly made
that besides consciousness there is another datum, "knowing,"
and even "looking," which, presumably, unites one being (the
conscious knower) with another (the known). This is even more
clearly implied in the following remarks:

How does the knower get beyond himself to a known? The question
is, we suggest, misleading. It supposes the knower to know himself
and asks how he can know anything else. Our answer involves two

[13] *Insight,* p. 320.

514

elements. On the one hand, we contend that, while the knower may experience himself or think about himself without judging, still he cannot know himself until he makes the correct affirmation, I am. Further, we contend that other judgments are equally possible and reasonable, so that through experience, inquiry, and reflexion there arises knowledge of other objects both as beings and as beings other than the knower. Hence, we place transcendence, not in going beyond a known knower, but in heading for being within which there are positive differences and, among such differences, the difference between object and subject. Inasmuch as judgments occur, there are in fact objectivity and transcendence; and whether or not such judgments are correct, is a distinct question to be resolved along the lines reached in the analysis of judgment.[14]

Had Lonergan also indicated, here or elsewhere, that the difference between the objectivity of the object and the subjectivity of the subject are the outcome, rather than the ontological precondition, of knowledge I would have accommodated other difficulties in the passage to the predominant sense that consciousness is not the attainment of an object, being, originally alienated from mind, but the self-differentiation of the self from the non-self. As it is, I am reduced to wondering whether this text does not mean much the same as that of Rahner quoted above, and whether according to Lonergan (a) although the problem of epistemology is not "how does the knower get beyond himself to a knower?", it is nevertheless, as it were, "how does the knower get to an unknown without getting beyond himself?", (b) this problem cannot be solved by looking at the act of knowledge from the outside, hence, (c) epistemology must proceed from an analysis of consciousness precisely as an act (indeed, as a phenomenon) and, finally, (d) if we so analyze consciousneess the problem disappears—that is, there can be no

[14] *Ibid.*, p. 377.

doubt about the reliability of the powers of knowledge in principle, and the Cartesian objections are without foundation in fact —because the knower does attain to an objective reality which is other than himself, although he does not do so by transcending himself but by following the spontaneity of his nature as being, which enables him not merely to establish cognitive relations with another but also to be conscious of these relations, i.e. to have "insight."

It is possible that I misconstrue Lonergan's thought when I interpret it as the conjunction of a sound idea of consciousness with an unnecessary pre-commitment to the classical concept of knowledge, paradoxical though this conjunction may be. But I think I find confirmation of this interpretation in Lonergan's doctrine of truth. According to Lonergan being is to be "identified with what is to be known through intelligent grasp and reasonable affirmation; but the only reasonable affirmation is the true affirmation; and so being is what is known truly. Inversely, then, knowing is true by its relation to being, and truth is a relation of knowing to being." [15] Admittedly, these expressions could be understood in more than one way, and they do not necessarily repeat the classical doctrines of Parmenides and Aristotle.[16] But the most obvious reading of the passage does bring to mind the classical doctrines, especially as Lonergan continues:

What is the relation [of knowing to being]? In the limiting case, when the knowing is identical with the known, the relation disappears to be replaced by an identity, and then truth consists in the

[15] *Ibid.,* p. 522.

[16] I have in mind particularly Parmenides, *Fragment 3,* and Aristotle, *Metaphysics* V, 7 (1017 a 32-34); VI, 4 (1027 b 18-28).

absence of any difference whatever between the knowing and the known being. In the general case, when there is more than one known and one of these is a knower, it is possible to formulate a set of positive and of negative comparative judgments and then to employ this set to define implicitly such terms as subject, object, and the principal notion of objectivity. Within this context there follows the traditional definition of truth as the conformity or correspondence of the subject's affirmations and negations to what is and what is not.[17]

I see no reason not to take these statements at face value. This is in every basic respect a re-statement of the traditional doctrine of truth, though it has been refined in some ways; for instance, it makes clear that the correspondence involved in the relation of truth is not between an objective content and its subjective reproduction, but between an objective content and the subjective act of knowing it. And this doctrine of truth is arrived at critically, that is, through an analysis of consciousness. But the analysis of consciousness is directed to a vindication of the traditional concept of knowledge—and in order to do so it must distinguish between consciousness and knowledge. This distinction, however, does not rest upon empirical grounds. It is an aprioristic distinction and, in my opinion, it is no more valid now than when Kant first used it as the basis of the very notion of *Kritik*. Like transcendental Thomists generally, Lonergan holds "tenaciously to an objectivists metaphysics" because at a fundamental level he admits unquestioningly an objectivist concept of knowledge—possibly because he first assumes that the only alternative to objectivism is subjectivism.

These criticisms, as I have said, are applicable to transcendental Thomists generally, and I believe one could find in Rahner's

17 *Insight*, p. 522.

517

work a parallel for each of the texts of Lonergan I have quoted. I wish to make separate mention, however, of the transcendental Thomist who in my opinion comes closer than any other to a radical criticism of the classical concept of knowledge. I refer to Emerich Coreth.

I will not expand on the considerable portion of Coreth's *Metaphysics* which I consider valid. Nor would I wish in any way to minimize Coreth's originality and depth of insight. Perhaps more clearly than other transcendental Thomists he distinguishes the transcendental method which is peculiar to transcendental Thomism from every other variation of it—on the one hand, from the transcendental methods of Kant, Hegel and Husserl, on the other, from that of Heidegger. The former, unlike Descartes, pose the question of epistemology taking account of the presence of the questioner to his own question. Hence, since Kant epistemology asks not about the possibility of valid transcendent intuition, but about the transcendental conditions of the possibility of the phenomenon of consciousness. Nevertheless, Kant, Hegel and Husserl, like Descartes, take as the indubitable fixed point of epistemological investigation the *content* of knowledge rather than its existential reality as an *act* of the knower. Heidegger, on the other hand,

uses the transcendental method in order to discover the conditions of possibility of human self-actuation. He tries to find what makes it possible for man to understand *Seiendes* (that which is). But because he considers only the act, not its content, because he overlooks the essence in his quest for real being, because he does not want to translate what he discovers into conceptual language, he gets lost in phenomenology and does not really penetrate into metaphysics.

From all this it is clear that we are confronted with a continual dialectic of *act* and *content*, both of which must be considered and investigated. The act and that which is unthematically co-affirmed in it must be expressed in concepts, transformed into content. Yet this conceptual thinking, the content, must never lose touch with the act, which always transcends it, which can never be exhaustively expressed in it. The concept must stay rooted in the act, explicit knowledge must feed on the knowledge implied in the act, on what we have called *exercised or lived knowledge*.[18]

Coreth does not avoid the dilemma with the allegation, for instance, that the distinction between act and content is subsequent to consciousness and that, therefore, it is not the condition of the possibility of human conscious experience but, on the contrary, a manifestation of its nature—that is the suggestion which would spontaneously occur to me if I were dealing with the question. Coreth accepts the polarity of content and act in much the same way as he accepts that of objectivity and subjectivity. His solution to the problem of how to steer between the Kantian Scylla and the Heideggerian Charybdys is the suggestion that the opposition between subject and object is not an opposition between one content actuated by its own act, and another content actuated by its own act, but that it is the opposition between act and content as these are found in the polar field created by the existential relations that obtain between existing objects and existing subjects. Thus, much of what Coreth states about the nature of human consciousness and its relations to reality is very much in line with the suggestions I have myself made in this book—very specially, as above with Lonergan, in whatever concerns the rejection of certain aspects of traditional epistemologies. In a passage strikingly parallel to those of Rahner and Lonergan which I have quoted above, Coreth explains:

[18] Emerich Coreth, *Metaphysics,* (New York, 1968), pp. 52–53.

Questioning or inquiring presupposes some *knowledge about being*. But this knowledge, through which we "anticipate" in the direction of being as a whole, is not a grasping possessive knowledge, but an anticipating projection knowledge; it is not a knowledge which possesses that which is known, but a knowledge which projects that which can be known. This presupposes that we already know about being or about the meaning of being. The origin of this knowledge lies in the act of questioning itself. Whenever we question, we know that we question, that we are the inquirer, that we perform the act of inquiring. In every act of inquiring or knowing, some being is given which coincides immediately with knowing, which knows itself as being. The act knows itself as being. Being knows itself as act. We have an immediate *unity of being and knowing in the very act of knowing*.[19]

Perhaps I should incidentally remark that here is the explanation why Rahner does not say, as I would, that *consciousness* is being present-to-self, but that "being"—I stress, *"being"*—is being-present-to-self." In any event, what does Coreth mean when he says that "being knows itself as act," and that "we have an immediate unity of being and knowing in the very act of knowing"? What he means, as I interpret it, is that the object-subject dichotomy is found in the phenomenal field and is, therefore, not *known* prior to its being found, *as an identity,* in the phenomenal field. Evidently, Coreth does *not* mean that the object-subject dichotomy is found *only* in the phenomenal field, or that it is not only not *known* prior to its being found in the phenomenal field but that it can *exist* only in the phenomenal field. Coreth does *not* mean, therefore, unless I misinterpret him, that the existential reality of consciousness and the selfhood of man emerge as the object-subject dichotomy is produced. Coreth *does* apparently mean, on the contrary, that the identity of subject and object

[19] *Ibid.,* pp. 69–70.

in the act of knowledge is *subsequent to their original isolation* in their pre-cognitive actuality in themselves:

> When we know, we know ourself as the knower and something else as that which is known. The duality of inquirer and that about which he inquires, of knower and that which he knows, is that of *subject and object.* Insofar as, in the one act of inquiring or of knowing, we know both of them, ourself and the other, both—subject and object —are posited in the same act. In the identity of the act we posit the difference of subject and object. This is true not of the subject and the object *in themselves,* but of the subject and the object *in the act* of knowing, that is, of the subject and the object insofar as in the unity of the self-knowing act they are posited and opposed to each other. But the difference of subject and object *in the act* presupposes the difference of the subject and the object *in themselves.*[20]

It is perfectly clear, thus, that according to Coreth what consciousness essentially and distinctively achieves is not the self-*differentiation* of the subject from the object. (The difference between object and subject it merely *reduplicates*—not, to be sure, by fashioning a reduplic*ate,* but by performing the act of reduplic*ation* which pertains essentially to the mind). What consciousness essentially and distinctively achieves is the *unity* of self and non-self (not, to be sure, in the coincidence of an objective content and its subjective conceptual reduplicate, but "in the identity of the act" by which is posited *for us* the difference which object and subject first hold *in themselves.*) It is possible I have misunderstood his meaning. But if I have not, then I would say: it appears that the classical concept of knowledge has managed surreptitiously to insinuate itself into the philosophy of Coreth.

Happily, Coreth does not consistently abide by the idea that

[20] *Ibid.,* pp. 71–72.

knowledge is essentially a remedy for the isolation of self-contained atomic intelligibilities, the idea that rules Hellenic-Western philosophy from Plato to Husserl through Aristotle, Aquinas, Descartes, Kant and Hegel. In much of Coreth's work this premise is ignored, and the conviction that effectively guides his reflections is the idea that consciousness is man's presense to himself. But Coreth's metaphysics suffers as a result of this inconsistency. This is most clearly evident in the fact that his overriding metaphysical doctrine constantly and unquestioningly assumes the identification of reality *with* and *as* being.

I have in this book suggested some reasons why the confusion of reality with being and, above all, the identification of reality as being, is invalid and particularly inadequate as a possible philosophical foundation for Christian theism today. The foregoing reflections on transcendental Thomism tend to confirm my previous conclusion that the reconceptualization of reality in a more adequate manner than metaphysics allows can be grounded only upon an epistemology which would depart from the very roots of Hellenic-Western metaphysical thought.

EPIGRAPH SOURCES

St. Thomas Aquinas, *De Caelo et Mundo*, I, 22.
Karl Rahner, "Theology and Anthropology," in T. Patrick Burke, (ed.), *The Word in History*, (New York, 1966), p. 1.
Arnold Toynbee, *Christianity Among the Religions of the World*, (New York, 1957), p. 63.

Index of Names

523